Organizational Communication: Approaches and Processes

FIFTH EDITION

Katherine Miller
Texas A&M University

WADSWORTH
CENGAGE Learning

Australia • Brazil • Japan • Korea • Mexico • Singapore
• Spain • United Kingdom • United States

WADSWORTH
CENGAGE Learning

Organizational Communication: Approaches and Processes, **Fifth Edition**
Katherine Miller

Publisher: Lyn Uhl

Executive Editor: Monica Eckman

Development Editor: Kate Scheinman

Assistant Editor: Kimberly Gengler

Editorial Assistant: Kimberly Apfelbaum

Associate Technology Project Manager: Jessica Badiner

Marketing Manager: Erin Mitchell

Marketing Assistant: Mary Ann Payumo

Content Project Manager: Jessica Rasile

Art Director: Linda Helcher

Production Technology Analyst: Jamison MacLachlan

Print Buyer: Susan Carroll

Permissions Editor: Roberta Broyer

Production Service/Compositor: Newgen–Austin

Cover Designer: Armen Kojoyian

Cover Image: © John Still

Library of Congress Control Number: 2007942791

ISBN-13: 978-0-495-56551-2
ISBN-10: 0-495-56551-2

Wadsworth Cengage Learning
25 Thomson Place
Boston, MA 02210

Cengage Learning products are represented in Canada by Nelson Education, Ltd.

For your course and learning solutions, visit **academic.cengage.com**.

Purchase any of our products at your local college store or at our preferred online store **www.ichapters.com**.

Printed in the United States of America
1 2 3 4 5 6 7 12 11 10 09 08

BRIEF CONTENTS

CONTENTS

PREFACE

Although the "ages" of scholarly fields are notoriously hard to pinpoint, most would agree that organizational communication has been around for six decades or more. The infancy of the discipline was marked by struggles for survival and nurturance from other disciplines. The teenage years saw a questioning of identity and fights for autonomy. Today, most would agree that organizational communication has reached a maturity few would have envisioned half a century ago, and the field now encompasses a healthy eclecticism in that a variety of theoretical approaches provide contrasting accounts of the ways in which communicating and organizing intersect. And this is definitely a good thing, for few would have predicted the changes that have occurred in our world—changes in politics, business, technology, values, the environment—during that time period. We need a solid but dynamic understanding of organizational communication to cope with this complex and changing world.

This book attempts to reflect the eclectic maturity of the field of organizational communication. When I began writing the first edition of this text over fifteen years ago, my first conceptual decision was not to advocate a particular approach to the field. Instead, I try to show that both traditional and contemporary perspectives provide potentially illuminating views of organizational communication processes. For example, a critical theorist, an ethnographer, and a systems researcher may all look at a particular organizational communication phenomenon—say, socialization practices—and see very different things. A systems theorist might see a cybernetic system in which the goal of organizational assimilation is enhanced through a variety of structural and individual communication mechanisms. A cultural researcher might see socialization as a process through which the values and practices of an organizational culture are revealed to—and created by—individuals during organizational entry. A critical theorist might see socialization as a process through which individuals are drawn into hegemonic relationships that reinforce the traditional power structure of the organization.

All these views of the organizational socialization process are partial in that each obscures some aspects of organizational entry. But each view is also illuminating. Thus, early chapters of this text cover a gamut of academic approaches—from classical through human relations and human resources to systems, cultural, and critical—as lenses through which organizational communication can be viewed. The strengths and weaknesses of each approach are considered, but no particular approach is presented as an inherently superior theoretical approach.

My second important choice in writing this book was deciding how to organize the burgeoning research literature on organizational communication. At the time I started this book—and even now—most textbooks had taken a "levels" approach, considering, in turn, organizational communication at the individual, dyadic, group, and organizational levels. I have been frustrated by this approach, both because there are some things that happen at multiple levels (for example, we make decisions alone, in dyads, and in groups) and because there are processes that are not easily linked to any of these levels. (For example, where does communication technology fit in? At what level do we consider emotion in the workplace?) Thus, the chapters in the second half of this textbook involve a consideration of organizational communication processes.

My goals in the "processes" portion of the book are threefold. First, I want the processes considered to be up to date in reflecting current concerns of both organizational communication scholars and practitioners. Thus, in addition to looking at traditional concerns such as decision making and conflict, this textbook highlights communication processes related to cultural and gender diversity, communication technology, organizational change, and emotional approaches to organizational communication. Second, I want to be as comprehensive as possible in describing relevant theory and research on each topic. Thus, each "process" chapter highlights both foundational and current research on organizational communication processes from the fields including communication, management, industrial psychology, and sociology. Third, I want students to understand that each of these communication processes can be viewed through a variety of theoretical lenses. Thus, Chapters 7 through 13 conclude with a section on the insights of the approaches considered in the first half of the book.

ORGANIZATION OF THE TEXT

This textbook explores the world of organizational communication in terms of both scholarship and application. The majority of chapters consider either approaches that have shaped our beliefs about organizational communication practice and study (Chapters 2 through 6) or chapters that consider specific organizational communication processes (Chapters 7 through 13). The first two chapters on "approaches" (Chapters 2 and 3) both consider prescriptive approaches on how organizational communication should operate (Classical Approaches, Human Relations and Human Resources Approaches) while the following three approaches chapters (Chapters 4 through 6) consider contemporary approaches regarding how we can best describe, understand, explain, and critique organizational communication (Systems Approaches, Cultural Approaches, and Critical Approaches). When we move on to the "processes" chapters, we first consider enduring processes that have always characterized communication in organizations in Chapters 7 through 10 (Assimilation Processes, Decision-Making Processes, Conflict Management Processes, and Change and Leadership Processes). Then, in Chapters 11 through 13, we look at emerging processes that have come into play in recent decades (Processes of Emotion in the Workplace, Organizational Diversity Processes, and Technological Processes). These chapters are sandwiched by an introductory chapter (Chapter 1) and a concluding chapter (Chapter 14) that put these approaches and processes into context by considering specific challenges in today's world and the ways in which the study of organizational communication can help us deal with these challenges.

Those familiar with this textbook will note a number of changes from the fourth edition that will enhance student understanding of organizational communication. All the chapters have been updated to include current research and theory, and further changes were made in a number of chapters. These include enhanced attention to resistance processes, communication during organizational crisis, knowledge management, diversity processes, and virtual organizing. A major addition to this edition of the textbook is a new Chapter 1, "The Challenge of Organizational Communication," that considers the complexity of organizational communication through a consideration of current issues such as globalization, climate change, terrorism, and demographic trends. This updating led to the addition of well over 100 new references, the vast majority from the past five years.

The fifth edition of *Organizational Communication: Approaches and Processes* continues from the first four editions many features that are designed to enhance students' abilities to integrate and apply the material. The fifth edition continues to include the "Spotlight on Scholarship" features, highlighting specific research that illustrates concepts considered in the chapter. In an effort to stay abreast of current research, however, three spotlights are new to this edition. Other pedagogical features are maintained from earlier editions, including explicit links among the "approach" and "process" chapters, tables and figures to illustrate key concepts, and case studies at the end of each chapter to apply conceptual material to real-life organizational communication situations. Two of the case studies are new to the fifth edition. One of my favorite features of this textbook—the "Case in Point" feature that began in the fourth edition—continues in the fifth edition. One of the most fun tasks during this process of revising the textbook has been discovering and writing about current events that reflect a variety of concerns about organizational communication. There are sixteen new Case in Point features as well as some from the fourth edition with which I couldn't part. Finally, the fifth edition adds one feature: learning objectives at the beginning of each chapter that help to focus attention on important content and concepts. Finally, like earlier editions, this fifth edition is accompanied by an Instructor's Manual that includes sample syllabi; paper assignments; key terms; chapter outlines; true/false, multiple choice, fill-in-the-blank, and essay test items; suggestions for effective use of the case studies; and helpful websites. The Instructor's Manual also includes Case Study, Spotlight on Scholarship, and Case in Point features from previous editions.

ACKNOWLEDGMENTS

When you are asked to write a textbook, you don't realize the work that will be involved in writing subsequent editions of that textbook. It is challenging to maintain the focus of earlier editions and keep what is foundational yet also provide the needed updates, restructuring, and "sprucing up" necessary for new groups of students. However, the daunting task of revision can be made relatively painless through the efforts of a great support system. First, the team at Wadsworth, a part of Cengage Learning, has been helpful throughout the process of revision. I am especially grateful for the support and assistance of Monica Eckman, Kimberly Gengler, Jessica Rasile, Kate Scheinman, and Smitha Pillai.

The comments of a number of organizational communication scholars were instrumental in shaping the direction, content, and presentation of this textbook. These include colleagues around the country who commented on the revision project at various stages: Elizabeth Alcock, Bristol Community College; Adam Earnheardt, Youngstown State University; Larry Erbert, University of Texas, El Paso; Katharine Hansen, Stetson University; Michelle Leacock, Seton Hall University; Meina Liu, University of Maryland; and Cynthia Stohl, University of California, Santa Barbara. I am also grateful for the comments of both undergraduate and graduate students at Texas A&M University and for the occasional colleague from around the globe who pops into my email in-box with helpful suggestions and comments.

Finally, my most heartfelt thanks go to my family for providing an environment in which writing this textbook was a pleasurable challenge. My daughter, Kalena Margaret Miller, was born while I was writing the first edition of this textbook. I'm amazed that she is now in high school—a young woman who continues to love learning and increasingly challenges my ideas with her own experience and insights. She is a delight and an inspiration. Finally, my husband, Jim Stiff, provided the inspiration to get started, the motivation to follow through, and—now more than ever—a wealth of examples of organizational communication in action. Both Jim and Kalena have kept me sane and grounded in recent years, and this book is dedicated to them.

Katherine Miller
College Station, Texas

The Challenge of Organizational Communication

CHAPTER 1

AFTER READING THIS CHAPTER, YOU SHOULD . . .

- Be able to describe how today's world is complicated by globalization, terrorism, climate change, and changing demographics
- Understand the concept of "requisite variety" and appreciate the need for complex thinking to cope with complex situations
- See ways in which we can complicate our thinking about organizations both by considering a variety of organizational forms and by viewing organizations that are often paradoxical and contradictory
- Understand the distinction between a "transmission model" of communication and a "constitutive model" of communication
- Be familiar with the seven conceptualizations of communication and the ways in which these domains of understanding can change our view of organizational communication

During the last few years, social networking sites such as MySpace and Facebook have caught the attention of college and high school students, others who are Internet savvy, and a wide range of commentators. One option for individuals creating Facebook profiles is to note that, in explaining the nature of a relationship, "It's complicated." That simple statement could be seen as defining much of our twenty-first century world and our lives within that world. Our relationships are complicated. Our families are complicated. Our work is complicated. Our politics and government are complicated. Our global economy is complicated. Our connections with other nation-states are complicated. Our beliefs about ourselves are complicated.

Nowhere is this complexity more apparent than in a consideration of communication processes or in a consideration of organizations, institutions, and social groupings. There is little doubt that our organizational world is much more complicated than the world of one hundred years ago (think of agriculture, increasing industrialization, and the birth of the assembly line) or the world of fifty years ago (think of moving to the suburbs, long-term employment, and *Father Knows Best*) or even twenty years ago (think of cross-functional work teams, the birth of the Internet, and the fracturing of the proverbial glass ceiling). Mark Penn (2007) contends that we have moved from the age of Ford, in which you could have a car in "any color, as long as it's black," to the age of Starbucks, in which the variety of beverages available is truly staggering. For an individual first confronting the array of offerings at Starbucks, this new world of choice is indeed complicated. However, this is not to say that past time periods have not taught us a great deal about ways to understand the complexity of our world today or provided us with strategies for coping with the high levels of complexity that confront us. Indeed, on a daily basis we as individuals, families, organizations, and societies find ways to live productively in this complicated world.

This textbook takes you on a journey of understanding into the complex world of organizational communication and the role of interacting individuals and groups within that world. This journey will involve trips to the past to consider how scholars and practitioners have historically approached issues relevant to organizational communication. It will also involve the consideration of a wide range of processes that make organizations complicated and that help us cope with that complexity. These include processes of socialization, decision making, conflict management, technology, emotion, and diversity. In this first chapter, however, we will take an initial look at ways in which today's organizational world is complicated. This initial look will be a brief and partial one, but it will introduce some of the ways in which participants in twenty-first-century organizations are confronted with confounding and challenging problems. We will then consider strategies for thinking about the concepts of "organization" and "communication" that will assist us on our journey as we explore approaches and processes in the understanding of organizational communication.

OUR COMPLICATED WORLD

There are myriad ways we could illustrate the complexity of today's world, and as we work our way through this textbook, we will discuss many of the "complicated" issues that confront us. In the last chapter, we will look at how the landscape of organizational communication has changed in recent years and will continue to change in the future. In this chapter, however, we consider four aspects of our world that were barely on the radar twenty years ago, but that today dominate much of our thinking—and our news coverage. They are globalization, terrorism, climate change, and changing demographics.

Globalization

It has become a truism to state that we now live in a global economy and participate in a global marketplace. As transportation and telecommunication systems improve, our world becomes ever more connected, both on a personal and an organizational level. The emergence of a global economy was facilitated by key political changes such as the end of the cold war and the development of the European Union and has included the emergence of a variety of institutions to help regulate the global economy, such as the World Trade Organization and the International Monetary Fund. The globalization movement has led to practices such as *outsourcing*, in which businesses move manufacturing and service centers to countries where labor is cheap. In a global economy, many organizations have a multinational or international presence, with employees of a single organization found in many locations worldwide. Further, in a global economy, businesses are no longer centered in a few Western nations, but are spread among nations throughout the developing world as well.

Some commentators see globalization as a largely positive—and clearly unstoppable—development. For example, in *The World Is Flat* (2005) Thomas Friedman argues that the global economy offers exciting opportunities for entrepreneurs with the requisite skills. Many others, however, argue that globalization can lead to problems such as domestic job loss, the exploitation of workers in third world nations, and environmental problems. David Held and others consider these issues in *Debating Globalization* (2005). Held et al. consider the complex issues of trade, economic development, security, and environmental protection that come into play as we consider global economic and industrial systems. What becomes clear from all sides of the debate is that our new world involves complex interconnections between business, political, and cultural systems, and these interconnections make it difficult to fully understand the ramifications of both globalization systems and the proposed means for making globalization "work" effectively. Joseph Stiglitz, who critiques economic institutions associated with globalization in his 2002 book, *Globalization and Its Discontents*, has noted more recently that there is at least hope for dealing with these complex problems. He argues that, "while globalization's critics are correct in saying it has been used to push a particular set of values, this need not be so. Globalization does not have to be bad for the environment, increase inequality, weaken cultural diversity, and advance corporate interests at the expense of the well-being of ordinary citizens" (Stiglitz, 2006, p. xv).

The field of organizational communication can contribute a great deal to these debates about globalization. The challenges of globalization are not just economic—they also concern messages, relationships, and systems of understanding. Some of the questions that organizational communication scholars now consider in the area of globalization include:

- How can organizational members communicate effectively in the contracted time and space of global markets?
- How can communication be used to enhance understanding in the multicultural workplaces that are a crucial feature of our global economy?
- How can communication processes in business, government, and non-governmental organizations be used to protect the rights of workers in the United States and abroad?
- How does "organizing" occur in the realm of the political and economic policy debates that are critical to the long-term direction of the global economy?
- How do corporations communicate about the balance between providing goods and services at a price preferred by consumers and providing a safe and economically secure workplace for their employees?

Case in Point: Toxic Toys

In today's global marketplace, a great deal of manufacturing is outsourced to nations such as India, Singapore, and, especially, China. The giant toy manufacturer, Mattel, closed its last U.S. plant in 2002 and now makes two-thirds of its toys in China (Harrop, 2007). Mattel owns some plants in China, but also contracts with outside vendors—factories over which the multinational company has little control. There's little doubt about what is driving this trend—a desire for profit on the part of organizations and a desire for low-cost products on the part of consumers. As Harrop (2007) summarizes: "Consider the whole picture. Big-box stores fight every penny increase in manufacturers' prices. That immediately knocks the American worker out of the game. One retailer has actually told its U.S. suppliers to move their factories to China. This price mania has also cost jobs in Mexico, where workers are still paid better than in Asia."

So, in the quest for profit and low price, the job of making toys—and the responsibility for keeping those toys safe—has been taken over by Chinese factories. And the quest for profit and price doesn't stop there,

as choices are then made to produce the toys with whatever subcontractors can do the job for the least money. Because of a lack of quality control, product safety suffers. Toys are exported with lead paint. Toothpaste is exported laced with antifreeze. Dogs and cats in the United States die because of poisoned pet food. And the safety record is even worse for Chinese goods that are *not* exported. Liu (2007) points out that while 1 percent of food exported to the West from China fails to meet quality standards, the flunking rate is much higher (20 percent) for food sold within China.

So what are the answers to these growing problems of product safety in the global marketplace? Within China, there is a clear need for increased government control over safety. For multinational corporations like Mattel there is a need to upgrade quality assurance systems. But as Harrop (2007) points out, there's enough blame to go around: "Rather than zero[ing] in on one country or company, let's zero in on ourselves. American consumers must understand that low prices come with a price."

Terrorism

The terrorist attacks of September 11, 2001, changed the world in profound ways. Subsequent attacks in London, Madrid, and elsewhere, combined with frequent news stories about attacks that have been thwarted and individuals arrested for planning more attacks, make it clear that terrorism will be a watchword in our lives for many years to come. As Oliver (2007, p. 19) notes, "in the wake of the attacks on the World Trade Center and the Pentagon on 9/11, the conventional wisdom was that 'everything has changed.'" However, as Rosemary O'Kane (2007) points out in her book *Terrorism: A Short History of a Big Idea*, terrorists have been around for many centuries, and terrorism can be perpetrated by individuals, groups, nation-states, and regimes. She notes that terrorism is not a particular ideology, but is a set of strategies that involves the use of unpredictable violence against individuals and thus creates ongoing fear and suspicion among large groups of people. The effectiveness of terrorism today can be enhanced both by the wide range of technological tools available to terrorists and by contemporary urban environments that have high concentrations of residents and mass transportation.

For individuals and organizations in the post-9/11 world, the implications of terrorism are everywhere, but can be seen, especially, in two widespread areas—the "war on terror" and "homeland security." Perhaps the most basic concern for organizational communication scholars in approaching the war on terror is gaining an understanding of how terrorist networks and terrorist organizations operate and grow (Stohl & Stohl, 2007). Such an understanding would involve a consideration of how terrorist organizations recruit and socialize their members, how terrorist cells make decisions and develop leadership, how terrorist networks form interconnections through technology and interpersonal contact. But a consideration of the war on terror has also come to encompass military interventions such as the wars in Afghanistan and Iraq. Thus, organizational communication scholars must also be cognizant of the complex communication processes involved in military actions and bureaucracy and the complexities of dealing with military personnel and their families during and after their service. The implications of the war on terror for organizational communication also include complex political negotiations with a wide range of government entities and the creation and dissemination of organizational rhetoric to connect institutional goals with public opinion.

Organizational communication scholars can also respond to the complexities of terrorism through a consideration of homeland security. When Brian Michael Jenkins of the RAND Corporation testified before Homeland Security Subcommittee of the U.S. House of Representatives on January 30, 2007, he made it clear that homeland security is, at its heart, a problem of organizational communication. He notes:

> Homeland security is not a television show about mysterious government agencies, covert military units, or heroes with fantastic cell phones that summon F-16s. It is an ongoing construction project that builds upon philosophy and strategy to ensure effective organization, establish rules and procedures, deploy new technology, and educate a vast army of federal agents, local police, part-time soldiers, private security guards, first responders, medical personnel, public health officials, and individual citizens. (Jenkins, 2007, p. 1)

For organizational communication scholars, then, critical questions revolve around how to develop communication systems to enhance border security, improve tracking of possible terrorist activities, and develop the ability of first-response organizations—police departments, fire departments, hospitals, military—to act quickly and appropriately in case of terrorist threats or attacks. But organizational communication scholars can go beyond this mandate to consider the role of the individual citizen as he or she encounters this organized effort of homeland security. At times, these questions will concern public relations and crisis communication, as we consider ways in which homeland security issues can best be framed and conveyed to a wide range of people. At other times, these questions will involve how organizations can manage the daily operations of homeland security, such as airport security or the passport application process, in a way that conveys understanding for the frustrations of ordinary citizens. At still other times, organizational communication scholars can contribute by enhancing our understanding of high-level policy debates in which conflicts arise between the need for security and the preservation of civil liberties.

Thus, in terms of the war on terror and in terms of homeland security, our post-9/11 world illustrates the complexity of questions that confront organizational communication scholars and students. These questions include:

- How do terror networks organize, recruit, and socialize members, and communicate across time and space?
- What communication systems can and should be put into place to best ensure the security of our boarders?
- How can we help prevent our fear of terror from becoming a fear of each other?
- How can we best deliberate policy and make decisions in the changed environment of our post-9/11 world?
- How can communication systems be designed to protect and enhance the well-being of individuals who serve as first responders in the war on terror?

Climate Change

In his best-selling book *An Inconvenient Truth* (2006), Al Gore argues that humanity's role in climate change is an issue that can no longer be denied and must be addressed by governments, businesses, and individuals. Though there are still some who contend that climate shifts are just part of larger natural patterns, most scientists and commentators now agree that recent changes in our climate—caused by the phenomenon known as "global warming"—can be attributed to the activities of individuals and organizations. As the U.S. Environmental Protection Agency notes:

> For over the past 200 years, the burning of fossil fuels, such as coal and oil, and deforestation have caused the concentrations of heat-trapping "greenhouse gases" to increase significantly in our atmosphere. These gases prevent heat from escaping to space, somewhat like the glass panels of a greenhouse . . . the Earth's average surface temperature has increased by about 1.2 to 1.4°F since 1900. The warmest global average temperatures on record have all occurred within the past 15 years, with the warmest two years being 1998 and 2005. Most of the warming in recent decades is likely the result of human activities ... If greenhouse gases continue to increase, climate models predict that the average temperature at the Earth's surface could increase from 2.5 to 10.4°F above 1990 levels by the end of this century. ("Climate Change," Environmental Protection Agency, 2007).

Scientists have already observed widespread effects from climate change. Sea levels are rising, glaciers are shrinking, permafrost is melting. These changes in the natural environment lead to additional changes in plant and animal life, as growth patterns change in response to shifting environmental conditions. These changes are occurring on land and underwater, as climate change affects vast ecosystems and threatens the survival of some, such as coral reefs. Global warming also influences weather events, such as hurricanes, which gain strength over warmer ocean waters. As Mooney argues, "human beings are already changing the environments in which hurricanes form and attain their terrifying strength, which means hurricanes will inevitably change, too" (p. 260). But these changes are not necessarily consistent across the globe or even predictable. This uncertainty is clear just within the United States, as "scientists believe that most areas will continue to warm, although some will likely warm more than others. It remains very difficult to predict which parts of the country will become wetter or drier, but scientists generally expect increased precipitation and evaporation, and drier soil in the middle parts of the country" ("Climate Change," Environmental Protection Agency, 2007).

The role of organizational communication in climate change and global warming is widespread. Much of the human contribution to climate change can be traced to factors that began with the Industrial Revolution, such as our systems of energy production, factory manufacturing, and petroleum-fueled transportation. Thus, when searching for ways to reverse or at least slow the process of climate change, these industrial organizations play a key role. Organizational communication is also implicated in the debates about global warming and what to do about it. These debates are global ones because countries such as China and India are rapidly becoming increasingly industrialized and there are arguments about nations' obligations to reduce greenhouse gases. In all countries, debates about the balance between economic opportunity and environmental health are rife. Organizational communication is also important in dealing with many of the effects of global warming such as the increased incidence of forest fires and weather disasters like hurricanes. Finally, addressing global warming and climate change can open up opportunities for businesses that want to raise their level of environmental responsibility and sell themselves as "green" companies to consumers. Thus, the field of organizational communication must be ready to deal with the complex questions that stem from climate change and global warming, including:

Case in Point: Green Travel

When considering industries that contribute to the problem of global warning, the travel and tourism sector can certainly be cited as an important culprit. Fossil fuels power transportation options such as planes, trains, ships, and cars, and when we get to our destinations, most hotels, motels, and resorts have large "carbon footprints" as they house, feed, entertain, and pamper us. Thus, it is not surprising that a number of organizations in the hospitality and travel industries are now making the decision to move to more "green" services and products. It's not only good for the planet; it's also good business.

One example of this trend is Virgin Airlines, whose chairman, Richard Branson, has pledged $3 billion of his company's profits over the next 10 years to combat global warming. The project—named Gaia Capitalism after the Greek goddess of the earth—will involve research and development in biofuel production, renewable-energy production, and alternative transportation options. Virgin Airlines is also looking at smaller changes that could make a big difference. Branson (2006, p. 48) notes several of these changes: "at JFK airport in New York, the average long-haul plane takes 60 minutes to get from the gate to takeoff, and burns seven tons of fuel in the process. By towing planes out to the takeoff point instead, we would save 10 percent of that fuel. By changing procedures for landing, so that planes wait on the ground for an available gate rather than circling in the air, we would save even more fuel."

There are also examples of the "greening" of the travel industry in the area of resorts and hotels. You may already be familiar with the "pillow-top" cards asking if you're willing to forego a daily change of sheets and towels as a way to help the environment. But some establishments are going even further in their green design and there is a movement to develop national standards for environmentally friendly hotels ("Green Your Getaway," 2007). In short, there are more and more options for green travel, and much of this can be tied to the linking of business sense with corporate responsibility. As Branson (2006, p. 48) sums up, "by making green investment a motive for success—rather than a charitable adjunct to companies' existence—humanity will dramatically increase the chance of its survival."

- How can organizations reinvent themselves to reduce or eliminate their contribution to global warming?
- How can government representatives engage in productive debate about ways nations can work together to influence climate change?
- How can entrepreneurs address the "greening of organizations" as an opportunity for both profit and social responsibility?
- As climate change increasingly affects local weather events and patterns, how should local, state, national, and international agencies coordinate their activities to cope with the human consequences of global warming?
- How can organizations effectively enhance awareness of the ways in which individuals can make a difference in influencing the process of climate change?

Changing Demographics

Compared to issues like globalization, terrorism, and climate change, the concept of demographics sounds pretty tame. *Demographics* refer to statistical descriptions of characteristics of a population—things like age, race, income, educational attainment, and so on. These descriptions are, in one sense, simplistic, but they are also undeniably important. Demographics describe who we are in the most basic of terms, and thus can have a foundational impact on how we communicate with each other, how we organize, how we address critical problems in our social world, and even what those problems are in a given time and place.

The most typical way to think about demographics is to consider distributions of the characteristics of people, and to look at those distributions in a comparative sense across either time or location. In the United States, the most complete record of demographic trends is found in the Bureau of the Census data, and the most recent national census was completed in 2000. Consider a few comparisons that can be drawn from census data (Smith, 2002):

- In 1990, 9 percent of the population was Hispanic, compared to 12.5 percent in 2000. In 1990, 12.1 percent of the population was black, compared to 12.3 percent in 2000. Hispanics have now surpassed blacks as a share of the U.S. population and their numbers continue to grow.
- In 1970, 40.3 percent of American households consisted of married couples with their own children; by 2000, that percentage fell to 24.1 percent. Similarly, the percentage of households with five or more people was twice as high in 1970 (20.9 percent) as in 2000 (10.4 percent).
- The 2000 census indicates continuing population shifts from rustbelt states in the northeast and Midwest to sunbelt states—especially to the new sunbelt states such as Nevada, Arizona, Idaho, Utah, Colorado, and Georgia.
- In 1930, 5.4 percent of the U.S. population was 65 years or older; by 2000, the number more than doubled to 12.4 percent of the population. It is anticipated that by the year 2050, more than 20 percent of the U.S. population will be 65 or older ("Statistics on Aging," Administration on Aging, 2007).

In terms of sheer description, then, the United States is a dramatically different place than it was in decades past, and these different descriptors of who we are, where we live, who we live with, and how long we live lead to dramatically different experiences as we encounter organizations and communicate in them. Consider, for example, the issue of age. Scholars often divide populations into "generational cohorts" that indicate similarities in birth year and associated similarities in experience (Schuman & Scott, 1989). Thus, my mother's experiences as a member of the "World War II Cohort" are very different from mine as a member of the "Late Baby Boomer Cohort" or my daughter's as a member of the "Generation Y Cohort." In terms of work experience, members of the World War II Cohort are known for dependability, long-term employment, and relationships with organized labor. Members of my cohort are known for their ambition but also their cynicism. Members of my daughter's generation are coming to be known as technologically savvy but also a bit spoiled in the ways of work. Clearly, a similar demographic analysis could be applied to ethnicity, family structure, social class, or household location.

Changing demographics do not just influence the organizational experience of individuals, though. They also create new challenges for organizational communication. Changing demographics result in multicultural workplaces, in workers with increasing responsibilities to aging family members, in workers with longer commutes, and in workers who telecommute. Changing demographics also pose the challenge of treating individuals from different ethnic backgrounds, races, ages, genders, disabilities, and sexual orientations in ways that respect these differences and create opportunities for meeting both individual and organizational goals. Thus, questions confronting organizational communication scholars as they consider these demographic shifts include:

- How can we communicate with members of a culturally diverse workforce in ways that respect difference and help achieve organizational and individual goals?
- How do members of the "sandwich generation" cope with the stresses of work and family concerns?
- What are the various communication patterns and needs of individuals from different age groups?
- How can we use communication technology to design virtual workplaces for employees in a variety of locations?
- How do we make the tough decisions regarding the roles of institutions and government in supporting an aging America?
- What role does communication play in assuring a level playing field for individuals with disabilities?

MEETING THESE CHALLENGES

So far in this chapter, we have briefly confronted a number of facets of our complex, changing world. The challenges of globalization, terrorism, climate change, and changing demographics were rarely considered in past decades, but today they point to the range of complex problems that must be met by individuals, groups, organizations, and institutions. The question, then, is how "organizational communication" can be conceptualized as a means for understanding and tackling these challenges.

In Chapter 4 of this text, we will learn more about a scholar named Karl Weick who has been an important influence on many organizational communication scholars. As we'll see, Weick has a lot to say about how we organize and make sense of organizing through ongoing interaction. At this point, though, it is helpful to consider one concept that Weick emphasizes: *requisite variety*. This concept suggests that successful organizations and groups need to be as "complicated" as the problems that confront them. For example, the organizational structure of a small catering service can probably be relatively simple. However, if that small catering service grows into a large restaurant or an even larger food service organization, the structure needed for decision making, payroll, customer service, training, and a myriad of other functions must become increasingly complex. The organization must be as complicated as the problem.

The same principle holds for our consideration of how we should see "organizational communication" as a means for approaching the challenges of today's world. We have talked about issues such as globalization, terrorism, climate change, and changing demographics as just a few of the complexities that must be dealt with through organizational communication. Thus, if we see these problems as complicated, we must also complicate our thinking about organizations and complicate our thinking about communication.

Complicating Our Thinking about Organizations

The first way of complicating our thinking about organizational communication is to complicate our thinking about organizations. In the first edition of this book (Miller, 1995), I defined *organization* as including five critical features, namely the existence of a social collectivity, organizational and individual goals, coordinating activity, organizational structure, and the embedding of the organization within an environment of other organizations. These critical features still hold today, but in complicating our thinking about organizations, it is important to stretch our understanding of each of these concepts. For example, when we think about the idea of "structure," we need to consider more than basic hierarchical structure, or even more complex team structures. We also need to consider structures based on collective and communal relationships, structures that eschew hierarchy in favor of flat organizational forms, and structures that cross boundaries of time and space. When we think of the concept of "goals" we need to move far beyond the economic goals that are often assumed in discussions of the "bottom line." The goals that drive many organizations and individuals today involve changing the world in big and small ways, or perhaps simply concern about "connection" itself.

When we work to stretch our thinking in these ways, we see that there are many examples of organizational types in today's world that were not often considered in past decades. To take a basic example, we often think about "businesses"—entities that are designed to make money—as the epitome of organizations, but scholars are now increasingly interested in the operations of *nonprofit organizations*. For both profit and nonprofit organizations, more and more organizations can be characterized as *service organizations* rather than manufacturing organizations. In areas around the globe, *nongovernmental organizations* (NGOs) are especially important in coordinating processes of change in first and third world nations. It is increasingly common for individuals with similar needs and goals to come together in organizations known as *cooperatives* (co-ops) that are often motivated by a concern for democracy, social justice, and environmental and global responsibility. Further, with advances in computer and communication technology, organizations often do without the "brick and mortar" physical location and operate as *virtual organizations*. It is also critical to stretch our thinking to understand that the features of an "organization" are also relevant for the consideration of *social organizations* such as fraternities and sororities, or even families or groups of friends who are coordinating around valued goals and tasks.

As we complicate our thinking about organizations, it is also necessary to acknowledge that organizations are not "simple" sites where goals are accomplished through straightforward cooperation in well-defined structures. Indeed, in recent years, scholars of organizational communication have increasingly understood organizations as places where the diversity of individuals, goals, and ways of doing things contribute to highly irrational processes. For example, according to Tretheway and Ashcraft (2004), organizational communication must be approached with an appreciation for paradox, irony, and contradiction. They contend that "[a]s organizational environments become more complex and turbulent, and as diverse institutional forms merge and emerge, organizations and their members are pulled or are purposefully moving in different, often competing directions" (Tretheway & Ashcraft, 2004, p. 81). These scholars believe the irrational aspects of organizational life have always existed, but that they are being intensified by current conditions in the organizational world.

Complicating Our Thinking about Communication

It is also important for us to complicate our thinking about communication if we are to deal with the complicated world that confronts us. Early models of communication were highly simplistic, arguing that communication could be conceptualized with a model like the S-M-C-R model in which a Source transmits a Message through a Channel to a Receiver. In the organizational context, this could be seen as a supervisor (source) asking for volunteers to work on the weekend (message) through an e-mail (channel) sent to all of her employees (receivers). Even when a "feedback loop" is added to this model (e.g., responses to the e-mail), it is clear that it fails to encompass the varying ways we need to think about communication. Communication is not just about sending simple messages to one or more receivers. Communication is also about the intricate networks through which computers link us to others. Communication is about the creation of meaning systems in families and cultures. Communication is about understanding a market segment to enhance persuasion and increase sales. Communication is about the multiple ways information must flow to provide aid when a natural disaster strikes. Communication is about framing information about a possible threat so that the public is warned but not panicked. Communication is about coming to an understanding within a community about issues that both unite and divide.

Robert Craig (1999) proposed a model of communication theory that helps sort out these various aspects of communication. First, he contrasts a transmission model of communication with a constitutive model of communication. In a transmission model, communication is a way of moving information from sources to receivers, similar to the S-M-C-R model considered above. In a constitutive model, communication is seen as a "process that produces and reproduces shared meaning" (Craig, 1999, p. 125). However, Craig suggests that this simple distinction is not particularly helpful. For one thing, he argues that it's not really a fair fight, as the transmission model is usually just presented as something easy to knock down. But Craig also believes that the transmission model *can* be useful to consider in some cases. For example, when the goal is to get evacuation information to residents in the path of a hurricane, the effective transmission of information is a lot more important than the creation of shared meaning. However, Craig doesn't think we should stop at the simple choice between a transmission model and a constitutive model. Instead, he suggests we complicate our thinking.

Craig argues that we should recast the constitutive model of communication as a *metamodel*, an overarching way of thinking about communication. That is, if we see the constitutive model as a "model of models," it is possible to constitute communication in a wide variety of ways. These different ways of constituting communication can provide different avenues for the development of theory and research. But more important for our purposes here, various ways of constituting communication can help us deal with the practical challenges that individuals face in organizations today. That is, there will be times when it is important to think about communication as a way of getting information from one person to another. There will be other times when it is important to think about communication as shared dialogue and a way to enhance understanding about self and others. There will be still other times when communication is best seen as a means of persuasion and motivation. Thus, Craig's metamodel of communication can help us to meet the practical challenges of today's organizational world.

Craig proposed seven domains of communication theory—seven different ways of thinking about how communication works in the world. These are presented in Table 1.1 and they range from the notion of communication as information processing (the cybernetic model) to communication as the experience of otherness and dialogue (the phenomenological model). Table 1.1 also considers how each way of thinking about communication might be put into play in the organizational context. It should be clear that these various approaches to communication allow us to answer—and perhaps more important, to ask—very different questions about how organizations and people work in today's complex society.

In summary, then, our world is becoming increasingly complex, and the intricate situations that arise with globalization, terrorism, climate change, and changing demographics require multifaceted approaches to understanding. Indeed, even without these issues, life in organizations is complex enough! Thus, it is critical to complicate our thinking and discussion about "organization" and "communication" in ways advocated by recent scholars such as Tretheway and Ashcraft (2004) and Craig (1999). In the final pages of this chapter, we will look ahead to the remainder of the book to consider how these ideas about organization and communication will be brought to bear on traditional and contemporary approaches to the study of organizational communication and on a wide range of organizational communication processes.

Table 1.1 | Approaches to the Concept of Communication

	Communication Theorized As:	Possible Use in the Organizational Context:
Rhetorical	The practical art of discourse	Considering the communication strategies of organizational leaders during times of crisis
Semiotic	Intersubjective mediation by signs	Studying the ways that organizations create and sustain identity through corporate symbolism
Phenomenological	Experience of otherness; dialogue	Using dialogue to mediate conflict between two employees
Cybernetic	Information processing	Finding optimal ways to set up communication network system for employees who telecommute
Sociopsychological	Expression, interaction, and influence	Using knowledge about personality and interaction style to improve conflict management programs
Sociocultural	(Re)production of social order	Looking at the intersection of organizational, national, and ethnic cultures in multinational organizations
Critical	Discursive reflection	Confronting the issue of sexual harassment in the workplace through programs designed to shift beliefs about gender and power

Portions adapted from R. T. Craig (1999). Communication theory as a field. *Communication Theory*, 9, 119–161.

LOOKING AHEAD

Chapters 2 and 3 will take us back to consider several "founding perspectives" that have influenced the study of organizational communication. These approaches originated in other academic fields (e.g., sociology, psychology, management) and in business and industry and provide the foundation upon which the field of organizational communication stands. Several aspects of these founding approaches are important to note. First, although these schools of thought provide the historical backdrop for our study of organizational communication, they are not "dead" subjects. Indeed, the influence of these approaches is widely seen in organizations today, and our discussion of them will consider both their historic and current significance. Second, these approaches are largely *prescriptive* in nature. That is, these theorists were primarily interested in prescribing how organizations *ought* to run rather than describing or explaining how they *actually do run*. Chapter 2 will take us back to the early part of the twentieth century to explore classical and bureaucratic approaches to the understanding of organizational communication. In Chapter 3, we will move to the middle and later years of the twentieth century to consider two related approaches: human relations and human resources. In human relations approaches, the spotlight is on individual needs; in human resources approaches it is on the role of employees as valued contributors to organizational functioning.

In Chapters 4 through 6 of this textbook, we will consider three additional ways of viewing organizations. In these more contemporary approaches—systems, cultural, and critical—the focus shifts from the founding approaches considered in Chapters 2 and 3. First, these contemporary approaches constitute ways to *understand* and *explain* organizational communication. In contrast to founding approaches, they are not prescriptive theories, but are theories that can be used to enhance our understanding of *any* organization, be it guided by classical, human relations, or human resources practitioners. Second, these approaches are primarily used by scholars rather than practitioners, although there are, of course, important pragmatic implications that stem from all of these approaches. Third, all three of these approaches continue to exert substantial influence today in terms of how organizational communication is studied. An organizational communication scholar would find research stemming from all three of these approaches in current academic journals.

Systems, cultural, and critical approaches provide very different frameworks for understanding organizations, however. The systems approaches we discuss in Chapter 4 look at organizations as complex interactions of systems components and processes. The cultural approaches we look at in Chapter 5 consider organizations as emergent networks of values, norms, stories, behaviors, and artifacts. Finally, the critical approaches we consider in Chapter 6 emphasize organizational power and aspire to the emancipation of marginalized voices within the organizational context.

In the second half of the textbook, we will move our focus from approaches that inform our understanding of organizational communication to the specific processes to which these approaches have been applied. What do I mean by *process*? Simply something that *happens* in an organization. Organizations are marked by constant activity. People learn about new jobs, make decisions, deal with conflict, cope with customers, program computers, form alliances, institute change, and cope with differences. All of these communication processes have been the focus of organizational communication scholars, and the last half of this book will consider our knowledge about *what* happens in these processes, *how* it happens, and *why* it happens.

The first four chapters that consider organizational communication processes can be seen as "enduring" processes because they consider things that have probably been happening in organizations for as long as there have *been* organizations. In Chapter 7, we will look at assimilation, or the processes through which individuals attach to—and detach from—organizations. Chapter 8 investigates how communication influences organizational decision making, and Chapter 9 presents theories and research on the role of communication in organizational conflict. Then, in Chapter 10, we look at communication and change processes and the leadership processes that are often crucial in terms of both change and stability.

Finally, in the last four chapters of the textbook, we will consider some of the organizational communication processes that have emerged in the last twenty to thirty years as the workplace has changed and evolved. These "emerging" processes in organizational communication certainly existed in past organizations, but current developments in the workplace have brought these issues to the forefront, and they increasingly demand the attention of both organizational practitioners and researchers. In Chapter 11, we will look at a fundamental shift in the way we have come to view organizations and the people in them. This is the shift from assuming organizations are always "rational" and "logical" to acknowledging the role of emotion in organizational life. In Chapter 12, we consider the phenomenon of cultural and gender diversity in the workplace, considering the experiences of women and people of color, and the challenges facing managers in diverse organizations. In Chapter 13, we examine communication technology in the workplace, and how technology has shifted the way we work and think about work. Finally, in Chapter 14, we conclude in much the same way we began, by considering trends that are changing the landscape of organizations.

Discussion Questions

1. How have organizations that you work in or have dealings with been affected by issues such as globalization, terrorism, climate change, and changing demographics? How do these issues have different effects on different people and different kinds of organizations?

2. Consider how airports deal with homeland security. What organizational communication processes have changed as a result of the threat of terrorism? Do you think airports and airlines have dealt effectively with these changes? Why or why not?

3. What kinds of organizational structures and processes stem from globalization? Why are these new structures and processes necessary? How do they enhance—or detract from—the quality of life for individuals working in or with the organizations?

4. How would each of the communication domains considered in this chapter approach the organizational issues that arose in the aftermath of Hurricane Katrina and the broken levies in New Orleans? How do these different lenses help us understand the complexity of organizational communication processes?

2 | # Classical Approaches

AFTER READING THIS CHAPTER, YOU SHOULD . . .

- Understand the ways in which a "machine metaphor" provides insight into organizational communication
- Appreciate the historical context of the early years of the twentieth century when classical approaches to organizing were proposed
- Be familiar with Henri Fayol's Theory of Classical Management, especially his principles of management regarding structure, power, reward, and attitude
- Know how Weber's Theory of Bureaucracy corresponds to Fayol's, and be able to discuss the forms of authority that Weber sees as existing in organizations and bureaucracies
- Be able to describe the key aspects of Frederick Taylor's Theory of Scientific Management and explain how his ideas responded to the concerns about industry in his time
- Understand how communication processes are influenced by the Theory of Classical Management and be able to recognize principles of classical organizing in contemporary organizations

Before the Industrial Revolution in the nineteenth century, most work was conducted by individuals or in small groups. Goods were created by individual artisans, by families, or in small "cottage industries" in which skilled workers accomplished large tasks from start to finish. Consider, for instance, a shoemaker during the eighteenth century. A cobbler during this time period would put together a shoe from tanned leather to finished product (and perhaps tan the leather, as well!). Clearly, this is a different type of organizational process from today's shoe factory.

With the advent of the Industrial Revolution in the late nineteenth century, common methods of producing goods began to change. Instead of cottage industries, increased mechanization and industrialization led to the organization of larger groups of people in factory and assembly-line settings. Scholars and consultants in the early twentieth century tried to make sense of these new organizational forms and to provide business and industry with advice about how best to organize in light of these new developments. A number of theories gained prominence during this period. Three of the more important ones are Henri Fayol's Theory of Classical Management, Max Weber's Theory of Bureaucracy, and Frederick Taylor's Theory of Scientific Management. Before we consider the details of each theory, let us consider what they have in common—the belief that organizations should be modeled after machines.

THE MACHINE METAPHOR

The Industrial Revolution had profound impacts on how people worked and even on how they thought about work. The world was moving from an agrarian society (centered around farming) to an industrial society. It is not surprising, then, that a machine metaphor is central to classical organizational theories.

The notion of a metaphor in organizational theorizing suggests that we can learn something about organizations by considering a disparate object that an organization "is like" (Morgan, 1986, 1997). For example, we might contend that "an organization is like a pizza" in that it must have people (flour), communication (water that holds the flour together), and goals (yeast that makes the dough rise). Although this particular metaphor is somewhat whimsical, any metaphor can be helpful in pointing out aspects of organizational functioning that we might not otherwise notice. Metaphors can also de-emphasize aspects of an organization. That is, a metaphor is a "partial view" of an organization that will both reveal and obscure important aspects of organizing.

As noted, classical theorists share a dedication to the machine metaphor. What does this metaphor suggest about organizations? What can we learn by considering the ways in which organizations are like machines? We will consider many detailed answers to these questions when we look at the theories of Fayol, Weber, and Taylor, which share the machine metaphor.

One aspect of the machine metaphor is the importance of *specialization*. Think about a machine like a car engine. Every part of the engine has a specific function. For example, the carburetor or fuel injector is responsible for producing the proper mixture of gasoline and air. The spark plug is then responsible for igniting the explosion that drives the piston. Thus, the fuel injector and spark plug play very specialized roles, both of which are necessary for the proper operation of the combustion engine. When we see organizations as machines, we see the same kind of specialization. Think, for instance, of a sandwich shop in which one worker is responsible for slicing the bread, a second is responsible for meats and cheeses, a third is responsible for vegetables and condiments, and a fourth is responsible for bagging and ringing up the order. This specialization of tasks—sometimes called division of labor—illustrates one way in which organizational functioning can be seen as machinelike.

A second aspect of the machine metaphor is *standardization*, which includes the related notion of *replaceability*. Machines are designed in such a way that the parts in one machine are the same as those in a similar machine and hence can be easily replaced. For example, if the belt in your vacuum cleaner snapped, you could easily buy a new one that would fit perfectly. When conceptualizing organizations as machines, the same principle holds for the human "parts" that work in the organization. That is, if a worker on an assembly line quits, a machinelike organization can easily replace that worker. The individuals who labor in the organization are seen as the "cogs" of the machine, and those cogs are standardized and interchangeable.

Finally, machines are *predictable*. There are rules that govern the way a machine is built and how it operates. When it breaks, a finite number of things might be wrong, and if we carefully and rationally think through the problem, we should be able to fix the machine. A quick perusal of any appliance operating manual illustrates this principle. An organization conceived as a machine has the same qualities. It runs according to specific rules and standards, and if the organization is dysfunctional, it can be fixed by a rational consideration of the manner in which the rules and standards are being applied or misapplied.

Thus, looking at organizations through the lens of a machine metaphor points out the ways in which organizations are specialized, standardized, and predictable. These aspects do not exhaust the insights we might gain about organizations by thinking of them as machines. Further, it should be very clear that in many ways organizations are not like machines. I will note the weaknesses of the machine metaphor later in this chapter and in subsequent chapters.

However, at the turn of the twentieth century, when industrialization was gaining a foothold, theorists generally looked at organizational functioning through this mechanistic lens. The next three sections of this chapter present the theorists who were the most prominent proponents of this trend: Henri Fayol, Max Weber, and Frederick Taylor.

HENRI FAYOL'S THEORY OF CLASSICAL MANAGEMENT

Henri Fayol, described by Koontz and O'Donnell (1976) as the "father of modern operational-management theory," was a French industrialist who lived in the late nineteenth and early twentieth centuries. His major work appeared in French in the early twentieth century and was translated into English several decades later (Fayol, 1949). Two aspects of Fayol's theory that have been particularly influential are his consideration of the *elements of management* and his consideration of the *principles of management*. Both of these components concern the managerial function of organizing. The elements of management deal with what managers should do, and the principles of management deal with how managers should enact these elements.

Elements of Management

Fayol proposes five fundamental elements of management—the "what" of managerial work. The first of these elements is *planning*, which involves looking to the future to determine the best way to attain organizational goals. Fayol (1949) believes that "[t]he plan of action facilitates the utilization of the firm's resources and the choice of best methods for attaining the objective" (p. 50). His second element of managing is *organizing*. Fayol looks at this element in terms of the arrangement of human resources (employees) and the evaluation of those employees. The third element Fayol emphasizes is the *command* element of management. This is the element through which managers set tasks for employees in order to meet organizational goals. The fourth element of management is *coordination*. It is through this element that "the separate activities of an organization must be harmonized into a single whole" (Miner, 1982, p. 365). The final element of classical management is *control*, which involves the comparison between goals and activities to ensure that the organization is functioning in the manner planned.

It is interesting to note that Fayol does not include communication as one of his "elements" of management. However, with the possible exception of the planning element, it is difficult to imagine the performance of these elements without communication. That is, the organizing, command, coordination, and control elements of classical management theory all require communication between management and workers. Thus, communication can be seen as an implicit part of Fayol's elements of management.

Principles of Management

In addition to discussing the *what* of management through a consideration of the elements, Fayol provides prescriptions regarding *how* management can best function. Although these principles of management are often presented as a simple checklist, let's group them into four sets, each of which deals with a different aspect of how an organization should be managed.

Principles of Organizational Structure

Many of Fayol's principles of management concern how the parts of an organization should be put together. Six principles deal specifically with organizational structure:

- *Scalar chain*: This principle proposes that an organization should be arranged in a strict vertical hierarchy and that communication should be largely limited to this vertical flow (i.e., move up and down the organizational chart).
- *Unity of command*: This principle proposes that an employee should receive orders regarding a particular task from only one supervisor.
- *Unity of direction*: This principle proposes that activities having similar goals should be placed under a single supervisor.
- *Division of labor*: This principle proposes that work can best be accomplished if employees are assigned to a limited number of specialized tasks.
- *Order*: This principle proposes that there should be an appointed place for each employee and task within the organization.
- *Span of control*: This principle proposes that managers will be most effective if they have control of a limited number of employees. Fayol generally suggests a limit of twenty to thirty employees for first-level managers and six employees for higher-level managers.

These six principles of management, taken together, propose an organization that is highly structured and hierarchical. The organization is divided into functional divisions (division of labor, unity of direction, and order principles). Within these divisions, managers command a specific number of employees (span of control

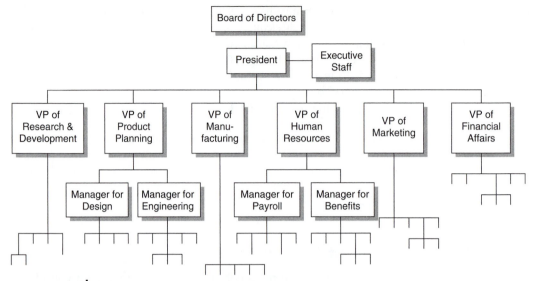

Figure 2.1 | Organizational Chart for Classical Organization

principle), and each employee has only one supervisor (unity of command principle). Throughout the organization, communication flows through vertical and highly structured channels (scalar chain principle). The type of organizational structure advocated by Fayol is illustrated in Figure 2.1.

One caveat is in order with regard to the structural principles proposed by Fayol. In general, Fayol advocated strict adherence to vertical communication flow within the hierarchical structure presented in Figure 2.1 However, he also recognized that horizontal communication across the hierarchy could sometimes facilitate organizational functioning. Thus, he proposed a structural "gangplank" (sometimes called Fayol's bridge) that would horizontally link employees at the same hierarchical level. Fayol proposed that such a link should be used only when authorized by a manager at the next highest level but should be used whenever such communication would aid in the accomplishment of organizational goals. "It is an error to depart needlessly from the line of authority, but it is an even greater one to keep to it when detriment to the business ensues" (Fayol, 1949, p. 36).

Principles of Organizational Power   The next three principles of management all deal with power relationships within the organization. These principles are:

- *Centralization*: This principle proposes that organizations will be most effective when central management has control over decision making and employee activities. However, Fayol believed that contingency factors such as firm size and the personal characteristics of the managers and employees could influence the optimal level of centralization (Miner, 1982).
- *Authority and responsibility*: This principle proposes that managers should hold authority that derives from both their position in the organization and

their personal characteristics (such as intelligence and experience). However, this principle also holds that responsibility must accompany authority in equal measure.

- *Discipline*: This principle proposes that all organizational members should be obedient to the rules of the organization and to the managers who enforce them.

These three principles describe Fayol's prescribed power structure for optimal organizational functioning. Fayol suggests that power should be relatively centralized in the managers, who hold both authority over and responsibility to the employees. The employees within this power structure should then submit to the rules and orders of the managers.

Principles of Organizational Reward   The third set of principles concerns Fayol's suggestions regarding appropriate rewards in organizations:

- *Remuneration of personnel*: This principle proposes that employees should be rewarded for their work with appropriate salaries and benefits. Kreps (1990) notes that "[t]his principle is based on the notion that organization members' primary motivation is financial and that work performance is dependent on the amount of remuneration they receive from the organization" (p. 69).
- *Equity*: This principle proposes that in remuneration (as well as in all organizational behavior) employees should be treated justly.
- *Tenure stability*: This principle proposes that the organization should guarantee sufficient time on the job for employees to achieve maximum performance. Fayol (1949) also notes that too much tenure stability could be counterproductive.

Thus, Fayol's principles of management suggest that employees are rewarded within the organization by the knowledge that their jobs are relatively secure and by the fair application of monetary rewards.

Principles of Organizational Attitude   Finally, Fayol sets forth three principles that consider the proper feelings and attitudes of organizational employees:

- *Subordination of individual interest to general interest*: This principle proposes that an organization can be effective only when the interests of the whole take precedence over the interests of individuals. Thus, individuals must always consider organizational goals first.
- *Initiative*: This principle proposes that managers should value and direct an employee's efforts to work in the best interest of the organization.
- *Esprit de corps*: This principle proposes—in the spirit of the Three Musketeers' "all for one and one for all" cry—that there should be no dissension in the organizational ranks.

Summary of Fayol's Theory

Ultimately, Fayol paints a picture of how an organization ought to be run. According to his principles of management, an effective organization is highly

Case in Point: Faster Food at the Cheesecake Factory

In recent years, the Cheesecake Factory has been one of the most successful and fastest-growing food franchises in the United States. Everything about the Cheesecake Factory is big, from its number of employees (over 18,000) to its number of menu items (over 200) to its portion size. And the Cheesecake Factory is successful because it uses modern technology in service of classical values like division of labor and efficiency (McGinn, 2004). Consider just a few examples:

- Lights flash behind the front counter when a table is expected to be open. That way, hosts and hostesses can "stage" guests to be ready for seating and waste little time on empty tables.
- Computers route customer orders to seven different cooking stations, each station staffed by two chefs and surrounded by all the necessary culinary supplies. If supplies run low, a separate staff member knows how to restock.
- An "expediter" keeps an eye on all the orders coming in to be sure that meals on the same order come out together and that nothing is delayed.
- Kitchen managers keep an eye on the quality of dishes that leave the kitchen and work to bail out any cooking station chefs who start to panic.

It's a crazy system, and some might not think it's worth it. Do we really need more than 200 menu items to choose from? But this culinary mix of high-technology equipment and assembly line values seems to be working. The chain is growing, employees are some of the most well-compensated in the industry, and waits at restaurants can be over two hours.

structured, and each individual knows where he or she fits. Clear structures facilitate the functioning of the organization and clear rules deal with these structures. Employees are rewarded through the equitable distribution of monetary rewards and are encouraged to labor strictly for the goals of the organization rather than for their own individual interests.

Let me emphasize again that Fayol's theory is *prescriptive* rather than descriptive or explanatory. In fact, relatively strong evidence demonstrates that this theory does not adequately describe or explain the ways in which organizations actually function (see Miner, 1982, for a review of empirical research results). To take one example, Fayol proposes that the elements of management are planning, organizing, commanding, coordinating, and controlling. However, in a classic study of what managers actually do, Mintzberg (1973) found ten work roles that had little to do with these functions. Instead, Mintzberg's roles included a number of interpersonal, informational, and decisional functions. However, in spite of the weakness of Fayol's theory as an explanatory or descriptive mechanism, the Theory of Classical Management has had a huge impact on how management is taught in schools and evaluated in the business world.

MAX WEBER'S THEORY OF BUREAUCRACY

The second classical management theory we'll consider was developed by Max Weber, a German sociologist, who lived in the same time period as Fayol. His ideas were introduced to the United States in English translations at approximately the same time as Fayol's (Weber, 1946, 1947). However, Weber is a very different kind of theorist than Fayol. Whereas Fayol provides prescriptions to managers about how organizations should be run, Weber takes a more scholarly approach. Weber's Theory of Bureaucracy has been termed an "ideal type" theory. An ideal type theory does not advocate a particular organizational form as best but rather lays out the features of an abstract—or idealized—organization of a given type. Thus, in his Theory of Bureaucracy, Weber enumerates the characteristics of a particular form of organization, the bureaucracy. Although skeptical about some of the tenets of bureaucracy, Weber believed that bureaucratic organizations would eventually dominate in society because of their technical superiority (Clegg, 1990).

Weber's Theory of Bureaucracy cannot be as easily divided into elements and principles as Fayol's can. However, six facets of bureaucracy permeate Weber's writing on the topic. Three of these are familiar from our discussion of Fayol. First, Weber believes that a bureaucracy should be operated through a *clearly defined hierarchy*. Second, Weber sees bureaucracy as characterized by *division of labor*. Third, he believes that bureaucracies are characterized by *centralization* of decision making and power. Because these notions are very similar to elements of Fayol's Theory of Classical Management, I will not consider them in detail here. However, three other aspects of Weber's Theory of Bureaucracy were not emphasized in Fayol's theory.

In addition to the categories of hierarchy, division of labor, and centralization, Weber emphasizes that bureaucracies are relatively *closed systems*. That is, to the extent possible, a bureaucracy will shut itself off from influences of the outside environment, because environmental interruptions could hamper its smooth functioning. Thompson (1967) extends this idea by proposing that organizations have "technical cores" that must be buffered from the environment through structural or communicative means. For example, in a physician's office the technical core is the interaction between physician and patient in the examining room. This technical core is buffered from environmental interruption by receptionists, rules about appointments, and nurses who monitor the flow of patients.

Weber's Theory of Bureaucracy also emphasizes the *importance of rules* for organizational functioning. Weber believes that rules should be rationally established and that there should be a rule for all possible contingencies in the organization. Further, he believes that these rules should be codified in written form.

Perhaps the most important aspect of Weber's Theory of Bureaucracy, though, is the attention he gives to the *functioning of authority*. Weber sees bureaucracies as working through a system of authority, power, and discipline. He postulates that such authority is based on one of three possible grounds:

- *Traditional authority* (sometimes called legitimate authority) is power based on long-standing beliefs about who should have control and is often vested in particular positions within an organizational hierarchy. For example, the queen of England has traditional authority that is based on age-old traditions within British society. Similarly, in some organizations the president or head of the board of directors may have power based on a tradition of authority rather than on actual abilities, actions, or behaviors.
- *Charismatic authority* is power based on an individual's personality and ability to attract and interact with followers. This kind of authority is highly unstable, as followers may become disenchanted with the leader's charismatic qualities.

Charismatic authority can be seen in the operation of many "cult" organizations in which a single individual draws in followers and demands obedience through the power of his or her personality. Business leaders such as Donald Trump have also been described as having charismatic qualities.

- *Rational-legal authority* is power based on the rational application of rules developed through a reliance on information and expertise. With rational-legal authority, power rests not in the individual, but in the expertise and rationality that have created a system of rules and norms. As Weber (1968) notes, "Every single bearer of powers of command is legitimated by the system of rational norms, and his [sic] power is legitimate insofar as it corresponds with the norm. Obedience is thus given to the norms rather than to the person" (p. 954).

Although Weber believes that all three types of authority (traditional, charismatic, and rational-legal) exist singly and in combination in organizations, he sees rational-legal authority as the type of power that dominates in the bureaucratic system. Traditional power and charismatic power rely on the position or the individual holding the position to define authority. Rational-legal power relies instead on rationality, expertise, norms, and rules. Thus, rational-legal power is far more impersonal than either traditional or charismatic authority. It is this reliance on rationality and impersonal norms that led Weber to advocate rational-legal authority as the basis of bureaucratic functioning.

In summary, Weber's theory concerns the "ideal type" features of the organizational form known as bureaucracy. He proposed that a bureaucracy is a closed system driven by rational-legal authority. Within this system, there is a strict reliance on rules, division of labor, and a clearly established hierarchy in which power is centralized. The result is a highly impersonal organization in which rationality is the guiding force and individuality is discouraged. As Miner (1982) summarizes: "Bureaucratic systems dominate through knowledge, and this fact gives them their rationality. The result is a climate of formal impersonality without hatred or passion and hence without affection or enthusiasm" (p. 391).

FREDERICK TAYLOR'S THEORY OF SCIENTIFIC MANAGEMENT

The third and final classical theory we consider in this chapter is one developed by Frederick Taylor in the early twentieth century. Taylor was a U.S. businessman, and, like Fayol, his goal was to provide prescriptions for how organizations could be better run. In contrast to Fayol's theory, however, Taylor concentrates on the "micro" level of organizational functioning. That is, Taylor is not concerned with organizational structure but with the relationship between manager and employee and the control of the individual at work. First we will discuss why Taylor developed his Theory of Scientific Management, then we will consider the detailed components of his system.

Impetus for the Theory of Scientific Management

Taylor developed his Theory of Scientific Management because he was frustrated with typical industry operations at the turn of the century. Several issues concerned him. First, most tasks in organizations were learned by newcomers watching more experienced workers at a particular job. This apprenticeship system, of course, would be effective only when the more experienced workers were doing the job in an efficient and effective manner. Thus, Taylor believed that learning tasks in this way could lead to work of uneven quality in the organization.

A second concern involved the manner in which individuals were rewarded for their work. At the turn of the century, piecework pay was the typical organizational reward system. That is, a bricklayer might be paid a penny for every five bricks he could lay. If he laid 100 bricks an hour, he would be paid 20 cents for that hour's work. Taylor was not concerned with the piecework pay system in and of itself. Rather, he was concerned with what could happen if a particularly efficient worker came on the job. For example, a group of workers might have established a norm of laying 100 bricks per hour. A new worker might come on the job and lay 200 bricks an hour (and hence earn 40 rather than 20 cents). A manager observing this productive behavior might conclude that everyone should be laying 200 bricks per hour and "bust the rate" down to a penny per 10 bricks rather than a penny per 5 bricks. More productive workers thus became known as "rate busters" because managers would often lower piecework pay as a result of their productivity.

Workers, of course, wanted to avoid having the piecework pay scale lowered. Therefore, a group of workers would often pressure each other to keep rate busting to a minimum. If productivity were kept down, wages would stay up. Taylor observed this social pressure to keep productivity down and wages up and labeled it "systematic soldiering." Thus, Taylor looked at organizational functioning and saw two impediments to optimal productivity. The first impediment was the *uneven work* that resulted from job training through custom and tradition. The second impediment was the *systematic soldiering* that resulted from rate busting and the system of piecework pay. To deal with these problems, Taylor developed his system of scientific management.

Components of Scientific Management

Taylor detailed his system in a book titled *The Principles of Scientific Management* (Taylor, 1911). In this book, he explains how his system has been successful in a number of organizations. For example, Taylor discusses the usefulness of scientific management at Bethlehem Steel Corporation. His system vastly improved the efficiency of this plant—the amount of material shoveled per day increased from 16 tons to 59 tons.

Like Weber's Theory of Bureaucracy, there are a variety of ways that Taylor's system can be broken down. In this section, we will consider four major tenets.

First, *there is one best way to do every job*. This tenet directly attacks the old system of learning through custom in which individual job skills were passed

Case in Point: Get Organized!

Frederick Taylor described organizations in which managers designed systems to make workers as efficient as possible in getting their jobs done. A century later, it appears that most of us are trying to be "managers" to ourselves, as we work to handle our increasingly busy lives in ways that minimize "wasted" time and motion. McGinn (2007) describes one case:

> Stefffany Mohan needs to be organized. The dentist from Des Moines, Iowa, runs her own practice, as well as a school for dental assistants on the side. She has three children under 8—and is expecting her fourth in a few weeks. Her husband is a busy surgeon. Not surprisingly, her desk is a jumble of in-process items. Her to-do list appears endless, and she's constantly struggling to make headway. (p. E8)

Increasingly, people like Steffany Mohan turn to "productivity consultants" and "time management gurus" to introduce order and efficiency to their lives. They buy books such as David Allen's *Getting Things Done* (2002), or Steven Covey's *First Things First* (1996). They use rules about how to deal with e-mail (the two-minute rule, or choices about whether to delete, delay, delegate, or diminish) or purchase special planners that help organize and prioritize their constantly expanding to-do lists.

Do these strategies work? Some would swear by them, while others have started to tout the dangers of being too organized and now advocate the value of chaos (Abrahamson & Freedman, 2007). But one thing is sclear. Taylor's practice of Scientific Management is far from passé—we've just turned it on ourselves.

down from generation to generation. Instead, Taylor believes that the one best way to do every job can best be determined through *time and motion studies*. Thus, a critical aspect of implementing his system is determining the most time-efficient way to accomplish the task at hand. For example, Taylor might analyze a dozen different methods of bricklaying to determine which method is the most efficient. That "one best way" would then be taught to all workers.

The second and third tenets of Taylor's system involve the importance of a proper fit between worker and job. His second principle requires the *proper selection of workers* for the job, and his third principle considers the importance of *training workers* in the manner suggested by time and motion studies. Taylor believes that workers should be scientifically selected and trained for each job and that only "first-class workers" should be retained. An inefficient bricklayer who was better suited to hauling dirt should be shifted to that job. If no "proper job" could be found for the inefficient bricklayer, he should be fired.

Fourth, Taylor believes that there is an *inherent difference between management and workers*. According to Taylor, organizational managers are best suited for thinking, planning, and administrative tasks. In contrast, organizational workers are best suited for laboring. He therefore advocates a strict division of labor in which workers perform physical labor that is planned and directed by management.

Thus, Taylor's system of scientific management is one in which scientific methods are used to determine the best way to do each job. After this best way is determined, workers are scientifically selected for their jobs and trained in the methods deemed most appropriate by time and motion studies. The organization functions by maintaining a strict distinction between workers and managers; workers are responsible for physical labor, and managers are responsible for thinking and organizing.

Taylor believed that this system effectively corrected the past problems of organizational functioning. The problem of *uneven work* would be eliminated by instituting the scientific investigation of work procedures through time and motion studies. The problem of *systematic soldiering* would be combated in two ways. First, although the scientific management system does not reject the practice of piecework pay, Taylor proposes that the piece rate should be based on minimum standards set through time and motion studies. Because these piece rates would be scientifically determined rather than capriciously set, management would not be free to bust the rate. Second, the social pressure of systematic soldiering would be

Spotlight on Scholarship

It is clear that in organizations ruled by "Taylorism" in the early years of the twentieth century, somebody was always watching the workers. Time and motion studies were being conducted to determine the "best way" to do various jobs, the bosses were on the lookout for laborers who might be engaged in dangerous "systematic soldiering" behaviors, and control systems were in effect to be sure that all workers were putting enough effort into accomplishing the goals of the organization. But those were the old days, right?

Scott D'Urso suggests that the old days may not have changed much in his recent article that explores "Who's Watching Us at Work?" D'Urso points out that issues of surveillance and monitoring are just as prevalent now—perhaps even more prevalent—than they were 100 years ago. There are several reasons for this trend. First, technology in the workplace (especially computer technology) both gives employees new opportunities for avoiding work and doing "social tasks" on the job and gives employers a new way of monitoring the extent to which this kind of activity is taking place. Further, new concerns in the post-9/11 world make issues of electronic monitoring and surveillance in the workplace even more salient. And, as D'Urso points out, "[a]lthough this type of government activity seems to go against rights guaranteed to the citizens of this nation, a cursory examination of the U.S. [C]onstitution reveals no explicit "right to privacy," despite the fact that this basic right is often thought to apply to nearly every aspect of civic life" (D'Urso, 2006, p. 282).

D'Urso begins his examination of this topic by considering the extent to which electronic monitoring occurs in the workplace. Consider just a few of the facts he raises:

- Almost 80 percent of major U.S. firms conduct surveillance on their employees. Half monitor phone calls either by listening or recording.
- Fifty-five percent of U.S. companies participating in a large survey in 2005 noted that they retain and review e-mail. This was an increase from 47 percent in 2001.
- In a survey, 90 percent of employees admitted that some of their e-mail at work is personal in nature. And in a separate survey, employees noted that they knew content on their computer was being tracked (23 percent) or were unsure of company policy on surveillance (40 percent).

Given the growing prevalence of electronic monitoring and surveillance on the contemporary organizational landscape, D'Urso argues that it is important for research to model the ways in which these practices might influence such outcomes as communication privacy, organizational control, organizational fairness, job performance, workplace satisfaction, and workplace communication. He proposes a model that considers issues such as the types of communication technologies used; organizational factors such as centralization, size, and climate; and policy factors. He hopes that his model will spur research into the ways in which we are still being watched as we move further into the twenty-first century.

D'Urso, S. C. (2006). Who's Watching Us at Work? Toward a Structural-Perceptual Model of Electronic Monitoring and Surveillance in Organizations. *Communication Theory*, 16, 281–303.

diluted by selecting specific workers for specific jobs. This selection process would often break up original work groups and hence eliminate the social interaction that sometimes led to systematic soldiering.

Taylor's theory and methods fell into some disrepute in the later part of his life, when he faced opposition from unions and became known as the "enemy of the working man." Though it is possible to read some of his writings as supporting laborers (for example, he discusses the importance of cooperation and harmony), it is also true that a great deal of his work indicates a low regard for the typical worker. Consider the following example:

> Now one of the very first requirements for a man who is fit to handle pig iron as a regular occupation is that he shall be so stupid and phlegmatic that he more nearly resembles in his mental make-up the ox than any other type . . . . He is so stupid that the word "percentage" has no meaning to him, and he must consequently be trained by a man more intelligent than himself into the habit of working in accordance with the laws of this science before he can be successful. (Taylor, 1911, p. 59)

Whether we consider Taylor a friend or an enemy of laborers, it is clear that his work has had a substantial impact on the way organizations function. Even in the twenty-first century, many organizations attempt to enhance efficiency through the scientific study of work processes. In combination with Fayol's and Weber's theories, Taylor's ideas give us a clear picture of organizational functioning in the classical mode. The next section of this chapter looks specifically at communication processes within organizations modeled after these classical standards.

COMMUNICATION IN CLASSICAL APPROACHES

It should be clear from our exploration of the work of Fayol, Weber, and Taylor that these theorists saw organizations through the lens of a machine metaphor. As I noted earlier, organizations run in a mechanistic manner will rely on the principles of standardization, specialization, and predictability in order to operate. In the theories we have considered thus far, these general principles are represented by the more specific ideas of organizational structure (such as span of control, scalar chain, hierarchy, division of labor), power (such as primacy of rational-legal power, importance of authority), work design (such as specialization and scientific design of jobs), and attitude (such as subordination of individual interest to organizational goals). It is no surprise that *communication processes* take on particular characteristics in these machinelike organizations. What is communication like in the organizations of Fayol, Weber, and Taylor? To answer this question let us con-

Table 2.1 | Communication in Classical Organizations

Content of Communication	Task
Direction of communication flow	Vertical (downward)
Mode/channel of communication	Usually written
Style of communication	Formal

sider several aspects of communication, including (1) the content of communication, (2) the direction of communication flow, (3) the mode or channel of communication, and (4) the style of communication. These are summarized in Table 2.1.

Content of Communication

In the classical theories we have considered, there are certain things that should be talked about and certain things that should not be talked about in the organization. Consider, for example, Fayol's principle of "subordination of individual interest to general interest." This principle suggests that employees should focus on the goals of the organization, not on their own individual needs and desires. It would follow from this principle, then, that communication within the organization should be focused on task-related topics.

In classical organizations, communication about task is very narrowly focused. For example, Farace, Monge, and Russell (1977) talk about three kinds of communication that often flow in organizational settings: task-related communication, innovation-related communication (communication about new ideas), and maintenance-related communication (communication on social topics that maintains human relationships). Obviously, social communication would be strongly discouraged in the organizations represented by classical theories. Such communication would be counterproductive to the achievement of organizational goals. It is interesting to note, however, that innovation-related communication would also be discouraged in these organizations—at least for the vast majority of employees. Consider a worker in an insurance company run according to Taylor's Theory of Scientific Management. This worker would not be encouraged to talk with co-workers about better ways to process insurance forms, as it is assumed that the best way has already been determined scientifically and that the worker is not capable of improving on these ideas. Thus, both social and innovation communication are discouraged in classically run organizations. The content of communication in these organizations is restricted to work-related issues.

Direction of Communication Flow

A second way to characterize communication in the classical theories is to consider how messages are routed through the organizational system. There are a number of possible directions in which communication can flow. For example, communication can flow vertically up and down the organizational chart, with supervisors talking to subordinates and vice versa. Communication can flow horizontally, with employees at the same level of the organization talking to each other. Or, communication can be free-flowing, in which all organizational members are encouraged to talk with all other members.

In the classical theories of Fayol, Weber, and Taylor, the most important route for communication is the *vertical flow* of information along the scalar chain of the organizational hierarchy. Further, in these classical theories, the vast majority of communication in the organization flows *downward* in the form of orders, rules, and directives. There is little feedback that moves upward from lower-level employees to higher-level management. (However, Fayol's gangplank allows the possibility of some horizontal communication.) The likelihood of horizontal and free-flowing communication does increase at higher levels of the organization as the tasks taken on tend to involve more planning and coordination. However, horizontal and free-flowing communication is the exception within classical theories. The rule for communication is the flow of information downward from managers to employees.

Channel of Communication

In addition to content and direction, a variety of channels can facilitate communication flow. To name just a few, information can be communicated through face-to-face channels, through written channels, or through a variety of mediated channels, including the telephone or computer. Although all of these modes of communication are possible within an organization run according to classical theories, it is likely that the *written* mode of communication is the most prevalent.

Several principles of classical theory point to the importance of written communication. Weber is most explicit about this issue in advocating the importance of rules and the importance of codifying them in written form. Taylor and Fayol also seem to favor written communication. For example, the notion of having "one best way" to do every job in scientific management lends itself to the production of written employee handbooks and instructions. For Fayol, the principle of "order" advocating a specified place for all employees and tasks in the organization would also suggest the importance of written instructions and guidelines. In short, because classical theories emphasize the permanence of rules and procedures for efficient organizational functioning, these organizations will probably also rely heavily on written communication in the form of employee handbooks, instructions, mission statements, rules, and performance evaluations.

Style of Communication

Finally, we can consider the *style* of communication that might be found in the organizations of these classical theorists. We have already noted that communication will tend to be top-down, written, and task-related. It is also likely that the tone or style of that communication will be highly *formal*. For example, forms of address will often be distant rather than familiar (for example, Mr. and Ms. rather than first names). Titles will be used (such as supervisor, secretary, or administrative assistant) to separate managers from other employees. The vocabulary chosen for messages will avoid slang and colloquial terms, opting instead for highly standard language. The formality of communication style in a classical organization might also be seen in nonverbal communication such as dress styles, where suits and ties or uniforms will be favored over more casual or individualized forms of attire. In short, the bureaucratic and professionalized climate of these organizations will often lead to formal—some might say sterile—styles of communication.

CLASSICAL MANAGEMENT IN ORGANIZATIONS TODAY

The theorists we have talked about in this chapter—Fayol, Weber, and Taylor—have all been dead for many years. These men created their theories in the early twentieth century with the organizations of that time period in mind. This could lead us to question whether these theories are totally outdated. Are classical theories of management only relevant for newly industrialized factories, or are these theories still applicable in today's world?

The answer to this question is clear. An examination of the vast majority of present-day organizations reveals the prevalence of classical management thought. Consider, for example, the process of registering for the organizational communication class in which you are currently enrolled. This registration process undoubtedly involved many of the principles discussed in this chapter, including rules for who can take a class and when, standardized procedures for signing up for the class, paperwork that may provide you with documentation of registration, and so on. Even registration that uses advanced technology like the Internet and World Wide Web could not proceed without highly systematized operations—indeed, standardization and systematic processing is especially important in designing the programs that allow technology to play a role in such a process.

If you go to a fast-food restaurant for lunch today, you will also see the principles of classical theorists at work. These organizations have determined the "one best way" to make a hamburger, and that procedure is followed religiously. There is also "one best way" to greet and serve customers—pity the poor counterperson who forgets to ask if you want fries with your order.

In short, your daily activities reveal the widespread use of classical principles in today's organizations. Let us consider two specific ways in which the tenets of classical management are still in popular use today.

Classical Structure in Today's Organizations

As we have noted, the structure advocated by classical theorists is one in which there is a well-defined division of labor and a strict hierarchy. In today's organizations, such a structure is most clearly represented by military organizations. The notions of scalar chain, unity of command, and span of control are the basis of organizing in the military, for without the checks and balances provided by hierarchy and rules, an individual could cause great harm by making an uninformed decision. These classical structures can also be seen in a great many manufacturing and service organizations in which various departments are responsible for specific tasks and in which these functional units are linked through a hierarchical and formalized organizational chart. In these settings, the core task is highly repetitive and routine, promoting the use of mechanistic principles. And even in nonprofit organizations, there is a press toward being as efficient as possible, so that donated money is spent with as little waste as possible (Quinn, 2006).

Of course, not all contemporary organizations use classical structure. In many organizations, division of labor is blurred through the use of cross-functional teams or through the "matrixing" of tasks. Many organizations now recognize that there is often value in communication that flows more freely among individuals with a variety of tasks, and hence these organizations reject the formalization of an organizational chart. It is clear, though, that the influence of classical management is still widely seen in the structural characteristics of many of today's organizations.

Classical Job Design and Rewards in Today's Organizations

Classical theorists, especially Taylor, advocate the scientific design of jobs, the routinization of those jobs, and the "fitting" of the employee to his or her optimal task. Although we would be hard-pressed to find an organization that uses scientific management to the extent proposed by Taylor, we do see many of his principles used in today's organizations. Consider, for example, an organization that is trying to computerize its system for dealing with accounts payable and accounts receivable. Such an organization will attempt to find the most efficient way to accomplish these tasks. Designers will look for the simplest system that reduces the number of keystrokes necessary for inputting information and keeps mistakes to a minimum.

In today's organizations—especially with the widespread use of computers and advent of robotic technology—we are often looking for the "one best way" to accomplish tasks. Organizations today also often follow Taylor's ideas about fitting the job to the individual, especially in terms of the match between the job and the psychological profile of an employee. For example, Lawler and Finegold (2000) argue for the importance of "individualizing the organization" in a way that accounts for personal differences in employee abilities, needs, and desires in the workplace.

Contemporary organizations also continue to be concerned with the role of financial rewards in the motivation of organizational members. Money will probably always be a critical factor in both recruiting employees and rewarding them, and commentators today debate about the extent to which various pay structures are "worth it" for the bottom line of a company. For example, there has been great debate in recent years about the huge payouts received by many CEOs. In 1994, CEOs made 142 times the average worker—by 2007 CEOs made 431 times the average worker. However, it can be argued that CEOs of contemporary organizations earn the extra money because they are managing much larger firms, taking more risks, and making decisions that touch a wide range of employees and the public (Foroohar, 2007).

SUMMARY

In this chapter, we have explored several classical organizational theories, all of which use a machine metaphor in which organizations are conceptualized as highly standardized, specialized, and predictable. The first theory we considered was Henri Fayol's Theory of Classical Management, which proposes that managing consists of the elements of planning, commanding, coordinating, controlling, and organizing. Fayol also proposes a number of principles to guide the structure, power relationships, reward system, and attitudes within an organization.

The second theory we considered was Max Weber's Theory of Bureaucracy. This theory has many features in common with Fayol's theory but in addition emphasizes the closed nature of bureaucracy, the importance of organizational rules, and the predominance of rational-legal authority in bureaucratic functioning.

We then considered Frederick Taylor's Theory of Scientific Management, a microscopic theory that considers relationships between management and workers and the manner in which jobs should be designed. In Taylor's system, jobs should be designed through time and motion studies, and organizations should be based on a strict division between workers and managers in which workers provide the physical labor and managers provide the mental planning of the work.

We then considered the nature of communication in organizations designed along classical lines. Communication in these organizations is charac-terized as primarily top-down, formal, task-related, and written. Finally, we looked at the existence of classical management principles in organizations today, exploring how both structure and job design in today's organizations often reflect the ideas expounded many years ago by classical theorists.

Discussion Questions

1. What aspects of a classical approach to organizing are revealed by the "machine metaphor"? What aspects are concealed or obscured? Are there other metaphors for organization and communication that could shed more light on how classical theorists thought about organizational communication?
2. What are areas of similarity and difference among the three major theorists considered in this chapter? Are the ideas of Fayol, Weber, and Taylor still relevant for today's organizations? Why or why not?
3. Thinking ahead to ideas beyond classical approaches to organizing, what are your major critiques of these ideas? How do you think the theories presented in this chapter misrepresent the nature of both people and organizations?

| CASE STUDY | The Creamy Creations Takeover |

THE SHOPPE

Creamy Creations Ice Cream Shoppe is a small and popular ice cream parlor in a midsize southern city. In 2002, Creamy Creations had been open for almost two years and was gathering a loyal clientele of families and students from the local community college. Creamy Creations specialized in fancy, individualized ice cream confections. Customers would order their base ice cream (or frozen yogurt) and the toppings they wanted to make their own "creamy creation." The toppings ranged from the typical (such as hot fudge, marshmallow, nuts, fruit syrups, and crushed candy bars) to the exotic (mango fruit chutney, chocolate-covered hazelnuts, and crystallized ginger). Each creamy creation was made start to finish by one of the high school or college students working behind the marble counter. Many customers had a favorite "creamy creator" and would wait for that person to be available to make a special sundae.

In the first 18 months of Creamy Creations' existence, it was owned by Bob Peterson, a local retiree who had started the business after 30 years in the military. However, after a year and a half of successful operations, Bob's wife talked him into selling the ice cream business "while it's hot" and buying a Winnebago to tour the country. Bob sold Creamy Creations to Burger Barn, a local fast-food chain that wanted to expand into other types of food service establishments.

THE TAKEOVER

When Burger Barn took over operations at Creamy Creations, they were pleased with what they saw. Creamy Creations had a solid customer base and had been making a modest profit almost since it opened. Customers spoke highly of the quality product and the friendly atmosphere. As a result, repeat business was high. Not surprisingly, though, Burger Barn thought that Creamy Creations could do even better. Burger Barn had built its reputation on high-quality food served in an efficient and friendly manner. When Burger Barn executives looked at Creamy Creations, they were pleased with the food quality and the friendliness but disturbed by the lack of efficiency. Customers would often have to wait 10 minutes before placing an order and would typically wait another 10 minutes for the order to be filled. This wait seemed excessive to Burger Barn executives, so they looked for ways to change the system in order to improve customer service.

After observing operations for several weeks, the Burger Barn managers decided that the best way to improve operations at Creamy Creations was to institute three "workstations" behind the counter. Customers would first order their base ice cream at the "scoop station," then move on to the worker at the "topping station" to have their sundae completed. Finally, the customer would move to the "pay station" to order drinks and have the bill rung up. Because workers were already trained in all facets of the Creamy Creations operation, they could shift easily from station to station. Burger Barn executives reasoned that this would keep them from being bored with their work and help maintain a high level of flexibility for scheduling.

THE AFTERMATH

After six months of operations under the Burger Barn umbrella, Creamy Creations was doing reasonably well. Profits were slightly higher than they had been before the takeover, though not as high as Burger Barn executives would have liked. Turnover had increased substantially, but Burger Barn executives did not see this as a troubling problem because there was a large labor market in the community capable of this type of unskilled work. Creamy Creations was still doing a brisk business, although there were many more customers getting their orders "to go" and fewer using the restaurant as a local gathering place.

When watching operations, Burger Barn executives were pleased that customers were served more quickly than before, though there was sometimes a bottleneck of customers at the toppings station, because this operation was more complex than activities at either the scooping station or the pay station. Burger Barn executives considered splitting the toppings station into two separate work areas ("syrup station" and "finishing touches") to improve efficiency further and avoid delays in customer service. They also considered eliminating some of the more bizarre topping options, because these toppings were very expensive, were rarely ordered, and tended to clutter up the work area and slow down operations.

All in all, the executives were pleased with the progress made in their acquisition. It was becoming clear that with the recent changes, Creamy Creations had the potential to become a profitable member of the Burger Barn family. They even thought of opening more Creamy Creations in surrounding communities.

CASE ANALYSIS QUESTIONS

1. The Burger Barn executives see a rosy future ahead for Creamy Creations. Do you see any reasons why they should not be so optimistic? What are the potential future pitfalls they should be watching out for?

2. How are the principles of classical management reflected in what has happened at Creamy Creations? Which tenets of Fayol's Theory of Classical Management, Weber's Theory of Bureaucracy, and Taylor's Theory of Scientific Management are in evidence? How have the advantages and disadvantages of the classical approach been played out at this business?

3. If you were called in as a communication consultant by Burger Barn executives, what kind of information would you gather in making an assessment about the likely future of Creamy Creations? What would you predict your findings might be, and how would these findings influence your recommendations to Burger Barn executives?

Human Relations and Human Resources Approaches

CHAPTER 3

AFTER READING THIS CHAPTER, YOU SHOULD . . .

- Know about the Hawthorne Studies and how they proved to be a springboard for the human relations approach
- Be familiar with Maslow's Hierarchy of Needs Theory and McGregor's Theory X and Theory Y as exemplars of the human relations approach
- Understand the ways in which the human relations approach was empirically inadequate and misused, and how these problems led to the human resources approach
- Be able to explain how the Managerial Grid and System IV management describe aspects of human resources management
- Be able to describe typical communication patterns in classical, human relations, and human resources organizations
- Appreciate the challenges of instituting human resources principles into today's organizations

As you discovered in Chapter 2, management theory in the early part of the twentieth century was marked by an allegiance to a machine metaphor and a search for ways to increase efficiency and productivity through systems of structure, power, compensation, and attitude. Indeed, many principles of classical management are still widely used today. It should be clear from our consideration of Fayol, Weber, and Taylor, however, that certain aspects of organizational communication are conspicuously absent from classical theories. For example, these theorists pay little attention to the individual needs of employees, to nonfinancial rewards in the workplace, or to the prevalence of social interaction in organizations. These theorists were also uninterested in how employees could contribute to meeting organizational goals through knowledge, ideas, and discussion—the only valued contribution was that of physical labor. Issues such as these drove the thinking of the theorists we will consider in this chapter: scholars and practitioners who represent the *human relations* and *human resources* approaches to organizational communication. In this chapter we will consider these two approaches that began more than eighty years ago and still influence values and practices today. We will first consider the human relations approach that emphasizes the importance of human needs in the workplace. We will then consider developments from this early movement—the human resources approach—that concentrate on the contributions of all employees in reaching organizational goals. In discussing each approach, we will consider the historical and scholarly context that led to the approach and representative theorists within the approach. We will then consider ways in which the human relations and human resources approaches influence communication in organizations and the ways in which these approaches are exemplified in today's organizations.

THE HUMAN RELATIONS APPROACH

From Classical Theory to Human Relations: The Hawthorne Studies

From 1924 to 1933, a number of research investigations were conducted at the Western Electric Company's Hawthorne plant in Illinois that have become collectively known as the *Hawthorne studies*. All but the first of these were conducted by a research team led by Elton Mayo of Harvard University (Roethlisberger & Dickson, 1939). Mayo and his research team were initially interested in how changes in the work environment would impact the productivity of factory workers. These research interests were quite consistent with the prevailing theories of classical management, especially Frederick Taylor's Theory of Scientific Management. That is, like Taylor and other supporters of scientific management, the research team at the Hawthorne plant attempted to discover aspects of the task environment that would maximize worker output and hence improve organizational efficiency. Four major phases marked the Hawthorne studies: the illumination studies, the relay assembly test room studies, the interview program, and the bank wiring room studies.

The Illumination Studies   The illumination studies (conducted before the entry of Mayo and his research team) were designed to determine the influence of lighting level on worker productivity. In these studies, two groups of workers were isolated. For one group (the control group), lighting was held constant. For the second (experimental) group, lighting was systematically raised and lowered. To the surprise of the researchers, there was no significant difference in the productivity of the control group and the experimental group. Indeed, except when workers were laboring in near darkness, productivity tended to go up in both groups under all conditions. It was at this point that Mayo's research team entered the scene to further investigate these counterintuitive findings.

The Relay Assembly Test Room Studies   To better understand the productivity increases seen in the illumination studies, Mayo and his team of researchers isolated a group of six women who assembled telephone relay systems. A number of changes were then introduced to this group, including incentive plans, rest pauses, temperature, humidity, work hours, and refreshments. All changes were discussed with the workers ahead of time, and detailed records of productivity were kept as these changes in the work environment were instituted. Productivity went up in a wide variety of situations. After more than a year of study, the researchers concluded that "social satisfactions arising out of human association in work were more important determinants of work behavior in general and output in particular than were any of the physical and economic aspects of the work situation to which the attention had originally been limited" (Carey, 1967, p. 404). Because productivity remained high under a wide range of conditions, Mayo and his colleagues believed the results could be best explained by the influence of the social group on productivity and the extra attention paid by the managers to the six workers in the group.

The Interview Program   The unusual findings for the relay assembly test room group led Mayo and his colleagues to conduct a series of interviews with thousands of employees at the Hawthorne plant. Although the goal of these interviews was to learn more about the impact of working conditions on productivity, the interviewers found workers more interested in talking about their feelings and attitudes. Pugh and Hickson (1989) note that "[t]he major finding of this stage of the inquiry was that many problems of worker-management cooperation were the results of the emotionally based attitudes of the workers rather than of the objective difficulties of the situation" (p. 174).

The Bank Wiring Room Studies   A final series of investigations involved naturalistic (nonexperimental) observation of a group of men in the bank wiring room. Observations revealed that the men developed norms regarding the "proper" level of productivity and exerted social pressure on each other to maintain that level. Slow workers were pressured to speed up and speedy workers were pressured to slow down. This social pressure (similar to the notion of systematic soldiering discussed in Chapter 2) existed in opposition to the organization's formal goals regarding productivity contained in production targets and incentive schedules. Mayo and his colleagues concluded that the social group's influence on worker behavior exceeded the leverage exerted by the formal organizational power structure.

Explanations of Findings in the Hawthorne Studies   A number of explanations can be offered to account for the findings of the Hawthorne studies. For example, productivity increases were often associated with changes in the work environment, such as work hours, temperature, lighting, and breaks. In the relay assembly test room studies, productivity also increased when pay incentives were offered to workers. Both of these explanations are consistent with classical approaches to organizing, and both were rejected by the investigating team at the Hawthorne plant.

Mayo and his colleagues instead turned to explanations that revolved around the social and emotional needs of workers. First, these researchers concluded that worker output increased as a direct result of the attention paid to workers by the researchers. This phenomenon, whereby mere attention to individuals causes changes in behavior, has come to be known as the *Hawthorne effect*. A second explanation proposed by the Hawthorne researchers is that worker output was in-creased through the working of informal *social factors*. Recall that the women in the relay assembly test room were separated from other factory workers during the experiment. Mayo and his colleagues concluded that these six women formed a tightly knit group and that social interaction in this group served to increase pro-ductivity. This explanation was enhanced through the observation of social pres-sure in the bank wiring room and the comments of the workers during interviews. Finally, the researchers believed that *management style* could account for some of the observed productivity changes. This conclusion was based on the impact of open communication between workers and managers in the relay assembly test room portion of the studies.

Were Mayo and his colleagues correct in their conclusions that productivity in-creases should be attributed to social factors, management style, and the Hawthorne effect? Subsequent analyses of the data from the Hawthorne studies clearly suggest that they were not (see, e.g., Carey, 1967; Franke & Kaul, 1978). Indeed, these reanalyses suggest that more traditional explanations, such as incen-tives, pressure from management, and worker selection, are better explanations of the Hawthorne findings. However, the questionable value of these findings and in-terpretations does not diminish the fact that at the time—and for many years after —it was *widely believed* that the results of the Hawthorne studies could be best ex-plained as a function of social factors and the satisfaction of the human needs of workers. These interpretations had a substantial impact on the thinking of organi-zational scholars in the 1930s. Because of these studies, theorists, researchers, and practitioners began to turn away from the mechanistic views of classical theories and consider, instead, the possibility that human needs and social interaction played an important role in organizational functioning. As Pugh and Hickson (1989) conclude: "Taken as a whole, the significance of the Hawthorne investiga-tion was in 'discovering' the informal organization which, it is now realized, exists in all organizations" (p. 175).

Thus, although the Hawthorne studies may have been lacking in scientific value and interpretive rigor, the sociological impact of the investigations cannot be underestimated. The Hawthorne investigations served as a springboard, moving or-ganizational theorists from classical theories to human relations approaches. These studies also began to highlight the role of communication, especially informal and group communication, in organizational functioning. The next two sections of this chapter present two representative theorists from the human relations movement: Abraham Maslow and Douglas McGregor.

Maslow's Hierarchy of Needs Theory

Abraham Maslow developed his Hierarchy of Needs Theory over a period of many years as a general theory of human motivation (Maslow, 1943, 1954). However, he and others have applied this theory extensively to organizational behavior, and it serves as a prototype of a human relations approach to organizing and management.

Maslow proposes that humans are motivated by a number of basic needs. The five types of needs that are consistently presented in his writing are listed next and presented in Table 3.1. The first three types are often referred to as lower-order needs and the final two as higher-order needs.

1. *Physiological needs*: These are the needs of the human body, including the need for food, water, sleep, and sensory gratification. In the organizational context, these needs can be most clearly satisfied through the provision of a "living wage" that allows individuals to buy adequate food and clothing and through physical working conditions that do not violate the physical requirements of the human body.

2. *Safety needs*: Safety needs include the desire to be free from danger and environmental threats. In the organizational context, these needs can, again, be satisfied through wages that allow employees to procure shelter against the elements and through working conditions that are protective and healthy.

3. *Affiliation needs*: This set of needs, sometimes referred to as "belonging needs" or "love needs," refers to the necessity of giving and receiving human affection and regard. These needs can be satisfied in the organization through the establishment of social relationships with coworkers and managers.

4. *Esteem needs*: Esteem needs refer to the desire of individuals to feel a sense of achievement and accomplishment. Esteem needs can be divided into external esteem, achieved through public recognition and attention, and internal esteem, achieved through a sense of accomplishment, confidence, and achievement. In the organizational context, external esteem needs can be met by compensation and reward structures. Internal esteem needs can be met by the provision of challenging jobs that provide employees with the opportunity to achieve and excel.

5. *Need for self-actualization*: Maslow characterizes this need as the desire to "become more and more what one is, to become everything that one is capable of becoming" (1943, p. 382). In the words of army recruitment ads, the need to self-actualize is trying to "be all that you can be." Clearly, this need will take different forms for different people. However, it is likely that an organization can facilitate the satisfaction of this need through the provision of jobs that allow an individual to exercise responsibility and creativity in the workplace.

Table 3.1 | Maslow's Needs Hierarchy in the Organizational Context

Need Level	Example of Need Satisfaction in Organization
Level 5: Self-actualization	Work allowing the exercise of creativity
Level 4: Esteem	Internal: Rewarding work External: Bonus pay
Level 3: Affiliation	Social relationships with coworkers
Level 2: Safety	Physically safe working conditions
Level 1: Physiological	"Living wage" to allow purchase of food, clothing

Maslow proposed that these five types of needs are arranged in a *hierarchy of pre-potency*. The notion of prepotency suggests that lower-level needs must be satisfied before an individual can move on to higher-level needs. For example, an individual will not attempt to satisfy affiliation needs until needs for physiological functioning and safety have been provided for. Thus, in the organizational context, social relationships on the job will not be satisfying if the organization has not provided adequate wages and working conditions.

Though there has been mixed support about its empirical accuracy (see, e.g., Kamalanabhan, Uma, & Vasanthi, 1999; Miner, 1980), Maslow's Hierarchy of Needs Theory is critical in its provision of a clear example of human relations principles and their possible application to the organizational context. Maslow's concentration on the satisfaction of human needs—especially the higher-order needs of esteem and self-actualization—reflects the shift in organizational theorizing that began when the Hawthorne researchers "discovered" the importance of social interaction and managerial attention in the workplace.

McGregor's Theory X and Theory Y

The second exemplar of the human relations movement that we will consider is Douglas McGregor's Theory X and Theory Y (McGregor, 1960). McGregor was a professor at Massachusetts Institute of Technology and one of the strongest advocates of the human relations movement. Theory X and Theory Y represent the divergent assumptions that managers can hold about organizational functioning. As you will see in the following list of propositions and beliefs, Theory X is representative of a manager influenced by the most negative aspects of classical management theories. In contrast, a Theory Y manager is one who adheres to the precepts of the human relations movement.

McGregor (1957, p. 23) spells out three propositions of the typical Theory X manager. These propositions argue that management is responsible for organizing money, material, and people for economic ends; that people must be controlled and motivated to fit organizational needs; and that without intervention and direction, people would be passive or resistant to the achievement of organizational needs. McGregor's Theory X postulates (McGregor, 1957, p. 23) about human nature are even more straightforward:

1. The average man is by nature indolent—he works as little as possible.
2. He lacks ambition, dislikes responsibility, and prefers to be led.
3. He is inherently self-centered and indifferent to organizational needs.
4. He is by nature resistant to change.
5. He is gullible, not very bright, and the ready dupe of the charlatan and the demagogue.

McGregor asserts that these beliefs are widely held by managers but are incorrect. He believes that managers should conceptualize workers as motivated by the higher-order needs in Maslow's hierarchy and as capable of independent achievement in the workplace. These managerial assumptions are represented in McGregor's presentation of Theory Y (McGregor, 1960, pp. 47–48):

1. The expenditure of physical and mental effort in work is as natural as play or rest.
2. External control and the threat of punishment are not the only means for bringing about effort toward organizational objectives. Man will exercise self-direction and self-control in the service of objectives to which he is committed.
3. Commitment to objectives is a function of the rewards associated with their achievement. The most significant of such rewards, such as the satisfaction of ego and self-actualization needs, can be direct products of efforts directed toward organizational objectives.
4. The average human being learns under proper conditions not only to accept but also to seek responsibility.
5. The capacity to exercise a relatively high degree of imagination, ingenuity, and creativity in the solution of organizational problems is widely, not narrowly, distributed in the population.
6. Under the conditions of modern industrial life, the intellectual potentialities of the average human being are only partially utilized.

Thus, a Theory X manager assumes that a strong and forceful hand is essential for harnessing the efforts of basically unmotivated workers. In contrast, a Theory Y manager assumes that workers are highly motivated to satisfy achievement and self-actualization needs and that the job of the manager is to bring out the natural tendencies of these intelligent and motivated workers. Not surprisingly, McGregor advocates the use of Theory Y management. He believes that behaviors stemming from these managerial assumptions (such as management by objectives and participation in decision making) would lead to a more satisfied and more productive workforce.

Like Maslow's Hierarchy of Needs Theory, McGregor's thinking emphasizes a conceptualization of employees as individuals characterized by needs for attention, social interaction, and individual achievement. Employees in human relations theories are not only motivated by financial gain but by the desire to satisfy these higher-order needs. Indeed, in comparison to the machine metaphor of classical theorists, a metaphor that could aptly be applied to the human relations approach is that of a *family*. Using this metaphor emphasizes the notion of relationships as central to our understanding of organizational functioning. Just as a machine thrives on precision and regularity, a family thrives when needs are fulfilled and opportunities are provided for self-actualization. It should be noted, however, that there are still distinctions among members of a family. Parents in a family—like management in a human relations organization—are held responsible for providing opportunities in which children's needs can be fulfilled and talents can be nurtured. And children in a family—like workers in a human relations organization—are often limited in terms of the power and influence they wield within the family unit.

Thus, human relations theorists share an allegiance to principles that highlight human needs and the satisfaction of those needs through interaction with others in the workplace and through the choices managers make about motivating and rewarding employees. Indeed, in moving from the classical theorists of the early twentieth century to human relations theorists of the mid-twentieth century, we shift from a belief that "workers work" to a belief that "workers feel." However,

Spotlight on Scholarship

The human relations approach to organizing high-lights the importance of finding the job factors and management practices that enhance employee satisfaction. Human relations theorists reason that satisfaction will then lead to more effective and productive employees and to organizational success. In the early years of the human relations approach, the search for factors that influenced satisfaction was relatively straightforward. Researchers could look at the nature of the job, relationships and communication in the workplace, and factors such as pay and promotion. These job factors, though, were usually "located" in the office building or factory being studied —just like the employees.

However, times have changed. People employed by a single organization now work in a variety of traditional and nontraditional work settings. As we'll explore further in Chapters 13 and 14 , technology—and the needs of a changing world—have led organizations to a variety of structural arrangements, including telework, virtual offices, and global organizations. But how do these changes in organizational form influence the more basic attitudes of interest to human relations theorists, such as job satisfaction? This question was explored recently by Rosenfeld, Richman, and May (2004) in their investigation of information and organizational culture in a "dispersed-network organization."

A dispersed-network organization is an emerging organizational form in which an organization includes both office personnel and field personnel at several different geographical locations. In this case, the organization studied was a health care provision organization (that the authors called "HCP") that included both a main office and branch offices. More important for this investigation, though, HCP included both personnel who worked in the office (typically performing clerical and administrative tasks) and field personnel who worked outside of the confines of the office (typically performing clinical tasks such as nursing care or social work). Rosenfeld et al. used a survey study to explore whether these two types of employees had different needs for information and different patterns of job satisfaction.

Though the results of this study were somewhat complex, one particular pattern stands out—employees working in the office reported job satisfaction based on different types of information than employees working in the field. For office personnel, satisfaction was predicted by receiving information about organizational policies, personal performance, and organizational performance. The satisfaction of field workers was also enhanced by information about organizational policy, but it was not influenced by information about personal or organizational performance. It appears that the nature of these workers' tasks—providing direct health care services for clients—was not as directly tied to organizational assessments of success. As Rosenfeld et al. state, "At HCP, in order to be satisfied with their work, field personnel need to have some distance from information regarding the organization's performance—presumably so that they can perform their client-based job responsibilities without worrying about the organization's bottom-line goal of profitability" (p. 45). Thus, this study clearly indicates that when it comes to satisfying the informational needs of employees, one size does not fit all. Probably this has always been true, but it is especially true in the complex organizations of today.

Rosenfeld, L. B., Richman, J. M., & May, S. K. (2004). Information Adequacy, Job Satisfaction and Organizational Culture in a Dispersed-Network Organization. *Journal of Applied Communication Research, 32*, 28–54.

there was yet another movement afoot following the human relations movement. This was a consideration of how workers can contribute to the workplace through more than just "working" or "feeling" but through thinking and participating in many aspects of organizational functioning. This approach—the human resources approach—is considered next.

THE HUMAN RESOURCES APPROACH

The approach to organizational communication we will look at in this section builds on the contributions of classical and human relationships theorists and adds an important twist. The *human resources approach* acknowledges contributions of classical and, especially, human relations approaches to organizing. Human resources theorists recognize that individuals in organizations have feelings that must be considered and also recognize that individual labor is an important ingredient for meeting organizational goals. What human resources theorists add to the mix is an emphasis on the cognitive contributions employees make with their thoughts and ideas. In this section, we first consider a few of the factors that led organizational theorists and practitioners from classical and human relations principles to the ideas at the center of the human resources approach to management and organizations. We then discuss two theories that provide early statements of some fundamental aspects of the human resources approach to organizing: Robert Blake and Jane Mouton's Managerial Grid and Rensis Likert's System IV.

Impetus for the Human Resources Approach

The Hawthorne studies served as a springboard that moved thinking about organizations from the classical school to the human relations school. Was there a similar watershed event that provoked disillusionment with the human relations school and led to the human resources approach? Not really. No single study or incident induced dissatisfaction with the ideas of human relations theorists—indeed, these views are still widely held today. However, in the fifties, sixties, and seventies, there was a growing feeling that models of employee needs were insufficient for describing, explaining, and managing the complexities of organizational life. In particular, there was concern about whether human relations principles really worked and whether they could be misused by organizational practitioners.

Do Human Relations Principles Work?
The principles of human relations theories are certainly intuitively appealing. We would like to believe that by assuming good things about employees, by treating them well with enriched and challenging jobs, and by fulfilling their needs for esteem and self-actualization, we could generate a climate in which worker satisfaction and productivity will flourish. However appealing, though, there is evidence that many of the ideas of human relations theorists simply do not hold up when put to the empirical test. This is true at the level of the individual study and theory, as there is limited support for the conclusions of the Hawthorne Studies or for the specific theoretical propositions of scholars like Maslow and McGregor. In addition, this lack of support can also be seen when we consider the general principles on which the human relations movement rests.

At its most basic level, the human relations approach posits that higher-order needs can be satisfied through job design, management style, and other organizational factors. When these higher-order needs are satisfied, employees should be happier. When employees are happier, they should be more productive. This general pattern is depicted in Figure 3.1.

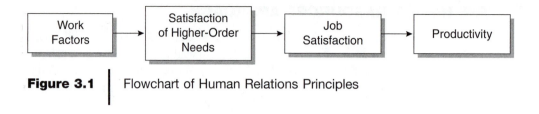

Figure 3.1 | Flowchart of Human Relations Principles

Let us now consider the various links in this human relations model. The first link is between aspects of the work environment and the satisfaction of higher-order needs. Evidence has shown that various job characteristics can serve as motivational factors, although aspects of the job that motivate may vary considerably by person and situation. Thus, this link of the human relations model seems to hold up. Evidence has also shown that job satisfaction will be the next step in the progression (e.g., Muchinsky, 1977). It is the third link in the model connecting job satisfaction and performance that is problematic. It seems "obvious" that employees who are more satisfied will also be more productive. However, years of research stemming from the human relations movement have failed to support this connection (see, e.g., Brief, 1998; Cote, 1999). Why aren't satisfied employees also more productive employees? Perhaps other motivations for hard work, such as financial reward or threat of punishment, take precedence over satisfaction. Whatever the reason, it is clear that "humans are complicated, choice-making animals whose decisions about the amount of effort they should spend on any particular activity are based on a myriad of personal considerations" (Conrad, 1985, p. 118).

Misuse of Human Relations Principles   Another factor that steered many to the human resources approach was the extent to which tenets of the human relations movement could be used in a superficial or manipulative way in organizations. For example, a manager who holds Theory X assumptions (e.g., that employees are inherently lazy and stupid) might adopt some superficial Theory Y behaviors in an effort to gain more control over the workforce. For example, the manager might ask for employees' opinions about an issue without having any intention of taking those opinions into account during decision making. Because this "pseudo-participation" is not based on a solid foundation of human relations principles, it is likely that it would backfire and be an ineffective organizational strategy. It is also likely that this manipulative use of human relations ideas would fail to satisfy worker needs.

Miles (1965) first highlighted this problem many years ago in his article "Human Relations or Human Resources." When Miles asked practicing managers about their *behaviors*, the managers reported a number of activities that would be endorsed by human relations theorists, such as participation in decision making and supportive and open communication. However, the *beliefs* of these managers did not match these behaviors. The managers did not think employees had sufficient abilities and talents to make high-quality decisions or to work independently. As the title of his article suggests, his study highlights the difference between *human relations* and *human resources*. Both human relations and human resources managers might advocate the same kind of organizational behavior but for very different reasons.

Consider the issue of participation. A human relations manager would institute participation to satisfy employee needs for affiliation and esteem and hope that this need satisfaction would lead to higher levels of productivity. In contrast, a human resources manager would institute participation to take advantage of the innovative ideas held by subordinates. This manager, in other words, sees employees as human resources that can be accessed to enhance the functioning of the organization and satisfy the needs of the individuals. It is also likely that the form of participation would distinguish a human relations manager from a human resources manager. A human relations manager might see a suggestion box or a weekly staff meeting as sufficient for meeting relevant employee needs. In contrast, a human resources manager would want to institute a form of participation that could fully tap the ideas and skills of organizational members.

Although Miles first raised this issue many years ago, organizational scholars continue to be concerned about the ways in which those in power in organizations might misuse participative programs. Wendt (1998) has eloquently pointed to this "paradox of participation" in his analysis of many contemporary organizational programs. He argues that "the team worker who constantly participates and contributes to problem solving but who, in the final analysis, has no control over the decision-making process becomes frustrated by a paradoxical dimension of

 ## Case in Point: Slashing ER Waiting Times

Many of us have been there. Sitting on hard plastic chairs in the waiting area of a hospital waiting room, hoping that you will finally "get in" to see the doctors and nurses and have your health emergency addressed. You've probably thought that there *must* be more efficient and effective ways to run an emergency room and provide care to people who are ill or who have experienced trauma. The employees at Parkland Hospital in Dallas, Texas, thought so, and started working in 2007 to streamline the admissions process. Their process of working through this problem is a clear reflection of what can happen when human resources principles are put into practice (Gordon, 2007).

In April of 2007, a committee was formed to improve the ER at Parkland by looking at issues such as patient transportation, bed turnaround times, discharge predictions, and the process through which medical orders are issued. Before this committee was

formed, three outside consultants had failed to have an impact, but in the two months after the problems were directly addressed by employees, Parkland has saved more than 2,000 hours of patient care. The average wait time has been reduced from three hours to one hour. How has this happened? Some of the changes have been as simple as moving X-ray services to a location closer to the emergency room. Others include more complex systemic changes. But what is clearly important is that the people making the changes are those who work in the hospital every day and who understand the challenges confronting the ER. Having these crucial "human resources" on board helps both with the substance of the changes and with getting them adopted in the hospital. According to Gordon (2007, p. 13), "[h]aving all parties involved helps increase buy-in and enables the committee to tackle larger issues." In other words, drawing on "human resources" makes a big difference.

empowered organizing" (p. 359), and further argues that "small tokens of recognition (the quality coffee cup) and freedom (jeans day) are strategic organizational symbols that may add somewhat to the quality of work life but do little to foster control and autonomy" (p. 359). In short, for a human resources approach to be truly empowering, it requires more than surface changes in communication patterns. It requires fundamental changes in assumptions about organizational functioning and fundamental changes in organizational structure and interaction.

There are several theories that illustrate this fundamental change. We will consider two seminal theories that represent this shift in thinking—Blake and Mouton's Managerial Grid and Likert's System IV.

Blake and Mouton's Managerial Grid

Robert Blake and Jane Mouton developed their *Managerial Grid* (now called the *Leadership Grid*) as a tool for training managers in leadership styles that would enhance organizational efficiency and effectiveness and stimulate the satisfaction and creativity of individual workers (Blake & McCanse, 1991; Blake & Mouton, 1964). They began with the assumption that leaders will be most effective when they exhibit both *concern for people* and *concern for production*, thus combining the interests of classical management (concern for production) and human relations (concern for people).

Blake and Mouton formed a grid in which concern for people and concern for production were gauged from low to high (see Figure 3.2). Both of these dimensions were numbered from 1 to 9. Any manager could then be "placed" on this grid, depending on his or her levels of concern. Although a manager could be placed on any portion of this grid, Blake and Mouton distinguished five prototypical management styles.

The first prototypical management style, *impoverished management*, is characterized by a low concern for people and a low concern for production (1,1 on the Leadership Grid scales). Such a manager cares little for either the goals of the organization or the people in it and would do the minimum necessary to get by. The second prototypical management style, *country club management* (1,9 on the Leadership Grid), is characterized by high concern for people and low concern for production. This kind of manager would concentrate efforts on the establishment of a pleasant workplace with friendly and comfortable human relations. The third prototypical management style, *authority-compliance* (9,1 on the Leadership Grid), is characterized by high concern for production and low concern for people. This manager—like those of scientific and classical management—would endeavor to arrange all components of the workplace, including people, in order to maximize efficiency and attain goals. There would be little concern for human needs. The fourth prototypical management style, *team management* (9,9 on the Leadership Grid), is characterized by high concern for both production and people. This type of manager believes that the best way to achieve organizational goals is through the interdependent action of committed, talented, and satisfied individuals. Thus, this manager tries to maximize both productivity goals and employee needs. Finally, *middle-of-the-road management* (5,5 on the Leadership Grid) describes a manager who attempts to balance concern for people and production without going too far

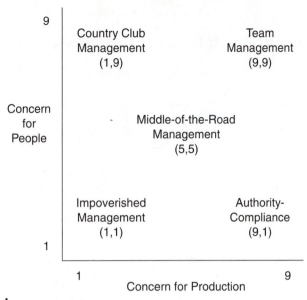

Figure 3.2 | The Leadership Grid

Adapted from *Leadership Dilemmas, Grid Solutions* by Robert R. Blake and Anne Adams McCanse (formerly *The Managerial Grid* by Robert R. Blake and Jane S. Mouton). Houston: Gulf Publishing Company, Copyright 1991 by Grid International, Inc.

for either goal. The watchword of such a manager would probably be "compromise." Not surprisingly, Blake and Mouton believe that all managers within an organization should adopt a team management approach, because such an approach would maximize concern for both production and people.

Likert's System IV

Blake and Mouton's Managerial Grid concentrates on how a manager can combine the values of the human relations school and the classical school into a leadership style that will maximize the potential of human resources within the organization. The second theorist we consider here works to specify the details of the organizational form that will incorporate the ideals of the human resources movement. Rensis Likert was the founder and longtime director of the Institute for Social Research at the University of Michigan. His work has been influential in a variety of academic fields. The contributions we will now discuss stem primarily from two of his books: *New Patterns of Management* (1961) and *The Human Organization* (1967).

Likert theorizes that there are a number of forms an organization can take and that these various forms are more or less effective in satisfying organizational and individual goals. He concentrates attention on the explication of four organizational forms, labeled System I through System IV. Likert believes that these four system types can be clearly differentiated in terms of motivational factors,

Case in Point: Retiring Resources

Many nuclear devices were developed by the military-industrial complex in the United States at the height of the cold war in the 1970s. Similarly, many nuclear reactors were built during the 1960s to cope with energy concerns. Who knows how to disarm those nuclear weapons and how to repair those nuclear reactors? The scientists and engineers who developed them. And what is happening to those scientists and engineers? They—like many members of the baby boom generation—are beginning to retire. And are these individuals passing their knowledge about these life-and-death issues to younger members of their organizations? Perhaps not. This scary scenario is one explored by David W. DeLong in his book *Lost Knowledge: Confronting the Threat of an Aging Workforce* (2004).

The human resources approach to organizing is based on the premise that organizational effectiveness is built on the knowledge and skills of individual workers. But what happens to that knowledge when those workers retire? DeLong argues that—given demographic trends—this is one of the most pressing problems facing organizations today. How can organizations transfer the important expertise and skills of workers before they walk out the door? DeLong points out that this may not be as easy and straightforward as it seems, as many executives are paying little attention to the problem, many younger workers might not feel older workers have much to teach them, and many older workers are reticent to share all they know. These challenges will require creative solutions, but it is essential to face them given the changing nature of our knowledge-intensive organizations.

communication, decision making, goal setting, control, influence structure, and performance:

- Likert's System I, called the *exploitive authoritative organization*, is characterized by motivation through threats and fear, downward and inaccurate communication, top-level decision making, the giving of orders, and top-level control. The exploitive authoritative organization includes all of the worst features of classical and scientific management.

- Likert's System II is called the *benevolent authoritative organization*. This organizational type is characterized by motivation through economic and ego rewards, limited communication, decision making at the top, goal setting through orders and comments, and top-level control. It is in many ways similar to a System I organization but does not incorporate the explicit goal of exploiting workers. However, the management style in this organization is still authoritative, because the managers believe that this style is "best for the workers."

- System III, the *consultative organization*, differs markedly from Systems I and II. In this organizational type, decisions are still made at the top and control still rests primarily at the upper levels of the hierarchy. However, before decisions are made, employees are consulted and their views are taken into consideration. Goals are set after discussion, and there is a high level of communication moving both up and down the hierarchy.

- System IV, a *participative organization*, provides a sharp contrast to the other system types. In a System IV organization, decision making is performed by every organizational member and goals are set by complete work groups.

Control is exercised at all levels of the organization, and communication is extensive, including upward, downward, and horizontal interaction. The contributions of all organizational members are strongly valued, and employees are rewarded through the satisfaction of a wide variety of needs.

These four system types, then, represent the move from the worst that scientific and classical management has to offer (System I) to an organizational type that values and encourages the contributions of all organizational members (System IV). Likert believes that a human resources organization (System IV) is more than just managerial attitudes. Rather, he advocates structural changes and practices that enhance the participation of individuals and the performance of the organization.

These two theorists provide a good initial look at human resources principles as they were developed in the mid-twentieth century. In some ways, these principles hark back to classical approaches because organizational effectiveness and productivity are again benchmarks of success. In other ways, the human resources approach is merely an extension of the human relations framework, as higher-order human needs for challenge and self-actualization are fulfilled through organizational activities. However, the human resources approach is distinct from both of the other approaches in two ways. First, it aspires to maximize *both* organizational productivity and individual need satisfaction. Second, in order to optimize both goals, the human resources approach emphasizes the contributions that employee ideas can make to organizational functioning. We will now consider ways in which both the human relations and human resources approaches are reflected in organizational communication goals and practices. These issues are summarized in Table 3.2.

Table 3.2 | Communication in Classical, Human Relations, and Human Resources Organizations

	Classical Approach	Human Relations Approach	Human Resources Approach
Communication content	Task	Task and social	Task, social, and innovation
Communication direction	Vertical (downward)	Vertical and horizontal	All directions, team-based
Communication channel	Usually written	Often face-to-face	All channels
Communication style	Formal	Informal	Both, but especially informal

COMMUNICATION IN HUMAN RELATIONS AND HUMAN RESOURCES ORGANIZATIONS

Content of Communication

In Chapter 2, we introduced the typology of Farace, Monge, and Russell (1977) that considered various types of communication in organizations. We noted that organizations following a classical model will emphasize task communication. As we consider human relations and human resources approaches, however, we see the other two types of communication content come into play. In human relations organizations, task-related communication still exists, but it is accompanied by communication that attempted to maintain the quality of human relationships within the organization—*maintenance communication*. And when we consider interaction in human resources organizations, the third type of communication in the Farace, Monge, and Russell typology comes to the forefront. This is *innovation communication*, which is interaction about how the job can be done better, new products the organization could produce, different ways of structuring the organization, and so on. Because the human resources approach to organizing places a premium on input from employees, the innovation content of communication is critical.

Direction of Communication Flow

In classical organizations, communication flows in a predominantly downward direction, as directives flow from management to workers. A human relations approach does not eliminate this need for vertical information flow, but adds an emphasis on *horizontal* communication. As discussed earlier in this chapter, human relations theorists believe that an important aspect of need satisfaction is communication among employees, so interaction that flows horizontally among employees is just as important as downward communication in the accomplishment of organizational goals. In a human resources organization, the goal is to encourage the flow of ideas from all locations throughout the organization. Thus, in the simplest sense, communication in this organizational approach will include all directional flows— downward, upward, horizontal, and diagonal. More specifically, this multidirectional communication flow often takes place in *team-based* settings in human resources organizations. That is, rather than restricting communication flow to the hierarchy of the organization (whatever the direction), a human resources organization will often reconfigure the organizational chart to optimize the flow of new ideas.

Channel of Communication

As you saw in Chapter 2, organizations run in a classical style are dominated by written communication, because a strong value is placed on permanence. In the human relations approach, in contrast, face-to-face communication takes center stage. This channel of interaction allows for more immediate feedback and more consideration of nonverbal cues. Thus, face-to-face communication is more appropriate for addressing the human needs emphasized in the human relations approach. In a human resources organization, it is unlikely that any particular channel of communication will be favored over others. Human resources theorists desire to maximize the productivity of the organization through the intelligent use of human resources. Sometimes these resources can best be utilized through face-to-face contact in meetings. Sometimes the situation calls for written memos or electronic mail. Thus, some scholars have suggested that effective managers will work to *match* the communication channel to the task at hand (Trevino, Lengel, & Daft, 1987). These researchers believe, for instance, that tasks with a high level of uncertainty require a communication channel that is relatively "rich" (e.g., face-to-face interaction), whereas tasks with a low level of uncertainty require a communication channel that is relatively "lean" (e.g., written communication).

Style of Communication

I noted in Chapter 2 that classical organizations emphasize formal communication, as standards of professionalism and bureaucratic decorum hold sway. In contrast, a human relations organization is likely to want to break down the status differential between managers and employees as a means of satisfying social needs. Thus, it is likely that informal communication—with less emphasis on titles, "business" dress, and bureaucratized language—will be emphasized. However, human resources organizations have the dual goals of enhancing organizational effectiveness and fulfilling human needs. On the needs side of the equation, an informal style is most likely to satisfy needs for affiliation. On the organizational effectiveness side, as well, an informal style will probably serve better than a formal one, because employees will probably feel more comfortable contributing in a relatively informal manner. However, a human resources manager would certainly not eschew the use of a formal style if it were the most appropriate for the task at hand.

HUMAN RELATIONS AND HUMAN RESOURCES ORGANIZATIONS TODAY

Human relations theories were proposed as a reaction to classical management systems and to evidence that meeting human needs is a critical aspect of organizational performance. The basic impetus of these ideas has certainly carried over the decades to today's organizations. For example, the influence of human relations ideas can clearly be seen in the general attitude of management toward employees. It would be difficult indeed to find managers today who would characterize their subordinates as interchangeable cogs whose needs play no role in organizational decisions. For example, if a manufacturing organization needed to shut down a factory, management would be likely to consider both economic issues and human factors such as the needs of workers and their families for severance pay, and job placement or retraining programs. Further, human relations principles can be seen in today's organizations in the area of job design. In many of today's organizations, an effort is made to enrich jobs by designing tasks that will satisfy some of the higher-order needs of workers through jobs that increase autonomy, variety, and task significance.

In general, though, it is the principles of human resources theorists that are most often reflected in today's organizations. Indeed, many of the ideas of early human resources theorists have been transformed in the light of the contingencies facing today's organizations. Theoretically, two of the most important developments in this area are the consideration of organizations as learning systems and the development of systems of knowledge management. Peter Senge and his colleagues (Senge, 1990; Senge, Roberts, Ross, Smith, & Kleiner, 1994) have made a distinction between *learning organizations* and those that could be seen as having "learning disabilities." Learning organizations are those that emphasize mental flexibility, team learning, a shared vision, complex thinking, and personal mastery. It is proposed that learning organizations can be promoted through participation and dialogue in the workplace. Scholars interested in *knowledge management* (see DeLong, 2004; Heaton & Taylor, 2002), see the organization as embodying a cycle of knowledge creation, development, and application.

Both of these approaches, then, have further developed the notion that effective organizations are those that can harness the cognitive abilities of their employees, and, indeed, these ideas developed from the kernel of the human resources approach are seen by many as the ideal way to run contemporary organizations. In the final sections of this chapter, we will look at how these abstract principles are often embodied in the practice of organizational life. We will consider first the question of what constitutes human resources management in today's organizations and then discuss how these programs can be instituted to enhance their effectiveness.

The "What" of Human Resources Programs

A number of organizational programs exemplify the use of human resources principles in today's organizations. These programs all emphasize *team management* and the importance of *employee involvement* in ensuring product or service quality and organizational productivity. Cotton (1993) defines employee involvement as "a participative process that uses the entire capacity of workers, designed to encourage employee commitment to organizational success" (p. 3). The goal is generally one of creating a "knowledge-enabled organization" (Tobin, 1998) in which the collective knowledge of workers facilitates high performance (Fisher & Duncan, 1998). Employee involvement is often fostered through team structures (Kinlaw, 1991; Tjosvold & Tjosvold, 1991).

Though specific programs of team management and employee involvement vary widely in terms of the specifics of human resources management, they all share the basic principle of trying to structure the organization in ways that maximize the contribution of employees, both individually and collectively. Pfeffer (1998) labels this important principle as "putting people first" in his book *The Human Equation* (see also Pfeffer & Veiga, 1999, for a summary). This book, based on both anecdotal evidence and social scientific research, highlights seven practices of successful organizations that serve as a useful summary of "what" is done in organizations today that follow human resources principles. These practices are presented in Table 3.3. As this table illustrates, the "what" of a successful human resources program includes many "nuts and bolts" issues regarding com-

Table 3.3 | Pfeffer's Seven Practices of Successful Organizations

Practice	Description
Employment security	Job security demonstrates commitment to employees and develops employees who understand the organization
Selective hiring	Employees who are a good "fit" for the organization—in terms of skills, abilities, and other attributes—will stay with the organization and enhance organizational performance
Self-managed teams and decentralization	Teams will permit employees to pool information and create better solutions, as well as enhance worker control over work processes
Comparatively high and contingent compensation	Contingent compensation connects performance outcomes with critical rewards
Extensive training	Front-line employees need training to identify workplace problems and contribute to innovative solutions
Reduction of status differences	By reducing both symbolic (e.g., language and labels) and substantive (e.g., pay) inequities, all employees will feel more valued
Sharing information	Employees can only contribute if they have adequate information about their own jobs and about the performance of the organization as a whole

Table developed from Pfeffer, J. (1998), *The Human Equation: Building Profits by Putting People First*. Boston, MA: Harvard Business School Press, and from Pfeffer, J., & Veiga, J. F. (1999), Putting people first for organizational success. *Academy of Management Executive*, 13(2), 37–48.

pensation, employment security, and organizational structure. This table also highlights the critical role of communication processes, both in terms of information sharing and teamwork and in terms of the communicative processes through which training occurs and status differentials are reduced.

The "How" of Human Resources Programs

There are clearly ways in which the principles of the human resources approach can be put into play in today's organizations. However, both our everyday experience and social scientific research suggests that these programs often *don't* work. As Jassawalla and Sashittal (1999) note with regard to collaborative teams, "[a]lthough they are formed with great optimism, few are managed for success." The chance of failure with human resources efforts can be seen in specific programs, as well. Consider total quality management (TQM), perhaps the most widely embraced program in the last thirty years. As Choi and Behling (1997, p. 37) summarize, "[t]he 1990s have not been good to TQM." They then enumerate evidence of the failures of TQM, including surveys of executives who do not believe TQM has enhanced competitiveness, programs that have been discontinued because of failure to produce results, and award-winning TQM programs that have stumbled (see, e.g., Becker, 1993; Doyle, 1992). It appears, then, that more than a belief in human resources principles is required for the success of human resources programs. The literature points to a number of ways in which the possibility for success in these programs can be enhanced. Although the following list is admittedly brief, it highlights some of the issues that should be taken into account when instituting the major change required by most human resources programs.

- Know when team-based management is appropriate. Many scholars and consultants suggest that there are times when team-based organizations will be particularly effective (see Forrester & Drexler, 1999; Mohrman, Cohen, & Mohrman, 1995). For example, work that cuts across functional lines, a diverse and complex organizational environment, a rapidly changing workplace in which innovation is critical—all of these factors suggest a need for team-based management.
- Consider the attitudes of top management. Although human resources programs involve the empowerment of workers throughout the organization, the impetus for change and the responsibility for dealing with change still often rest with top management.
- Deal with cynicism about change. Especially today, employees are often dismayed by the prospect of yet another "program of the month" at their organization. Reichers, Wanous, and Austin (1997) recommend that cynicism about organizational change can be minimized by keeping people involved in plans, by seeing change from the employees' perspective and providing opportunities to vent, by rewarding supervisors for effective communication, and by minimizing surprises. (See also the discussion of organizational change processes in Chapter 10.)
- Facilitate the translation process. Every new program in an organization will require a new "language" to be learned. In TQM, for instance, employees must understand terms such as "just in time," "pareto charts," and "statistical methods quality indicators." Programmatic changes in the organization can be accomplished only if members understand the terminology of the program (Fairhurst & Wendt, 1993) and if managers frame the change in a way that helps members enact their roles in the organization in viable and effective ways (Fairhurst, 1993).

SUMMARY

In this chapter, we looked at two related approaches to the study and practice of organizational communication, the human relations approach and the human resources approach. The human relations approach was inspired, in large part, by the Hawthorne Studies, that pointed scholars and practitioners toward the importance of human needs and the consideration of management practice and job design to meet those needs.

The human relations approach was illustrated by Maslow's Hierarchy of Needs Theory and McGregor's contrast between Theory X and Theory Y assumptions. However, there was often limited support for human relations theories and the principles of human relations were often instituted in half-hearted and manipulative ways. The human resources movement that emerged from these frustrations emphasizes the need to maximize both organizational productivity and individual employee satisfaction through the intelligent use of human resources. Human resources ideas were illustrated through the models of Blake and Mouton (the Managerial Grid) and Rensis Likert (System IV).

We then examined the nature of communication in human relations and human resources organizations by considering factors of commu-

nication content, direction, channels, and style. Finally, we considered ways in which human relations and, especially, human resources principles are utilized in today's organizations. We discussed the "what" of human resources management by looking at both specific programs and general principles for "putting people first." We concluded with some ideas about "how" human resources programs can be instituted.

Discussion Questions

1. A great deal of research has discredited many of the findings from the Hawthorne studies. Given this research, why were the Hawthorne studies influential when they were conducted? Are they still influential today? Why or why not?

2. In jobs you have had, what aspects of the workplace did you find particularly satisfying? What role did managers have in making the organization a satisfying place? How do your experiences, then, fit in with the ideas of Abraham Maslow and Douglas McGregor?

3. In Chapter 2 we noted that the classical approach follows a "machine metaphor" and in this chapter we associated human relations theorists with a "family metaphor." What metaphor would you use to describe the human resources approach? What are the strengths and weaknesses of the metaphor you propose?

4. Is the human resources approach more appropriate for some kinds of jobs and organizations than others? Why or why not? Can human resources principles be adapted for a variety of workplaces?

CASE STUDY | **Teamwork at Marshall's Processing Plant**

Marshall's is a large plant in the midwestern United States that processes corn into the fructose syrup used in many soft drinks. Marshall's is a continuous processing plant, running 24 hours a day, 365 days a year. There are two major components of the plant. In the wet mill, where 75 employees work, the corn is soaked. Then the soaked corn moves on to the refinery (employing 80 employees), where the soggy corn is processed into fructose syrup. Marshall's is a computerized state-of-the-art plant, and much of the work in the wet mill and refinery consists of monitoring, maintenance, cleanup, and troubleshooting. There are also 30 staff members who work in the office and in various other support positions. All the

employees except the support staff work 12-hour shifts.

Three years ago, Marshall's instituted a "team management" system to enhance productivity in the plant and improve worker morale. The program included two types of teams. First, work teams met on a weekly basis to consider ways of improving the work process within their own portion of the plant. In addition, the plantwide "Marshall Team" met on a monthly basis to consider decisions about issues facing the plant as a whole, such as benefit and compensation plans, company policies, and capital equipment purchases. Each work team elected one member to serve on the Marshall Team. Management at Marshall's regarded the teams as "consultative" bodies. That is, management used team suggestions as input but retained the right to make final decisions about all plant operations.

For the first three years of the team program, the same set of people participated heavily in team meetings and the same people tended to get elected to the Marshall Team. These go-getters took their roles very seriously and liked having a voice in company decisions. However, management at Marshall's was becoming concerned about the people who did not participate in the team program. After evaluating the problem for a while, management decided that it was a complicated issue and that there were three kinds of employees who were not participating in the team program.

First, one group of employees complained that the program led to too many meetings and a lot of extra busywork. This group was epitomized by Shu-Chu Lim. Shu-Chu was a hard worker and was well respected at the plant, but she was also a no-nonsense kind of person. When asked about participating in work teams and the Marshall Team, she said, "I don't have time to sit around and shoot the breeze. When I'm on the job, I want to be working, not just chit-chatting and passing the time."

A second set of workers resented the fact that they had to deal with so much of their own work situation. These employees believed that management was not providing enough input and was counting on the work teams to figure everything out. Consider, for example, Bill Berning. Bill had lived near the Marshall's plant all his life and liked working there because the pay was good. However, he saw his job simply as a way to earn money that he could spend on the great love of his life, motorcycles. When management started asking him to do more and more on the job, he just clammed up. After all, he argued, management was getting paid to make the decisions, not him.

Finally, a third set of employees refused to participate because they did not think their input would be listened to. In many ways, this was the group that most disturbed higher management because many of these people had participated in team activities in the past. Harvey Nelson was a prime example. When the team management system was instituted, Harvey was

very active in his area's work team and was even elected to the Marshall Team several times. However, after a couple of years, Harvey stopped participating. When asked, Harvey said: "I thought that the team idea was great at first, but then I realized that management is just going to do what it wants regardless of what we say. I can live with autocratic managers—I just don't want them to make me wake up early for a team meeting and then ignore what I have to say. If the teams are just window dressing, it's not worth it to me."

Marshall's wants to have a team management system that really works, and they know that they need to get more participation in order to have this happen. However, they've now realized that the problem is more complex than they realized at first. You have been called in as a consultant to help them fix their program. What kind of suggestions will you make?

CASE ANALYSIS QUESTIONS

1. Do the original goals of the team management system used at Marshall's comport more with the philosophy of human relations or human resources management? How would the theorists discussed in this chapter (Maslow, McGregor, Likert, and Blake and Mouton) analyze the current situation at Marshall's?

2. Employees identified three reasons for not participating in the program at Marshall's. How would you deal with each of these problems? Is it possible (or desirable) to satisfy all groups of employees and achieve full participation? Would human relations and human resources theorists have different ideas about the importance of these various reasons for not participating in the team management system?

3. What changes would you make in the team management system at Marshall's that would increase participation? What changes would you make to enhance the effective use of human resources at Marshall's? How would you institute these changes and communicate them to employees?

Systems Approaches

CHAPTER **4**

AFTER READING THIS CHAPTER, YOU SHOULD . . .

- Recognize the differences between a "machine metaphor" and a "systems metaphor" for describing organizational processes
- Be able to explain systems components, systems processes, and systems properties and illustrate these ideas with organizational communication examples
- Be familiar with cybernetics as a systems theory that can help explain goal-related communication in organizations
- Appreciate Weick's theory of organizing as an important way to "make sense" of the workings of organizational communication
- See the ways in which ideas from "new systems theory" can transform processes of organizational understanding
- Know about research methods for studying systems, especially the details of network analysis

Back in Chapter 2, we considered classical and scientific management approaches to organizational communication theory. You found that these theories are based on a mechanistic metaphor. That is, classical theorists thought that organizations could best be understood by comparing them to machines that are predictable and comprised of replaceable parts. The human relations and human resources approaches we considered in Chapter 3 objected to this model because of the way it conceptualized workers—as individuals who should be considered as laborers without feeling or thought. In addition to these concerns about employee treatment and involvement, however, many theorists also continue to find the machine metaphor to be an unsatisfying model for explanation and understanding because organizations—to a large extent, at least—do not behave in predictable and machinelike ways. A new metaphor has thus emerged to explain organizations, this *systems* or *organismic* metaphor views organizations not as self-contained and self-sufficient machines but as complex organisms that must interact with their environment to survive. As Morgan (1986) notes:

> The problems of mechanistic visions of organizations have led many organizational theorists away from mechanical science and toward biology as a source of ideas for thinking about organization. In the process, organization theory has become a kind of biology in which the distinctions and relations among *molecules, cells, complex*

organisms, species, and *ecology* are paralleled in those between *individuals, groups, organizations, populations (species) of organizations*, and their *social ecology*. (pp. 40–41, emphasis in original)

In this chapter, we explore the systems approach by considering how an organismic metaphor can provide insight into organizational communication processes. A systems approach to the study of organizational communication is different from those we have considered so far because it shifts our attention away from how people should behave in and manage organizations to the question of how we should study them. We will first consider some basic systems concepts and apply these to the organizational arena. We will then look at three theoretical applications of systems concepts: cybernetics, Karl Weick's theory of organizing, and the study of "new science" systems. Finally, we will look at a variety of methodologies that have been used by systems theorists in organizational communication.

THE SYSTEMS METAPHOR AND SYSTEMS CONCEPTS

Systems theory did not originate in the study of organizations but rather in the fields of biology and engineering. One of the key founders of the systems movement was Ludwig von Bertalanffy, a theoretical biologist who was interested in the study of "living systems" within his own academic field. Von Bertalanffy was also concerned, however, with the extent to which intellectual disciplines were isolated from one another, and he argued that systems concepts could be applied to a large number of fields in both the natural and social sciences. In 1968, he published *General Systems Theory*, a book espousing a systems theory that he believed was as appropriate for the social sciences as it was for biology (von Bertalanffy, 1968).

The study of systems was eagerly adopted by organizational theorists. Perhaps the most influential application of systems theory to organizational processes appeared in 1966 with Katz and Kahn's *The Social Psychology of Organizations*. Katz and Kahn (1978) argue that organizations should be conceptualized as complex open systems requiring interaction among component parts and interaction with the environment in order to survive. Another early and influential application of systems theory to organizational functioning is Thompson's (1967) *Organizations in Action*. In the field of communication, one of the first comprehensive applications of systems theory came with Farace, Monge, and Russell's *Communicating and Organizing* (1977), an application of structural-functional systems theory to communication processes within organizations. In short, the 1960s and 1970s were marked by extensive attention to the systems metaphor as a way of understanding the processes of organizational behavior and communication.

If you were to peruse some of these influential books, you would find substantial variety in the details presented about systems theory. However, almost all systems theories embrace certain aspects of the systems metaphor. In the following sections, we consider a number of concepts that are endorsed by a wide range of systems theories. We first look at what systems are made of—system components. We then consider how systems work—system processes. Finally, we discuss the unique characteristics that arise from these components and processes—system properties.

System Components

At its most basic level, a system is an assemblage of parts, or components. In a biological system, these parts include cells and organs. In an organizational system, these components are the people and departments that make up the organization. We could also think about the larger society as a system. In this case, the parts would be the organizations and institutions that make up the society. Regardless of what particular system we look at, the first task of a systems theorist is to identify the relevant components that comprise the system. After the components of the system have been identified, it is interesting to look at how these parts are arranged and how they work. Three concepts characterize system components: hierarchical ordering, interdependence, and permeability.

Hierarchical Ordering   A system is not simply an undifferentiated set of parts thrown together. To the contrary, system components are arranged in highly complex ways that involve subsystems and supersystems—a *hierarchical ordering*. If you think about your body as a system, you can observe this hierarchy. Your body is made up of a number of subsystems—the cardiovascular system, the digestive system, the neurological system, and so forth. In turn, these systems are also made up of subsystems—for example, the cardiovascular system includes the heart, lungs, and blood vessels. We could take this even further with a consideration of organ components, cells, and so on.

The same hierarchical ordering can be seen when considering the organization as a system. Let us, for example, look at a hospital as an organizational system. A hospital is made up of a number of departmental subsystems, including surgical units, recovery units, the emergency room, laboratories, and offices. These subsystems, in turn, are composed of smaller work groups and individuals. We could also move in the other direction and see that the hospital is part of a larger supersystem, the health care industry. This supersystem would include organizations such as hospitals, clinics, insurance companies, and pharmaceutical companies. Note that the concept of "hierarchy" has a different meaning here than when the same term is used by classical management theorists. A classical theorist sees hierarchy as the relatively straightforward lines of authority represented by the organizational chart. In contrast, hierarchical ordering within systems theory means that when we look at any system we can see how that system is made up of smaller subsystems and is embedded within a larger supersystem.

Interdependence   A second concept that characterizes system components is *interdependence*. The notion of interdependence implies that the functioning of one component of a system relies on other components of the system. Think again of the human body. The brain needs a constant supply of blood in order to function, but this supply would not be possible if it weren't for the heart's pumping action. In turn, the heart relies on the lungs to bring in the oxygen that fuels the blood. Both the heart and the lungs rely on the brain for the neurological signals that facilitate functioning. In short, the body is a highly interdependent system in which the breakdown of one component would lead to breakdowns in other components and in the system as a whole.

An organization, as a system, is also highly interdependent. In our hospital, for instance, the surgical units could not function effectively without laboratories to provide important test results. The laboratories rely on the purchasing department for supplies such as test tubes and chemicals. Many hospital units are dependent on the personnel and business offices to deal with the paperwork of compensation and insurance. Thus, no component within the hospital can function effectively without active assistance from other system parts.

At levels higher than the individual organization, interdependence can be seen by considering the complex relationships among organizations within a given business sector or in related sectors. This interdependence is particularly apparent in today's highly connected global economy. For example, Browning and Shetler (2000) conducted a case analysis of the semiconductor industry. This industry is highly competitive on a global level and for many years organizations within this sector wanted to maintain a clear sense of independence. However, the U.S. government formed a consortium called Sematech that worked to improve relationships and communication among a wide range of semiconductor companies. This move from suspicious independence to cooperative interdependence shows a shift in thinking toward a global-systems view of the industry.

Permeability   A third characteristic of system components is that they have *permeable boundaries* that allow information and materials to flow in and out. The degree of permeability varies from system to system—some are relatively closed, whereas others are extremely open. However, all biological and social systems require some degree of permeability to survive. Permeability refers both to the system as a whole—which must be open to its environment—and to the components within the system. For example, the human body must be open to its environment in order to take in the air, food, and water necessary for survival. The components of the human body must also be permeable to allow the flow of materials among organs and organ systems. In our hospital, too, we can observe both system and component permeability. The hospital must be open to its larger environment so that patients, information, and resources can move into and out of the organization. Similarly, hospital units must be open to each other to facilitate the flow of people, information, and materials.

Of course, permeability to the larger environment can cause problems for a system, too. If the body is taking in poisonous gas, for example, permeability to the environment can be extremely detrimental. For organizations, permeability can be toxic as well. Garner (2006) argues in a recent case analysis that the *Columbia* space shuttle disaster in 2003 can be partly explained in these terms. In the years leading up to the disaster, NASA had become increasingly dependent on other organizations in the environment, including government, contractors, and space station partners. NASA felt the power of these partners through its permeable boundaries, especially regarding the pressure to launch. A more closed system might have made different decisions than those that led to the *Columbia* disaster.

System Processes

Let's now look at how these hierarchical, interdependent, and permeable components function in a system. At the most basic level, systems are characterized by *input–throughput–output* processes (Farace, Monge, & Russell, 1977). That is, a system "inputs" materials or information from the environment through its permeable boundaries. The system then works on these inputs with some kind of transformational process; this is "throughput." Finally, the system returns the transformed "output" to the environment. For example, a furniture manufacturer will input raw materials such as wood and fabric, transform these inputs into chairs and couches, and output these products to the buying public through retail outlets. Organizations input and transform information, as well. For example, an insurance claims adjuster must gather information about relevant damages, make decisions based on insurance coverage, and then output that information (and, hopefully, a check!) to the policyholder.

Two kinds of processes characterize input–throughput–output operations. The first of these—the process of *exchange*—is apparent in both input and output activities. That is, both the input of materials and information and the output of transformed materials and information require a process of exchange with the environment outside the system. Obviously, this process of exchange is intimately related to the permeability of system boundaries. Some organizations have highly permeable boundaries to facilitate the exchange process, whereas others are relatively closed. For example, throughout the Cold War era, many manufacturers worked primarily as defense contractors for the government, and operated as relatively closed systems with regard to other markets. However, when the Cold War ended, defense contracts were in shorter supply. At this point, these organizations —if they were to be successful—needed to develop an awareness of consumer needs and exchange information regarding markets in other business sectors. By increasing system permeability and exchange, many of these businesses switched their emphasis to consumer-oriented applications such as communication satellites and satellite dishes. In so doing, these companies enhanced their chances of survival in a rapidly changing organizational environment.

A second type of process—*feedback*—is critical to the throughput portion of organizational functioning. Throughput involves the interdependent components of a system acting together. Feedback is information that helps to facilitate the interdependent functioning of system components. Two types of feedback are important to system functioning. The first of these is variously referred to as *negative* feedback, *corrective* feedback, or *deviation-reducing* feedback. This kind of feedback helps to maintain steady system functioning. Suppose, for instance, that a restaurant supervisor notices that one of the waiters is telling patrons about yesterday's specials instead of today's specials. The supervisor might inform the waiter about his error so he can change his message to the diners. This is corrective feedback that serves to keep organizational functioning on a steady course.

A second type of feedback is known as *positive*, *growth*, or *deviation-amplifying* feedback (see Maruyama, 1963). This is information that serves to change system functioning through growth and development. Our restaurant supervisor, for example, might notice that more and more patrons are bothered by smoke while dining. Our supervisor, then, might suggest to higher management that the restaurant be transformed into a nonsmoking establishment. This kind of feedback serves to change the entire system rather than to maintain it in a steady state.

There are, of course, times when these feedback systems get out of control or don't work effectively. For example, just as intense interaction and feedback can yield "codependent" relationships in some families, organizations can also exhibit codependence (McMillan & Northern, 1995). In these dysfunctional organizations, there can be a reliance on a limited set of feedback relationships that keep circulating and emphasizing the same information. For example, an organization that constantly provides feedback about the need to work harder and an obsession with the bottom line might create dangerous situations of workaholism. In these situations, the positive construct of "interdependence" is morphed into the dangerous construct of "codependence."

System Properties

Now we will consider system properties that emerge from the interaction of these components and processes. Four properties are particularly relevant: holism, equifinality, negative entropy, and requisite variety.

Holism   The property of holism suggests that a system is "more than the sum of its parts." Systems have this property because of the interdependent nature of their components and the information that flows through the processes of feedback and

Case in Point: Navigating a Complex System

A systems approach to organizational communication emphasizes the complexity of organizations, the interdependence of system components, and the importance of relationships between the organizational system and the environment. Indeed, as society becomes more complex, organizational systems often mirror this complexity. This might be necessary, but in some industries we clearly yearn for less complexity and simpler times.

The U.S. health care industry, based increasingly on principles of "managed care" (see Miller & Ryan, 2001), is a clear illustration of such a complex system. Garr (2004) compares his experiences in the French medical system when his wife had a serious stroke with his subsequent experiences in the managed care system of the United States. The hospital in Nice, France, provided a one-page invoice for a two-and-a-half-week hospital stay and was puzzled when

asked for further itemization. In contrast, once back in the United States, a much longer set of invoice statements were required just to sort out the extra equipment ordered for a wheelchair. As Garr states, "everything in American medical care is a la carte, and the invoices are so dense with codes and abbreviations, it's a wonder anyone can decipher them" (2004, p. 19). Dealing with the system requires contacts with physicians, nurses, office staff, hospital business staff, insurance representatives, and perhaps lawyers. And the person left to navigate this complex system is the health care consumer who is already, of course, dealing with myriad stresses in his or her personal life.

Many years of grappling with these issues indicate that answers are not easy. But the problems of managed care clearly point to the problems that can confront an individual dealing with an overly complex system.

exchange. Imagine, for instance, that five individuals are asked to solve an organizational problem. These individuals may come up with many interesting and innovative ideas while sitting alone in their respective offices. However, if these five people are placed in an interdependent system, it is likely that many more and different problem-solving ideas will emerge from their interaction.

Equifinality The system property of equifinality states that "a system can reach the same final state from differing initial conditions and by a variety of paths" (Katz & Kahn, 1978, p. 30). This, again, is a result of the interdependent operation of system components. Because the components of the system are integrated in highly complex ways, a variety of means exist to reach any system goal. Consider an organization that wants to increase sales by 10 percent. This sales increase could be accomplished through the interaction of many different system components. A change in the training of salespeople might serve to increase sales. Alternatively, supervisors might exert tighter control over procedures to reach the goal. In short, because a system is complex and interconnected, there is more than a single path to any system outcome.

Negative Entropy Entropy is the tendency of closed systems to run down. For example, if a body is totally closed to its environment (and receives no food, water, or oxygen), it will quickly deteriorate. Open systems, however, are characterized by negative entropy, or the ability to sustain themselves and grow. Negative entropy is possible because of the flow of information and materials between the environment and the system. As Buckley (1967) notes, "That a system is open means, not simply that it engages in interchanges with the environment, but that this interchange is an essential factor underlying the system's viability" (p. 50). For example, U.S. auto companies in the 1960s were relatively closed to their environment, ignoring information about world conditions and consumer preferences. If the auto companies had remained closed, they would have deteriorated and gone out of business. It was only through the intake of information from the environment that the automakers were able to survive. This is the principle of negative entropy in action—a system fights off deterioration and perhaps thrives through active exchange with the system's environment.

Requisite Variety A final system property again deals with the relationship between a system and its environment. The property of requisite variety states that the internal workings of the system must be as diverse and complicated as the environment in which it is embedded. This "matching complexity" allows the organization—or team or group within the organization—to deal with information and problems in the environment. Morgan (1997, p. 113) argues that this "is not just an abstract concept . . . If a team or unit is unable to recognize, absorb, and deal with the variations in its environment, it is unlikely to evolve and survive." Consider the contrast, for instance, between two political campaign organizations. In one campaign, the candidate is running unopposed. In the second campaign, a bitter battle is being waged between a Republican, a Democrat, and a third-party candidate. The first campaign organization could be relatively small and simple, because the political environment of an unopposed campaign is uncomplicated.

The second campaign organization, however, would need more complex subsystems to monitor, evaluate, and react to the quickly changing politics that surround a hotly contested three-person race.

To summarize, when we look at an organization as a system, we see it as a collection of system components that are hierarchically arranged, interdependent, and permeable to each other and the environment. The organizational system is characterized by input–throughput–output processes that require exchange with the environment and positive and negative system feedback. Because of the openness and interdependence of organizational systems, they are characterized by the properties of holism, equifinality, requisite variety, and negative entropy.

These basics of the systems approach are summarized in Table 4.1.

Table 4.1 | Summary of Systems Basics

System Components	Principle
Hierarchically ordered	A system consists of smaller subsystems and is embedded within larger supersystems.
Interdependent	System components *depend on each other* for effective functioning.
Permeable	A system is open to its environment and system components are open to each other.

Input–Throughput–Output Processes	Principle
Exchange processes	Input and output processes require exchange between the system and the environment. Throughput processes require exchange among system components.
Feedback processes	System control is maintained through feedback. *Corrective (negative)* feedback serves to keep a system on a steady course. *Growth (positive)* feedback serves to transform or change a system.

System Properties	Principle
Holism	Because of component interdependence, a system is more than the sum of its parts.
Equifinality	Because of component interdependence, there are multiple paths to any system outcome.
Negative entropy	Because of system openness, a system has the ability to avoid deterioration and thrive.
Requisite variety	Because of system openness, a system should maintain the internal complexity necessary to cope with external complexity.

THREE SYSTEMS THEORIES

A great many theories relevant to organizational communication have been based on systems concepts, including open systems theory (e.g., Katz & Kahn, 1978), structural functionalism (e.g., Farace, Monge, & Russell, 1977), and sociotechnical systems theory (e.g., Trist, 1969). In this section, we look at three examples that emphasize different aspects of systems theory and principles. The first of these, cybernetics, was developed many years ago in the engineering and physical sciences but has been applied to organizations. The second was developed by Karl Weick specifically to enhance our understanding of organizational systems. The third is an approach emerging in a variety of fields, including organizational science—the study of "new science" systems.

Cybernetic Systems Theory

The term *cybernetics* derives from the Greek word for a boat's steersman. As this name implies, cybernetic systems theory deals with the process through which physical, natural, and organizational systems are steered toward reaching system goals. Cybernetic systems theory was developed by Norbert Wiener (1948, 1954) and was initially applied to self-regulation within physical systems. However, as you will see, cybernetic concepts also can be readily applied to organizational and human systems.

A cybernetic system consists of several interrelated components. The first of these is the *system goal* located in the control center. The system goal is a target for a particular aspect of system operation. For example, the human body has a system goal of maintaining a temperature of approximately 98.6 degrees Fahrenheit. The system uses a variety of *mechanisms* that help to maintain this system goal. However, there will be times when system behavior does not match the system goal. For example, when the body is infected, its temperature will rise higher than 98.6 degrees. At this point in cybernetic processing, *feedback* is sent to the control center and compared to the goal. If there is a difference between the goal and the feedback (e.g., the body's temperature is either higher or lower than 98.6 degrees Fahrenheit), new mechanisms will be instituted to adjust the behavior of the system. For example, if body temperature is higher than 98.6, an individual will sweat. If body temperature is lower than 98.6, an individual will shiver. Sweating and shivering are mechanisms that serve to regulate system behavior and keep it aligned with the system goal.

Since this model seems rather complex, let's apply it to a specific aspect of organizational communication. Let's look at the process of a performance review and attempt to model it as a cybernetic system.

Gina is a pharmaceutical salesperson who sits down with her supervisor, Rick, to discuss her job performance. Together, Rick and Gina decide that she should aim to improve her sales by 10 percent over the next quarter, and they map out some strategies for attaining this goal. They decide that Gina should make more sales calls and improve the service she is providing to her accounts. Over the next three months, Rick monitors Gina's performance via the sales reports she files. At their next performance review meeting, Rick and Gina discuss the fact that her performance has improved, but only by 2 percent. Because they still feel that the goal of 10 percent improvement is reasonable, they decide that Gina may have to work on her sales pitch and begin using new telemarketing strategies to improve her performance.

All of the components of the cybernetic systems model are apparent in this scenario (see Figure 4.1). The *system behavior* under consideration is level of sales. The goal set for this behavior is 10 percent improvement. Initially, the *mechanisms* of increased sales calls and account service are used to change system behavior. When *feedback* from the sales report indicates that these strategies have not been entirely effective, additional mechanisms of telemarketing and an improved sales pitch are instituted. We could also continue to analyze Gina's performance with the use of a cybernetic model, mapping out differences in goals, mechanisms, performance, and feedback over time.

Cybernetics emphasizes some aspects of systems theory and de-emphasizes others. In considering the system processes we discussed earlier, a cybernetic system emphasizes the role of feedback—especially corrective feedback—in maintaining system functioning. Cybernetics also emphasizes the interdependence of system parts, because the mechanisms are intimately related to the goals. However, some aspects of system functioning are de-emphasized. For example, the basic cybernetic model does not account for the growth of systems nor does it incorporate the role of the environment in influencing system processes. The next theory we consider,

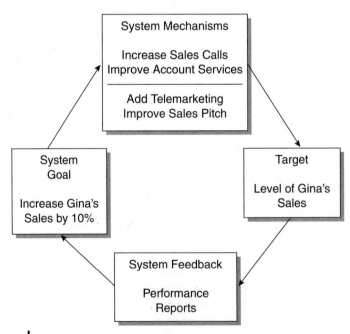

Figure 4.1 | An Organizational Example of a Cybernetic System

Karl Weick's theory of organizing, is a very different type of systems theory and emphasizes different aspects of the general systems approach.

Karl Weick's Theory of Organizing

Karl Weick's scholarship—and in particular his books *The Social Psychology of Organizing* (1979) and *Sensemaking in Organizations* (1995)—has had a profound impact on organizational theory, especially in the area of organizational communication. His highly complex model seeks to illuminate the process of organizing, and he draws on a variety of theories in developing his perspective. These include evolutionary theory, information theory, and general systems theory (see Kreps, 1990). Weick defines the process of organizing as "the resolving of equivocality in an enacted environment by means of interlocked behaviors embedded in conditionally related processes" (Weick, 1969, p. 91). This is a rather dense and complex definition. Let's try to clarify it through a look at its critical components.

Central to Weick's theory of organizing is the idea that organizations exist in an environment. Weick is clear, though, that this environment is not merely a physical environment but is an *information environment*. Furthermore, the information environment of an organization does not exist "out there" in an objective manner. Rather, individuals create the environment that confronts them through the process of *enactment*. The process of enactment suggests that different organizational members will imbue information inputs with different meanings and hence create different information environments. As Weick (1995) explains, "There is not some kind of monolithic, singular, fixed environment that exists detached from and external to people. Instead, people are very much a part of their own environments." For instance, if you and a coworker were both asked to "see the boss as soon as

Case in Point: Making Sense of My Money

When we think about organizational sensemaking, we often consider the ways in which interpersonal communication with those around us reduces confusion about organizational events. However, the Internet connects us in ways that can both heighten our distress over equivocality and provide us with important new sources for understanding and support.

Andrew Herrmann made this point in his study of "Stockholders in Cyberspace" (2007). In recent years, more and more individuals have started investing in the stock market, and media outlets with information about various options for investing have flourished. If your head has ever started spinning while watching the multiple crawls and pop-ups on CNBC or similar financial cable networks, you understand that there is

a lot of information out there and it would be fair to characterize much of the financial data as highly equivocal.

How is an individual to "make sense" of this huge influx of information? Hermann suggests that many people turn to discussion boards and chat rooms on the web for help, and he analyzed one message board (discussing Warren Buffett's Berkshire Hathaway Inc. on the Motley Fool website) to demonstrate this. The messages show individuals drawing on a wide array of media sources—and, especially, each other—to make sense of complicated financial data. Herrmann doesn't know if the bank accounts of these individuals were increased, but it appears that their equivocality was reduced.

possible," you might imbue the situation with very different meanings, depending on your past experiences, goals, personalities, and so on.

In Weick's model, the major goal of organizing is the reduction of equivocality in the information environment. *Equivocality* is the unpredictability that is inherent in the information environment of an organization. In an equivocal information environment, there are many interpretations that could be used for a particular event. For example, in the "go see the boss" example above, an individual might be able to attach many logical (and probably many illogical!) explanations for the requested meeting. According to Weick, reducing equivocality—or making sense—is central to the process of organizing. Some organizations are likely to be generally predictable. However, for organizations in highly competitive or quickly changing business environments or for any organization during a time of crisis (see, e.g., O'Connell & Mills, 2003), equivocality is likely to be high.

How, then, is sense made in these equivocal information environments? Weick proposes that organizational members use *assembly rules* and *communication cycles*. Assembly rules are procedures (sometimes called "recipes") that can guide organizational members in set patterns of sensemaking. For example, a personnel director might always ask applicants for a résumé in a particular form in order to simplify the information environment. Assembly rules are particularly useful for sensemaking when the information environment is not especially equivocal. However, when equivocality in the environment is high and there are many possible explanations for an event, organizational members engage in communication cycles. Through communication cycles, organizational members introduce and react to ideas that help to make sense of the equivocal environment. The use of assembly rules and communication cycles is most prevalent during the selection stage in Weick's model, although the process of sensemaking is an ongoing one.

The selected assembly rules and communication cycles will sometimes be effective in reducing equivocality in the information environment and sometimes will be ineffective. When sensemaking is effective, Weick proposes a *retention* process in which rules and cycles are saved for future organizational use. Rules and cycles can be retained in the form of *causal maps* that are used to make sense of future equivocality in the information environment. Weick's model of organizing is presented in Figure 4.2.

Weick's model of organizing is obviously highly complex and abstract. At the risk of oversimplifying his ideas, let's look at an organizational communication

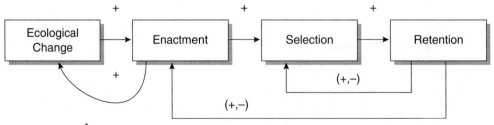

Figure 4.2 | Weick's Model of Organizing.

Reprinted with permission of McGraw-Hill, Inc., from Weick, K. E. (1979), *The Social Psychology of Organizing*, p. 132.

Spotlight on Scholarship

As we have discovered in this chapter, Karl Weick's systems view of organizing sees organizational life as a social process in which individuals and groups are consistently confronted with opportunities for sensemaking. Of course, there are times when equivocality is low, and organizational actors can rely on established ways of doing things and thinking about events. However, there are other times when there is a "shock" or "rupture" in organizational life—when taken-for-granted ideas about how things should work are put into serious question. At these times, the need for sensemaking is particularly strong. When something surprising or shocking happens, should we just try to smooth it over as a part of organizational life? Or does the surprise require a radically different way of thinking about what we are doing?

Alexandra Murphy (2001) explored these questions with regard to a particularly important kind of "organizational rupture." Specifically, she looked at how flight attendants cope with "breaches" in the ongoing and regular routine of air travel. How do flight attendants "make sense" of the disruption of unruly passengers, mechanical failure, or dangerous weather? And how does the sensemaking of flight attendants influence their interaction with pilots, passengers, and other flight attendants?

The "dilemma" of the flight attendant is a particularly interesting one, because the job of the flight attendant is—in large part—to perpetuate the story that air travel is as safe and secure as sitting in one's own living room. All of the "dominant rituals of flight" are designed to decrease the perception of risk. As Murphy points out, the statement "the cabin pressure is carefully controlled for your comfort" really means that enough oxygen is pumped into the cabin so passengers can breathe (p. 38). For flight attendants, perpetuating the story of risk-free flight often involves the performance of a feminized role of giving comfort and service rather than ensuring safety. As a participant in Murphy's research stated, "We are on board the airplane 80% for safety and 20% for service. But, the passengers don't want to know that. They want to see it as 80% for service and 20% for safety. They want us to give them a pillow and blanket and make them feel comfy" (Murphy, 2001, p. 39).

Thus, when there is a "rupture" in this safe and comfortable world—perhaps an unruly passenger, bad weather, or mechanical failure—flight attendants must make sense of that rupture and make a choice: to uphold the dominant rituals of flight or to break the established routine and do something about the rupture. Murphy's analysis of many hours of observation, extensive interviews, and archival data points to the challenges of this sensemaking activity. Further, she notes that there are barriers to sensemaking, especially rules that limit communication between flight crews and flight attendants and cost-control efforts by airlines that often lead to attendants serving with different flight crews for each leg of a flight. Without relational connections between pilots and flight attendants, it is difficult for crews to "make sense" of emergencies in the best way possible. As Murphy (2001, p. 50) concludes, "The importance of open communication in air travel cannot be stressed enough, as literally lives are on the line." And though this was certainly true in February of 2001 when this article was published, we know even better since September 11 of that year that air travel can be a risky business. Making sense through communication has never been more important.

Murphy, A. G. (2001). The Flight Attendant Dilemma: An Analysis of Communication and Sensemaking During In-Flight Emergencies. *Journal of Applied Communication Research*, 29, 30–53.

situation that exemplifies some of them. In a recent study of a midwestern hospital, Miller, Joseph, and Apker (2000) looked at a group of nurses who were coping with major changes in the health care environment. The hospital where they worked was encountering increased competition within the new "managed care" payment environment, and hence decided to develop a new system emphasizing interdisciplinary health care. The nurses in the study were designated as "care coordinators" but were given little guidance about what this new role would entail. The nurses in this situation were placed in a highly equivocal situation—they had to "make sense" of new roles that could be interpreted in a wide variety of ways. The Miller et al. (2000) interviews with these nurses suggest that some relied on simple assembly rules (e.g., I'll just assume that "care coordinator" is the same thing as "discharge planner"). Other nurses—perhaps the more successful ones in the long run—relied instead on intense interaction with each other and with others in the hospital environment to craft and make sense of their new organizational roles. This example illustrates both the importance of sensemaking and the selection of various communication strategies for making sense in an equivocal organizational environment.

This presentation has, of course, oversimplified Weick's model and has left out a number of his innovative ideas about the processes through which organizational members make sense of their environments. However, even from this cursory look, it should be clear that Weick's theory of organizing emphasizes a number of relevant systems theory concepts. The notions of environment and permeability are critical to his theory, as is the concept of system component interdependence. The sensemaking process proposed by Weick also highlights the concept of requisite variety. That is, simple decision rules and structures can be used in sensemaking when equivocality is low, but more complex communication cycles and systems are needed to make sense of highly uncertain information environments.

"New Science" Systems Theory

In recent years, a new area of systems theorizing has begun to gain prominence in organizational research. Based on work in fields such as physics and cosmology, this area of theorizing has branches that are known by such labels as *chaos theory* (e.g., Coveney & Highfield, 1995), *complexity theory* (e.g., Lewin, 1992), and *self-organizing systems theory* (e.g., Contractor, 1994). When applied to the study of communication and organizations, all of these areas suggest new ways of thinking about organizations as "different kinds" of systems, and as a group these ideas can be considered "new science" systems theory (Merry, 1995; Wheatley, 1992).

The heart of new science ideas is the notion that not all systems in nature and society are like those described by classical physics. That is, systems in the new sciences are not seen as necessarily linear and striving toward equilibrium. Rather, new science systems are complex and adaptive systems in which order can emerge from disorder, in which time makes a difference, in which complex systems are often preserved in fractal form, and in which large effects can come from very small changes. New science systems are not always logical and they are not always predictable. Rather, this approach to systems emphasizes the importance of complexity, fluctuating information, and the innovativeness that can emerge when a system is at "the edge of chaos." As Horgan (1996) explains:

> The basic idea of the edge of chaos is that nothing novel can emerge from systems with high degrees of order and stability, such as crystals; on the other hand, completely chaotic . . . systems such as turbulent fluids or heated gases, are too formless. Truly complex things—amoebas, bond traders, and the like—happen at the border between rigid order and randomness. (pp. 196–197)

So what do these new science systems theories have to do with communication in organizations? Some theorists and consultants (e.g., Stacey, 1996; Wheatley, 1992) argue that if ideas from chaos theory, complexity theory, and self-organizing systems theory are taken to heart in the organizational realm, it means an altogether different way of communicating in organizations. Miller (1998) lays out some of these ideas with regard to Meg Wheatley's book, *Leadership and the New Science*. Ideas for organizational communication derived from the new sciences include:

- *The importance of relationships in organizations.* This factor is derived from new science ideas about the interconnectedness and interdependence of entities in quantum physics.
- *The importance of participation in organizational processes.* This factor is emphasized because of the participatory nature of the universe and because "participation, seriously done, is a way out from the uncertainties and ghostly qualities of this nonobjective world we live in" (Wheatley, 1992, p. 64).
- *The appreciation of organizational change and instability.* Wheatley argues that "organizational change, even in large systems, can be created by a small group of committed individuals or champions" (p. 96).
- *The importance of being open to the information environment.* In the new sciences, change occurs at the edge of chaos when we are open to the swirl of ideas around us. As Wheatley states, "we need to open the gates to more information, in more places, and to seek out information that is ambiguous, complex, and of no immediate value" (p. 109).

Thus, new science approaches to systems theory open up ideas about how the complex and chaotic nature of organizational systems might lead to the emergence of new and innovative organizational forms and processes. These theories emphasize, not the "logic" of organizational systems, but rather the interconnectedness of systems, their openness to the environment, and the interdependence that must be acknowledged in both physical and social systems. This kind of theorizing may be particularly important as we move to increasing complexity in our global world. For example, Houston and Jackson (2003) argue that self-organizing system theory can be especially helpful in understanding how citizens of developing nations adopt and talk about information and communication technologies.

METHODS FOR STUDYING ORGANIZATIONAL SYSTEMS

In the late 1960s and 1970s, systems theory enjoyed a great deal of popularity among organizational communication researchers. This is not surprising, because systems theory emphasizes the notions of exchange, feedback, and interdependence —concepts critical to communication theory. Unfortunately, research methodologies at the time could not account for these complex processes (Monge, 1982; Monge, Farace, Eisenberg, White, & Miller, 1984). However, several research techniques have emerged—or gained prominence—in the last few decades that are particularly appropriate for the investigation of systems explanations of organizational functioning. In this section, we briefly review three of these research approaches: network analysis, modeling techniques, and case analysis. Although these three research approaches are very different, each tries to capture the complexity of systems in its explanatory technique.

Network Analysis

One of the hallmarks of systems theory is the denotation of the interconnections among system components and the arrangement of those components into subsystems and supersystems. When the components of systems are people and social groups, the "mapping" of relationships among people becomes crucially important. *Network analysis* provides a means for creating and analyzing those maps of relationships. Monge and Eisenberg (1987) differentiate between the positional tradition of network analysis and the relational tradition. Typifying the positional tradition is the formal organizational "chart" that defines the prescribed flow of communication within an organization (see McPhee & Poole, 2001, for more on formal structure and hierarchy in organizational communication research). However, Monge and Eisenberg note that the formal chart is often a poor reflection of the actual system of communicative relationships. Thus, the relational tradition considers the actual communication relationships that emerge through the activity of the organizational system.

Properties of Networks   Put as simply as possible, a network consists of a system of links among components (e.g., individuals, work groups, organizations). The purpose of network analysis is to map out the flows that move among these network members. There are a number of ways we can characterize a network as a whole, including network content, network mode, and network density. *Network content* refers to the "stuff" that is flowing through the linkages in the network. For example, Tichy, Tushman, and Fombrun (1979) see network content as falling into four major categories: goods and services, information, expressions of affect, and attempts to influence or control. *Network mode* refers to the communication medium through which network linkages are maintained. Early research often differentiated between written and face-to-face modes, although the advent of communication technologies has increased the number of possible network modes dramatically. Consider, for example, how network connections can change and expand as wireless connections become so common that entire campuses, neighborhoods, and even cities are "wired." Third, the network as a whole can be characterized in terms of its *density*. A highly dense network is one in which there are many interconnections among network members, whereas a less dense network is more loosely interconnected. Finally, the network can be considered in terms of its *level of analysis*. Intraorganizational networks will look at connections among individuals within a given organization, whereas interorganizational networks will consider links among many organizations (see Eisenberg et al., 1985). In a global and complex society, interorganizational networks—of businesses, governments, and nongovernmental organizations—become particularly important (see, e.g., Doerfel & Taylor, 2004).

Properties of Network Links   It is also possible to characterize the connections that link members of a network together. There are many ways to consider network links (see Monge & Contractor, 2001, p. 442) but three of the most often used identifiers involve the properties of strength, symmetry, and multiplexity. Link *strength* has been defined in a variety of ways. For example, a strong link might be one in which there is a great deal of communication flowing between two people, one that has endured over a long period of time, or one in which the exchange is deemed important by network participants. The *symmetry* of a communication link refers to whether the two people involved in the link have the same kind of relationship with each other. For example, the supervisor–subordinate relationship is asymmetrical, whereas the coworker relationship is symmetrical. Last, the *multiplexity* of a link refers to the number of different kinds of content (e.g., work-related, social, innovation ideas) that flow through a particular link.

Network Roles   Finally, it is possible to look at the individual actors within a network. Each "node" within a network can be described in a variety of ways (e.g., how central the node is in the network; see Monge & Contractor, 2001, p. 443). However, one of the most interesting ways to consider the individual actors in a network is to consider network roles. Network roles define the ways in which individuals are connected with each other. Consider the hypothetical network represented in Figure 4.3. By looking at this diagram, it is clear that individuals are connected in very different ways within the network. For example, compare the connections of Mike, Tomas, and Ernest. Mike doesn't talk to anyone in the network, and he would be characterized as an *isolate*. Tomas talks to a number of highly interconnected individuals (Dan, Yun-Mi, Natalie, and Stefan), and all of these people would be characterized as *group members*. Within this group, Dan serves as a *bridge* to individuals outside of the group. Finally, Ernest talks to

Case in Point: Nowhere to Hide Connectedness

A network approach to understanding organizational systems emphasizes the interconnected communication patterns that join individuals within organizations and across organizational boundaries. This connectedness—and an ability to understand it—is enhanced through technologies such as computers, cell phones, and global positioning systems (GPS).

Consider, for example, the technology of "Work-track" developed by Aligo, a company in Mountain View, California. Levy (2004) describes the system like this:

> The system is sold to employers who want to automate and verify digital time-logs of their workers in the field . . . Workers have cell phones equipped with GPS that pinpoint their locations to computers in the back office. Their peregrinations can be checked against the "Geo

> Fence" that employers draw up, circumscribing the area where their work is situated . . . "If they're not in the right area, they're really not working," says Aligo CEO Robert Smith. "A notification will come to the back office that they're not where they should be." (p. 76)

In other words, the technology creates a system where the whereabouts and connections among workers can be constantly tracked. Though Aligo president Smith claims that "workers like the technology because it insures they get credit for the time they spend on the job" (Levy, 2004, p. 76), one could also argue that the "freedom" gained from mobile technology has been turned on its head. Those systems of interconnections may tie workers more and more closely to those in control.

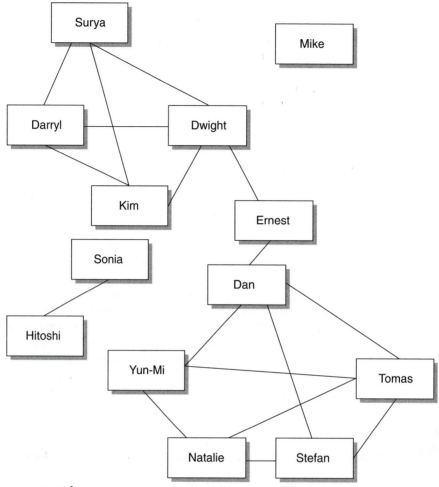

Figure 4.3 | A Hypothetical Communication Network

two people who have radically different connections within the network, and he would be characterized as a *liaison*.

In summary, we can look at emergent communication networks by considering the characteristics of the full network (its content, mode, and density), by considering the characteristics of network links (their strength, symmetry, and multiplexity), and by considering network roles. It is worth emphasizing that though we often think about a network as a "snapshot" of the group, organizational, or interorganizational structure, these network configurations often change over time, and these changes can make a big difference for network functioning and the effect of the network activity on individuals. For example, Shumate, Fulk, and Monge (2005) found that an interorganizational (and international) network of organizations coping with the HIV-AIDS crisis changed substantially over a period of eight years. As for the individual, Susskind (2007) recently found that involvement in communication networks over time was important in helping employees cope with being "survivors" in a corporate downsizing.

Modeling Techniques

Network analysis is useful in drawing and analyzing the maps that characterize organizational communication systems. However, systems theory concepts also incorporate complex *processes* of behavior. In order to better understand how organizational communication systems work, scholars have turned to statistical techniques that attempt to model patterns of communicative behavior and events in an organization. These models take many forms, and their complexity precludes a full discussion in this text (see Miller, 2001, for a more complete discussion). However, it is important to note that modeling techniques allow researchers to assess complex relationships among variables through the evaluation of causal models (McPhee & Babrow, 1987) or to assess changes in organizational communication systems through the use of time-series analysis and related techniques (Monge, 1990).

Perhaps one of the most exciting developments in organizational communication systems research is the use of computer simulations of organizational communication processes (Poole, 1996). Researchers using this technique program the computer with the "rules" of a particular system and starting values, and then see what happens to the system when it is taken to its logical conclusion. For example, Contractor and Seibold (1993) have explored how a "self-organizing system" would work in the context of group decision making. In a self-organizing system, order is purported to "emerge" in chaotic systems when conditions are right. Using computer simulations allows researchers to explore a variety of permutations that might emerge in such complex systems. These permutations would be impossible to explore through the isolated observation of actual organizational communication processes.

Case Analysis

Both of the research techniques discussed so far—network analysis and modeling techniques—involve relatively sophisticated statistical analyses. But mathematical techniques are not the only ones available to the systems researcher. Indeed, some scholars have argued (e.g., Sypher, 1997) that complex systems are best understood through individual cases. A case analysis approach suggests that the richest understanding of organizational systems can be obtained by closely observing specific organizations grappling with specific issues. By collecting a variety of data through observation, interviews, questionnaires, and archives, the analyst can come to a more finely grained understanding of how and why an organizational system develops and behaves as it does. For example, a case analysis of a system using principles from complexity theory (Miller, 1998) highlighted the stress created for employees when the organization was trying to enhance innovation at "the edge of chaos."

Case analyses have been particularly useful in developing aspects of Weick's theory of organizing, presented earlier in this chapter. For example, Weick (1993) uses a historical case to enhance our understanding of times when systems of sense-making fail. In 1949, thirteen firefighters and smoke jumpers died in the Mann Gulch fire in Montana. Weick uses writings about this disaster to develop a complex case analysis assessing the unraveling of this firefighting group. By discussing reasons for the failure of sensemaking (e.g., problems with role structure, the disintegration of the group in the face of panic), Weick is able to extend his theory of sensemaking and provide suggestions for how groups can become more resilient and less vulnerable to sensemaking collapses.

SUMMARY

In this chapter, we have reviewed the systems approach to the study of organizational communication. The systems approach works from the metaphoric concept that an organization is like an organism. We looked at a number of basic systems concepts, including the nature of system components, the nature of system processes, and the properties that emerge from the conceptualization of organizations as interdependent and open sets of interacting components. After our review of basic system properties, we explored three exemplary but very different systems theories. The first of these, cybernetic systems theory, highlights the importance of feedback and regu-lation in goal-directed systems. The second, Weick's theory of organizing, emphasizes how organizational interaction revolves around making sense of equivocal information environments. The third, systems theory from the "new sciences," emphasizes the chaotic and complex nature of "self-organizing" systems. Finally, we considered several methodological approaches that are useful to organizational communication scholars in the systems tradition. These methods —network analysis, modeling techniques, and case analysis—all provide avenues for understanding the complex nature of organizational communication systems.

Discussion Questions

1. How does the systems metaphor for organizing move us from a prescriptive consideration of organizational communication to a descriptive and explanatory approach? Which aspects of the systems metaphor are particularly helpful, for you, in explaining organizational communication processes?
2. What aspects of the systems metaphor are highlighted in a cybernetic approach to understanding? Which aspects are highlighted in Weick's theory of organizing? Which aspects are highlighted by "new science" system theories?
3. What kinds of research questions could be answered by the kinds of systems research methodologies outlined in this chapter? Are these methods mutually exclusive or can you see ways in which they could be usefully combined?

CASE STUDY | **Sensemaking after the Acquisition**

Helen Adams hung up the phone slowly and sat at the desk in her home office. She was surrounded by piles of documents relevant to various projects she was organizing for Sales Infomatics, the marketing firm she worked for. As an independent contractor, Helen had the freedom to work at home and set her own hours. However, she had traded this flexibility at a cost of limited job security and benefits.

And now she was especially concerned about her precarious position. Sales Infomatics, a small family business, had just been acquired by Marketron Inc., a publicly held firm with more than 500 employees in satellite offices around the country. Helen had just been informed about the sale by Les Kelsey, the long-time owner and manager of Sales Infomatics. Les assured her that her job was safe and that the Marketron people would be contacting her soon with employment information.

Though Helen felt a little better with these reassurances, after the phone conversation she had a multitude of questions swirling through her head.

Later that night at dinner, Helen enumerated her concerns to her husband, Glen. "I don't even know if I'll be an employee or an independent contractor. And what will working for Marketron be like? It's not like working for SI when I could just pick up the phone and talk to Les. And will we have to move to one of their office locations? Which office is the best for my work? Which is the best for us? Or for your career? Or should I even work for them? Maybe I could go off on my own, or maybe someone else at SI would go with me?"

"Whoa, slow down!" laughed Glen. "I know you're really concerned about this change. I am, too. But there's no point getting into a tizzy about it now. I'm sure someone from this Marketron place will call you tomorrow and you can start figuring out all the details of the acquisition and how it will affect you. In the meantime, just keep doing your work. It will keep you busy and show Marketron what a valuable employee you are."

But no one from Marketron called the next day. Or the next day. Or the next. Not that Helen didn't talk with anyone about the acquisition. Quite to the contrary, Helen seemed to talk about nothing but the acquisition. The other SI employees fed Helen all sorts of rumors about what was going on at Marketron. From Sara, an SI data analyst, Helen heard that all of the Marketron offices worked under different project models and that getting in with the "right" office was a key to success. From Lance, an SI project manager, she heard that the incentive system

was going to change radically, but the exact form of the future system was still up in the air. From Gretel, the receptionist at the SI office, she heard that the movers had come and gone and that all SI employees were being reassigned to various Marketron offices. But Helen heard nothing from Marketron.

After two weeks, Helen decided to take matters into her own hands. She called Akiba Jaffe, the vice president for employee relations at Marketron. "Mr. Jaffe," Helen began, "you don't know me, but my name is Helen Adams, and I'm an independent contractor with Sales Infomatics."

"Of course, I know who you are, Helen," Akiba replied. "I've talked with Les Kelsey about you on many occasions. I hear you do incredible work and I anticipate that you'll be a valued member of the Marketron team."

Helen was surprised. "Great, Mr. Jaffe! Perhaps, then, we could take a few minutes to talk about my employment relationship with Marketron. I have a lot of questions for you, and I'd like to start getting some things settled in my mind. We could meet in person, if you'd like, or I have a list of questions prepared that we could consider now. For example . . ."

"Well, you know, Helen," Akiba interrupted, "I'd love to talk right now, but I have a lot on my plate to deal with first. Our plan is to get to the arrangements with independent contractors in the next week or so, after we settle the transition plans with permanent employees. Be patient, and we'll get back to you then."

Helen was patient for the next week. And the next. And the next. She continued to do her work and complete the projects she'd been working on for Sales Infomatics. She continued to get dribs and drabs of information from former SI employees. She learned that they had all received employment contracts, though many were unsatisfied with the nature of the contracts. She learned that many of the SI "ways of doing things" were changing. But she still heard nothing about her own future at Marketron and she began to update her résumé just in case she had to hit the streets and look for a job.

Finally, six weeks after the acquisition, Helen talked again with Les Kelsey. "Les," Helen began, "I hate to be pesky about this, but I'm still trying to figure out where I stand with Marketron."

Les quickly broke in. "But I heard from Akiba Jaffe that he talked with you and assured you that you would be an important part of the Marketron team. He's really the person you need to talk with now about all the details." Helen hung up the phone, frustrated once again. If Les didn't have the answers, who could she turn to?

CASE ANALYSIS QUESTIONS

1. How would you use Weick's model of sense-making to describe Helen's experiences since Sales Infomatics was acquired by Marketron? What kind of information environment confronts Helen? And what options does she have to successfully cope with that information environment?

2. Do Helen's experiences reflect any of the systems factors identified by theorists using "new science" principles? Or could these principles help Helen change or adapt to the situation she has found herself in?

3. How does Helen's role in the communication networks at Sales Infomatics and Marketron influence her ability to cope with life after the acquisition? How would you describe the networks and her roles within them?

4. Think about Helen's situation as a cybernetic model in which the goal is enhanced information about life as an employee of Marketron. What kind of feedback is Helen now receiving? And what kinds of mechanisms could she use to enhance her knowledge about the new company?

Cultural Approaches

CHAPTER **5**

AFTER READING THIS CHAPTER, YOU SHOULD . . .

- Know about how the cultural metaphor for understanding organizations was first developed as a prescriptive model for improving organizational performance and be able to describe the weaknesses of this prescriptive approach
- Appreciate ways of describing organizational cultures as complicated, emergent, unitary, and ambiguous
- Understand Schein's definition and model of organizational culture and be able to use that model to analyze cultural factors in organizational communication
- See ways in which the cultural metaphor requires alternative research methods such as ethnography and the writing of cultural tales

Several of the approaches in the previous chapters have looked at organizations and communication through the lens of a metaphor. Classical approaches conceptualize organizations as machines, and systems approaches look at the organismic aspects of organizational structure and functioning. In this chapter, we look at an additional metaphor by regarding organizations as *cultures*. The cultural metaphor derives from the field of anthropology, where for years scholars have studied the cultures of nations, tribes, and ethnic groups.

What is a culture? When we think about the culture of a nation, many things come to mind. Consider U.S. culture, for example. We might think of some of the values that many Americans hold—freedom, independence, hard work, or achievement. We might think of some of the symbols of U.S. culture—the stars and stripes, the bald eagle, baseball, and apple pie. We might think of the rites and rituals of Americans—Fourth of July picnics, blowout wedding receptions, or Super Bowl parties. We might think of the daily life of Americans—early mornings on the family farm, ninety-minute commutes on the Los Angeles freeways, or long days balancing the demands of work and family. But, of course, the notion of American culture is not always straightforward and uncontested. Especially in our post-9/11 world, there are debates about what it means to be American both within our own borders and as a part of the interdependent global world. In short, when thinking about U.S. culture, we think about a complicated patchwork of values, symbols, and behaviors that define "America" in various ways for various people.

In using a cultural metaphor for the investigation of an organization, we are again looking for the qualities that make an organization "what it is." What makes IBM different from Apple? What makes McDonald's different from Burger King? What makes the University of Texas different from Texas A&M University? What makes the Delta Gamma house on your campus different from Alpha Chi Omega's? As Pacanowsky and O'Donnell-Trujillo (1983) note, "Each organization has its own way of doing what it does and its own way of talking about what it is doing" (p. 128). To discover these ways of doing and ways of talking is to investigate organizational culture.

In this chapter, we consider two different ways of thinking about culture. The first, originating in the popular business press, looks at culture as something an organization has. According to this approach, having the "right" kind of culture can make or break an organization. The second approach considers culture as something an organization is. Following the discussion of these two ways of thinking about culture, I will explicate one model of culture in more detail. This model, developed by Edgar Schein (1992), conceptualizes culture as the assumptions, values, behaviors, and artifacts that an organization exhibits as it attempts to adapt to internal and external organizational contingencies. Finally, we will take a look at the research methods typically used to investigate organizational culture.

PRESCRIPTIVE VIEWS OF CULTURE

During the last part of the twentieth century, organizational scholars and practitioners became fascinated with the concept of "organizational culture." As Eisenberg and Riley (2001, p. 291) note, "the speed at which 'organizational culture' emerged as a significant lens for communication scholars and other academics to examine or otherwise engage with organizations and institutions was astounding." The concept of "culture" took the business and academic community by storm for several reasons. First, the metaphor of culture clearly resonated with both academics and practitioners. It simply made sense to see organizations as complex arenas of stories and values rather than as entirely rational institutions. Second, the cultural metaphor opened up new and fruitful areas of research, as you will discover in this chapter. And finally, culture quickly became a part of everyday talk in carpools and around watercoolers. As Eisenberg and Riley (2001, p. 292) point out, "organizational discourse was soon peppered with such statements as 'The culture here won't allow us to . . .' or 'Our culture is very intense—we work hard and play harder.' "

The early popularity and widespread use of cultural terminology can be traced back to two popular books published in the early 1980s. These books were *Corporate Cultures: The Rites and Rituals of Corporate Life*, by Terrence Deal and Allen Kennedy (1982), and *In Search of Excellence: Lessons from America's Best-Run Companies*, by Tom Peters and Robert Waterman (1982). Both books propose that successful companies can be identified in terms of their cultures.

Deal and Kennedy's "Strong Cultures"

Deal and Kennedy (1982) argue that business success can be enhanced through the development of a "strong" culture. If an organization has the components of a strong culture, it will be a better place for individuals to work and will improve individual and organizational performance. Deal and Kennedy identify four key components of a strong culture:

1. *Values* are the beliefs and visions that members hold for an organization. For example, 3M Corporation espouses a value for innovation, whereas Prudential Insurance represents a value of stability.
2. *Heroes* are the individuals who come to exemplify an organization's values. These heroes become known through the stories and myths of an organization. For example, Steve Jobs is a hero who exemplifies innovation and market savvy at Apple.
3. *Rites and rituals* are the ceremonies through which an organization celebrates its values. An organization that values innovation may develop a ritualistic way of rewarding the new ideas of employees. In other organizations, rites and rituals might include a company picnic or an awards banquet for outstanding employees.
4. Finally, the *cultural network* is the communication system through which cultural values are instituted and reinforced. The cultural network could consist of both formal organizational channels, such as newsletters, and the informal interactions of employees.

Peters and Waterman's "Excellent Cultures"

A second book that made a big impact on the business community in the 1980s was *In Search of Excellence*, by Peters and Waterman (1982). Like Deal and Kennedy, Peters and Waterman were attempting to identify aspects of organizational culture that were prevalent in high-performing companies. They studied sixty-two organizations deemed "excellent" by employees and organizational experts. They then identified "themes" that characterized the cultures of these organizations. These themes are presented in Table 5.1. As this table indicates, the themes emphasize the importance of people (e.g., "close relations to the customer" and "productivity through people") and downplay bureaucratic structure and values (e.g., "autonomy and entrepreneurship" and "simple form, lean staff").

Both *Corporate Cultures* and *In Search of Excellence* had an enormous impact on organizational practice. These books emphasize the importance of organizational intangibles, such as values and heroes, and signal a move away from strictly rational models of organizing. However, the books were not as widely embraced by the academic community, primarily because they provide *prescriptions* for managerial practice rather than descriptions or explanations of organizational life. For example, Deal and Kennedy's book argues that a strong culture held by all employees is the only route to success in the business world. Similarly, individuals reading Peters and Waterman's book would conclude that excellence could best be achieved through the themes laid out in Table 5.1. Indeed, some scholars later called this

Table 5.1 | Peters and Waterman's Themes for Excellent Organizations

Theme	Description
1. A bias for action	Excellent organizations react quickly and do not spend excess time planning and analyzing.
2. Close relations to the customer	Excellent organizations gear decisions and actions to the needs of customers.
3. Autonomy and entrepreneurship	Excellent organizations encourage employees to take risks in the development of new ideas.
4. Productivity through people	Excellent organizations encourage positive and respectful relationships among management and employees.
5. Hands-on, value-driven	Excellent organizations have employees and managers who share the same core value of productivity and performance.
6. Stick to the knitting	Excellent organizations stay focused on what they do best and avoid radical diversification.
7. Simple form, lean staff	Excellent organizations avoid complex structures and divisions of labor.
8. Simultaneous loose-tight properties	Excellent organizations exhibit both unity of purpose and the diversity necessary for innovation.

approach "value engineering" because it espouses the belief that "effective cultural leaders could create 'strong' cultures, built around their own values" (Martin & Frost, 1996, p. 602). Others have emphasized that this *integration* approach to culture is only one lens through which a culture might be viewed (Martin, 2002).

It is important to stress that the values prescribed in this view of culture are, in large part, ones that can—and do—make positive contributions to organizational performance and to the work lives of organizational members. For example, there is little doubt that customer service organizations will be more successful if they gear decisions and actions to customer needs (Theme 2 from Table 5.1) or that it is dangerous to try to do too many different things within one organization (Theme 6 from Table 5.1). Indeed, more recent popular press management books have continued to echo many of the themes first set forth in these early books (see, e.g., Collins, 2004).

However, these prescriptive approaches to culture also fall short in two important respects. First, it is naive to assume that there is a single cultural "formula" for achieving organizational success. For example, although a "bias for action" may have proven effective for the organizations studied by Peters and Waterman, there are certainly times when a more contemplative approach to organizing would be appropriate. Thus, prescriptions for the "correct" culture oversimplify the complexities of organizational life. Second, these prescriptive approaches treat culture as a "thing" that an organization "has." This objectification of culture is risky be-cause when we objectify culture we de-emphasize the complex processes through which organizational culture is created and sustained. When we objectify culture, we also tend to simplify it. For example, we might assume that *all* organizational participants share the same culture and that the organization's culture is relatively stable over time.

Because of these problems, most scholars who adopt a cultural approach to the study of organizations avoid the prescriptive tack taken by these writers. Instead, cultural researchers seek to *describe* and *understand* the complex ways in which organizational culture is developed and maintained. The next section considers these alternative approaches to culture.

 ## Case in Point: Red Sox Nation

I am a citizen of Red Sox Nation.

How did this happen to a lifelong Detroit Tigers fan? A woman who, as a girl, listened to the venerable Ernie Harwell broadcasting Tigers games through a transistor radio under the pillow? A woman who named her dog after Mickey Stanley, a 1960s Tiger centerfielder? A woman who, in 1985, reprised the 1968 Detroit Tigers' fight song on a Lansing, Michigan, radio station in order to win a free gallon of ice cream?

Well, part of my change in nationality came from marrying a lifelong Red Sox fan. And having a daughter with a closet full of Red Sox (and anti-Yankee) shirts makes a difference, too. But the power of the culture of "Red Sox Nation" was clearly an influential factor in my changing allegiances. For the Red Sox organization embodies a strong culture that reaches from the front office, to the field, to the streets of Boston, and to citizens of Red Sox Nation around the world.

At the beginning of the 2004 season, Mark Starr (2004) highlighted some of the characteristics of the Red Sox culture that include intense rivalry (with the hated Yankees, of course), a singular setting (Fenway Park and the green monster), and a shared history of maddeningly dashed hopes. The power of this culture has been heightened in more recent years by owner-ship that balanced tradition and change, a talented and sometimes quirky team, and widespread television coverage of games on the New England Sports Network.

It all came to fruition in late October 2004. The Red Sox came back from a three-game deficit to win the American League pennant over the Yankees and then swept the St. Louis Cardinals to win their first World Series in 86 years. They reversed the "Curse of the Bambino" and the power of the Red Sox Nation culture was felt all over Boston and, indeed, across the country. I was there for the second game of the World Series and the excitement was palpable at Fenway and throughout Boston. Looking back from the distance of several years, one might wonder if such a culture can maintain its strength. Judging from ticket sales, media coverage, and sports memorabilia, the answer is clearly yes. And as I sit in my living room waving a Red Sox foam finger in the post-season of 2007, I can assure you that the power of this culture has not weakened a bit. I'm now making my final revisions, several months after the Red Sox won the 2007 World Series. I rejoiced in the victories, celebrated while watching the parade through Boston, and laughed as Jonathan Papelbon danced his river dance. Apparently, the curse of the Bambino has been reversed, and the culture of Red Sox Nation will endure.

ALTERNATIVE APPROACHES TO CULTURE

Today, most scholars interested in organizational culture eschew the simple prescriptive approaches discussed above. Rather than seeing culture as a "thing" that can and should be "managed," these researchers see culture as the emerging and sometimes fragmented values, practices, narratives, and artifacts that make a particular organization "what it is." Putnam (1983) introduced this interpretive approach in the communication discipline, noting that this approach requires a consideration of "the way individuals make sense of their world through their communicative behaviors" (p. 31). Although this chapter cannot fully explore the multitude of positions taken by those trying to describe and understand organizational culture (see Eisenberg & Riley, 2001; Martin, 1992, 2002; and Martin & Frost, 1996), four issues highlight the distinction between prescriptive approaches to culture and the approaches taken by most cultural scholars today: (1) culture is complicated; (2) culture is emergent; (3) culture is not unitary; and (4) culture is often ambiguous.

Organizational Cultures Are Complicated

The complexity of organizational culture is demonstrated by the wide variety of "markers" that scholars use to investigate it. We will consider just a few. Beyer and Trice (1987) argue that an organization's culture is revealed through its rites, and they differentiate among rites of passage, rites of degradation, rites of enhancement, rites of renewal, rites of conflict reduction, and rites of integration. Dandridge (1986) looks at organizational *ceremonies* as indicators of culture. Quinn and McGrath (1985) focus on the role of *values* and *belief systems* in the transformation of organizational cultures. Smith and Eisenberg (1987) consider the *metaphors* of employees and management in a study of the culture at Disneyland. Boje (1991) and Meyer (1995) contend that culture can best be revealed through the *stories* that organizational members tell. Schall (1983) and Morley and Shockley-Zalabak (1991; Shockley-Zalabak & Morley, 1994) investigate *communication rules* in the development of culture. Even organizational *hallway talk* can be a lens for viewing culture (Gronn, 1983).

Rites, ceremonies, values, belief systems, metaphors, stories, communication rules, and hallway talk are just a few of the windows through which researchers attempt to gain a glimpse of an organization's culture. Moreover, some scholars concentrate on a single cultural marker whereas others attempt to examine the ways in which a variety of cultural manifestations are woven together (Martin & Frost, 1996). Given this diversity of cultural markers, it is not surprising that most scholars see organizational culture as a highly complex phenomenon.

Organizational Cultures Are Emergent

A second point of agreement among most organizational culture scholars is the notion that cultures are socially created through the interaction of organizational members. This idea is central to a communication focus on culture in which culture is not merely transmitted through communication but in which communication is "constitutive of culture" (Eisenberg & Riley, 2001, p. 294). Putnam (1983) took this position many years ago, arguing that social reality is a symbolic process "created through ongoing actions and intersubjective meanings attributed to those actions" (p. 44). Pacanowsky and O'Donnell-Trujillo (1983) took this emergent approach into the cultural realm in their work on "Organizational Communication as Cultural Performance." These scholars argue that a study of organizational culture should concentrate on the communication processes through which culture is created. They further argue that these communication processes can be best conceptualized as "performances" that are interactional, contextual, episodic, and improvisational.

Cultural performances are *interactional* in that they require the participation of multiple organizational members. Cultural performances are *contextual* in that they are embedded in organizational situations and organizational history. Cultural performances are *episodic* in that they are "nameable as distinct events" (Pacanowsky & O'Donnell-Trujillo, 1983, p. 133). Finally, cultural performances are *improvisational* because there are no scripts that guide organizational members. By pointing to the importance of "cultural performance," Pacanowsky and O'Donnell-Trujillo highlight the communicative processes through which organizational cultures emerge and shift over time.

Organizational Cultures Are Not Unitary

Most organizational culture researchers agree that it is impossible to characterize an organization as having a *single* culture. Rather, most scholars agree that organizations are characterized by a multitude of subcultures that "may co-exist in harmony, conflict, or indifference to each other" (Frost, Moore, Louis, Lundberg, & Martin, 1991, p. 8). Martin (2002) highlights this aspect of culture in her discussion of a *differentiation* approach in which inconsistencies among cultural views are expected and often seen as desirable.

But where are these various subcultures found in an organization and how do they work? Louis (1985) addresses these questions in her consideration of the *sites of culture* and *cultural penetration*. Louis first argues that there are a number of sites where culture might develop in an organization, including a "vertical slice" (e.g., a division), a "horizontal slice" (e.g., a particular hierarchical level), or a specific work group. Martin (2002) also points out that subcultures might emerge around networks of personal contacts or demographic similarity. These cultural sites all "serve as breeding grounds . . . for the emergence of shared meaning" (Louis, 1985, p. 79). Thus, a wide range of subcultures could spring up at various sites in a single organization. For example, Marschall (2002) recently conducted an ethnographic study of a software development firm and found that skilled workers in the Internet economy created their own occupational community. This community—though perhaps divided by geography—shared work practices, ideas about what was important in the workplace, and even adopted a distinct language and vocabulary.

One additional consideration of the nonunitary nature of organizational culture is that various subcultures within an organization may represent important differences in power and in interests (see, e.g., Alvesson, 1993). In other words, not

Spotlight on Scholarship

From smoky newsrooms to loud and dirty press-rooms to sitting around on the police beat, the newspaper business has traditionally been viewed as a "man's world." This has changed to some extent, of course, since the 1970s, as women have entered the workforce in greater numbers. However, these changes have come slowly in journalism. "[C]ompared to the U.S. civilian workforce in 2000, women journalists are considerably less prevalent than women in other professions. Women journalists are also less likely to be managers than women in other areas of the professional work force (Everbach, 2007, p. 478). Indeed, Al Neuharth, while CEO of Gannett Co., one of the largest U.S. newspaper companies, commented that "Too many middle-aged white men still make the decisions" in newsrooms around the country (Everbach, 2007, p. 478).

But what happens when there *are* women in control of a large newspaper? Does their leadership make a difference? Does the kind of news produced change? Does the organizational culture change? Tracy Everbach (2007) explored these questions in her recent article, "The Culture of a Women-Led Newspaper: An Ethnographic Study of the *Sarasota Herald-Tribune*." In this study, Everbach conducted interviews and made observations at a large Florida newspaper that was the first in the country to have an all-women management team. Her findings illustrate many of the concepts regarding organizational culture discussed in this chapter.

First, Everbach found that having a women-led management team definitely made a difference in terms of the organizational culture. The workplace was marked by more family-friendly policies, more openness in communication patterns, and more participative and egalitarian decision making. As Ever-

bach (2007, p. 484) notes, "the female leaders at the *Herald-Tribune* made a point of welcoming employee input, offering open-door conversation policies, and coming out of their offices to communicate with the staff." All of these processes have been identified as more "feminine" forms of management, and the editors at the newspaper very consciously saw themselves as role models for these kinds of policies and behaviors. Workers at the paper also identified negative aspects of a "feminine" culture. Some staffers believed that assertive reporting behaviors were discouraged and others thought that the atmosphere had become more "gossipy" and "catty."

It is interesting, though, that in spite of this large change in the culture attributed to a women-led organization, there was little change in the product of that organization. As Everbach (2007, p. 479) points out, "the *Herald-Tribune*'s front page, local news, business, sports, and lifestyle sections represented few women, so the female management team clearly did not change news values regarding content selection." This may point to the limits of a local organizational culture to influence the values of an industry or occupation. The value for hard news becomes almost hardwired into journalists. Everbach (2007, pp. 480–481) notes, "[f]emale journalists are socialized to view these [masculine] standards as journalistic objectivity, allowing the news to become 'masculinized' even when reported by women." The values of leaders can make a big difference, but shifting the larger professional values of an occupation is clearly a long-term process.

Everbach, T. (2007). The Culture of a Women-Led Newspaper: An Ethnographic Study of the *Sarasota Herald-Tribune*. *Journalism and Mass Communication Quarterly*, 83, 477–493.

only can the subcultures of the corporate boardroom and the assembly line be described as "different," these differences also point to fundamental schisms in power and ideology in the organization. For example, at your own university, the student population might have a distinct subculture that is quite different from those of faculty or staff (see Kramer & Berman, 2001). However, it is likely that the values espoused through the student culture hold less sway than those espoused by others.

(These differences in power and ideology are discussed in much greater detail in Chapter 6.)

Organizational Cultures Are Often Ambiguous

Finally, scholars of organizational culture recognize that there is not always a clear picture of the organization's culture—or even of its various subcultures. There may be multiple manifestations of culture that are difficult to interpret. Martin (2002) discusses this approach to culture as the *fragmentation* perspective, and argues that fragmentation studies will see an ambiguous culture as "a normal, salient, and inescapable part of organizational functioning in the contemporary world" (p. 105).

This notion that culture is oftentimes ambiguous, fragmented, and hard to pin down is particularly important when considering organizations that are rapidly changing. Many scholars argue that we now live in a "postmodern world" that is multifaceted, fragmented, fast-moving, and difficult to understand (see, e.g., Holstein & Gubrium, 2000). In such an environment, it is not surprising that organizational culture might also be in a state of flux. For example, Risberg (1999) analyzed the culture of a Swedish manufacturing company that had just been acquired. Risberg noted that "a post-acquisition process cannot be understood in one clear way. There are ambiguities in interpretation of situations and statements. These ambiguities illustrate the multiple realities within the organization and during the post-acquisition process" (Risberg, 1999, p. 177). These ambiguities can be

Case in Point: Leadership and Deaf Culture

There are times when cultural factors beyond the organization itself have a huge impact on organizational processes—and vice versa. Such is the case at Gallaudet University in Washington, D.C., the leading school for the deaf in the United States. In 1988, students at Gallaudet launched the concept of "deaf culture" when they objected to the appointment of yet another hearing president. These objections were heard, and I. King Jordan was appointed as the first deaf president at Gallaudet. When Jordan announced his retirement in 2006, the university's board of trustees began to search for a new president, and soon announced the planned appointment of Jane Fernandes. Shortly after this announcement, students were once again protesting the appointment, leading to widespread campus conflict (Childress, 2006).

In this case, though, the conflict was not over appointing a hearing president or about the nominee's experience with the school. Indeed, Fernandes was born deaf and had been serving as Gallaudet's provost. Instead, these protests point to the ways in which the values of both societal cultures and organizational cultures shift over time. For one of the major concerns of the protestors was whether Fernandes was sufficiently committed to promoting deaf culture (though concerns with leadership style were also raised). Fernandes didn't learn to sign until she was 23, and American Sign Language is seen as a crucial component of deaf culture. Childress (2006, p. 44) notes that "some [protestors] worry that she will focus too much on technology to 'fix' deafness rather than embrace it." In the end, the protestors had their way, as Robert Davila was appointed as interim president. This situation, though, points to the changing nature of organizational culture and the interplay between values in society and values in specific organizations. In 1988, the important step was to have deaf leadership at Gallaudet University—by 2006, the cultural stakes had become much more complex.

particularly challenging for individuals as they try to forge their own identities within these reconfigured organizational cultures (Pepper & Larson, 2006).

In summary, current organizational culture scholars take an approach to culture that seeks to understand the ways in which communication and interaction create a unique sense of place in an organization. These scholars look for the complex web of values, behaviors, stories, rules, and metaphors that comprise an organization's culture, acknowledging that culture is socially created through the communicative performances of organizational members. These scholars also look for the similarities and differences among various subcultures that exist simultaneously in any organization, and acknowledge that culture is often ambiguous and in a state of flux. In the next section, we review one specific model of organizational culture. Although this model does not capture all of the nuances of contemporary approaches to culture, it provides a helpful lens for analyzing organizational cultures and subcultures.

SCHEIN'S MODEL OF ORGANIZATIONAL CULTURE

Edgar Schein is a management scholar and consultant interested in the role of leaders in the development and maintenance of organizational culture. His 1992 book, *Organizational Culture and Leadership* (first edition published in 1985), describes a model of culture that pulls together several of the notions we have already considered in this chapter.

A Definition of Culture

Schein (1992) first defines the culture of a social group—an organization or other collective—in the following way:

> a pattern of shared basic assumptions that the group learned as it solved its problems of external adaptation and internal integration, that has worked well enough to be considered valid, and, therefore, to be taught to new members as the correct way to perceive, think and feel in relation to those problems. (p. 12)

This definition raises several critical issues. First, Schein defines culture as a *group phenomenon*. An individual cannot have a culture, because cultural formation depends on communication. However, cultural groups can exist on many levels, ranging from civilizations and countries to small organizational or social groups. Schein acknowledges that not all groups develop an "integrated" culture and that cultures are often fragmented, as we discussed above. However, Schein believes that it is important to highlight the human need for stability, consistency, and meaning. Thus, he argues that "cultural formation, therefore, is always a *striving toward patterning and integration*, even though the actual history of experiences of many groups prevents them from ever achieving a clear-cut paradigm" (Schein, 1992, p. 11).

Second, Schein defines culture as a *pattern of basic assumptions*, suggesting that the beliefs that make up culture are relatively enduring and difficult to change. Indeed, individuals may not even be aware of the cultural assumptions they hold. As we will see in the model he developed, Schein acknowledges that organizational culture also encompasses values, behaviors, rules, and physical artifacts. However, he believes that the core of culture is its basic assumptions and that values, behaviors, and so on are better seen as *reflections* of that culture.

Third, Schein sees culture as an *emergent* and *developmental* process. According to his definition, cultures are learned or invented as a group meets internal and external challenges. Consider, for instance, the trajectory of Internet startup firms in the 1990s and early part of the twenty-first century. In the mid- to late 1990s, many fledgling Internet companies were riding high, looking for venture capitalists to finance grand schemes of expansion. The culture of such a company would reflect the contingencies of this environment. It might be aggressive, confident, fast-moving, perhaps even brash. But when the economy—and particularly the Internet economy—contracted in 2000 and 2001, the culture at these companies probably changed substantially. In short, the culture was shaped by the circumstances of the organization and its environment.

Finally, Schein's definition highlights the *socializing* aspect of organizational culture. We will discover more about this topic in Chapter 7. At this point, though, it is enough to point out that when individuals enter an organization, a major part of "learning the ropes" consists of developing an understanding of the assumptions and values that make up that organization's culture. This is not to suggest that newcomers are blank slates upon which culture is written, however. Indeed, Schein believes that in many cases "the new members' interaction with old members will be a more creative process of building a culture" (Schein, 1992, p. 13).

A Model of Culture

After presenting his definition of culture, Schein sets forth a model that sorts out the various elements of culture into three distinct levels. This model is presented in Figure 5.1.

Level 1: Artifacts   The most visible level of culture in Schein's model consists of the physical and social environment that organizational members have created. A number of different cultural indicators could be included at this observable level. The most obvious of these are the artifacts—or things—displayed by organizational members and the overt behavior of organizational members. A researcher attempting to investigate and understand an organization's culture would normally begin by considering these overt manifestations. An investigator looking at artifacts might consider such diverse items as architecture, furniture, technology, dress, written documents, and art. An investigator looking at behaviors might consider communication patterns such as forms of address, decision-making styles, communication during meetings, and network configuration. These items, and the questions a cultural investigator might ask about them, are included in Table 5.2.

Of course, as Schein (1985) notes, "whereas it is easy to observe artifacts— even subtle ones, such as the way in which status is demonstrated by members— the difficulty is figuring out what the artifacts mean, how they interrelate, what deeper patterns, if any, they reflect" (p. 15). Hence, even this outer layer is labeled as "difficult to decipher" in Schein's model. Imagine, for instance, that you notice that the faculty in a communication department all address each other by formal titles (e.g., "Professor Jones" or "Doctor Smith") rather than by first names. How

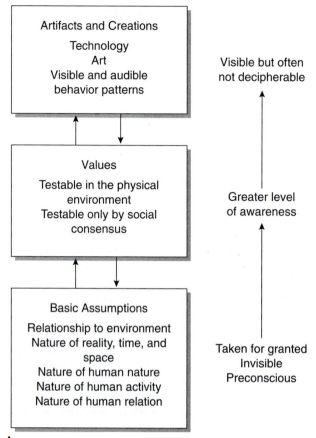

Figure 5.1 | Levels of Culture and Their Interaction.

Reprinted with the permission of Jossey-Bass Inc. Publishers, from Schein, E. H. (1985), *Organizational Culture and Leadership.*

are you to interpret this observation? Perhaps faculty members hold each other in such high esteem that the use of titles seems natural and appropriate. Perhaps formality is the rule throughout the university. Perhaps faculty members are trying to set an example for students. Perhaps faculty members dislike each other intensely and hence try to maintain a distant relationship.

Any of these explanations might be plausible and each says very different things about the organizational culture. Thus, to get a better handle on the cultural meaning of observable behaviors and artifacts, we must move to Schein's second level of culture.

Level 2: Espoused Values   The second level of Schein's model of culture is composed of individual and group values. Values represent preferences or what "ought" to happen. For example, an individual with a value for hard work will probably spend long hours at the office. A manager who values innovativeness will reward workers who come up with new and better ideas for getting the job

Table 5.2 | Cultural Artifacts and Behaviors

Artifact/Behavior	Possible Questions of Cultural Researcher
Architecture	Is the floor plan open? Do the offices have windows? Who has the large offices? What part of the building does the company occupy?
Furniture	Is the furniture functional? Is the furniture comfortable? How is the furniture arranged? Does the furniture match? How is furniture distributed among employees of various hierarchical levels?
Technology	What kind of phone system is used? How up-to-date are the computer systems? What are the usage patterns of computers, fax, and phone systems? Is telecommuting allowed or encouraged?
Dress	Is there a dress code? Do men wear suits and ties? Do women wear dresses? Does dress vary by position? Does dress vary by day of the week?
Written documents	Is all activity documented? Handwritten, typed, or electronic? How are forms processed and filed? Are there rules in place for document creation and destruction?
Art	Is public art classical? Modern? Impressionistic? Do employees decorate their own spaces with posters and photos? What do those personal spaces look like?
Forms of address	Are titles or first names used? Do forms of address vary by job level? Do forms of address change over time? Does everyone follow the same rules for address?
Decision-making style	Do managers make decisions autocratically or through participative means? Do managers consult with employees on decisions? Are decisions made quickly or after much deliberation?
Communication during meetings	How formal are meetings? Is there always an agenda? Do participants stick to it? Are decisions made in meetings? How is technology used during meetings?
Network configuration	Who talks to whom? Does the network pattern vary for work and social communication? Has the network pattern changed over time?

done. Thus, this level of culture represents a mosaic of beliefs about how things ought to be done in an organization.

Several interesting points should be raised about this second level of culture. First, organizations do not have values, individuals do. The individuals in an organization may hold a wide range of values whose variety will contribute to the existence of the organizational subcultures that we considered earlier. However, not all values will hold equal "weight" in an organization. Indeed, many scholars believe that the values of the organizational founder or chief executive officer (CEO) play a critical role in shaping the organization's culture. In discussing the values and behaviors of the CEO, Bennis states that "[h]e or she is the one clearly responsible for shaping the beliefs, motives, commitments, and predispositions of all executives—from senior management to the operators of the organization" (1986, cited in Morley & Shockley-Zalabak, 1991, p. 425). In support of this, Morley and Shockley-Zalabak (1991) determined that founder values exert a strong influence on the values held by other employees.

A second point about the value level of culture is that sometimes individuals say they hold a particular value but their behavior belies that statement. Thus, Schein labels the "middle" level of culture "espoused values" (see Argyris & Schon, 1978), emphasizing that stated value and behavior don't always match. For example, a manager might say that she values the contributions of her employees in decision making. However, that same manager might consistently make decisions without seeking employee input. Thus, when studying an organization's culture, it is critical to look at the correspondence between the behaviors and artifacts of Level 1 and the values of Level 2. If there is a strong match between these two levels, it is likely that both the behaviors and the values are indicators of underlying cultural assumptions. However, if espoused values do not match artifacts and behaviors, it is possible that the values are really "either rationalizations or only aspirations for the future" (Schein, 1992, p. 21). Because of the contradictions that might be found at this value level of culture, it is often important to look even further, to the third level: the basic assumptions of organizational members.

Level 3: Basic Assumptions   Schein's third level of culture is the "core" assumptions that individuals in a group hold about the world and how it works. As indicated in Schein's definition of culture, these assumptions have become "taken for granted" because they have been reinforced time and time again as the group deals with internal and external problems. These basic assumptions are uniformly held by cultural or subcultural members. However, individuals can rarely articulate them because they have become such a natural part of "the way we are" or "the way we do things around here." Schein discusses six areas around which these basic assumptions typically revolve. These are:

1.   Assumptions about the nature of reality and truth
2.   Assumptions about the nature of time
3.   Assumptions about the nature of space
4.   Assumptions about the nature of human nature
5.   Assumptions about the nature of human activity
6.   Assumptions about the nature of human relationships

Clearly, these basic assumptions are not specific to organizational functioning but deal, instead, with how people view the world and humanity's relationship to it. Schein believes that an examination of the basic assumptions might reveal a coherent paradigm that guides a strong and united culture. Or, the cultural assumptions might be fragmented and contradictory and point to problems of adapting to external and internal organizational problems. As Schein (1985) states: "Unless we have searched for the pattern among the different underlying assumptions of a group and have attempted to identify the paradigm by which the members of a group perceive, think about, feel about, and judge situations and relationships, we cannot claim that we have described or understood the group's culture" (p. 111).

Schein's definition and model, then, represent culture as a complex pattern of assumptions, values, behaviors, and artifacts. The cultural pattern that develops over time in a group might be a consistent one. That is, underlying assumptions about the world might be reflected in a set of values that in turn generates behaviors and artifacts. In this case, Schein's model might be seen as an "onion" with interconnected levels. Consider, for example, the "onion" pattern of assumptions, values, and behaviors illustrated in Figure 5.2. In this illustration, the organization has an underlying assumption that change is good. This underlying assumption might be reflected in the valuing of innovation in products and services. On the outside layer of the onion, then, are behaviors and artifacts that reflect this value. These might include bonuses for new ideas, suggestion boxes spread around the office, and a relaxed atmosphere that encourages creative thinking.

Of course, organizations will also exist in which the assumptions do not match the espoused values or where the values are not reflected in observed behavior and creations. These cases might indicate the existence of fragmented subcultures or a

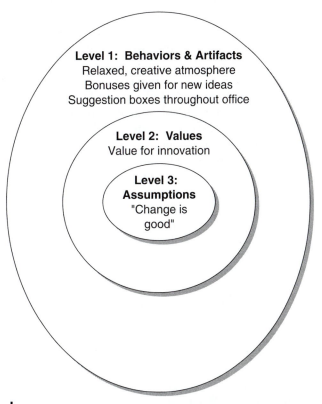

Figure 5.2 | An "Onion Model" Example of Organizational Culture

culture in transition from one set of assumptions and values to another. Further, underlying assumptions can lead to dysfunctional behaviors or can fail to shift as the contingencies of the organizational environment change. Consider, for example, the rapid rise and fall of Enron. Sloan (2002) noted that the underlying cultural assumption of "confidence and aggressiveness" led to beliefs and behaviors of "cockiness and arrogance." Thus, "[w]hat made Enron successful—innovation and daring—got the company into trouble" (Sloan, 2002, p. 21).

Schein's model, of course, oversimplifies the nature of organizational culture and the role of communication in creating and sustaining that culture. As we discussed in considering research related to the descriptive approach to culture, theorists and researchers increasingly see culture as a fragmented and often ambiguous phenomenon, and Schein's model can obscure this complexity. However, Schein's model provides a helpful heuristic for looking at the multiple indicators of organizational culture and how these indicators might—or might not—be indicative of more enduring values and assumptions (see, e.g., Schein, 2004).

METHODS FOR STUDYING ORGANIZATIONAL CULTURE

In our discussion of organizational culture, several points have been emphasized. First, an organizational culture is reflected in a complicated set of assumptions, values, behaviors, and artifacts. Second, organizational cultures change over time as groups adapt to environmental contingencies. Third, organizations are usually composed of subcultures existing in varying degrees of harmony or competition. Fourth, organizational cultures are created and maintained through the communicative interactions of organizational members. Research methods used to investigate culture, then, need to account for these facets of culture.

Although a variety of analytical tools have been used to investigate organizational culture, many researchers believe that qualitative methods are the most appropriate for gaining an understanding of the complicated, fragmented, and changing nature of cultural groups (see Strauss & Corbin, 1990). In particular, because the metaphor of culture was borrowed from the field of anthropology, many scholars have turned to an anthropological method, ethnography, for the investigation of organizational culture.

The term *ethnography* means the "writing of culture," and ethnographic methods differ dramatically from traditional social science techniques (Goodall, 2000). To begin with, an organizational ethnographer approaches an organizational culture as a "text" to be read (Brown & McMillan, 1991). In order to decipher this cultural text, an ethnographer will try to become immersed in organizational life. For example, an ethnographer attempting to learn about the culture at a fast-food restaurant might get a job flipping burgers ("participant observation"); might spend a great deal of time watching interactions at the restaurant ("nonparticipant observation"); might examine training manuals and work-related memos ("archival analysis"); or might talk with employees about their values, heroes, metaphors, rules, and stories. Actually, the ethnographer would probably do several or all of these things. Whatever the specific observational technique, the goal is to *minimize* the distance between the researcher and the culture being investigated. It is assumed that a rich understanding of culture can be garnered only through personal experience (Jackson, 1989).

Through this intense observation of the cultural group, the ethnographer begins to develop an understanding of the values and assumptions at work. In other words, through the observation of organizational behaviors and artifacts (Level 1 of culture) and discussion about organizational values (Level 2 of culture), the researcher develops ideas about the assumptions that drive organizational members (Level 3 of culture) and how all three levels of culture interrelate. Bantz (1993) systematizes this inference process in his "organizational communication culture method." This method suggests that the researcher should first gather organizational communication messages, then analyze these messages in terms of their vocabulary, themes, and symbolic forms (e.g., metaphors and stories). Inferences can then be made from these messages and symbolic forms with regard to organizational norms, roles, motives, and style.

Through these methods of observation and inference, the ethnographer thus creates a mini-theory that is grounded in observations of a particular organizational culture (Glaser & Strauss, 1967). Consider again, for instance, the communication department in which the faculty always address each other by using formal titles. If an ethnographer were studying this department, she might observe many other behaviors and artifacts. She might note that male professors always wear suits and ties when lecturing and that female professors always wear skirts or dresses. She might observe that faculty members socialize together and engage in much more informal behavior outside of the university setting. In talking to faculty members, our ethnographer might find that they often refer to their university and profession in reverential tones. From these and other observations, our ethnographer might begin to build a grounded theory about the department's culture. This theory might revolve around the importance of scholarly tradition in this culture and discuss the manner in which behaviors and artifacts reflect this basic value.

Once a cultural researcher has developed a grounded theory about an organization's culture, the ethnography of that culture can be written. For a cultural researcher, the writing of the research report rarely takes the form of a traditional social science article (e.g., literature review, methods, results, discussion). Rather, the ethnographer is trying to tell a "cultural tale" to help the reader understand the organization in all of its rich and varied detail. Van Maanen (1988) has discussed three kinds of cultural tales that can be told about an organizational culture. The first, a *realist tale*, is like a documentary, as the ethnographer tries to provide a complete and relatively objective account of what was observed in the organization (e.g., Carbaugh, 1988). The second, a *confessional tale*, is as much about the ethnographer as about what was observed. That is, the researcher talks personally about how he or she experienced the culture under investigation (e.g., Goodall, 1991). Finally, an *impressionist tale* is a narrative in which information about the culture is slipped into a story that could stand on its own dramatic merits (e.g., Goodall, 1989). *Critical tales*—narratives with the express goal of uncovering the deep power structures implicit in organizational functioning—could also be added to this list (e.g., Wendt, 1994).

Thus, research regarding organizational culture is often quite different from traditional social science research. The researcher usually uses qualitative methods of observation, including participant observation, nonparticipant observation, and interviews. The researcher then tries to gain an understanding of the culture that is grounded in these local and detailed observations. Finally, the researcher shares this cultural understanding with readers through tales that reflect the complex, emergent, and interactional performance of a particular organizational culture.

SUMMARY

This chapter has presented approaches that view organizations and communication through the lens of a cultural metaphor. We began by considering two books about business practices that popularized the notion of "organizational culture." These books, *Corporate Cultures*, by Deal and Kennedy, and *In Search of Excellence*, by Peters and Waterman, conceptualize culture as a "thing" that belongs to an organization. In this view, having the "right" organizational culture is a prescription for success.

This prescriptive view of culture, however, has been largely rejected by academics. Instead, scholars now take an approach that emphasizes the *description* and *understanding* of culture. This approach emphasizes that cultures are very complex, are socially constructed through the communicative interaction of organizational members, are composed of fragmented subcultural units, and may be fraught with ambiguity.

We then considered an approach developed by Schein that emphasizes the emergent and complex nature of culture. Specifically, Schein argues that cultures can best be conceptualized as having three levels: behaviors and artifacts, espoused organizational values, and taken-for-granted assumptions about how the world works.

Finally, we looked at the research methods used by researchers of organizational culture. We noted that cultural investigators—ethnographers—typically use qualitative methods to build a grounded theory that enhances cultural understanding. Research results are then communicated to the audience through the telling of cultural tales.

Discussion Questions

1. Why is "organizational culture" such a powerful concept for both practicing managers and those who want to have insight into organizational functioning? In what ways does this metaphor for organizing provide a better (or at least different) lens for looking at organizations than the metaphors we've considered in previous chapters of this book?

2. What are the key differences between prescriptive and descriptive approaches to culture? Is Schein's model of organizational culture a descriptive model or a prescriptive model?

3. Think about an organization you know well. This could be a workplace, a church, or perhaps the school you attend. What would you look for in developing a "cultural profile" of this organization? How would you link your observations about this organization with conclusions about the culture? And what specific conclusions would you draw?

| CASE STUDY | The Cultural Tale of Two Shuttles |

The first space shuttle flight occurred on February 18, 1977, with the launch of *Enterprise*. It was a proud day for NASA, and the beginning of a new age in space exploration. Less than 9 years later, on January 28, 1986, the nation was stunned when the space shuttle *Challenger* disintegrated 73 seconds after launch. All seven crew members perished. The technical explanation for this disaster was the "O-ring" problem—a crucial shuttle component was compromised by the cold weather on that launch day. Subsequently, it became clear that there were voices speaking against the launch because of worries about the O-ring problem. However, there were pressures to launch and a belief in the infallibility of the decision-making process. Thus, the voices speaking against launch were silenced.

During the late 1980s and 1990s, there were a plethora of studies considering the *Challenger* disaster, and many pointed to the organizational culture at NASA as a crucial contributing factor leading to the launch decision (McCurdy, 1992). For example, in 1990, the U.S. government issued the "Augustine Report" on the future of the U.S. space program (U.S. Advisory Committee, 1990). This report was built largely on the premise that organizational culture directly contributes to organizational performance. The report notes that "[t]he most fundamental ingredient of a successful space program . . . is the culture or work environment in which it is conducted" (U.S. Advisory Committee, p. 16). This committee also worked from the assumption that the culture at an organization like NASA needs to be fundamentally different from that at many organizations. NASA works with the most complex of technologies, and the stakes are incredibly high. As McCurdy notes, "[e]rrors that might be forgotten in other government programs can produce in NASA a myopic space telescope or an exploding space shuttle" (McCurdy, 1992, p. 190). Given these assumptions, the report pointed to many specific aspects of organizational culture at NASA, and made recommendations regarding cultural beliefs and assumptions that should characterize a successful space program. These include the beliefs that:

- The success of a mission should take precedence over cost and deadlines. Mission success is more important than the role of any individual or group.
- Space flight requires open communication in which individuals are encouraged to report on problems or anomalies. Issues need to be "put on the table" for consideration.
- The space program cannot succeed in an environment where "avoiding failure" is seen as an important goal. Instead, the risky nature of the operation must be acknowledged.
- The space program should not get "spread too thin" by working simultaneously on different projects such as flight, research and development, and design. "Either operations dominates to the detriment of research and development, or employees working on new projects neglect operations" (McCurdy, 1992, p. 190).

NASA seemed to be following these "cultural guidelines" in the 1990s. The first "post-*Challenger*" mission occurred on September 29, 1988, with the launch of *Discovery*. The 100th shuttle mission occurred on October 11, 2000. However, as we all know, there was yet another tale of shuttle disaster to be written. On February 1, 2003, the space shuttle *Columbia* disintegrated during reentry. Pieces of the shuttle fell over eastern Texas and all seven crew members died. The sense of déjà vu was mournful and unavoidable. And the reports dissecting this disaster came quickly.

Of course, a different technical problem led to the *Columbia* disaster. In this case, a piece of foam fell off during launch and ripped a hole in the left wing. During reentry, this allowed superheated gases to enter the wing interior, and the wing frame melted. But were the underlying cultural traits that led to the *Columbia* disaster similar to the ones that doomed *Challenger*? Sadly, the Columbia Accident Investigation Board concluded that the cultural themes of the two tales were much the same. Indeed, "[t]he board's final report said that NASA had done little to improve shuttle safety since it lost the shuttle *Challenger* in 1986" ("Concerns Raised that Changes in NASA Won't Last," 2003). This report

CASE STUDY | **The Cultural Tale of Two Shuttles** *continued*

listed specific cultural traits that contributed to the *Columbia* disaster, including ("Concerns Raised," 2003):

- Reliance on past success as a substitute for sound engineering practices.
- Organizational barriers that prevented effective communication of critical safety information and stifled professional differences of opinion.
- The evolution of an informal chain of command of decision making that operated outside the organizations rules.

So had NASA learned at all from the *Challenger* disaster? Had the organization learned and just fallen back into old bad cultural habits? The chairman of the Investigation Board, Harold Gehman Jr., thought that this was possible. He noted, "Over a period of a year or two, the natural tendency of all bureaucracy, not just NASA, to migrate away from that diligent attitude is a great concern to the board because the history of NASA indicates that they have done it before" ("Concerns Raised," 2003).

Perhaps the most poignant comment during this time period came from Jonathan Clark, a NASA flight surgeon whose wife, Laurel Clark, died in the *Columbia* disaster. "I wasn't here during the *Challenger* disaster but I certainly talked to a lot of people who were. And, yes, there were similarities, as Diane Vaughn pointed out earlier in her book [*The Challenger Launch Decision*, 1996]. You could almost erase the O-Ring problem and put in the tile shedding and

put '*Columbia*' instead of '*Challenger*'" ("Columbia Spouse: Report a Prescription for Change," 2003).

Fourteen brave Americans lost. The separate tales of two destroyed space shuttles linked by one organizational culture. The first post-*Columbia* launch occurred on July 25, 2005, and shuttle launches are planned to continue until 2010. Let's hope NASA heeds Jonathan Clark's advice: "I think we are really going to have to look very carefully at what lessons we didn't learn from *Challenger* and make sure we absolutely learn them this time" ("Columbia Spouse," 2003).

CASE ANALYSIS QUESTIONS

1. What factors in NASA's culture contributed to the *Challenger* and *Columbia* shuttle disasters? Using Schein's "onion model" of culture, is it possible to show how basic assumptions are linked to beliefs and values and then to potentially fateful behaviors?

2. Cultural change was obviously difficult at NASA. Can you think of specific things that could have been done to make cultural changes more lasting or more effective?

3. Are there particular aspects of NASA that might make cultural change particularly challenging? Are bureaucracies particularly susceptible to these difficulties of cultural change? Do organizations involved in high-risk tasks face special challenges?

Critical Approaches

CHAPTER **6**

AFTER READING THIS CHAPTER, YOU SHOULD . . .

- Understand the distinctions between a critical approach and the other approaches we have thus far considered
- Appreciate the centrality of "power" to the critical approach and be able to describe how power is represented through the modes and means of production and through organizational discourse
- Be familiar with the critical concepts of "ideology," "hegemony," "emancipation," and "resistance" and be able to describe how these concepts fit together for critical theorists
- Be able to describe how feminist approaches to organizational communication and the theory of concertive control represent important concepts to critical scholars
- Understand deconstruction as a critical method and how critical activism requires particular "modes of being" in the world

We have gone down a long road in the last four chapters in learning about various approaches to the study of organizational communication. We began with classical approaches that conceptualize organizations as machines and emphasize rationality and efficiency. We next considered human relations and human resources approaches, which, respectively, emphasize the needs of employees and the contributions those employees could make to organizational functioning. We then looked at two relatively contemporary approaches to organizational communication, conceptualizing organizations first as systems and then as cultures. As we traveled along this road, we highlighted the differences among these approaches. Indeed, these approaches to organizational study *are* quite distinct. However, common threads underlie all of them.

The first of these underlying threads involves the "political" frame of reference used to understand the organization. Burrell and Morgan (1979) distinguish among unitary, pluralist, and radical frames of reference. In the *unitary* frame of reference, emphasis is placed on common organizational goals. Conflict is seen as rare and negative, and power is the natural prerogative of management. In the *pluralist* frame of reference, the organization consists of many groups with divergent interests. Conflict is seen positively, as "an inherent and ineradicable characteristic of organizational affairs" (Morgan, 1997, p. 202). Finally, in the *radical* frame of reference the organization is viewed "as a battleground where rival forces (e.g., management and unions) strive for the achievement of largely incompatible ends" (Morgan, 1997, p. 202). Conflict and power are seen as reflections of larger class struggles in society.

The approaches to organizational communication we have considered so far have utilized unitary or pluralist frames of reference. For example, classical approaches clearly adopt a unitary frame of reference. This is true to a lesser extent of human relations and human resources approaches. Systems and cultural approaches tend to take pluralist approaches by considering the management of divergent subgroup interests. None of the approaches we have looked at so far, however, have used the radical frame of reference to understand organizational communication processes.

A second underlying thread involves the role of the theorist in approaching organizational life. For classical, human relations, and human resources approaches, the role of the theorist is typically one of finding effective techniques for organizing. For systems and cultural scholars, the role of the theorist is to *understand* or *explain* organizational communication phenomena. Of course, this understanding or explanation can take very different forms, depending on the approach. The systems theorist aims for an objective explanation of causal relationships, whereas the cultural theorist attempts to gain a subjective understanding of the organization from the viewpoint of an insider. Both of these theorists, though, would balk at stepping in and attempting to *change* the organization in their role as theorist. As Bernstein (1976) notes, "while the theorist may be passionately interested in the fate and quality of social and political life, he [*sic*] must bracket this practical interest in his [*sic*] pursuit of theory" (p. 173).

The approaches we consider in this chapter take a turn away from these commonalities. Specifically, *critical approaches* adopt a radical frame of reference by considering organizations as *sites of domination*. Furthermore, these approaches see theory as a force that can emancipate individuals from these dominating organizational forces or consider how employees resist organizational dominance. Thus, the theorist takes an activist role in instigating and encouraging organizational transformation. We first look at historical and contemporary framing assumptions that are used by most critical theorists. Next, we consider two specific approaches to critical theory—concertive control and feminist theory—that have been widely used in the field of organizational communication. We then survey the analytical techniques often used by critical scholars.

CRITICAL APPROACHES

Although the roots of critical scholarship can be traced to a variety of influential thinkers including Georg Hegel and Max Weber (see Miller, 2005, for review), some of the most important roots of critical theory in organizational communication can be found in the work of Karl Marx. Marx, a German intellectual who lived in the nineteenth century, examined the relationship between owners and workers in a capitalist society and theorized that there was an inherent imbalance in this relationship and that eventually workers would rise up in revolt against the capitalist system. Marx believed that "critique" would lead to revolution because it would reveal fundamental truths about the human social condition. He noted that "what we have to accomplish at this time is all the more clear: relentless criticism of all existing conditions, relentless in the sense that the criticism is not afraid of its findings and just as little afraid of the conflict with the powers that be" (Marx, 1967, p. 212).

Marx's political influence has been, of course, widespread. Theoretically, his thoughts have also shaped the work of theorists taking a "critical" approach to social research. Perhaps the most widely known of these are researchers from the Frankfurt school of critical theory. Scholars aligned with the Frankfurt school (including Max Horkheimer, Theodor Adorno, Herbert Marcuse, and Jurgen Habermas, among others) pursued social and political critiques that would lead to "the development of normative alternatives which might enable humans to transcend their unhappy situation through critical thought and action" (Huspek, 1997, p. 266).

It would be impossible to provide a thorough review of the various strands of critical theory (see Alvesson & Deetz, 1996; Morrow, 1994; Mumby, 2000). At the risk of oversimplifying, however, critical theorists tend to agree on the following: First, critical theorists believe that certain societal structures and processes lead to fundamental imbalances of power. Second, these imbalances of power lead to alienation and oppression for certain social classes and groups. Third, the role of the critical theorist is to explore and uncover these imbalances and bring them to the attention of the oppressed group. Emancipation is then possible, either through direct political action, individual resistance, or awareness of the oppressed individuals.

In the next few sections of this chapter, we will "unpack" this explanation of critical theory by considering several key concepts. First, we look at power and how power can be seen as residing in the social structures and processes that make up organizational life. Second, we look at the impact of these power relationships by considering the related concepts of ideology and hegemony. Third, we examine the concept of emancipation within critical theories of organizational communication. Finally, we consider ways in which processes of resistance often work against the dominance of the powerful in the workplace.

The Pervasiveness of Power

No concept is as important as *power* for the critical theorist. As Mumby (2001, p. 585) argues, critical theorists see power as "a defining, ubiquitous feature of organizational life." The concept of power is typically equated with the related constructs of control and domination (Pierce & Dougherty, 2002), and these ideas are central to all critical theories. In exploring the concept of power, it is useful to examine three approaches to the topic outlined by Conrad and Ryan (1985). The *traditional approach* considers power to be a relatively stable entity that people or groups possess. Researchers adopting a traditional approach ask questions about the factors that lead to organizational power and the impact of power on outcomes such as job satisfaction and performance. These scholars often equate power with control over resources or with hierarchical status in the organization (Hardy & Clegg, 1996). The *symbological approach* (see also Mumby, 2001, for related discussion of the *interpretive approach*) views power as a product of communicative interactions and relationships. Researchers taking this approach are interested in how communication constitutes understandings of power through socially constructed organizational relationships (Mumby, 2001, p. 594). In reference to the approaches we have thus far discussed in this textbook, the traditional approach to power would be adopted by classical and human relations theorists, whereas the symbological approach would be adopted by cultural theorists.

The third approach to power, the *radical-critical approach*, is most germane to the theorists considered in this chapter. In this approach, the theorist is concerned with the "deep structures" that produce and reproduce relationships in organizational life. Furthermore, these theorists contend that there are inherent contradictions between the "surface structure" and the "deep structure" of power that must be explored. The role of the radical-critical theorist, then, is to explore the ways in which economic, social, and communicative relationships produce and maintain organizational power relationships.

What, precisely, are the structures that serve to shape power relationships in the organization? Morgan (1997) explored fourteen sources of power within the organizational setting, presented in Table 6.1. This table presents just a sampling of the sources of power in the organization; others could probably be added. As Hardy and Clegg (1996) note, "All resource lists are infinite, however, since different phenomena become resources in different contexts" (p. 626). This table is instructive, though, in pointing out the wide range of power sources that can be drawn on in the organization. Some of these sources of power are relatively overt and tend to be the focus of traditional theorists. These include, for example, formal authority, control of scarce resources, and control of knowledge and information. Other sources of power, however, are less obvious to the casual observer; these covert and unobtrusive forms of power in organizations tend to be the focus of critical theorists. We will now consider two sources of power in more detail. The first of these, control of modes and means of production, is associated most clearly with the Marxist tradition of critical theory. The second, control of organizational discourse, highlights concerns most typically associated with critical theorists in the communication discipline.

Control of Modes and Means of Production Classic Marxist theory examines the ways in which capitalist owners have control over the modes and means of production in the workplace (see Clegg & Dunkerley, 1980). The modes and means of production constitute the *substructure* of society—its economic and production base. The term *modes of production* refers to the economic conditions that underlie the production process. For example, Marx argues that the capitalist mode of production is based on owners expropriating surplus labor from workers. However, owners and workers in a capitalist system are not necessarily aware of this process. As Deetz and Mumby (1990) explain:

> To Marx, the surplus value of labor was hidden from both workers and capitalists. The capitalist would understand the realization of profit as coming from the investment in the plant and equipment, with the amount of profit determined by market conditions rather than by unpaid labor. The worker being paid a wage would not be in a position to determine the portion of the value of the product that was a result of his or her labor and hence could not recognize unpaid labor. (p. 20)

Table 6.1 | Sources of Power in Organizations

The following are among the most important sources of power:

1. Formal authority

2. Control of scarce resources

3. Use of organizational structure, rules, and regulations

4. Control of decision processes

5. Control of knowledge and information

6. Control of boundaries

7. Ability to cope with uncertainty

8. Control of technology

9. Interpersonal alliances, networks, and control of "informal organization"

10. Control of counterorganizations

11. Symbolism and the management of meaning

12. Gender and the management of gender relationships

13. Structural factors that define the stage of action

14. The power one already has

These sources of power provide organizational members with a variety of means for enhancing their interests and resolving or perpetuating organizational conflict.

Used by permission of Sage Publications, Inc., from Morgan, G., *Images of Organization* (1986), p. 159.

These hidden imbalances, then, create conflict between workers and owners. According to Marxist theory, the continuing existence of this conflict (the *thesis* in the material dialectic model of Hegel and Marx) would lead to the revolt of the working class (*antithesis*) and a transformation of the economic system (*synthesis*).

The term *means of production* refers to actual work processes—how products are made and services rendered. According to Deetz and Mumby (1990), "In Marx's view, industrialization brought with it dehumanization and alienation from work and work products ... the division of labor, the treatment of labor as a commodity, and the separation of the individual from his or her product produced a fragmented, lost person, estranged from his or her own production activities" (p. 20). This controlling aspect of means of production has been further elaborated by Braverman (1974), who argues that as the workplace becomes more technologically sophisticated, workers become "deskilled" and alienated from their work. For example, assembly-line production leads to highly specialized, fragmented, and monotonous jobs. Retail and service jobs often involve repeating the same simple tasks over and over again. Office work often has similar characteristics, as computer software programs often break down jobs and take autonomy and freedom away

Spotlight on Scholarship

This chapter has pointed to the centrality of the concept of "power" for a critical understanding of organizational communication and to the various resources that organizational participants use to marshal power. Power comes from control of resources, from control of time and tasks, and from control of gender issues. But perhaps most important for communication scholars, power comes from the control of discourse—from the stories we tell as a part of organizational life. Often, these stories are told "about" the organization or "in" the organization. There are stories from around the proverbial watercooler, stories of behavior in meetings, and stories of individuals in their lives outside of the organization. But in some organizations, the story *itself* is the central product of the organization, and the narratives of these organizations can wield particular power within the organizational context. Faye Smith and Joann Keyton provide a fascinating case study of one such organization.

In the late 1980s, *Designing Women* was one of the most popular situation comedies on television. For its first several years, producer Linda Bloodworth-Thomason wrote almost all of the show's scripts with an eye toward an "ensemble" show that highlighted the nature of relationships among contemporary women and current social issues. According to Smith and Keyton (2001), however, tension developed between Bloodworth-Thomason and one of the actresses on the show, Delta Burke. This tension, apparently, revolved primarily around Burke's increasing popularity with fans and hence her desire to emerge as a "star" within the ensemble, and it was also influenced by Burke's weight gain during this time period. In short, there was a power struggle emerging between Bloodworth-Thomason and Burke, and that struggle came to a head at the end of the 1989–1990 season.

In this power struggle, both Burke and Bloodworth-Thomason had resources. Both had the "resources" embedded within the contract that bound Burke to the show, and there was power derived from relational ties among the series' actresses and producers. But Burke was developing an additional source of power through her fan base and was "demanding star treatment" through the renegotiation of her contract (Smith & Keyton, 2002). What power did Bloodworth-Thomason have that Burke did not? The power of storytelling, as Bloodworth-Thomason wrote all of the scripts for the show. And for the final episode of the 1989–1990 season, Bloodworth-Thomason wrote a script that highlighted Burke's weight gain and culminated in a verbal and physical fight among the characters in a resort spa mud bath. Bloodworth-Thomason embedded lines in the script that seemed to target her conflict with Burke, such as "Just because this place is not exactly what you envisioned ... you now want to spoil it for the rest of us!"

Smith and Keyton (2002) analyze the script and production of this episode within the historical and relational context of *Designing Women*. Though the authors acknowledge that a variety of interpretations are possible with regard to these cultural events, their analysis is fascinating in highlighting the role of a highly public narrative (what could be more public than national television—not to mention years in syndication!) in playing out personal struggles of power and identity in the workplace. In noting the striking parallels between the lines in the script and the ongoing drama of the workplace, they conclude, "organizational scholars should look for issues of power and identity in the least expected of places" (p. 176).

Smith, F. L., & Keyton, J. (2001). Organizational Storytelling: Metaphors for Relational Powers and Identity Struggles. *Management Communication Quarterly*, 15, 149–182.

from individuals. Telemarketers are provided specialized scripts they must follow, and data entry workers can have their jobs broken down to the individual keystroke.

But what is the outcome of this monotonous and fragmented work? Surber (1998, p. 77) explains: "Anyone who has worked for an hourly wage at some repetitive and mechanical task will realize not only how one's own physical activity can come to appear alien but also how easily she or he can be replaced by another person willing to do the same work." In short, when owners and managers have control over workplace processes and technologies (the means of production), critical theorists believe the result will be an alienated and oppressed workforce. Alienation can occur through the repetitive and boring jobs created by technology; oppression can occur as workers are replaced or limited in advancement by robotics or other technical achievements. Further, the mechanization of the workplace allows management to constantly monitor the behavior of workers. Think, for instance, of how many times you hear the phrase "this call may be monitored for quality-control purposes" when calling an organization for sales or service help. This kind of surveillance is one more example of how management maintains its domination over employees (see D'Urso, 2006, in Chapter 2's "Spotlight on Scholarship").

Control of Organizational Discourse   Critical scholars in the communication field argue that power relationships are produced and reproduced through organizational discourse (Mumby, 1988, 1993). Like cultural researchers, these scholars believe that organizational reality is socially constructed through communicative interaction. However, critical researchers go further, suggesting that the reality created through discourse is the site of domination. Mumby (1989), for instance, plays off Geertz's (1973) definition of culture as "webs of significance." Mumby (1989) comments:

> If we extend Geertz's own web metaphor a little further it might be suggested how power relations are fundamentally structured into all social relations. After all, a spider's web is not simply an intricately constructed and beautiful product of nature; it is itself a site of struggle. The very existence of the web structures and instantiates a particular kind of power relationship between the spider and its prey. (p. 292)

There are a number of ways in which organizational discourse can be seen as creating and recreating power structures in the workplace. For example, the use in our culture of particular phrases to describe work can be seen as reinforcing dominant power structures. Clair (1996) examined the ways in which the phrase "real job" (as in "when are you going to get a real job?") serves a political function within the organization by implying that the kind of jobs held by college students (e.g., waiting tables, retail clerking) are not as important as other types of employment. Thus, this phrase—and the meanings that surround it—serves to define power relationships in the workplace.

Mumby (1987, 1993) extends this view by looking at how organizational narratives (i.e., stories) can function in power-laden ways in the organization. Mumby (1987) argues that "narratives provide members with accounts of organizing. Such accounts potentially legitimate dominant forms of organizational reality and lead to discursive closure in the sense of restricting the interpretations and meanings that can be attached to organizational activity" (p. 113). Thus, the stories people tell make sense of the organization in a way that often supports the dominant organizational coalition. Mumby (1987), for example, analyzes a famous, oft-told IBM story in which a lowly security worker refuses to let the company president into a restricted area without the proper identification. Mumby argues that although this story is held up as showing the strength of the "little people," it also serves to strengthen the dominant coalition by highlighting the importance of bureaucratic rules and regulations.

Tompkins and Cheney (1985) make a related point, arguing that *decision premises* serve as a source of unobtrusive control in organizational life. Like narratives, the options available to a decision maker serve to restrict choice and provide an interpretation for organizational activity. For example, if decisions are always made with the bottom line as the criterion for a quality decision, any decision made will serve to support the dominant coalition in the organization.

Finally, Zoller (2003) argues that entire industries can be influenced by the discursive constructions found in regulatory materials. She considers the discourse of the Occupational Safety and Health Administration (OSHA), arguing that OSHA standards act to establish control by defining occupational injury and illness in particular ways—ways that support the power of management. For example, Zoller notes that the terms "cumulative stress disorder" and "repetitive strain injuries" are being replaced in OSHA standards by the term "upper extremity musculoskeletal disorder" because the latter term does not imply that the workplace caused the physical problem. Similarly, the term "accident" is used to describe an injury because it does not suggest any culpability on the part of management.

Ideology and Hegemony

In the last section, we explored how the economic structure of the workplace and organizational discourse can serve as instruments of domination and control. Later in this chapter, we will explore some other sources of power such as identification with the organization and control over gender relationships. But what are the outcomes of these control structures and processes? Critical theorists argue that these processes of control will lead to a shaping of ideology and to hegemony. Let's define these concepts and talk about how they fit into the models of critical theorists.

Ideology refers to "the taken-for-granted assumptions about reality that influence perceptions of situations and events" (Deetz & Kersten, 1983, p. 162). This definition has several important facets. First, ideology refers to more than a set of attitudes or beliefs. Rather, ideology "structures our thoughts and controls our interpretations of reality" (Eisenberg & Goodall, 1997, p. 153). As Therborn (1980, p. 18) argues, ideology shapes our understanding about what *exists*, what is *good*, and what is *possible*. Second, ideology involves assumptions that are rarely questioned or scrutinized. Deetz and Kersten (1983) provide an example of this in considering our ideological beliefs about organizational structure. As they note, "most people assume that organizational hierarchy is a necessary and useful arrangement. When a person encounters superior-subordinate situations, he or she views them as normal, acceptable, and unproblematic" (p. 162). Third, by shaping our view of the world, an ideology can also influence our behaviors. As Bernstein (1976) observes, "The *power* of ideologies is related to the way in which they are used to justify and legitimize actions" (p. 108).

For critical theorists, though, ideology is not a neutral concept but is intimately tied to systems of power and domination (Mumby, 1989). This leads us to the concept of *hegemony*, originally developed by Gramsci (1971). Hegemony refers to a process in which a dominant group leads another group to accept subordination as the norm (Hall, 1985). It is "manufactured consent" (Habermas, 1971) in which employees willingly adopt and reinforce hierarchical power structures. As Mumby (2001, p. 587) argues, "Hegemony does not refer to simple domination, but rather involves attempts by various groups to articulate meaning systems that are actively taken up by other groups." Hegemonic control is typically accomplished by shaping ideology in such a way that the controlled group accepts and actively participates in the control process. For example, most organizational members accept the legitimacy of rules and may actively participate in formulating them. However, these rules serve as a source of managerial control over organizational members. This is an example of hegemonic control, in which the subjugated group becomes complicit in the control process.

A study of the "Japanese model" of team participation in a U.S. automobile plant provides a telling illustration of hegemony in today's organizations (Graham, 1995). Graham first presents the arguments often presented for team-based management, which is that workers will benefit from increased control on the floor and will be more satisfied with cooperative workplace relationships. She then argues that worker selection, orientation, and participative processes within these systems often serve as hegemonic devices to control workers. And, because the Japanese model often undermines existing union systems and future unionization efforts, workers in these "participative" systems may ultimately have little voice in the workplace. More on this issue will be considered when we discuss "concertive control" later in this chapter.

For the critical theorist, then, social structures and processes allow the dominant class to shape organizational ideology. The result of this ideological monopoly is a hegemonic relationship in which one group is controlled by another through coercion, acceptance, or even active participation. What is to be done about these social imbalances? For critical theorists, the next step is emancipation of the oppressed group. For participants in these organizational structures, the next step might be activities of resistance. These two concepts are discussed next.

Emancipation

The ultimate goal of the critical model is *emancipation*, or "the liberation of people from unnecessarily restrictive traditions, ideologies, assumptions, power relations, identity formations, and so forth, that inhibit or distort opportunities for autonomy, clarification of genuine needs and wants, and thus greater and lasting satisfaction" (Alvesson & Willmott, 1992, p. 435). Although some critical theorists in the Marxist tradition advocate overt political action and "bloody revolution" (see Burrell & Morgan, 1979), most see emancipation as a process of emerging awareness and communicative action on the part of the oppressed.

Habermas (1971) has compared the role of the critical theorist in the emancipation process to the role of the psychoanalyst. A psychoanalyst's job is to help a client break down resistances and gain a deep level of self-understanding. As

Bernstein (1976) notes, "The success of therapy ultimately depends not on the analyst's understanding of the patient, but on the extent to which the patient by his [*sic*] own self-reflection can appropriate this analytic understanding and dissolve his [*sic*] own resistances" (p. 201). By analogy, the role of the critical theorist is to reveal the social structures and processes that have led to ideological hegemony. When alienated people are able to consider their condition critically, emancipation will be possible. For organizational communication theorists, then, it is important to find ways that people can participate in free and open communication about power and control in the organizations where they work. In discussing such structures, Deetz (2005, p. 99) argues that "minimally, forums would be available for discussion and decision making, and no individual or group would be excluded arbitrarily from the opportunity to participate."

The possibility for emancipation is further emphasized in Giddens's (1979) notion of a *dialectic of control*. Giddens argues that "relations of autonomy and dependence (power relations) are never fixed; that is, subordinates can always exercise some degree of control over the conditions of hegemonic reproduction" (Stohl & Sotirin, 1990, p. 65). Consider, for example, Mumby's idea that power relationships are produced and reproduced through the stories that organizational members tell. The current stories in an organization might be serving to support managerial interests in the workplace. However, if workers become aware of this process, they can create their own narratives that can shift the balance of power in the organization.

Resistance

Within critical communication research, the dialectic of control is most clearly illustrated in work on *resistance* in the workplace. We have talked extensively about how power and control are exercised in organizational settings—the concept of resistance considers how workers can exert counterpressure on this exercise of power and control. Mumby (2005, p. 21) notes that scholarship in organizational communication has been moving in this direction for a number of years: "While early critical studies focused almost exclusively on organizational processes of control and domination, more recently the pendulum has swung more toward a focus on —perhaps even a celebration of—possibilities for employee resistance." However, Mumby argues that these ideas shouldn't be seen in an "either/or" way and are better conceptualized as intimately linked in organizational communication processes. He illustrates this with a Malaysian proverb: "When the great lord passes, the wise peasant bows deeply and silently farts" (Mumby, 2005, p. 20). Domination (the bow) and resistance (the silent fart) are intimately linked in processes of organizational communication.

Resistance is sometimes seen in collective and organized processes such as unionization, strikes, boycotts, and large-scale social movements. For example, protestors at the World Trade Organization meeting held in Seattle in 1999 are often credited with stopping a multilateral economic agreement that protestors believed was contrary to the interests of workers (Ganesh, Zoller, & Cheney, 2005). But organizational communication scholars are more often interested in resistance undertaken by the individual. For example, Murphy (1998) considered ways in which flight attendants would go along with the rules of the airline in public (e.g., serving pilots beverages before takeoff to avoid dehydration) but communicate their resistance to the rules through the "hidden transcripts" (Scott, 1990) of backstage and ironic forms of communication (e.g., joking with pilots about their "hydration" needs). Bell and Forbes (1994) documented how office workers sometimes decorate their cubicles with cartoons that signal resistance (e.g., cartoons reading "I Have PMS and a Handgun . . . Any Questions?" or "When I Woke Up This Morning I Had One Nerve Left, and Damned If You Ain't Got On It!").

Two recent studies suggest the complexity of resistance processes that have sprung from changing organizational forms and evolving technologies. Drawing on theories of gender and resistance, Ashcraft (2005) describes the changing job of commercial airline pilots. Traditionally, the job of an airline captain was one with unquestioned power and control. However, in recent years there have been industry-wide efforts toward a model of cockpit resource management (CRM) that "endeavors to institutionalize a shift in crew roles, from captain as infallible 'god' to empowering manager and from crew as compliant minions to active, even questioning partners" (Ashcraft, 2005, p. 77). However, many pilots have resisted this change in their workplace through a process of redefinition. Specifically, the pilots structure these organizational changes as a program they have generously agreed to

Case in Point: Wake Up Wal-Mart?

A critical approach to the study of organizations advocates a careful look at how powerful corporations might negatively influence a wide range of stakeholders. These stakeholders could include customers, employees, suppliers, communities, and the general public. No corporation has received more of this scrutiny in recent years than Wal-Mart. For example, recent documentaries such as *Wal-Mart: The High Cost of Low Prices* (Greenwald, 2005) and *Frontline: Is Wal-Mart Good for America?* (Young, 2004) critique the practices of Wal-Mart on many fronts. These critiques are also detailed in a popular website—WakeUpWalMart.com—that provides numerous channels for community and grassroots resistance to Wal-Mart's dominance. This website also provides "facts and research" on issues including:

- Community Impact
- Cost to Taxpayers
- Worker Injuries
- Health Care
- Child Labor
- Gender Discrimination
- Benefits

- Anti-Union Policy
- Undocumented Immigrants
- Port Security

These voices are loud and clear in denouncing the dominance of Wal-Mart, particularly with regard to labor and employment policies, practices in the global community, and the impact on smaller retailers when "Wal-Mart comes to town." However, this isn't the only side of the story. Samuelson (2006, p. 39) argues that "on any list of the nation's major concerns, the giant retailer would not rank in the first 50," noting that the evils of Wal-Mart can be countered with the argument that the store serves the needs of middle- and working-class Americans with prices that save consumers an average of 20 percent. Similarly, another recent documentary, entitled *Why Wal*Mart Works and Why This Makes Some People C-R-A-Z-Y*, defends Wal-Mart (Galloway, 2005). In other words, when considering issues of power, control, and dominance—especially with regard to the world's largest retailer—there are always multiple viewpoints fighting to be heard.

go along with, maintaining their perceived power and enhancing their perceived sensitivity. Thus, the pilots maintain symbolic power even when sharing control in the cockpit.

Another example of how the contemporary workplace shapes resistance practices is offered by Gossett and Kilker (2006). These researchers considered the new phenomenon of "counterinstitutional websites" in a study of RadioShackSucks .com. On this website, many members of the Radio Shack community (employees, past employees, customers) shared their dissatisfaction with Radio Shack management and policies, vented frustrations, and suggested actions that could be used as more active resistance strategies. For example, posters to the website facetiously suggested things that should "not" be done after quitting a job at the company: "I have decided NOT to remove every price tab in the store on MY last day . . . Nor will I break off the key in the cage padlock" (Gossett & Kilker, 2006, p. 77). Thus, Internet technology provided a forum for widespread and anonymous organizational resistance.

TWO CRITICAL APPROACHES IN COMMUNICATION

The underlying assumptions of critical approaches provide a view that is both sobering and hopeful. The view is sobering because it highlights the many ways that individuals can be controlled and dominated in organizational settings. The view is hopeful because its ultimate aim is the emancipation of oppressed groups through critical reflection and action, and because avenues of resistance are revealed that provide insight into the tension inherent in workplace domination processes. This coexistence of critique and hope also permeates several specific critical approaches that have been used extensively in organizational communication. In this section, we consider two of these approaches—concertive control theory and feminist theories.

A Theory of Concertive Control

In Chapter 3, we noted the increasing prevalence of team-based structures within today's organizations. Following human resources principles, these team-based structures are intended to distribute participation and accountability throughout the organization and facilitate a more "democratic" organizational form. But do team-based organizational structures actually fulfill these democratic ideals? This is the question addressed by an important theory in organizational communication —the theory of *concertive control* (see Miller, 2005, for a review of the theory). This theory, which originated with the work of James Barker, George Cheney, and Phil Tompkins, attempts to explain how power relationships can be transformed in an era of team-based and "alternative form" organizations. Three concepts are particularly important to an understanding of this theory—*control, identification*, and *discipline*.

Control   Concertive control theorists (Barker, 1993, 1999; Barker & Cheney, 1994) begin with organizational strategies of control originally enumerated by Edwards (1981). Edwards identifies three broad strategies for exerting control in the modern organization. *Simple control* involves the direct and authoritarian exertion of control in the workplace. *Technological control* involves control exerted through technological workplace processes such as assembly lines or computer programs. *Bureaucratic control* is based on the power of hierarchical structure and the rational-legal rules (Weber, 1968) that emanate from the bureaucratic structure. These three forms of control have long exemplified typical forms of power in organizations. However, some theorists propose that in team-based organizations, a new form of control has emerged—*concertive control*. Daniels, Spiker, and Papa (1997, p. 196) define concertive control systems as those in which

> the locus of control in an organization shifts from management to workers, who collaborate to create rules and norms that govern their behavior. The role of top management in this process is to provide a value-based corporate vision that "team members use to infer parameters and premises (norms and rules) that guide their day-to-day action." (Barker, 1993, p. 413)

Identification   The second key concept for understanding concertive control systems is *identification*. Identification refers to "the perception of oneness with or belongingness to [a collective], where the individual *defines* him or herself in terms of the [collective] in which he or she is a member" (Mael & Ashforth, 1992, p. 104). Thus, when an individual identifies with an organization or a work group, that individual takes on the concerns of the organization or group and accepts those concerns as his or her own. Organizational identification represents "the point at which the individual and the collective merge . . . the point of transcendence for the natural differences between individual identity and collective identity" (Barker, 1999, p. 128). Thus, within a concertive control system, an individual identifies with the values of the organization or work group and hence will act in accordance with those values even in the absence of simple, technological, or bureaucratic control.

Discipline   A final concept important for understanding the theory of concertive control is *discipline*. Barker and Cheney (1994) draw on the work of Foucault (1976) in seeing discipline as embedded within the "discursive formations" of a social group. That is, through communicative interaction, work groups develop techniques to reward and punish behavior that conforms with or deviates from the values identified as important by the work group. These disciplinary techniques might include direct criticism, the use of silence, social pressure, or a host of other interaction strategies. What is important to note is that although the values being upheld may emanate from management, the discipline is meted out by the work group. Thus, a concertive control system is established in which workers identify with organizational values and then discipline behavior in accordance with those norms.

These various aspects of a concertive control system come together in an organization analyzed by Barker (1993; Barker & Cheney, 1994). This organization was moving from a traditional hierarchical model to a team-based organizational system. Barker describes how team members came to identify with values developed by management (e.g., quality, on-time shipment, team responsibility) and then disciplined team members who were not behaving in accordance with those values. Indeed, Barker notes that, ironically, the discipline enacted by the teams was often more powerful, more difficult to resist, and less obvious than similar discipline enacted in a bureaucratic control system. Consider, for example, the comments of "Danny" describing how his team dealt with problems of punctuality:

> Well we had some disciplinary thing, you know. We had a few certain people who didn't show up on time and made a habit of coming in late. So the team got together and kinda set some guidelines and we told them, you know, "If you come in late the third time and you don't wanna do anything to correct it, you're gone." That was a team decision that this was a guideline that we were gonna follow. (Barker, 1993, p. 426)

In summary, the theory of concertive control argues that power is embedded in a system of identification and discipline. Workers identify with the values and norms of management and then use these values as a basis for making workplace decisions and for disciplining other members of the work team. For example, Papa, Auwal, and Singhal (1995) considered the Grameen Bank Cooperative in Bangladesh and found that fieldworkers highly identified with the bank's goal of uplifting the poor and thus disciplined each other to keep loan recoveries up. As Papa et al. (1995, p. 209) recount, these workers "do not receive pressure from upper management if their loan recovery rate falls below 99% but they place incredible pressure on one another." Thus, even in a workplace designed with democratic and participatory ideals (or with the culture of a "family" or "team"—see Casey, 1999), the ideology of management is upheld through the everyday practices of organization members.

Feminist Theories of Organizational Communication

One of the first researchers to approach the issue of gender in the organizational setting was Rosabeth Moss Kanter (1977) in her book *Men and Women of the Corporation.* Kanter explores a variety of gender-related issues, ranging from tokenism (the promotion of a few women into highly visible positions) to the role of the "executive secretary" and the "corporate wife." Her analysis makes it clear that gender issues permeate organizational life. In recent years, an increasing number of organizational communication scholars have adopted feminist theory as a backdrop for their work (Ashcraft & Mumby, 2004; Buzzanell, 1994; Mumby, 1996).

Many feminist scholars have noted that organizations—in their traditional and bureaucratic forms—are inherently patriarchal (see, e.g., Ferguson, 1984). They further note that women have distinct ways of viewing the world and creating meaning through interaction. For example, Buzzanell (1994) argues that traditional views of organizational communication highlight the importance of individualism, cause-and-effect thinking, and autonomy. In such a bureaucratic workplace, the most valued commodities are the stereotypical male characteristics of logic, aggressiveness, and competitiveness. In contrast, stereotypical female characteristics such as emotion, empathy, intuition, connectedness, and cooperation are likely to be downplayed in organizational life. Feminist scholars also argue that the concepts used to understand organizational life (such as rationality and hierarchy) tend to be male-biased (see, e.g., Mumby & Putnam, 1992) and that the very structure of language is patriarchal (see, e.g., Penelope, 1990). In short, feminist scholars believe that women in organizations can become marginalized in organizational life because of the dynamics of gender relationships within patriarchal organizational structures.

It should be noted, though, that not all see feminist work in the organizational communication field as situated within critical theory. Indeed, Ashcraft (2005) argues that it is better to look for the roots of the feminist organizational communication studies within the larger feminist movement, as this movement emphasizes activism. As Ashcraft (2005, p. 145) argues, feminist work within organizational communication "reflects an entrenched commitment to do more than talk within the walls of an ivory tower; it embodies the desire for tangible forms of justice that enhance the lives of real people." Even within this focus on activism and emancipation, however, there are a variety of views regarding what should be done (see Buzzanell, 1994; Mumby, 1996). For example, *liberal feminists* believe that remedies for female subordination should come from within the system and that women should work to gain their fair share of control in institutions currently run by men. Other feminists balk at this approach, arguing that it only serves to support the patriarchal nature of society. *Radical feminists* believe that emancipation for women can occur only through the destruction of male-dominated institutions or through the total separation of women from these institutions. Other feminists argue for more symbolic courses of action. *Standpoint feminists* work to enhance the opportunity for a variety of marginalized voices to be heard within societal dialogue, and *postmodern feminists* attempt to "deconstruct" male-dominated meaning systems in order to highlight women's perspectives. Recently,

Case in Point: Using the F Word

In recent years, the word *feminist* has fallen into disrepute. As Anna Quindlen (2003) states in a column entitled "Still Needing the F Word," people see the word *feminist* as inappropriate, offensive, or simply off-putting. In part, this reputation can be attributed to commentators who see feminists as activists for an unwanted agenda ("femi-nazis"). However, this current disregard for feminism also stems from the belief that we are now in an era in which all the battles have been won. As Quindlen states, "conventional wisdom has it that we've moved on to a postfeminist era, which is meant to suggest that the issues have been settled, the inequities addressed, and all is right with the world" (p. 74).

However, recent research suggests that feminists have not progressed as far as they would like (e.g.,

pay inequity remains a major problem and women still struggle against sexual harassment in the workplace) and may even have taken a few steps backwards. For example, Quindlen argues that although women in the past felt pressured to be the perfect housewife and mother, women today strive to be models of perfection in the workplace while maintaining the same old pressures at home. In *The Second Shift* (1993), Arlie Hochschild argues that women still do the majority of domestic work even while taking on enhanced responsibility at work. In other words, says Quindlen, "women have won the right to do as much as men do. They just haven't won the right to do as little as men do" (p. 74).

Ashcraft (2000) has argued for a hybrid form of feminism that she calls *pluralist feminism*. Ashcraft's research suggests that even in "feminist" organizations there are pragmatic contingencies that constrain an idealistic view of feminism. In developing pluralist feminism, scholars could become "responsive to the needs of organizations that seek social change yet cannot fully embrace antibureaucratic, countercapitalist ideals and practices" (Ashcraft, 2000, p. 381).

Feminist scholarship within organizational communication research is expanding rapidly. Some researchers consider specific practices that illustrate the gendered nature of organizations, and some consider the ways in which the social fabric of life in the workplace can influence the professional and personal identities of women. Others consider the ways in which gender intersects with race and class in organizational life (Parker, 2003). Still others investigate whether there are communicative differences between traditional bureaucratic organizations and woman-controlled and nonhierarchical organizations. We will briefly consider three studies to provide a sampling of feminist scholarship in organizational communication.

The "Framing" of Sexual Harassment   One early investigation in the feminist tradition (Clair, 1993b) examined the narratives of women talking about sexual harassment in the workplace. Clair examined the "framing devices" women used in the telling of these harassment stories. For example, a woman could frame her story as "simple misunderstanding," or she could trivialize the event. The framing devices examined, and their definitions, are presented in Table 6.2. Clair argues that certain framing devices serve to accentuate or confront the hegemonic experience of women in organizations:

> How these personal narrations of organizational life are framed contribute to or challenge the dominant ideology of organizational life. Certain framing techniques either reinforce or challenge the dominant ideology. Specifically, the subjugated group, in this case female targets of sexual harassment, framed their stories in such a way that sexual harassment incidents were generally sequestered or kept out of the mainstream of organizational communication. (1993b, p. 131)

Thus, through the examination of women's stories, Clair uncovered an important hegemonic aspect of relationships between men and women in the workplace. In the very ways that women talk about harassment, they often normalize it and suppress further discussion of harassment as an oppressive feature of the workplace.

Discourse at a Woman-Owned Business   Many feminist scholars argue that life can be different in an organization that exemplifies feminist values such as cooperation, emotion, and support. Paige Edley (2000) examined this assumption in her study of a woman-owned interior design firm that employed mainly women (the only men were part-time delivery and warehouse workers). Edley's long-term participant observation study of this organization resulted in an interesting picture of life in a woman-owned business. One of her major findings, for example, was that though everyone in the organization "talked the talk" of a cooperative and flexible workplace (e.g., one in which family concerns were taken seriously), the owner of the business often did not "walk that talk." Instead, the

Table 6.2 | Framing Devices on Sexual Harassment Narratives

Framing Device	Explanation
Accepting dominant interests	Sexual harassment accepted or justified as a less important problem than other managerial concerns
Simple misunderstanding	Sexual harassment accepted or justified as "mere flirting"
Reification	Sexual harassment accepted or justified as "the way things are"
Trivialization	Sexual harassment accepted or justified as "a harmless joke"
Denotative hesitancy	Sexually harassing encounter not defined by the term *sexual harassment*
Public/private expression— public/private domain	Sexual harassment described as part of private, rather than public, life or described using private forms of expression (e.g., embarrassment, fear)

Based on Clair, R. P. (1993b). The use of framing devices to sequester organizational narratives: Hegemony and harassment. *Communication Monographs*, 60, 113–136.

owner often publicly derided those who took off too much time for family concerns or kept those individuals from key work assignments.

Second, though Edley found that communication in this organization was often marked by emotion and conflict, such interaction was often labeled as simply the way women talk. Edley (2000, p. 293) reports that "conversations were filled with references to women as cranky and moody and blaming nonverbal expressions of anger on PMS [premenstrual syndrome]." By blaming their anger and emotional outbursts on "the way women are," workers in this organization could downplay the importance of conflict in the organization.

Thus, Edley found that in many ways the women in this organization played into the sexual stereotypes of women. Through their discourse, they constructed an idealized organization of support and flexibility that, in many ways, didn't really exist. Through their discourse, they also submerged conflict, blaming emotional communication on PMS or the stereotypical emotionality of women. This sounds, in many ways, like a very negative construction of women within this woman's organization. However, Edley argues that there were rewards for the women as they saw themselves as working in an ideal workplace in which they could speak and act as women.

Disciplined Bodies Finally, recent work by Angela Tretheway (1999, 2000) has examined how the organizational context, as well as society and culture in general, serves to discipline women in terms of bodily display. For example, she reviews research that has considered the ideal body for white, middle-class women. These bodies have a particular size and shape that must be maintained through diet and exercise regimes. These bodies must pay careful attention to nonverbal movement—walking, sitting, and gesturing in particular ways. And these bodies must be displayed with makeup and clothing that exhibit the appropriate level of femininity.

Tretheway then argues that women are faced with a conundrum in the workplace: although a "professional body" is strong and competent, such a body might contradict the nurturing and soft body of traditional femininity. How are women to manage this dilemma? Tretheway's interviews with a wide range of professional women provided several answers to this question. First, women clearly saw a "professional body" as a fit body that symbolized discipline and endurance. Second, women believed they needed to control their nonverbal displays in a way that communicated strength—but that was nonthreatening. For example, one of Tretheway's respondents said, "we still need to have that firm handshake, but don't overdo it" (Tretheway, 2000, p. 119). Finally, women talked about the need to control and discipline the female body's tendency to "leak out through unruly clothing, menstrual bleeding, pregnancy, or emotional displays" (Tretheway, 2000, p. 20). Such a leaking body calls attention to the feminine and private nature of a woman's body in a public context that values control.

RESEARCH METHODOLOGY IN THE CRITICAL APPROACH

In this chapter so far, we have considered a wide range of scholarship that has investigated power, discipline, control, and resistance in organizational settings. Clearly, there are challenges in learning about these issues, as many of the processes considered are "below the surface" and may not be easily accessed through typical organization research. How, then, do critical scholars do their work in organizational communication? In the most general sense, the research methodology employed by critical theorists is "ideology critique" (Alvesson & Deetz, 1996). That is, through their scholarship, critical theorists attempt to show "how specific interests fail to be realized owing partly to the inability of people to understand or act on those interests" (Alvesson & Deetz, 1996, p. 198). The specific data and analytical techniques that contribute to this critique can vary substantially across different research efforts. Quantitative data can contribute to such critiques by showing how resources are distributed in organizations and how individuals perceive their lives within organizations. More often, critical theorists use interpretive research techniques similar to those used by cultural scholars (see Chapter 5; see also Taylor & Trujillo, 2001). As Eisenberg and Goodall (1997) explain, "[a] critical theorist . . . gathers interpretive cultural data about language, motives, and actions, and makes judgments about the power relationships that exist in the organization" (p. 168).

One research technique unique to critical theorists—and to postmodern critical theorists, in particular—is known as *deconstruction* (Derrida, 1976; see also Linstead, 1993). Deconstruction involves "taking apart" a text in order to reveal social and political meanings. Specifically, Derrida argues that in any text, certain meanings and interpretations are "privileged" while others are "marginalized." For example, an employee handbook might privilege male interpretations by referring to a manager as "he," or a rational approach to organizing may be privileged through the decision-making processes prescribed by an organization. The process

Table 6.3 | Examples of Privileged and Alternative Meanings

Study	Discourse	Privileged Meaning	Alternative Meaning Revealed through Deconstruction
Clair (1996)	"A Real Job"	Paid jobs (typically white-collar) through established organizations are the only ones that "count"	Other jobs should also be honored such as volunteer work, temporary work, blue-collar work, and care giving to children, elderly, or disabled people
Clair (1993a)	"Keep a Record"	Women who are sexually harassed should carefully document all details of the harassment incident	Women must keep a record because—in a bureaucratic organization—her account will not be believed if the man has a different story
Mumby & Putnam (1992)	"Bounded Rationality"	Decision makers in an organization attempt to be rational but are limited by cognitive and organizational factors	Perhaps rationality should not be the goal of organizational life and we should honor emotion instead
Zoller (2003)	"Accident-proneness" and "Compliance"	When something goes wrong with safety in the workplace it is because the worker is clumsy or didn't properly follow the rules	These phrases divert attention from work processes that might be inherently dangerous

of deconstruction, then, involves "dismantling the apparent fixed meaning of a text" (Mumby & Putnam, 1992, p. 468). Table 6.3 considers several examples of how organizational communication discourse has been "deconstructed" by scholars attempting to provide alternative meanings to those that are typically privileged.

It is worth emphasizing, however, that critical scholars do more than "take apart" organizations for study. Indeed, a central tenet of critical scholars is to strive to improve the lives of organizational constituents through social activism and education. Thus, Deetz (2005) argues that the most important aspect of undertaking a critical approach in organizational communication is to live a life characterized by *critical modes of being*. Specifically, Deetz believes that critical scholars should be "filled with care" in their empathetic approach to others, "filled with thought" in their consideration of the social and political ramifications of organizational experience, and "filled with good humor" in appreciating the irony and contradictions that are always a part of organizational life.

SUMMARY

At the beginning of this chapter, we noted two threads that underlie classical, human relations, human resources, systems, and cultural approaches to organizational communication: (1) organizations consist of unitary or pluralist systems of control, and (2) the organizational theorist's job is to understand and explain. The critical approaches we considered in this chapter have questioned these basic assumptions. Specifically, critical theorists take a radical frame of reference and believe that the theorist's job is to change organizations through the emancipation of oppressed social groups. We examined

important concepts such as power, ideology, hegemony, and resistance and considered two bodies of work within organizational communication —concertive control theory and feminist theory —to illustrate how a critical lens can be placed on organizational communication processes. We concluded our discussion by briefly considering research methods used by critical theorists. The critical theorist's general goal of ideology critique can be achieved through a variety of research techniques, especially interpretive research and deconstruction, and should be constantly tempered through critical modes of being.

Discussion Questions

1. Many abstract concepts are important to critical work in organizational communication. How do these concepts fit together? For example, how is ideology related to hegemony? How is power related to discourse? How is emancipation related to resistance?
2. Think of how the terminology used in an organization, or the stories told in an organization, contributes to power imbalances.

What are ways of fighting against these imbalances?
3. If you are a woman, do the studies of feminist organizing described in this chapter ring true for you? Do you have other stories about the challenges of being a woman in a patriarchal organization? If you are a man, are these studies revealing to you? Do you think men

| CASE STUDY | **Talking Turkey** |

Brandon and Gabriella Houston were both home from college for Thanksgiving weekend. Brandon, a senior, attended a state university about 90 miles from home. Gabriella, a sophomore, attended a small college in a neighboring state. Both were home for the first time during the school year and were spending some time catching up. As they lounged in the living room watching football, the smell of roast turkey wafted through the house and assorted relatives milled around munching on celery sticks and green olives.

Brandon and Gabriella's parents contributed the lion's share of their children's college expenses, footing the bill for tuition and the majority of room and board. However, both Brandon and Gabriella had to pitch in a small portion of the housing tab and cover any incidental expenses they might incur. Thus, both held part-time jobs while going to school. Brandon worked 20 hours per week at the Baxter Company, a small manufacturing firm that assembled corrugated boxes. It was boring but dependable work and paid slightly better than minimum wage. Gabriella worked for

CASE STUDY | **Talking Turkey** *continued*

Personal Greetings, a small company that specialized in personalized party greetings, including singing telegrams and "strip-o-grams." Gabriella worked eight to ten jobs per week (each job lasted about an hour) and earned $25 per job plus tips. Brandon was mortified when he heard what Gabriella was doing to earn her college money. "Gabs, I can't believe you're taking off your clothes for money! Does Mom know what you're doing?"

"Well, not exactly, but I don't think she'd mind. Mom and Dad are pretty liberal about these things, and I don't actually take off all my clothes. It's really pretty innocent—just some entertainment for people who like to have a good time. Unlike you, brother dear. Besides," Gabriella added, "I make great money. I usually pull in over $400 a week for about 10 hours' work. Can you say the same?"

"The money isn't the point. And neither is being liberal or conservative, for that matter. The point is that you're being exploited. You may be making $400 a week, but you can bet that Personal Greetings is making a lot more than that. And they're making it off of your body. How can you be a woman in this day and age and allow people to do this to you—isn't this the very thing that feminists have been fighting against for years?"

"Well, maybe the feminists are wrong about this," Gabriella replied. "It seems to me that everyone is benefiting from this situation. I make great money and can support myself while I get an education and move on to something else in my life. The company is highly successful and can keep paying people like me a good wage. And the customers are getting a service that they're eager to pay for. Who loses? If you want to see someone being exploited, you should just look at yourself, Brandon."

"What do you mean? I'm doing good honest work. I may not be paid a lot, but at least I'm keeping my clothes on!"

"Yeah, I'm stripped of my clothes, and you're just stripped of your dignity," Gabriella retorted while Brandon stared back in disbelief. "The Baxter Company is making money hand over fist, and they've got you working for minimum wage. They

set your hours, they give you boring work to do, they control when you can take a break and who you can talk to on the job. And you just shuffle along and pick up your paycheck and feel good because you're doing 'honest work.' Maybe your kind of job is the American way, but I'd rather wiggle my butt for a living and have a lot of free time to study and have some fun!"

Gabriella and Brandon's mother stood at the doorway. "I think dinner's ready, kids. We've got turkey, cornbread dressing, cranberry sauce, green bean casserole, corn, and three kinds of pie. I don't think anyone will go hungry today!"

Brandon led the way past his mother into the dining room. As he left, he turned back for one last parting shot. "Sounds great, Mom, and I'll take an extra portion of dressing. Given Gaby's current line of work, I don't think she'll be wanting any."

CASE ANALYSIS QUESTIONS

1. How would you evaluate the argument between Brandon and Gabriella? Are either or both of them being exploited? If so, how?

2. How does this discussion illustrate the concepts of power, ideology, and hegemony?

3. What oppressive structures of organization and communication are in evidence in the jobs held by Brandon and Gabriella? Do either Gabriella or Brandon participate in a system of "concertive control"?

4. Does a feminist approach serve to shed any additional light on the job held by Gabriella? Would different types of feminist theory reach different conclusions about the nature of her job?

5. How would a critical theorist work to achieve emancipation for Brandon and Gabriella? Would either of them want to be emancipated? How could either Brandon or Gabriella exercise resistance in their work?

7 | # Assimilation Processes

- Appreciate the importance of understanding processes of organizational socialization and exit
- Know the three major phases of organizational socialization—anticipatory socialization encounter phase, and metamorphosis—and know which critical communication processes are active in each of phase
- Be familiar with the types of information typically learned during socialization and understand the processes (such as information seeking) through which this information can be gained
- Understand the functions of an employment interview and the different roles that the interviewer and interviewee play
- Be able to explain the processes through which roles are developed and negotiated over time in organizational settings
- Understand the implications of demographic and cultural changes for organizational exit and be familiar with how exit often happens in organizations

In times past, people would often work for one organization throughout their entire life. Perhaps it was a family business, a farm, or a corporation that nurtured long-term relationships with employees. Today, however, in the United States, the odds are that you will work for several or many organizations in your lifetime. Our society has become increasingly mobile, and people switch jobs, and even careers, with great frequency. With all of these organizational "comings and goings," it becomes useful to understand the processes through which individuals and organizations adapt to each other.

Fred Jablin and his colleagues use the term *assimilation* to refer to "those ongoing behavioral and cognitive processes by which individuals join, become integrated into, and exit organizations" (Jablin & Krone, 1987, p. 712). Assimilation is a dual process. On the one hand, the organization is trying to influence the adaptation of individuals through formal and informal *socialization* processes. For example, socialization occurs when an individual learns about the requirements of the job or decides that dressing formally will help her or him fit into the organizational culture. On the other hand, the employee may try to change some aspect of the organization to better suit his or her needs, abilities, or desires. This type of change happens through the process of *individualization*. Individualization might occur, for example, if a new employee develops an improved strategy for collecting payments on overdue accounts or if a group of new employees start a new tradition of going out for beers on Friday after work. These two assimilation processes—socialization and individualization—play out over time as an individual encounters and becomes a part of an organization.

In this chapter, we consider the role of communication in organizational assimilation. In the next few pages, we first look at models of assimilation that lay out the stages and the content of socialization. Then, for the largest share of the chapter, we look at some key communication processes that occur during assimilation. We first consider the dynamics of the employment interview. Then we look at how individuals entering organizations obtain information through formal and informal channels. Next, we consider the ongoing "role development" processes that characterize a person's continuing adaptation to the organization. Finally, we look at communication processes during organizational exit.

MODELS OF ORGANIZATIONAL SOCIALIZATION

The processes through which individuals adapt to organizational life are complicated. These processes develop over a great span of time and involve many organizational members and activities. Thus, a number of scholars have attempted to better understand organizational socialization by developing theories that model portions of the socialization process. We consider two aspects of socialization in the following sections. We first look at how socialization unfolds over time, and then we consider what is "learned" during the assimilation process.

Phases of Socialization

When an employee joins an organization, adaptation is not automatic and immediate. Rather, adjusting to organizational life takes place gradually. Scholars considering this process often divide socialization into three phases. Of course, these phases are not cut-and-dried across people or time. Indeed, the socialization process is undoubtedly marked by "turning points" in which individuals become more (or less) connected to the organization (Bullis & Bach, 1989). These turning points will be different for each individual and may include events such as promotions, changes in job responsibility, or perhaps a new boss or coworker who changes the atmosphere in the workplace. In this sense, then, socialization is a process that may have many ups and downs and sometimes may not seem to follow a distinct pattern. However, despite the individual nature of the socialization process, the consideration of phases has proven to be a useful tool for studying many of the processes that individuals experience as they enter organizations. In this section, then, we will consider three such phases: *anticipatory socialization*, the *encounter phase*, and the *metamorphosis phase*. These phases are summarized in Table 7.1.

Table 7.1 | Stages of the Socialization Process

Stage	Description
Anticipatory socialization	Socialization that occurs before entry into the organization. Encompasses both socialization to an occupation and socialization to an organization.
Encounter	Sensemaking stage that occurs when a new employee enters the organization. The newcomer must let go of old roles and values in adapting to the expectations of the new organization.
Metamorphosis	The state reached at the "completion" of the socialization process. The new employee is now accepted as an organizational insider.

Anticipatory Socialization Anticipatory socialization refers to socialization processes that occur before an individual actually enters an organization (Van Maanen, 1975). There are several aspects to anticipatory socialization: learning about work in general, learning about a particular occupation, and learning about a particular organization.

In a very basic sense, we grow up learning about what "work" means. This knowledge can come from a variety of sources. Children might learn about the nature of "work" through participating in household chores or completing school

Case in Point: Hustling Cookies

If you grew up female in America, there's a reasonably good chance your first experience with work processes such as recruiting customers, making sales, and going after incentives came from selling Samoas, Do Si Does, Tagalongs, and the venerable Thin Mints. Hustling Girl Scout cookies has been a rite of passage for many girls, as they go door-to-door, set up tables outside of grocery stores, or send sales sheets with their parents to work. Stephen Woodburn (2007) describes the experience of accompanying his daughter on sales calls, noting that "[t]he Girl Scouts emphasize how cookie sales build young girls' confidence through setting goals and working to achieve them" (p. E4). The experience also builds skills in the nuances of the sales pitch. Woodburn recounts: "My daughter knows it's a hustle, because the customer is already hooked. She asks not, 'Would you like to buy?' but 'Do you have a favorite kind?'—knowing

that most people do. And unless they're diabetic or got tapped by another Girl Scout, they're going to order something" (Woodburn, 2007, p. E4).

The experience has become much more complicated since (decades ago) I tried to hit up all my neighbors before my friends and sisters. There are now reward systems (other than bragging rights) that accompany sales goals. Safety concerns have led to increased sales through cookie booths rather than door-to-door encounters. And these days, cookies are usually just one step in a fund-raising sales career that may begin in preschool and continue through high school. These may not be changes for the better, but they are changes that reflect today's world of work better than the simpler sales process I experienced in the 1960s and 1970s. Thus, hustling cookies may still be one of the best ways around for young girls to learn about the world of work.

assignments (Bowes & Goodnow, 1996). For an 8-year-old, a parent's or teacher's order to "get your work done" has a great deal of meaning and recent public debates about "appropriate" levels of homework suggest that some believe this socialization into the rigors of work may come too quickly. The meaning of work is also developed through part-time employment during the teen years (Barling, Rogers, & Kelloway, 1995; Greenberger, Steinberg, Vaux, & McAuliffe, 1980), through interactions with friends, and through media contact. Indeed, as we discussed in Chapter 6, Clair (1996) argues that by the time an individual in the United States reaches college, the notion of having a "real job" has taken on a very specific meaning imbued with the values of a capitalist economy.

Anticipatory socialization also involves ideas about the nature of specific careers and occupations. Before even starting school, many children have an answer to the question "What do you want to be when you grow up?" One girl might dream of being a veterinarian because she loves her dog so much, a boy might want to be a police officer because of what he has seen on television. Undoubtedly, these children's occupational visions are highly idealized and inaccurate. However, it is clear that ideas about possible occupations begin early in life. As the child grows up, he or she learns more about what it means to work in a particular field. Our vet-to-be, for instance, might read books about working with animals or visit the local small-animal clinic. When she goes to college and vet school, she learns even more about her chosen occupation. Thus, from childhood onward, she is being socialized into an occupational role.

The third portion of anticipatory socialization involves learning about a particular organization. For example, many college graduates go through the ritual of interviewing with prospective employers through the campus placement center and investigate possible job sites through the Internet. Consider a college senior contemplating work with CompuStuff, a computer software company. Before even signing up for an interview, she is likely to learn a great deal about CompuStuff through its website and through media coverage of CompuStuff. Information obtained in this way might include the company's structure, goals, and financial position. Then, through the interviewing process, she enhances her understanding of CompuStuff by learning more about what it might be like to work for CompuStuff—job responsibilities, salary, even the social culture. Before setting foot on company grounds, she is able to anticipate what life at CompuStuff might be like.

Encounter The second phase of socialization occurs at the organizational "point of entry," when a new employee first encounters life on the job. Louis (1980) describes the encounter experience as one of change, contrast, and surprise, and argues that the newcomer must work to make sense of the new organizational culture. In order to interpret life in the new organization, the newcomer relies on predispositions, past experience, and the interpretations of others (Louis, 1980). This phase of socialization can cause a great deal of stress for the newcomer, especially if he or she has ideas about what an organization "should" be like that are contrary to current practices and as a result experiences "reality shock" (Hughes,

Spotlight on Scholarship

The socialization models discussed by scholars often assume well-defined stages of socialization that are experienced by all newcomers. For example, in this chapter we consider a three-stage model of anticipatory socialization, encounter, and metamorphosis. Research on socialization often also considers employees who initially have little familiarity with the organization and employees who are being socialized into white-collar or pink-collar occupations. Recent work by Melissa Gibson and Michael Papa turns away from these scholarly templates and gives us new insight into communication during the organizational socialization process.

Gibson and Papa's study is a qualitative investigation of blue-collar workers at a company they call "Industry International." Industry International is a medium-size manufacturing organization and a market leader in its sector. Gibson and Papa interviewed more than 50 blue-collar workers and also considered observational data and archival documents. Through their analysis, they came to some interesting conclusions about how socialization may work for blue-collar workers in settings such as Industry International.

Gibson and Papa first argue that it is impossible to understand the socialization process without understanding the nature of the organization and the nature of the workers. They point out that Industry International embodies the norms of the "old social contract" in which "employees remain loyal to an organization for their lifetime" (pp. 75–76) and are rewarded through high pay earned through a piecework pay system. The workers at Industry International are extremely loyal and marked by a strong work ethic. These workers believe they are "uniquely geared to the rigors of life at Industry International" (p. 76) and label themselves "the mud, the blood, and the beer guys" (p. 77). It is also notable that many workers grew up in the ideological shadow of Industry International; more than two-thirds of those in the study sample indicated that they had a family member who either was working or had worked for Industry International. Thus, at an early age, workers received anticipatory socialization into both job-related and cultural aspects of work at Industry International.

This strong anticipatory socialization meant that the encounter and metamorphosis stages of socialization were almost "nonevents" and marked by little of the "surprise and sensemaking" that often characterize organizational entry. Gibson and Papa thus coin the term *organizational osmosis* to refer to "the relatively effortless absorption of organizational values, beliefs, and understandings on the basis of preexisting socialization experiences" (p. 84). They also note that this osmosis process may well speed up and strengthen the formation of identification with the organization. Workers who had "grown up" with Industry International strongly identified with its values and goals, and thus disciplined others who did not. This strongly suggests that initial and ongoing socialization experiences might be very different for newcomers with different ideological and experiential groundings. As one 31-year employee in Gibson and Papa's study compared newcomers, "Don't get me wrong. Bob's kid works here and he's a damn good worker. I have no problems with him. It's the kids who don't know anything about this place or don't know how to work" (p. 81). This points out just one more complexity in the processes through which individuals are socialized into—or perhaps just absorb—the roles and culture of organizational life.

Gibson, M. K., & Papa, M. J. (2000). The Mud, the Blood, and the Beer Guys: Organizational Osmosis in Blue-Collar Work Groups. *Journal of Applied Communication Research*, 28, 68–88.

1958). Thus, the encounter phase encompasses learning about a new organization and role, and letting go of old values, expectations, and behaviors.

The encounter phase can involve a wide variety of formal and informal communication processes. These include organizationally designed orientation programs (Van Maanen & Schein, 1979), formal and informal mentoring (Kram, 1985; Zey, 1991), and information seeking on the part of the employee (Miller &

Jablin, 1991). We will deal more extensively with the proactive role of the individual in the encounter phase later in this chapter.

Metamorphosis The final stage of the socialization process occurs when the new employee has made the transition from outsider to insider. "During this stage the recruit begins to become an accepted, participating member of the organization by learning new behaviors and attitudes and/or modifying existing ones" (Jablin & Krone, 1987, p. 713). This is not to suggest, however, that the relationship between the individual and the organization is static at this point, because there is always some measure of flux and uncertainty in employees' understandings of organizational roles and culture.

This flux within the metamorphosis stage is demonstrated in work by Michael Kramer (1993a, 1993b, 1995, 1996) analyzing the process of adjusting to job transfers within an organization. When individuals transfer from one job to another within an organization, they typically are not seen as "new" employees and thus are not provided formal socialization experiences. Yet these individuals still must cope with new job requirements, new social relationships, and sometimes a new location. Kramer's work has highlighted the ways in which transferring from one job to another constitutes part of the continuing assimilation experience and how communication with the supervisor and coworkers in the new job can serve to ease the transition experience.

Content of Socialization

In addition to considering the socialization process over time (the *when* of socialization), researchers have also looked at the content of socialization—what must be learned in order to adapt to the organizational context. For example, Louis distinguished two classes of information that must be grasped during the socialization process: *role-related* information and information about the *organizational culture*. Role-related information encompasses the information, skills, procedures, and rules that an individual must grasp to perform on the job. For example, a new secretary might need to learn about the organization's word processing programs, filing system, and bookkeeping procedures to adapt to his or her role in the organization.

A new organizational member must also learn about the organizational culture. Learning about the organizational culture can be much more complex than comprehending role-related information, as formal documentation regarding cultural norms rarely exists and current organizational members might have a difficult time articulating these values for the newcomer. Indeed, Stohl (1986) found that much of socialization occurs through the communication of "memorable messages"—narratives and cultural truisms that stick with employees as they continue on in their employment with the organization (see also Dallimore, 2003).

Recently, Myers and Oetzel (2003) proposed a model that provides greater detail about the processes involved in socialization. Though these processes involve more than just the "content" of socialization, they are useful for considering the various issues that newcomers must cope with when entering an organization. Specifically, these processes are:

1. Developing a familiarity with others
2. Acculturating, or learning the culture of the organization
3. Feeling recognized by others
4. Becoming involved in the organization
5. Developing job competency
6. Role negotiation

Myers and Oetzel (2003) developed this typology from a study of individuals in a wide range of industries, including banking, advertising, hospitality, and social service organizations. Myers (2005) then applied this typology in a study of socialization among firefighters who work in what is known as a "high reliability organization" (HRO). HROs are organizations "that continually operate under conditions of high danger but are able to avoid catastrophe through careful planning and leadership" (Myers, 2005, p. 344). Myers found that, for firefighters, the area of "role negotiation" was not important, but that establishing trustworthiness was critical in the socialization process. This suggests that, not surprisingly, organizational context plays a critical role in what individuals need to experience to become socialized into the organizational environment.

Summary of Socialization Models

In summary, a variety of models have been proposed to help us better understand the organizational socialization process. Phase models of socialization help us understand the "when" of socialization—how individuals move from anticipating occupational and organizational life to becoming integrated organizational members. Content models of socialization help us understand the "what" of socialization by differentiating between role-related and cultural information. Embedded within these notions of "when" and "what" are a variety of processes through which assimilation occurs—formal training programs, mentoring, interviewing, outside research, and relationships with managers, coworkers, and subordinates.

In the next section we look more carefully at the role of communication in the socialization process. We first examine three aspects of socialization in which communication plays a crucial role. The first of these, communication during the employment interview, is closely tied to anticipatory socialization. We then consider the second aspect: ways newcomers seek information during the encounter phase of socialization. Next, we discuss the third aspect, which is the ongoing communication in the role-development process that characterizes the metamorphosis stage of socialization and the sense of identification that individuals develop with their organizations and careers. In the final section of the chapter, we will consider communication processes during organizational exit, a "forgotten phase" of the assimilation process.

COMMUNICATION PROCESSES DURING ASSIMILATION

The Employment Interview

Although there are a variety of contexts in which new employees can be recruited and screened, the employment interview is one of the most widely used (Powell &

Goulet, 1996). In an employment interview, an organizational representative (or, perhaps, a group of representatives) and a potential employee come together for questions, answers, and conversation. The setting for the interview might be a college placement center, an employment office, the organization itself or the interview might take place over the phone. The outcome of the interview might be an offer of employment, a chance at a second interview, or a polite "thanks but no thanks." Regardless of the setting or outcome, the employment interview is an important step in the anticipatory socialization process.

The employment interview serves three basic functions. First, as an organizational representative, the interviewer is using the interview to recruit potential employees and make decisions about the quality of those recruits. Second, the applicant is using the interview as a way to find out more about the organization. Third, as a point of first contact between the organization and the applicant, the interview serves as a socialization tool—that is, as a way to facilitate the adaptation of the applicant should he or she be hired.

The Interview as a Recruiting and Screening Tool   From the organization's perspective, the main function of the employment interview is the recruiting and screening of potential employees. In an interview, the organizational representative often has only thirty minutes to make assessments about the interviewee's background, knowledge, motivation, communication skills, and personality. Although there are, of course, differences in style from interviewer to interviewer,

Case in Point: The New Job Hunt

It used to be so easy. You'd look in the classified ads —or perhaps on the job board at your local college or university—and find a job you were qualified for. You'd submit your application and résumé, interview with the hiring officer, and promptly find out whether you were hired. Well, maybe it was never quite that easy, but it's clear that hunting for a job now is more complicated than ever.

The complexity begins with the first step: submitting an application. Many companies now require applicants to submit their applications online. After you fill out all the proper forms, your credentials might well be sorted by a "data extractor," which is designed to pull out all of the essential information to match you with the job and company. However, as Ramer (2003) points out, the algorithm used by the extractor might not "read" your qualifications correctly or might downplay experiences that you think

are key to the job. Thus, technology might keep you from even getting a chance to talk to a human and make your case about your qualifications.

But the job search is also more difficult once you get a chance to interview. As McGinn (2003) points out, the interview process has become increasingly reliant on technical and problem-solving questions and on personality testing. For example, William Poundstone (2003) describes an interview in which an applicant for an engineering position is asked to describe November. "After some blather about orange leaves and Thanksgiving, the interviewer lowered the boom: bad answer. Engineers should be precise, like 'November consists of the 30-day period situated 20 days before the winter solstice.'" The bottom line: In a tight job market and a technological world, people face challenges in many phases of their search for work.

research points to some definite patterns in how the interview is used to recruit and screen applicants.

First, most interviewers gather information in relatively structured ways. Indeed, reviews of the research literature (Campion, Palmer, & Campion, 1997; McDaniel, Whetzel, Schmidt, & Maurer, 1994) indicate that highly structured interviews are better predictors of future job performance than unstructured ones. Some structured interviews are highly formulaic (e.g., the "situational interview," the "behavior description interview," or even the "stress interview"), whereas others involve a variety of questions and answers arranged in a structured form. For example, many interviews follow an inverted-funnel approach in which closed-ended questions are used at the beginning of the interview followed by open-ended questions as the interview progresses (Tengler & Jablin, 1983).

Second, research suggests that interviewers often "cue" applicants about appropriate responses through the use of directed or leading questions (Jablin & Miller, 1990). For example, an interviewer might say, "We are a national company with the need for high-mobility employees. Would you be willing to relocate as part of your job?" The preferred answer is clear from the nature of this question.

Third, a great deal of variability marks the content of interview questions among different employers and industries (Jablin & Miller, 1990). One interviewer might concentrate on college courses and activities, whereas another might ask about behavior in hypothetical organizational situations. A third might take an even more abstract approach and ask how the interviewee might describe a sunset to someone who had never experienced one. This variability in question content is not surprising given the wide variety of characteristics deemed important for employability by recruiters. It is interesting to note, however, that one characteristic that seems important to almost all interviewers is the ability to communicate. Jablin (2001, p. 750) reports that "fluency of speech, composure, appropriateness of content, and ability to express ideas in an organized fashion" are all frequently cited as critical factors in recruiters' decisions.

The Interview as an Information-Gathering Tool   From the interviewee's perspective, the interview provides a glimpse of a possible future employer. Indeed, Ralston (1993) has found that applicant satisfaction with the interview is a good predictor of the acceptance of second interviews. The ability of the interview to serve this purpose is limited, however, because most interviewees assume that they should play a relatively passive role in the interview process. Indeed, few interviewees ask any questions during the interview until such questions are requested by the interviewer (Babbitt & Jablin, 1985). According to Jablin and Miller (1990), "The average applicant asks about ten questions in an interview, most of which are succinct and closed-ended in form, asked after their interviewers formally seek applicants' questions, and focus on single versus multiple topics" (p. 75).

In spite of limited questioning activity, however, recruits do form impressions during the interview process. For example, McComb and Jablin (1984) have found that if interviewers used probing questions, the recruit perceived the interviewer to be an empathic listener. Applicants were also more satisfied when open-ended questions predominated and when they were given an opportunity to express themselves (Jablin & Miller, 1990). Interviewees receiving second interview offers were likely to be those who confined their questions during the interview to job-related issues (Babbitt & Jablin, 1985). Finally, it is quite possible that interviewees form an opinion about the company based on the questions that are asked and the behavior of the recruiter. For example, interviewees form more positive impressions from interviews that concentrate on job and organization-related information (DeBell, Montgomery, McCarthy, & Lanthier, 1998) and from recruiters who have a warm, open, and interested demeanor (Golitz & Giannantonio, 1995).

The Interview as a Tool for Socialization   Finally, the employment interview can serve to ease a newcomer's adaptation to the organization should she or he be offered a job. Wanous (1992; Wanous & Colella, 1989) develops this position in his support of realistic job previews (RJPs). The idea behind RJPs is that if new recruits are provided a realistic picture of their future job, they will be less likely to be disappointed if inflated expectations are not met. Thus, RJPs should serve to reduce voluntary turnover. For example, if a potential receptionist is "warned" about monotony, overload, and abusive clients through an employment interview, that employee is less likely to quit after a few weeks on the job. A comprehensive review of research found support for this relationship between unmet expectations and both job satisfaction and organizational commitment (Wanous, Poland, Premack, & Davis, 1992).

The effectiveness of RJPs may depend on what information is communicated during the interview and how the interaction occurs. As Ralston and Kirkwood (1995) note, "Whatever transpires between the participants can mold expectations about communication within the organization" (p. 85). Popovich and Wanous (1982) suggest that RJPs should be viewed as persuasive communication. This view highlights choices made about message source (e.g., job incumbent vs. recruiters), message content, and communication medium (e.g., electronic vs. written materials vs. oral presentation). This view of realistic recruiting also carries risks, however. Rynes (1990) has argued that some recruits may view negative job characteristics as a challenge and hence not self-select out of inappropriate jobs.

Newcomer Information-Seeking Tactics

A second communication process critical to the adaptation of newcomers occurs primarily during the encounter phase of socialization and emphasizes the *proactive* role of organizational newcomers (Miller & Jablin, 1991; Morrison, 2003; Reichers, 1987). In this view, newcomers are seen as more than passive recipients of training programs and organizational handbooks. Instead, newcomers actively seek information that will help them adapt to their new roles and the norms and values of the organizational culture.

Miller and Jablin (1991) have developed the most complete typology of newcomer information seeking. These scholars posit seven modes through which newcomers seek information. These information-seeking strategies are presented and defined in Table 7.2. As this table indicates, newcomers can seek information in obvious ways (e.g., asking overt questions or questioning third parties) or in a more covert manner (e.g., through observation, surveillance, or disguised con-

Table 7.2 | Newcomer Information-Seeking Tactics

Tactic	Definition
Overt questions	Newcomer solicits information by asking direct questions of information targets.
Indirect questions	Newcomer solicits information by asking noninterrogative questions or by hinting.
Third parties	Newcomer solicits information by asking a secondary source (e.g., coworker) rather than a primary source (e.g., supervisor).
Testing limits	Newcomer solicits information by breaking or deviating from organizational rules and observing reactions.
Disguising conversations	Newcomer solicits information by disguising the information-seeking attempt as a natural part of the conversation.
Observing	Newcomer solicits information by watching behavior in salient situations.
Surveillance	Newcomer solicits information by making sense of past observed behavior.

Adapted from Miller, V. D., & Jablin, F. M. (1991). Information seeking during organizational entry: Influences, tactics, and a model of the process. *Academy of Management Review*, 16, 92–120.

versations). For example, a newcomer trying to learn about norms for weekend work might use an overt question by asking, "Are we expected to work on weekends?" Alternatively, the newcomer might drive by the company on a Saturday to check on cars in the parking lot (observation tactic) or engage in conversations about upcoming weekend activities with coworkers (disguised conversation).

According to Miller and Jablin (1991), use of these information-seeking tactics will vary depending on the extent to which uncertainty needs to be reduced and the social costs of seeking information. The social costs for seeking information might include embarrassment about not knowing something or fear of irritating coworkers with repeated requests for information. For example, a new employee might be interested in knowing how the log-on and password system works on the company's internal computer network. Uncertainty about this issue might be high, and it is unlikely that the newcomer would perceive a high level of social costs associated with inquiries about the local-area network. Thus, the new employee would probably use a relatively straightforward information-seeking tactic such as an overt question. In contrast, if a newcomer were trying to learn about the appropriate level of formality in addressing supervisors, a more covert tactic (e.g., observation, testing limits, or asking third parties) might be used. Several studies have investigated the use of information-seeking tactics by organizational newcomers (Comer, 1991; Morrison, 1993; Teboul, 1995) and have been relatively supportive of the ideas about the influence of uncertainty and social cost. For example, Teboul (1995) found that information seeking by new employees was influenced by the perception of social costs, and that those perceptions were created through socialization and social support processes.

Role-Development Processes

The final communication process we will discuss in this chapter is an ongoing one that begins at organizational entry and continues through the metamorphosis stage of socialization. This process is concerned with how individuals interact to define and develop their organizational roles. The model was developed by George Graen and his colleagues. Graen (1976) began with the assumption that "organizational members accomplish their work through roles" (p. 1201), and theorized that individuals develop those roles through interaction with others in the organization. Graen and his colleagues believe that the supervisor–subordinate dyad is critical in the process of role development. They argue that a role is developed by an organizational member through a social exchange process with his or her leader. Hence, this theory has been labeled Leader-Member Exchange (LMX) Theory. Graen and colleagues (see, e.g., Dienesch & Liden, 1986; Graen, 1976; Graen & Scandura, 1987) argue that the role-development process begins when a newcomer enters an organization (or a new organizational role) and continues through ongoing interactions with the supervisor and other organizational members. The LMX model divides role development into three interrelated phases: role taking, role making, and role routinization.

Role-Taking Phase   The role-taking period is "the sampling phase wherein the superior attempts to discover the relevant talents and motivations of the member through iterative testing sequences" (Graen & Scandura, 1987, p. 180). During this phase, the leader will request a variety of activities of the member. By observing how the member responds to these requests, the leader will begin to evaluate the talents, skills, and motivation of the subordinate. For example, imagine that Josh is a new sales representative for a pharmaceutical company. Josh's supervisor, Laura, may initially ask Josh to update the client list to include local health maintenance organizations. By watching how Josh accomplishes this task, Laura can reach conclusions about Josh's organizational and communication skills and the extent to which he can perform tasks independently. Laura can continue this process by assigning Josh a wide variety of organizational tasks.

Role-Making Phase   The second phase of the role-development process marks an evolution from the one-way activity in which the supervisor "gives" the role and the subordinate "takes" it, to a process in which the member seeks to modify the nature of the role and the manner in which it is enacted. For example, Laura might want Josh to take on more responsibility for supervising telemarketing in the office. When she asks him to do this, Josh might respond that he needs a break from other organizational responsibilities or that he needs clerical help to accomplish the task. Through interaction, Josh and Laura will negotiate this and other aspects of Josh's role.

The role-making process involves a social exchange in which "each party must see the other party as valuable and each party must see the exchange as reasonably equitable or fair" (Graen & Scandura, 1987, p. 182). The member can offer time, skills, and effort to the role-making process. The leader can offer formal rewards as well as informal resources such as information, support, and attention. By exchanging these resources, leader and member work together to develop the member's organizational role.

Role-Routinization Phase The third phase of the role-development process represents the point at which the role of the subordinate and expected behaviors of the supervisor are well understood by both parties. The sampling of the role-taking phase and the negotiation of the role-making phase have led to an established relationship between supervisor and subordinate. It is important to note, however, that each development process is unique. Thus, a single leader can develop very different types of relationships with different subordinates. Indeed, some scholars suggest that supervisor–subordinate relationships can be arrayed along a continuum from "in-group" relationships, which are characterized by high levels of trust, mutual influence, support, and formal/informal rewards (Fairhurst & Chandler, 1989), to "out-group" relationships, which are characterized by low levels of trust, support, and rewards, and the use of formal authority rather than mutual influence (see Figure 7.1).

Some of these differences in role development might be attributable to the role negotiation process. Role negotiation is the interactive process through which individuals create and alter expectations about how a job is to be done (Miller, Jablin, Casey, Lamphear-Van Horn, & Ethington, 1996), and this process is likely to be key in predicting "the newcomer's chances of successfully individualizing his or her role in the organization" (Jablin, 2001, p. 781). In other words, Josh's success in creating and maintaining a meaningful role in the organization might depend both on his job-related skills and efforts and on his ability to communicate effectively in interactions with Laura in the workplace.

Beyond the Leadership Dyad It is also critical to note that while the leader-member exchange model—and the role negotiation process—is considered in terms of interaction between a supervisor and subordinate, these dyadic exchanges are always embedded within the larger organizational context (see Sias & Jablin, 1995). For example, Teboul and Cole (2005) developed an evolutionary model of workplace integration that highlights social relationships with peers. Recent scholarship has also pointed to the importance of the workgroup in the socialization process. Myers and McPhee (2006) found that workgroup communication was particularly important to assimilation in high reliability organizations where trust among crew-members is critical. Apker, Propp, and Ford (2005) also found that the team was critical in the socialization of nurses, particularly in today's complex health care environment. They note that "nurses who identify the varying role expectations of team member constituencies and develop a repertoire of communicative strategies to manage those expectations may be better equipped to meet the multiple challenges presented in modern nursing roles" (Apker, et al., 2005, pp. 110–111). In other words, when jobs are complex and stressful—as the jobs of firefighters and

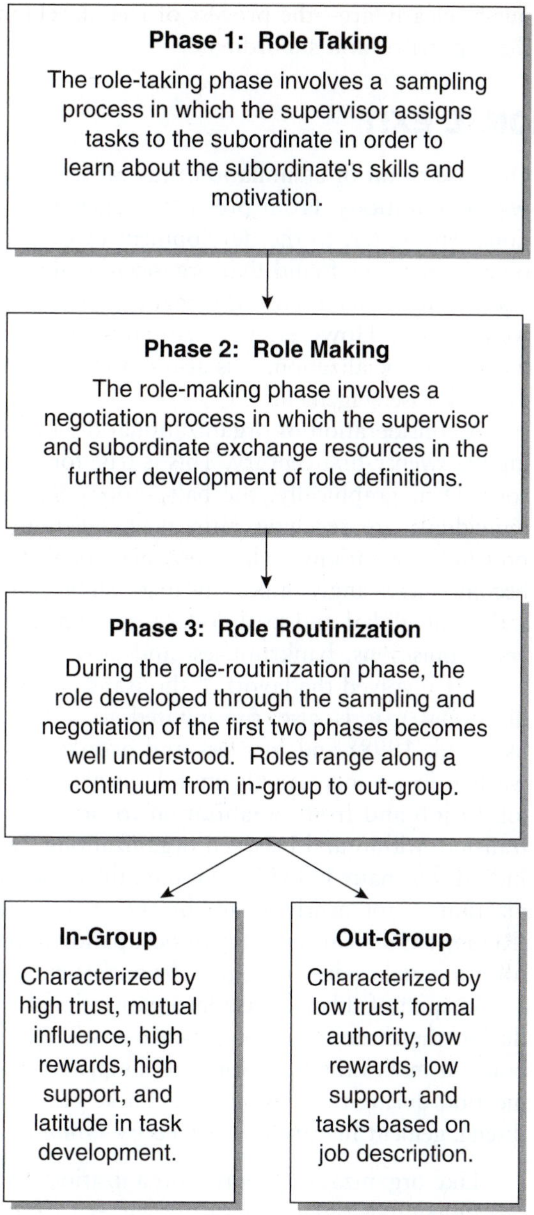

Phase 1: Role Taking

The role-taking phase involves a sampling process in which the supervisor assigns tasks to the subordinate in order to learn about the subordinate's skills and motivation.

Phase 2: Role Making

The role-making phase involves a negotiation process in which the supervisor and subordinate exchange resources in the further development of role definitions.

Phase 3: Role Routinization

During the role-routinization phase, the role developed through the sampling and negotiation of the first two phases becomes well understood. Roles range along a continuum from in-group to out-group.

In-Group

Characterized by high trust, mutual influence, high rewards, high support, and latitude in task development.

Out-Group

Characterized by low trust, formal authority, low rewards, low support, and tasks based on job description.

Figure 7.1 | The Leader-Member Exchange Role-Development Process

nurses clearly are—the process of role development is one that cannot involve just the supervisor and subordinate.

ORGANIZATIONAL EXIT

Our discussion of assimilation thus far has focused on processes involved in *entering* organizations. From pre-entry anticipation, through the surprises of organizational encounter, to the development of ongoing relationships and roles within an organization, we found that organizational socialization was a communicative process through which sense was made of work life and varying levels of identification were forged. However, the "comings and goings" of organizational life involve more than socialization. It is also critical to consider the "goings" of organizational exit and disengagement.

A consideration of organizational disengagement is particularly important during the twenty-first century. This is true for demographic, economic, and social reasons. Demographically, the baby boom generation is aging, and more and more individuals are reaching retirement age (and often retiring at earlier ages than previous generations). Thus, organizational disengagement through retirement will become increasingly important (e.g., Shultz, Morton, & Weckerle, 1998). Economically, the global and postmodern marketplace is one often characterized by mergers, acquisitions, bankruptcies, and downsizing. For example, the "fall of Enron" in 2001 involved the layoff of thousands of workers (Schwartz, 2001). Thus, organizational exit is also precipitated to a large extent by downsizing (Folger & Skarlicki, 1998) and mergers and acquisitions (Howard & Geist, 1995). Finally, we live in an increasingly mobile society in which people move frequently from job to job and from organization to organization. Thus, exits precipitated by job transfers within and between organizations (Jablin & Kramer, 1998) are common. Indeed, for many individuals today, the notion of a connection to a particular organization is not nearly so important as a connection with a career or occupation (Russo, 1998). This primacy of occupational identification over organizational identification makes disengagement from particular jobs all the more likely.

In spite of this increase in organizational exits, the research on communication during the disengagement process is still quite thin (Jablin, 2001). Thus, at this point, it makes the most sense to simply offer a few generalizations about communication during the exit process. These generalizations are based on organizational disengagement literature reviewed by Jablin (2001).

- Like organizational entry, organizational exit is a process, not an event. Individuals often anticipate their exit from an organization, perhaps for many years (in the case of retirement) or for shorter time spans (in the case of job transfers). Even layoffs that are seen from the outside as "sudden" are often anticipated well in advance by organizational insiders.
- Organizational exit is a process that influences both those who leave and those who are "left behind." We often concentrate our attention on the person who has crossed the organizational boundary (the leaver), but those who remain in the organization (the stayers) may experience such diverse emotions as happiness or relief (if the leaver was a disliked coworker), resentment (if the stayer

must take on additional work), or even "survivor's guilt" (if the stayer was spared in a layoff or downsizing).

- Further, organizational exit can have profound effects on the families of those who leave the organization. For example, Buzzanell and Turner (2003) interviewed men who had recently lost their jobs, and they also questioned their families. The interviews suggested that the men and their families had to work to control (or express) feelings of anger and often struggled to maintain a sense of "normalcy" and to construct a continuing masculine role within the family structure.

- Communication plays a critical role in the disengagement process. At times, communication might spur disengagement, as when messages from coworkers or an unpleasant communication environment motivate an employee to leave (Cox, 1999). Communication also serves as a sensemaking resource, particularly when the organizational exit is unexpected or confusing (e.g., in downsizing or mergers and acquisitions). Third, communication patterns might change as the leave-taker's role shifts from insider to outsider. For example, Roth (1991) found that the period between an announced departure and the actual exit provided the communicative space to discuss numerous "taboo" topics in the organization. Finally, communication in the form of social support is critical for relieving the stress that often occurs in the postexit stage for both leavers and stayers (Lim, 1996).

SUMMARY

In this chapter, we have looked in detail at the processes through which individuals assimilate to organizational life. We began by considering models of socialization phases and content. We then looked at communication processes that occur during socialization. We looked at the employment interview during the anticipatory socialization phase. We then considered information seeking during the encounter phase and the process of role development. Finally, we explored communication during organizational exit and disengagement. In closing, it is instructive to look back at the six approaches to the study of organizational communication considered in the first half of this book and consider how these approaches would investigate organizational assimilation processes. A number of ideas are presented in Table 7.3.

Most of the research on assimilation discussed in this chapter has taken a classical, human resources, or cultural approach. For example, the research on realistic job previews takes a mainly

classical view in its emphasis on reducing employee turnover. The work on socialization content and tactics is based in large part on human resources approaches to organizations. That is, its goal is to understand the ways in which socialization programs can be developed to maximize the ability of employees to become contributing members of the organization. In contrast, work on information-seeking strategies is based to a large extent on cultural approaches, because an emphasis is placed on how the newcomer can seek information proactively to make sense of the new culture.

The use of other approaches might deepen your understanding of the organizational assimilation process. For example, at the beginning of this chapter, organizational assimilation was described as consisting of the reciprocal processes of socialization and individualization. Most scholars have concentrated on socialization, but a critical theorist might enhance our knowledge of individualization processes by looking at how

Table 7.3 | Approaches to the Assimilation Process

Approach	How Assimilation Would Be Considered
Classical	Assimilation seen as a way to ensure that employees are properly trained for maximum effectiveness and efficiency. Research might evaluate training programs or consider realistic recruitment as a means of reducing the inefficiencies of employee turnover.
Human Relations	Assimilation seen as a way to maximize the possibility that employees will be highly satisfied organizational members. Research might evaluate the extent to which socialization practices help employees satisfy higher-order needs.
Human Resources	Assimilation seen as a way to maximize the contribution employees can make to the organization. Research might consider the extent to which socialization practices empower employees or the extent to which selection processes "choose" recruits who can contribute to organizational goals.
Systems	Assimilation seen as a boundary transition between the "outside" and the "inside" of the system. Research might consider the effect of boundary permeability on this process, or the role of communication networks on the adaptation of newcomers.
Cultural	Assimilation seen as a process through which newcomers come to understand the assumptions, values, and norms of the new organizational culture. Research might consider the strategies individuals use to make sense of the new culture or differences in socialization practices within different organizational cultures.
Critical	Assimilation seen as a process through which organizational owners and managers develop and maintain hegemonic relationships with employees. Research might consider how socialization tactics serve as instruments of unobtrusive control or processes of emancipation through individualization.

newcomers can change the organization to emancipate themselves from oppressive organizational practices. For example, Bullis (1993a) argues that a feminist interpretation of socialization could allow us to focus on "muted voices as resources for resistance and change" (p. 12). A feminist approach is also advocated by Allen (1996), who argues that a black woman's experience of socialization in the academic environment is very different from the experience of whites and/or men.

Other insights might be made in the study of socialization by looking in more detail at systems concepts such as boundary permeability, subsystems and supersystems, and communication networks. In short, although our knowledge of communication during the socialization process is already well established, the use of alternative perspectives might broaden and enhance our knowledge of this important organizational communication process.

Discussion Questions

1. Anticipatory socialization is a process that begins early in childhood as kids learn about work, careers, and organizations. When you were a child, what did you want to be "when you grew up"? How realistic were your aspirations? How have they changed based on anticipatory socialization processes?

2. Think about organizations you have worked for or groups you have been a part of. To what extent do your experiences reflect the "stages" of socialization discussed in this chapter?

3. If you worked for the career center on campus, what advice would you give to individuals signing up for job interviews? What advice would you give to organizations interviewing candidates on your campus? How could the interview process be improved so it would be more productive—and less stressful—for all involved?

CASE STUDY | **The Church Search**

SCENE ONE: OCTOBER, A SUNDAY SCHOOL ROOM IN MICHIGAN

Lisa sighed in frustration. "Why did Joe have to leave? He was a great pastor—he was why I came to this church and stayed here. And now we have to look for someone new. I'll do it. I'll be a part of this search committee. But that doesn't mean I have to like it."

"Well, you could always turn to that old saying of God opening a window when he closes a door," countered Jason. "I'm not happy that Joe left, either, but it was a great opportunity for him—we can't begrudge him wanting new challenges. And maybe this provides new opportunities for our congregation—perhaps we've become a bit complacent with Joe's ministry and this is just what we need to think about where we want to go and what we want to do."

Many at the table nodded in agreement. Seven were gathered around the table, all members of a midsized congregation of a Protestant church. Their longtime pastor had recently accepted a calling to a new church, and these seven had been selected as the search committee for the new pastor. They had a lot of work ahead of them and chose Nancy to head the committee. She got straight to the point.

"Okay," said Nancy. "Let's get to work. We need to start by developing a profile of our church and congregation. Who we are, what we do, and where we think we're going. And then we need to think carefully about what kind of pastor we want for our future. What are the critical characteristics for our new minister? Is preaching the most important? Evangelism? Spiritual development? Community service and social justice? And then we need to think about the questions we'll ask when we get to the interview process. Who will be involved? What kinds of activities should we include? And then we need to think about how we'll welcome the new pastor once we make a decision about who it will be. And then . . ."

Everyone at the table began to laugh as Nancy's list of "and thens" grew longer and longer. "Uh, Nance," interrupted Rick, "we only scheduled a two-hour meeting. Sounds like you'd like to have us here through the night."

"Nope," responded Nancy, looking at the circle of already tired faces. "We'll just have to have a lot more meetings. But let's get to work for now. And let's have a quick prayer before we get started. I think we'll need it."

SCENE TWO: FEBRUARY, A LIVING ROOM IN MISSOURI

Marsha sat in the middle of the floor, surrounded by piles of spiral-bound documents. "Who knew that so many churches could be looking for a pastor? I mean, it's good news for someone like me, but it makes the whole process so much more confusing."

Marsha's husband, Ron, also sprawled on the floor, rifled through some of the papers. "We just have to be systematic in looking through these profiles and think about what you want in a position and where you can best serve. You have gifts in music ministry and youth ministry that could make a big difference for some congregation." Ron looked up from one profile. "This one, for example, would probably be a bad fit. It's a big church and they've really divided up the ministerial jobs. I'm not sure you'd ever see the kids in the church much, let alone get to work with them in the way you'd want to."

Marsha looked up. "I know, we should just be careful about looking through everything. It's just such a scary prospect. I've been really comfortable in my role as a youth minister and moving to a larger role seems like a big step." She started laughing. "I know, we've been through all this before and we'll go where God calls us. But this discernment thing is really tough sometimes!"

Half an hour later, Marsha and Ron were both engrossed in the church profiles. "Hey," said Marsha. "Here's a good possibility. It's not a very big church, but the values and mission really match a lot of my own commitments. And they're clearly big on encouraging music and youth programs. What do you think about moving to Michigan?"

SCENE THREE: APRIL, A RESTAURANT IN MICHIGAN

Nancy looked across the table at Marsha. "I'm so glad to finally have the chance to meet you in person after all our time comparing profiles and talking on the phone. This process is sure a lot more complicated than I ever anticipated!"

Marsha smiled in agreement. "You're telling me— I've almost been tempted to change denominations to one where pastors are appointed by the conference. Sure would make this process simpler."

"True," said Nancy. "But I must admit that I like a system that empowers the congregation and the pastor. I mean, I love our conference minister and have great respect for him, but I've never liked that idea of 'matchmaking' for the church."

Nancy then pulled out a notebook and began sorting through some pages. "As you know, Marsha, we've got a pretty full weekend ahead of us. After we finish dinner, we'll head over to the church where you'll meet with the entire search committee. And then, we have more meetings with the committee in the morning and we'll give you a chance to tour the community and see what life here is like. And then, on Sunday, we've arranged for you to preach at a 'neutral pulpit' so committee members can hear you. And then, the committee will be able to make a recommendation to the congregation and you can think and pray about what you want to do. And then ..."

Marsha laughed. "Rick told me you were the queen of 'and thens.' But yes, it looks like we have a busy weekend ahead of us and a lot of challenges to consider. Let's start with supper."

CASE ANALYSIS QUESTIONS

1. How have Marsha's experiences so far represented aspects of the anticipatory socialization process? Is it also possible to consider anticipatory socialization from the point of view of the church searching for a new pastor? What does anticipatory socialization look like from the organization's point of view?

2. During the weekend ahead, what questions should Marsha anticipate during the interview process? What questions should she ask? What are the various functions that the interview will serve for both Marsha and the congregation?

3. Assuming that Marsha eventually takes on the role of pastor with this church, what should she anticipate during her first few months in her new role? Are there steps that she can take before and after moving to Michigan to ease her transition? Are there steps the congregation can take to help her "make sense" of life in the new church?

4. A pastor's role is one in which the "supervisor" could be seen as the congregation. How could the leader-member exchange model be adapted to account for these kinds of organizational positions?

Decision-Making Processes

CHAPTER **8**

AFTER READING THIS CHAPTER, YOU SHOULD . . .

- Appreciate how rational decision making is often hampered by individual and organizational limits and know alternative ways to understand individual and group decision making
- Be able to describe phase models of group decision making and know alternatives to these models
- Be familiar with the concept of "groupthink" and with models of effective decision making that could help organizations deal with groupthink and similar challenges.
- Be able to compare and contrast the affective and cognitive models of participative decision making
- Be familiar with various ways that participation has been instituted in organizations and be especially aware of the challenges of organizational democracy
- Understand knowledge management systems—both information-based and interaction-based—as ways that contemporary organizations move beyond simplistic visions of decision making

One of the most critical activities in any organization is decision making. Decisions might involve the strategic direction of the organization (e.g., a decision about a possible merger or acquisition) or might simply deal with the daily activities of employees (e.g., a decision about new procedures for greeting clients on the telephone). Decisions might be made after months of information gathering and deliberation or in an instant with little or no consideration. Decisions might be made by individuals either alone, through consultation with relevant organizational members, or in participative groups. And, decisions will vary in their level of effectiveness. Indeed, Nutt (1999) concluded that half of all decisions made in organizations fail because of the poor use of decision-making tactics by managers as well as problems with communication.

In this chapter, we explore the role of communication in organizational decision making. First, we look at general models of the decision-making process, considering the movement away from rational models toward those based on intuition and other less "logical" premises. Then, we discuss the small-group context in which many organizational decisions are made. Next, we consider one way in which values about decision making are embedded into organizational work life: the study of participation in decision making and workplace democracy. We close the chapter with a look at knowledge management processes that move us beyond the decision-making process.

MODELS OF THE DECISION-MAKING PROCESS

Rational Models of Decision Making

In classical theories of organizational behavior, decision making is an entirely rational and logical process. First, organizational members notice a problem that necessitates a decision. After carefully defining the problem, the decision makers then search for all the relevant information that might bear upon it. Next, the decision makers develop a set of decision options and evaluate them according to carefully developed criteria for decision effectiveness. The decision-making process concludes when an optimal decision is identified and decision implementation can begin.

Nutt (1984) discusses this rational and logical model of decision making as the *normative* method recommended for executives in most management textbooks. This normative model includes five stages: formulation, concept development, detailing, evaluation, and implementation.

Consider, for instance, a team of managers trying to make a decision about adopting a new server for the company's network of computers. In the *formulation stage* (Stage 1), the team might do a survey of organizational members to determine computing needs and desires. In the concept *development stage* (Stage 2), the management team would generate alternative ways for dealing with the problem. At this point they might look at the various types of servers and ways individual computers could be configured in local-area networks. During the *detailing process* (Stage 3), subgroups might be assigned to get more detail on the pros and cons of various options, and their workability might be tested. During the *evaluation stage* (Stage 4), the information gathered during detailing would be placed under intense scrutiny by the group in order to quantify the costs and benefits of each type of computer system. Finally, in the *implementation stage* (Stage 5), the server system that came out ahead during evaluation would be put in place by the management group.

Alternatives to Rational Models

This rational and logical process sounds like the ideal way to make an organizational decision. However, scholars long ago recognized that this model was *not* a good representation of how organizational decision makers actually work. The first theorists to suggest an alternative to this model were March and Simon (March & Simon, 1958; Simon, 1960), who characterize the traditional approach to decision making as an *optimizing* model in which decision makers are attempting to find the single best solution to an organizational problem. They believe that it is more realistic to look at organizational decision making as a *satisficing* process in which the search is not for a single optimal solution but for a solution that will work well enough for dealing with the situation. As Pugh and Hickson (1989) explain:

Most decisions are concerned not with searching for the sharpest needle in the haystack, but with searching for a needle sharp enough to sew with. Thus, administrators who "satisfice" can make decisions without a search for all the possible alternatives and can use relatively simple rules of thumb. In business terms, they do not look for "maximum profit" but "adequate profit"; not "optimum price" but "fair price." This makes their world much simpler. (p. 138)

March and Simon (1958) propose that organizational decision makers use satisficing strategies because it is not *possible* to make the ideal rational solution. Rather, organizational decision makers are characterized by *bounded rationality*. That is, decision makers attempt to make logical decisions, but they are limited cognitively (e.g., humans are not always perfectly logical) and by the practical aspects of organizational life (e.g., limits in time and resources). For example, a manager might need to make a decision about what word processing program to adopt. If this manager were optimizing, she would undertake a search of all possible programs and evaluate these options against a set of carefully developed criteria. However, there is rarely time or motivation to do this. Instead, our manager might talk to a few colleagues about software to find a program adequate for the organization's needs. Thus, March and Simon propose that decision makers still use logic, but do so under personal and organizational constraints.

More recently, March and Simon have proposed models of decision making that are even further removed from optimizing models than is satisficing. For example, Simon (1987) has proposed that a great deal of organizational decision making can be attributed to the *intuitive processes* of managers. Simon harkens back to early work by Barnard (1938), who suggests a distinction between logical and nonlogical management processes. Barnard argues that decision makers are often forced to make quick decisions without the opportunity for information search

Case in Point: Personal Finance Decisions

Decisions made in the workplace have important implications for organizations and the people who work in and for them. But for the individual, the most important "work" decisions might be those involving what to do with the money earned on the job. Such decisions will influence the individual's lifestyle, date of retirement, and charitable activities.

You would think, then, that rationality would be front and center in making these decisions that are so important for our lives and our futures. Not so, say experts in "behavioral finance," a field of study investigating the role of motivation and psychology in investment decisions (Bernard, 2004). Instead, most individuals rely on mental shortcuts—"heuristics"— that undercut rational principles of probability in investing. For example, people tend to feel more secure

following the lead of other investors, tend to focus too much on what has happened recently, tend to develop irrational "anchor points" for decisions, are reluctant to realize losses, and tend to treat money differently depending on its source. All of these tendencies can lead to flawed investment decisions.

So what's an investor to do? Well, following the steps for "rational" decision making laid out in this chapter would make sense. But because we don't have perfect information, unlimited time, or a perfectly rational approach to our own lives and money, this can be difficult. Thus, consulting an expert decision maker might be well advised. As Bernard (2004, p. E5) concludes, "[t]aking the emotion out of the decision increases the chance that it will result in a rational move."

and debate. Managers in these situations often make decisions without conscious knowledge of how these decisions are made. Barnard (1938) notes that

> The sources of these non-logical processes lie in physiological conditions or factors, or in the physical and social environment, mostly impressed upon us unconsciously or without conscious effort on our part. They also consist of the mass of facts, patterns, concepts, techniques, abstractions, and generally what we call formal knowledge or beliefs, which are impressed upon our minds more or less by conscious effort and study. This second source of non-logical mental processes greatly increases with direct experience, study and education. (p. 302)

Simon (1987) points out that though intuitive decision making is not "logical," neither is it "illogical." Rather, this kind of decision making is based on past experience in similar contexts. One could say that this kind of decision making is *analogical*. That is, a manager faced with making a decision will consider what has worked in similar situations in the past. By analogy, a similar solution should work again. As Simon (1987) notes, "The experienced manager . . . has in his or her memory a large amount of knowledge, gained from training and experience and organized in terms of recognizable chunks and associated information" (p. 61). Intuitive decision making depends on the decision maker accessing the relevant "chunk" of information and putting it to use.

A study of intuitive decision making (Burke & Miller, 1999) supports many of Simon's ideas. Indeed, when managers were asked how often they used intuition in decision making, only 10 percent said "seldom" or "rarely." Indeed, practicing managers believed that many decision-making situations called for intuitive methods and that intuitive decision making could yield benefits including expediting the decision-making process, improving the quality of the decision, facilitating personal

Case in Point: Crunching the Data

This chapter so far has made the argument that many decisions in organizations are not made rationally, through the careful, logical analysis of data. Rather, decisions are often made through intuitive processes or by considering similar situations and past decisions. Further, part of what limits our rationality in decision making is our inability to access and process all of the information that would be required for a truly rational decision. Well, it turns out that might be changing, thanks to high-powered computers and lots of disc space.

In a new book entitled *Super Crunchers*, Ian Ayres (2007) argues that we are in the midst of a powerful trend: "the replacement of expertise and intuition by objective, data-based decision making, made possible by a virtually inexhaustible supply of inexpensive information" (Adler, 2007, p. 42). Ayres points out

that the vast quantities of information gleaned from electronic sources, together with sophisticated algorithms for analyzing those data, can assist in decisions made in disparate areas such as marketing, criminal justice, agriculture, and medicine. We are probably all familiar with the use of information to track our online buying preferences, and Ayres tracks this trend in many phases of organizational life. Though these developments may lead to decisions that are "better" (or at least more thoroughly based on evidence and data), they also take some of the challenge out of people's work. As Adler states, "jobs that used to call for independent judgment, especially about other people, are being routinized and dumbed down" (p. 42). In other words, there's less chance of charming that loan officer or convincing her that you're a good risk. Your credit score will say it all.

development, and promoting decisions compatible with the culture of the organization.

Another alternative to rational decision making has been proposed by March and his colleagues (Cohen, March, & Olson, 1972). In their garbage can model of decision making, these theorists venture far from the rational norm, proposing that decision making is a process wherein problems, solutions, participants, and choices are all dumped together in a relatively independent fashion. A decision is made when "a suitable collection of problems, solutions, participants, and choices coincide" (Pugh & Hickson, 1989, p. 145). Thus, a manager might have a pet plan for a new billing procedure that happens to coincide with a colleague's need to revamp accounts receivable. The "decision" that arises in this situation is not one of logical search and solution but merely happy coincidence. March and colleagues believe that organizational behavior often occurs in just such an irrational manner and it is only after the fact that the "decision-making process" is constructed. This belief is similar to Weick's notion of sensemaking, discussed in Chapter 4.

In summary, theory and research suggest that decision making is not a perfectly rational process of information search and decision choice. Instead, decision makers typically use truncated decision procedures and rely on intuition, satisficing solutions, and the collision of problems and answers. In the next section, we consider the small-group context in which a great many organizational decisions are made.

SMALL-GROUP DECISION MAKING

According to an old adage, a camel is a horse designed by committee. This saying points to the pitfalls that can arise in group decision making. However fraught with problems the process might be, though, the fact remains that a vast majority of organizational decisions are made in the context of a small group, whether that group is a standing committee, a self-managing work team, an ad hoc task force, or a group of colleagues standing around the coffeemaker. In this section, we first explore models that describe the group decision-making process. We then consider factors that contribute to effective or ineffective decisions in small groups.

Descriptive Models of Small-Group Decision Making

Most models of group decision making propose that groups go through a series of phases as they systematically attempt to reach decisions. One representative model was proposed by B. A. Fisher (1970). He identifies four phases: orientation, conflict, emergence, and reinforcement. In the *orientation* phase, group members become acquainted with each other and with the problem at hand. During the *conflict* phase, possible solutions to the problem are presented and debated. After this, the group will arrive at some level of consensus during the *emergence* phase, and the decision will be supported during the final group phase, *reinforcement*. Similar phase models have been proposed by Bales and Strodtbeck (1951) and Tubbs (1978).

In some ways, these phase models of group decision making mirror the rational model of decision making we considered above. As Poole and Roth (1989a) note, stage models "explain decision behavior as the result of the group following a systematic logic" (p. 325). Stage models also assume a rigid and unitary sequence of group activities. That is, decision making always begins with orientation to the problem and ends with the emergence and reinforcement of a solution. A number of theorists have objected to this type of model. For example, Cissna (1984) argues that phases do not exist, and Morley and Stephenson (1977) argue that phasic development will vary depending on the type of decision being made by the group. Gersick (1991) has developed a "punctuated equilibrium" model that highlights both the underlying deep structure and the revolutionary shifts that occur in groups.

The most complex response to rational phase models has been mounted by Poole and his colleagues (Poole, 1983; Poole & Doelger, 1986; Poole & Roth, 1989a, 1989b). Poole has advanced a *multiple sequence model* that represents the variety of decision paths taken by groups. By coding the continuous interaction of decision-making groups, Poole and Roth (1989a) developed a typology of decision paths typically adopted. The three major types of group decision paths are presented in Table 8.1.

As Table 8.1 indicates, less than a quarter of the groups studied exhibited the rational sequence prescribed by most stage models. Groups were more likely to engage in complicated sequences of cycles (i.e., breaking the problem down into subproblems and processing these one at a time) or to focus on the solution with little regard to problem definition or discussion. Note the similarity between this and our discussion of alternatives to the rational model of decision making presented earlier. It appears that regardless of the context, decision making is rarely a linear and rational process in which organizational members carefully search for and evaluate decision options.

Effective Small-Group Decision Making

Poole's multiple sequence model is useful in highlighting the varying communicative patterns small groups use when making decisions. However, this model says little about what types of communication lead to *effective* decisions. Is a group better off following the rational model? Should a group concentrate on solutions?

Table 8.1 | Typology of Small-Group Decision Path Types

Decision Path Type	Frequency	Explanation
Unitary sequence path	23%	Group interaction generally followed traditional sequence of orientation, problem analysis, solution, and reinforcement.
Complex cyclic path	47%	Group interaction consisted of multiple problem–solution cycles.
Solution-oriented path	30%	Group interaction involved no activity related to problem definition or analysis.

Based on Poole, M. S., & Roth, J. (1989a). Decision development in small groups IV: A typology of group decision paths. *Human Communication Research*, 15, 323–356.

How should a group distribute its energy among the wide range of tasks that must be accomplished? What interaction patterns lead to bad decisions? These questions have been the focus of a number of group theorists.

Probably the best-known analysis of dysfunctional decisions has been presented by Janis (1972, 1982). Janis studied a number of historically noteworthy decision disasters (e.g., the Kennedy administration's decision to invade Cuba at the Bay of Pigs) and concluded that interaction in these groups was characterized by the property of *groupthink*. Other more recent high-level decisions—such as the space shuttle disasters involving both *Challenger* and *Columbia*—have also been attributed to groupthink (see Case Study for Chapter 5 for more detail on these decisions and the culture that created them). Groupthink refers to "a mode of thinking that people engage in when they are deeply involved in a cohesive in-group, when the members' striving for unanimity overrides their motivation to realistically appraise alternative courses of action" (Janis, 1982, p. 9). Thus, in a group characterized by groupthink, there is more concern with appearing cohesive and maintaining group relations than there is with making a high-quality decision. The major symptoms of groupthink identified by Janis are presented in Table 8.2.

This table clearly indicates the pitfalls that can result from pressure toward uniformity in an overly cohesive group. However, besides group cohesion, Whyte (1989) has speculated that decision fiascoes might also be attributed to the tendency of groups to make more extreme decisions than individuals and the tendency of groups to frame some decisions in negative ways. Hirokawa and Scheerhorn (1986) have proposed that low-quality decisions can result from factors including the improper assessment of the situation and goals, the establishment of a flawed information base, and faulty reasoning.

Table 8.2 | Symptoms of Groupthink

Groupthink Symptom	Description
Illusion of invulnerability	The belief that nothing can go wrong within the group
Illusion of morality	The self-righteous belief that the virtues of the group are above reproach
Stereotyping	The categorizing of others *outside* of the group in ways that see their views as unacceptable
Self-censorship	The overt restraint of group members against offering opinions counter to the prevailing thought in the group
Illusion of unanimity	The statement of group agreement while private doubts and disagreements are suppressed
Direct pressure on dissidents	The coercive force that obliges group members to behave and think in similar ways
Reliance on self-appointed mind guards	The protection of the group from contrary information from outside influences

A recent and profound example of these problems can be found in the organizational decision making that led to the United States' invasion of Iraq in 2003. The bipartisan Senate Intelligence Committee report released in the summer of 2004 suggested that the decision making regarding Iraq might have been driven by a preferred solution rather than by a detailed and rational consideration of the available evidence. As Isikoff (2004) summarizes, "U.S. intelligence officials repeatedly embellished fragmentary and ambiguous pieces of evidence, making the danger posed by Iraq appear far more urgent than it actually was" (Isikoff, 2004, p. 37). Even at the highest levels of government, decision makers are influenced by the human desire for things to turn out in a particular way and may therefore see things in a preferred light.

How, then, can a group improve its chances of making an effective decision? Several answers to this question have been proposed by researchers of small groups. Some scholars have suggested that a group's manner of dealing with conflict can influence decision quality. For example, Amason (1996) found that "cognitive conflict" (task-oriented disagreements about how to achieve common objectives) enhanced decision-making quality, while "affective conflict" (emotional disagreements focused on personal incompatibility) detracted from effectiveness. Similarly, Kuhn and Poole (2000) found that groups that worked through their conflicts in collaborative and integrative ways (see discussion in Chapter 9) made more effective decisions. Jabs (2005) has recently argued that individuals and groups need to be consciously aware of the communication rules to be followed, as this will keep people from following social norms that might have undesirable effects.

Perhaps the most complete explication of the role communication plays in enhancing decision quality comes from Randy Hirokawa and Dennis Gouran in their *Functional Theory of Group Decision Making* (see Gouran, Hirokawa, Julian, & Leatham, 1993; Gouran & Hirokawa, 1996; Hirokawa & Salazar, 1999). Functional theory argues that effective decision making depends on groups attending to critical functions through group communication. Specifically, these functions are as follows (from Gouran et al., 1993, p. 580):

- The group should have a correct understanding of the issues to be resolved.
- The group should determine the minimal characteristics required in order for any alternative to be acceptable.
- The group should identify a relevant and realistic set of alternatives.
- The group should carefully examine the alternatives in relation to each previously agreed-upon required characteristic.
- The group should select the alternative that is most likely to have the desired characteristics.

As this list indicates, functional theory works through the same phases identified as necessary for effective individual decision making (i.e., understanding the problem, identifying alternatives, and determining criteria for evaluating those alternatives) and identifies how group communication can enhance the likelihood of success. A statistical review of research testing the functional group approach to decision making suggested that two factors—problem definition and the negative evaluation of alternatives—were key in leading to high-quality decisions (Orlitzky &

Hirokawa, 2001). Interestingly, this review also suggested that generating many possible solutions (i.e., "brainstorming") was not strongly linked to high-quality decisions.

Technological solutions can also enhance the likelihood that groups will make good decisions. In addition to the ability of computers to gather and process vast amounts of information (see "Case in Point: Crunching the Data" earlier in this chapter), communication and computer technology can also assist humans in the decision-making process through *Group Decision Support Systems* (GDSSs). With these systems (see Scott, 2003) group members are located together in one room and linked via the technology. The technology allows for parallel input of comments (reducing the chance that a few people "take over" the meeting), allows for anonymous input and voting, and provides tools for helping to sort out various decision options. Rains (2005) recently found that groups using these systems experience greater participation and equality and generated more ideas than groups meeting face-to-face.

Beyond Rational Group Processes

Though research on group decision-making processes and effectiveness has led to a number of important findings, there have also been critiques leveled against these structured and rational approaches to group decision making. For example, group decision-making literature has been critiqued as being overly concerned with the *task* functions of groups and for ignoring the socio-emotional and relational aspects of group interaction. One theory that has been proposed to help consider these relational issues is *symbolic convergence theory* (see, e.g., Bormann, 1996); this theory considers the role of communication such as stories and jokes in creating a feeling of group identity. Theories of group decision making have also been critiqued because they often ignore organizational context by studying contrived decision situations using groups of college students. The *bona fide groups perspective* (see, e.g., Putnam & Stohl, 1996) deals with this critique by proposing that group research consider factors such as shifting membership, permeable group boundaries, and interdependence within an organizational context. One study of decision making stemming from a bona fide groups approach considered the importance of "backstage" communication in decision making for an interdisciplinary geriatric health care team (Ellingson, 2003). This research suggested that "hallway conversations" among team members were just as important in the decision-making process as was interaction in formal group meetings.

PARTICIPATION IN DECISION MAKING

Thus far, we have examined the process of making decisions—*how* decisions are made by individuals and small groups. We will now consider the question of *who* makes the decision, with a look at the voluminous theory and research on participation in decision making (PDM) and a look at the growing academic interest in workplace democracy. We first discuss some of the founding research on PDM and the proposed effects of participation. We then look at two models that attempt to explain why participation should produce valuable organizational outcomes. We conclude with a consideration of how participation can be brought to life in organizations through workplace democracy programs.

Effects of Participation in Decision Making

The first major study of participation in decision making was conducted by Coch and French in 1948. These researchers were interested in factors that would enhance employee commitment to organizational decisions and found support for their hypothesis that participation in organizational decisions would make employees less resistant to change. Since this early study, researchers have considered a wide range of attitudinal, cognitive, and behavioral effects of participation (see Miller & Monge, 1987; Seibold & Shea, 2001, for reviews).

The most widely studied attitudinal effect of participation is job satisfaction. Other attitudinal effects thought to be the result of participation in decision making (PDM) include job involvement and organizational commitment. The cognitive effects proposed for PDM include enhanced use of information from a wide range of organizational members and a greater employee understanding of decisions and the organization as a whole. Finally, proposed behavioral impacts of participation include improved productivity and an increase in the effectiveness of decisions. One meta-analytic literature review of the most often-studied effects of PDM (Wagner, 1994) concludes that participation has significant and consistent—but relatively small—effects on satisfaction and performance.

Models of the Participation Process

In addition to looking at the possible effects of PDM, it is important to consider the processes through which PDM may produce these outcomes. Miller and Monge (1986) have summarized several models that explicate links between participation, job satisfaction, and productivity. Two of these models—the *affective model* and the *cognitive model*—use notably different frameworks to link PDM to these outcome variables. Both models are described below.

The Affective Model   The affective model of participation is based on the work of human relations theorists (see Chapter 3). This model proposes that PDM is an organizational practice that should satisfy employees' higher-order needs (e.g., esteem needs and self-actualization needs). When these needs are met, job satisfaction should result. Ritchie and Miles (1970) state that proponents of this model "believe simply in involvement for the sake of involvement, arguing that as long as subordinates feel they are participating and are being consulted,

Figure 8.1 | The Affective Model of Participative Decision Making

their ego needs will be satisfied and they will be more cooperative" (p. 348). Supporters of this model would then argue that satisfied workers are more motivated and hence more productive (French, Israel, & As, 1960). The affective model is presented in Figure 8.1.

To illustrate this model, consider Frank, an assembly-line supervisor who needs to make a decision about how to improve product rejection rates at the factory. Frank decides to involve his subordinates in this decision. He reasons that including them in the decision will make them feel needed and important and hence engender satisfaction with the job. Believing that "happy workers are effective workers," Frank figures that improved productivity is sure to follow.

The Cognitive Model   The cognitive model is based on principles of the human resources approach (see Chapter 3). This model proposes that PDM improves the upward and downward flow of information in the organization. The improvement of upward information flow rests on the notion that individuals close to the work (i.e., at the "bottom" of the organizational hierarchy) know the most about how to accomplish the work. Thus, when these individuals participate in the decision-making process, a decision is made with higher-quality information. The improvement of downward information flow rests on the idea that individuals who participate in decisions will be better able to implement the decisions down the road. When decisions are made with a better pool of information and are better implemented, productivity should improve. Increased employee satisfaction is then seen "as a by-product of their participation in important organizational decisions" (Ritchie & Miles, 1970, p. 348). The cognitive model is presented in Figure 8.2.

To illustrate this model, let's look at Rosie, another assembly-line supervisor at Frank's factory. Rosie also decides to involve her subordinates in decisions about improving rejection rates, but she does so for different reasons than Frank. Rosie realizes that her workers spend all their work hours on the line and probably

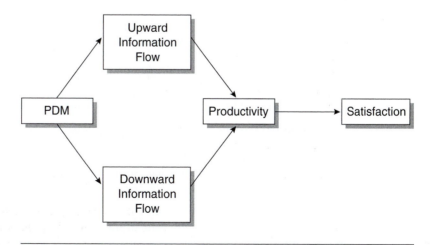

Figure 8.2   The Cognitive Model of Participative Decision Making

know more about why quality control is slipping than anyone else. She wants their input. She also realizes that changing inspection procedures will be far easier if her workers have had a hand in the change process. Thus, she reasons, productivity will improve through participation. Because her philosophy is "busy hands are happy hands," she assumes her subordinates will be satisfied as well.

Evidence for Models of Participation   Some support exists for both of these models of participation. The strongest evidence for the *affective model* comes from the ample research finding a link between general perceptions of participation in decision making and employee satisfaction (see Miller & Monge, 1986, for a review). This indicates that working in a "participative climate" can meet workers' needs and increase satisfaction. Evidence for the *cognitive model* comes from research linking participation in organizational decisions with productivity increases (Miller & Monge, 1986), and research linking participation with organizational knowledge (Marshall & Stohl, 1993). This research suggests that participation positively influences performance by leveraging pools of knowledge in the workplace.

Participative Applications in Organizations and Workplace Democracy

Participation in decision making can be instituted in the workplace in a wide variety of ways. Cotton, Vollrath, Froggatt, Lengnick-Hall, and Jennings (1988) have noted that management participation can range from the short-term and informal (e.g., a manager casually asking a subordinate for input) to formal representative systems and employee ownership. Seibold and Shea (2001) considered five types of participation programs often used by organizations and reviewed the research on the effectiveness of these programs. These programs vary greatly in terms of their structure and goals, but all attempt to enhance organizational effectiveness through participation. Seibold and Shea's results are summarized in Table 8.3.

In recent years, communication scholars (e.g., Cheney, 1995; Deetz, 1992; Harrison, 1994) have become increasingly interested in *workplace democracy*—the participative ideal for organizations. More than just participation, workplace democracy involves realizing the standards for a democratic society in the workplace. Indeed, Collins (1997) argues that from an economic and political standpoint, participatory management is both inevitable and ethically superior to authoritarian alternatives. Cheney (1995) defines workplace democracy as

> a system of governance which truly values individuals' goals and feelings . . . as well as typically organizational objectives . . . which actively fosters the connection between those two sets of concerns by encouraging individual contributions to important organizational choices, and which allows for the ongoing modification of the organization's activities and policies by the group. (pp. 170–171)

In other words, participation within a democratic workplace is based on more than mere expediency—it is based on humanistic ideals about how individuals should be treated and involved in society. Participation in such an organization will typically include an actual (rather than just apparent) influence on a large range of organizational processes and issues, and democracy at all levels of the organization.

Table 8.3 | Forms of Participation in Decision Making

	Quality Circles (QCs)	Quality of Work Life (QWL) Programs	Employee Stock Ownership Plans (ESOPs)	Scanlon Gainsharing Plans	Self-Directed Work Teams (SDWTs)/New Plant
Type of program	Voluntary Formal	Voluntary Formal	Voluntary Formal	Voluntary Formal	Voluntary Formal
Effectiveness	Low	Moderate	Moderate	High	High
Degree of participation	Low	Low	Low to moderate	Moderate to high	High
Type of influence	Consultative	Consultative	Varies with program	Consultative and full participation (can implement some decisions without management approval)	Consultative and full participation (can implement many decisions without management approval)
Content of decision making	Work itself Immediate work area	Work itself Working conditions Company policy (on occasion)	Varies (usually vote for representatives to sit on board of directors)	Work itself Working conditions Company policy Financial bonuses	Work itself Working conditions Schedules and budgets Hiring at team level Compensation
Social range of participation	Group/department (Employees from specific department or work area)	Group/organization (Employees, managers, union representatives across organization)	Individual/organization (Full-time employees, managers across organization)	Group/organization (Employees and managers work together across all levels)	Group/organization (Employees from specific areas across organization)
Financial component	No	No	Yes (indirect)	Yes (direct)	(varies)

From Seibold, D. R., & Shea, B. C. (2001), Participation and decision making. In F. M. Jablin & L. L. Putnam (Eds.), *The New Handbook of Organizational Communication: Advances in Theory, Research, and Methods* (p. 670). Thousand Oaks, CA: Sage. Reproduced with permission of Sage Publication Inc. Books via Copyright Clearance Center.

Spotlight on Scholarship

Instituting and maintaining participative decision-making processes—particularly those that could be characterized as "organizational democracy"—introduces new challenges in each organizational setting.

The challenges faced by a large hierarchical corporation will be distinct from those faced by a small family business. Thus, it is instructive to consider case analyses of how various organizations "do" democracy to better understand how decision-making practices can be enhanced in a range of workplaces.

Mary Hoffman provides one such analysis in her study of two communities of Benedictine nuns. Though religious women's organizations may differ in significant ways from other workplaces, in others they represent a growing segment of contemporary organizations. As Hoffman (2002, p. 203) notes, "Benedictine communities carry out the same functions as other contemporary organizations—they recruit and select members, assign jobs, oversee budgets and property, run subsidiaries such as hospitals and colleges, implement building projects and mergers, and manage large-scale organizational change." Further, Benedictine communities represent the growing trend of feminist organizations that are often nonprofit service agencies. Thus, it is likely that a great deal can be learned from how these women's religious organizations manage to enhance participative decision making and organizational democracy.

Hoffman argues that there are three critical ways in which organizational democracy is enhanced. The first is through shared values. Of course, because Benedictine nuns take vows, these shared values could, perhaps, be assumed. However, what's interesting is the way in which these religious values are relevant to organizational democracy. For example, "the vow of obedience, seemingly out-of-place in a democratic organization, is interpreted to mean a commitment to attentive listening and mutual responsibility" (Hoffman, 2002, p. 209). Thus, it is critical that organizational members share fundamental values such as equality, participation, support, and the dignity of all contributions.

The second critical way that organizational democracy is enhanced is through structures. In particular, Hoffman points to structures that maximize cooperation (e.g., rules for election), and structures that encourage individual participation (e.g., open microphones at meetings, straw tallies). Together, these structures provide a way for individuals to be empowered through "challenge in a climate of trust" (Pacanowsky, 1988, p. 378). In addition, Hoffman found it was important that the communities instituted structures requiring a periodic review of participative processes. The third critical way that organizational democracy was fostered was through resources possessed by members of the community. For example, many of the nuns were highly educated, and the community encouraged additional training. Further, resources were provided prior to individual meetings and decisions through specific reading and an advanced agenda.

This attention to participative values, structures, and resources did not always lend itself to efficient decision making. As one sister expressed in frustration, "sometimes it takes forever to make a decision" (Hoffman, 2002, p. 214) but most of the members thought that trading some efficiency for higher-quality decisions—and consensus about what was important and what should be done—was clearly worth it.

Hoffman, M. F. (2002). "Do All Things with Counsel": Benedictine Women and Organizational Democracy. *Communication Studies, 53,* 203–218.

Workplace democracy involves collaboration among "multiple stakeholders" (Deetz, 1995), including workers, investors, consumers, suppliers, host communities, and the world economic community. According to proponents of workplace democracy, shared decision making among *all* of these stakeholders is crucial in today's complicated organizational world.

Of course, workplace democracy and participation are not easy-to-enact panaceas for the ills of today's organizations. Stohl and Cheney (2001) considered the paradoxes that arise in instituting democratic and participative systems. These paradoxes point out situations in which "the pursuit of an objective involves actions that are themselves antithetical to the desired end" (Stohl & Cheney, 2001, p. 354). Stohl and Cheney highlight fourteen paradoxes of participation that fall into four categories, described in Table 8.4. These paradoxes present a cautionary note about the complexity of instituting participation and democracy within organizations. Ultimately, however, these theorists are hopeful about organizational democracy, and they provide creative, productive ways to handle these paradoxes that could eventually "lead to a much better situation for social actors than had those actors never encountered the paradox in the first place" (Stohl & Cheney, 2001, p. 356).

Beyond Decisions: Knowledge Management Systems

Finally, it is important to note that, to an ever-increasing extent, organizations no longer see decision making as an isolated process but rather as an ongoing system that is integrated into structures and behaviors throughout the organization. This is clear from the ideas we have considered about organizational democracy—a process that involves a clear conceptual shift by all stakeholders in an organization. This move toward a more overarching view of decision-making processes in organizations can also be seen in the move toward knowledge management systems that we briefly considered in Chapter 4's discussion of human resources approaches to organizational communication.

Knowledge management involves "identifying and harnessing intellectual assets" to allow organizations to "build on past experiences and create new mechanisms for exchanging and creating knowledge" (Heaton, 2008). Knowledge management involves the use of explicit knowledge that is saved in documents, systems, and programs and tacit knowledge that is held by individuals in an

Table 8.4 | Paradoxes of Participative Democracy

Paradox Type	Definition	Employees Are Told:
Structure	Paradoxes involving how organizational democracy is planned, designed, and formalized	"Be spontaneous, creative, vocal, and assertive in the way we have planned!"
Agency	Paradoxes concerning an individual's sense of responsibility, autonomy, and cooperation within the participative system	"Do things our way but in a way that is still distinctly your own!"
Identity	Paradoxes concerning issues of inclusion, boundaries, and interests within the participative system	"Be *self*-managing to reach *organizational* goals!"
Power	Paradoxes concerning how control and leadership are exercised within the participatory system	"Be independent, just as I have commanded you!"

Adapted from Stohl and Cheney (2001).

organization. Nonaka and Takeuchi (1995) argue that a successful system of knowledge management will do two things. First, a successful system will allow individuals in an organization to convert their tacit knowledge into explicit knowledge that can be shared and used in organizational decision making and operations. Second, a successful system will allow organizational members to find ways to make the codified knowledge meaningful once it has been retrieved from organizational systems. For example, knowledge management regarding customer service at a restaurant will involve statistics about restaurant operations *and* the stories of waiters and waitresses about service encounters.

Iverson and McPhee (2002) have argued that the need for both kinds of knowledge has led to two distinct approaches to knowledge management processes. Information-based knowledge management is most concerned with tracking data and developing processes for cataloguing and retrieving those data. In contrast, interaction-based knowledge management is concerned with the tacit knowledge that organizational actors hold and—especially—how interaction patterns in organizational networks can facilitate the sharing of that information. Effective organizational decisions can only emerge when these two kinds of knowledge management are linked.

SUMMARY

In this chapter, we looked at the activities through which organizational members and groups make decisions. We first considered several models of the decision-making process, noting that most scholars have rejected a strictly rational depiction of decision making in favor of models that include intuition and other nonrational components. We then looked specifically at the small-group context in which a great many organizational decisions are made. Again, we found that most theorists now eschew linear models of decision making in favor of descriptive models that incorporate the complex ebb and flow of communication in small groups. We also looked at group communication processes that result in effective and ineffective decisions, noting that attention to key communication functions in group communication can decrease the risk of groupthink in decision-making collectives. Finally, we considered the question of "who" makes the decisions by examining the literature on participative management. We first examined two models of participation in decision making (PDM)—the affective model and the cognitive model. Then we looked at programs that could be used to institute PDM within the organizational

context. We also considered the ideal of workplace democracy and the movement toward systems of knowledge management.

Table 8.5 summarizes the work on decision making in terms of the six approaches to organizational communication we have discussed in this textbook. It should be clear that the early models of decision making we considered have their roots in the classical approach to organizational communication. The rational models of decision making and the phase models of small-group processing assume that an ideal decision can be made if organizational decision makers are careful in following "correct" procedures. These models of decision making have been largely rejected, however, in favor of models more in line with human relations, human resources, and systems approaches. The affective and cognitive models of participation, for example, are clearly predicated, respectively, on human relations and human resources principles. The influence of systems approaches can be seen in the work of Poole on decision paths and in the functional theory of Gouran and Hirokawa, who see the small group as a decision-making "system" characterized by complex processes of interdependence and information exchange.

Until a few years ago, little research had approached decision making from either a cultural or a critical vantage point. However, as our discussion of the paradoxes of participation above indicates, more recent work has begun to remedy this situation. For example, a volume edited by Conrad (1993) emphasizes the role of individual and organizational values in the decision-making process. In one chapter of this volume, for instance, Bullis (1993b) demonstrates that personal, professional, and organizational values can often conflict with each other and these "interpenetrating streams of culture" (p. 99) can have a strong impact on decision making. From a critical stance, Tompkins and Cheney (1985) argue that when employees make decisions based on decision-making premises endorsed by management, they are, in effect, succumbing to unobtrusive control:

> We believe that much of the communication in this entire process is tacit; that is, there are many kinds of suppressed premises, and this is what makes the . . . process so elusive, subtle, pervasive, and, from the organization's standpoint, effective. Organizational members often "fill in" premises while nearly always accepting the "master premise" of putting the organization first. (p. 196)

The critical approach also shows great promise for a reconsideration of PDM in team-based management systems. In Chapter 6, we discussed the concept of "concertive control," and its relevance is particularly apparent in relation to decision making. For example, Barker's (1993) study of an organization moving from a hierarchical to a team-based system concluded that, through the

Table 8.5 | Approaches to the Decision-Making Process

Approach	How Decision Making Would Be Considered
Classical	Decision making is seen as a rational and logical process. Emphasis is placed on procedures through which decision makers can reach an optimal solution as efficiently as possible.
Human relations	Participation in the decision-making process is seen as an avenue for the satisfaction of workers' higher-order needs (e.g., esteem needs and self-actualization needs). Satisfied workers will then be more productive.
Human resources	Participation in the decision-making process is seen as an avenue for eliciting valuable information from employees and for ensuring effective implementation of organizational decisions.
Systems	Decision making is seen as a complex process involving multiple and varied stages. Both information and organizational members seen as part of knowledge management systems.
Cultural	Decision making is seen as a set of practices that reflect and constitute organizational values and assumptions. Conflicts in decision making are seen as possible indications of different values within organizational subcultures.
Critical	Decision making is seen as a process through which management can exert control over employees. When employees participate in decision making, they accept the decision premises of the organization and contribute to hegemonic relationships in the organization.

influence of PDM processes, a team-based organization can exert even stronger control over workers than a hierarchical one. Wendt (1994) has made similar observations about how total quality management can exert hegemonic control over organizational workers. Thus, although the majority of research on decision making stems from human relations, human resources, and systems approaches, emerging work from cultural and critical schools of organizational communication is beginning to shed a new light on the process of organizational decision making.

Discussion Questions

1. Think about a decision you've recently made. Did you make that decision in a rational and logical way? If yes, how did you structure your decision-making process? If no, in what ways was your decision-making process not rational?
2. In what ways does group decision making parallel individual decision making? How does group interaction change and influence the decision-making process? If the group is part of an organization, how do organizational factors influence decision making?
3. Is organizational democracy merely a utopian goal, or is it something that can be achieved in the workplace? What steps would you take to make an organization that you're a part of more democratic?
4. How are people and data linked in systems of knowledge management? Can you think of a job you have had in which your "tacit" knowledge was different from the "explicit" knowledge available to organizational decision makers? How can these two kinds of knowledge be linked through organizational communication processes?

CASE STUDY | **Too Many Majors**

Chelsea McGuire is the chairperson of a communication department at a university in the southeastern United States. She has been chair for more than five years and has built a successful department. But Chelsea has worried for some time that the department is too successful. Over the last few years, the number of communication majors in the university has steadily increased. When Chelsea took over as chair there were 500 communication majors. There are now more than 800 such majors, with no indication that this trend will change. Unfortunately, university support for the department has not increased at the same pace, and with only 15 department professors, Chelsea knows that some kind of action will soon need to be taken.

A month ago, she appointed two separate groups to study the problem and formulate enrollment management plans. First, she formed an ad hoc enrollment management committee to investigate the problem. Second, she asked the standing undergraduate curriculum committee to consider avenues for handling the preponderance of communication majors.

Chelsea now has a memo from each of these committees on her desk and has scheduled a meeting of the full faculty to discuss options and come to a decision about enrollment management. Let's first take a look at the memos from the two committees:

To: Dr. Chelsea McGuire
From: Dr. Walter Staniszewski,
         Chair, Ad Hoc Enrollment
         Management Committee
Date: March 23, 2008
Subject: Enrollment Management Plan

The Ad Hoc Committee on Enrollment Management has met on three occasions in the last month and conducted extensive research into enrollment management systems around the campus. Our goal was to determine the optimal system for stemming the flow of majors into the communication department. In order to reach our goal, we conducted a systematic survey of all other campus departments to determine if they, too, had experienced problems with over-enrollment in the past ten years. If they had experienced this problem, we inquired about plans that had been instituted to deal with the problem and established how well these plans were working. We also carefully compared the characteristics of other campus departments with relevant attributes of the communication department in considering options for dealing with our own enrollment management problems.

After committee evaluation of possible solutions, we have determined that three options are worthy of further departmental consideration:

- Many departments have instituted additional course requirements for majors. These have served to make the major less attractive to many students. Specifically, we might want to consider instituting a requirement of two years of a foreign language or a requirement of math and computer competency courses.
- Some departments have instituted strict grade point requirements for entry into the major. Although the university does not encourage this type of plan, the departments believe it to have been highly successful. Specifically, we might want to consider instituting a 2.5 GPA requirement for entry into the major and continuation in the major.
- A few departments have instituted an "application process" for admitting students to the major. Although this system would require additional paperwork on the part of the department, it would discourage students who were not truly interested in being communication majors from becoming majors.

The Ad Hoc Committee on Enrollment Management is looking forward to a careful evaluation of these options at the upcoming faculty meeting.

To: Professor Chelsea McGuire
From: Professor Jerry Gluesing Chair,
          Undergraduate Curriculum
          Committee
Date: March 25, 2008
Subject: Enrollment Management Issue

At its biweekly meeting, the Undergraduate Curriculum Committee took up the issue of enrollment management. We had a lively discussion on the issue, and it quickly became clear that a number of perspectives were possible. The committee was particularly persuaded by the position of Dr. Tanaka, who, as you know, has been with the department for more than 30 years. Dr. Tanaka pointed out that we have had these "crises" of too many majors (or too few majors) many times in the past, and have often spent an inordinate amount of time looking for the proper "solution" to the problem. Dr. Tanaka argued convincingly that enrollment ups and downs are part of the natural life cycle of an academic department and that we would be rash to institute major curricular or policy changes at this point. Indeed, as Dr. Tanaka pointed out, we have made few major changes to the program in the past 25 years, and over the long haul, enrollment has remained at a healthy but manageable level. Thus, although we would certainly enjoy discussing alternative ideas, our committee would suggest that no action be taken at this point. If necessary, we can revisit the issue next year at this time.

With these two memos in hand, Chelsea McGuire is now getting set to lead a faculty meeting where the sole agenda item is discussion of an enrollment management system. Her leadership in the past has always been highly participative. She has generally gone along with the "will of the faculty" in making departmental decisions, and she has been pleased with the effect of this decision-making style on both the quality of decisions made and on faculty morale. However, she is now concerned that this style might not work for the enrollment management decision, and she is going into this meeting with a bit of trepidation.

CASE STUDY | **Too Many Majors** *continued*

CASE ANALYSIS QUESTIONS

1. How would you characterize the decision-making styles of the two committees that considered the enrollment management problem? Would you characterize either of these processes as more effective or appropriate to the decision under consideration?

2. What advice would you give to Chelsea McGuire for the upcoming faculty meeting? Should she retain her typically participative decision-making style? What are the advantages and disadvantages of this kind of style in this type of decision-making situation?

3. Are there specific decision-making strategies that would be helpful in making an effective decision regarding enrollment management? What communication behaviors would you watch for in the upcoming meeting to assess whether an effective decision-making process is being used?

4. How might a "symbolic convergence" perspective on social and emotional communication in the group influence your assessment of the situation? How might a "bona fide group" perspective on the way the group is embedded in organizational structures (e.g., the department, the university, professional institutions) influence your assessment of the situation?

Conflict Management Processes

CHAPTER 9

AFTER READING THIS CHAPTER, YOU SHOULD . . .

- Be able to define organizational conflict and explain its stages and the various levels at which it might occur in the organization
- Be able to recognize various conflict styles, identify their effectiveness, and appreciate ways in which a styles approach might fall short in analyzing organizational conflict
- Know about the role of "third parties" in conflict negotiation, especially the processes of mediation and arbitration
- Understand how personal, relational, organizational, and cultural factors influence the conflict process
- Appreciate the need for an alternative approach to conflict, such as the approach suggested by feminist theorists and practitioners

A manager and an employee of a consulting firm disagree about how to best organize a report for a client. Two coworkers at a fast-food restaurant find themselves in a heated discussion about who is going to be stuck working the weekend shift. Representatives of a school district and a teachers union sit down to hammer out the details of a labor agreement. An automobile company's manufacturing division strongly opposes a set of design changes proposed by research and development.

All of these scenarios are examples of a pervasive part of organizational life— *conflict*. Conflict can be both destructive and productive. It can destroy work relationships or create the impetus for needed organizational change. Through communication, organizational members create and work through conflicts in ways that can be either functional or dysfunctional. In this chapter, we explore the role of conflict in organizational life. First, we conceptualize the issue by defining conflict and then discuss levels of conflict and phases in the conflict process. Following this, we look at communicative processes for managing conflict by considering individual conflict styles, the processes of negotiation and bargaining, and the role of third parties in settling organizational disputes. We then look at personal, relational, and organizational influences on the conflict management process. Finally, we consider an alternative view of conflict and negotiation derived from feminist organizational theory that shifts us from exchange models to a focus on dialogue and community.

CONCEPTUALIZING THE CONFLICT PROCESS

Defining Conflict

What exactly is conflict? Roloff (1987, p. 485) has noted that there is "no shortage of definitions" in the research literature. However, Putnam and Poole (1987) have developed a definition that is useful in highlighting several critical components of conflict in the organizational arena. They define conflict as "the interaction of interdependent people who perceive opposition of goals, aims, and values, and who see the other party as potentially interfering with the realization of these goals" (p. 552). This definition highlights three general characteristics that we might think of as the "three I's" of conflict: incompatible goals, interdependence, and interaction.

The notion of *incompatible goals* is central to most definitions of conflict (see, e.g., Deutsch, 1973). In the organizational setting, the nature of this "goal incompatibility" can vary substantially. For example, many organizational conflicts stem from contradictory ideas about the distribution of organizational resources. Management and labor negotiate about the distribution of payroll and benefits, or the top executive team argues about what capital investments to make in the coming fiscal year. Incompatibility can also disrupt organizational procedures. For example, a manager who believes in strict adherence to the time clock might clash with a new employee who believes in getting the work done on a more flexible schedule. Or, conflict might stem from different value orientations. For instance, in mergers and acquisitions, conflict often arises if the culture of the acquiring company is based on values different from those of the acquired company. In short, the basis of organizational conflict lies in the perception of incompatibility regarding a variety of organizational issues.

However, incompatibility is not a sufficient condition for organizational conflict to result. It is only when the behaviors of the organizational members are *interdependent* that conflict arises. Consider a situation in which one manager supports participative decision making while another believes in an authoritative management style. This incompatibility can exist harmoniously until interdependencies develop between the two managers. For example, if the two managers are asked to work together on a project or if their subordinates begin to "compare notes" about bosses, a conflict could well ensue. However, until behaviors are interdependently entwined, incompatibility need not result in conflict.

Finally, our definition of conflict highlights the role of *interaction* in organizational conflict. That is, conflict involves the *expression* of incompatibility, not the mere existence of incompatibility. This idea highlights the importance of communication in the study of conflict. As Putnam and Poole (1987) argue:

> Communication constitutes the essence of conflict in that it undergirds the formation of opposing issues, frames perceptions of the felt conflict, translates emotions and perceptions into conflict behaviors, and sets the stage for future conflicts. Thus communication is instrumental in every aspect of conflict, including conflict avoidance or suppression, the open expression of opposition, and the evolution of issues. (p. 552)

Thus, it is through communication that conflict is instantiated, and through communication that conflict is dealt with in productive and constructive—or sometimes unproductive and destructive—ways.

Levels of Organizational Conflict

As we have seen, organizational conflict can take place at a variety of levels. By far, the most research attention has been paid to the *interpersonal* level of conflict, the level at which individual members of the organization perceive goal incompatibility. However, conflict can also be present in the form of intergroup conflict and interorganizational conflict.

Intergroup conflict considers aggregates of people within an organization (e.g., work teams, departments) as parties in the conflict. As an illustration, two divisions fighting over scarce fiscal resources are involved in intergroup conflict. Not surprisingly, intergroup conflict can become complicated when members of a single group hold varying views about the conflict. For example, in labor negotiations, dissension often occurs among members of the union or members of the management team regarding how the conflict should be resolved. This suggests that intergroup conflict often involves both communication within the group in establishing a coherent position and communication between groups in negotiating differences.

Interorganizational conflict involves disputes between two or more organizations. This kind of conflict can involve both competition in the marketplace, perhaps between two stores competing for the same market share or two firms trying to get the same consulting contract. The more interesting interorganizational conflicts, however, may be those among organizations that are *working together*, perhaps in joint operating agreements or community consortiums. This level of conflict, then, emphasizes the role of "boundary spanners"—individuals on the "edges" of organizations who have significant interorganizational contact. For boundary spanners, interorganizational conflict is particularly stressful, because they are asked to understand the needs of both organizational insiders and the outsiders with whom the negotiation takes place (Adams, 1980).

Phases of Organizational Conflict

Individuals in organizations do not move suddenly from peaceful coexistence to conflict-ridden relationships. Rather, as Pondy (1967) has suggested, people move through phases as conflicts develop and subside. Pondy has suggested five phases that characterize organizational conflict. A summary of these is presented in Table 9.1.

As Table 9.1 indicates, organizational conflict can go through several phases before it becomes manifest in communicative interaction. The first phase, *latent conflict*, involves a situation in which the conditions are ripe for conflict because interdependence and possible incompatibility exist between the parties. The second phase, *perceived conflict*, occurs when one or more of the parties believes that incompatibilities and interdependence exist. It is possible, of course, to have latent conflict without perceived conflict. For example, two coworkers might have different ideas about the best way to organize a report, but this difference of opinion

Table 9.1 | Phases of Organizational Conflict

Phase	Description
Latent conflict	Grounds for conflict exist because parties are interacting in interdependent relationships in which incompatible goals are possible.
Perceived conflict	One or more parties perceive that their situation is characterized by incompatibility and interdependence.
Felt conflict	Parties begin to personalize perceived conflict by focusing on the conflict issue and planning conflict management strategies.
Manifest conflict	Conflict is enacted through communication. Interaction might involve cycles of escalation and de-escalation as various strategies are used.
Conflict aftermath	Conflict episode has both short-term and long-term effects on the individuals, their relationship, and the organization.

Based on Pondy, L. R. (1967). Organizational conflict: Concepts and models. *Administrative Science Quarterly*, 12, 296–320.

might not be an issue for either of them. It is also possible to have perceived conflict without latent conflict. This situation would exist, for instance, if a manager and a subordinate believed they had different standards about weekend work but actually had the same values.

During the third phase of conflict, *felt conflict*, the parties begin to formulate strategies about how to deal with the conflict and consider outcomes that would and would not be acceptable. These strategies and goals are enacted in communication during the *manifest conflict* phase. (Much of the rest of this chapter expands on what goes on during this conflict phase.) Finally, the last phase discussed by Pondy, *conflict aftermath*, emphasizes that conflicts can have both short-term and long-term consequences. Even after a conflict is "settled," it can change the nature of the individuals, their relationship, and their functioning within the organization.

MANAGING ORGANIZATIONAL CONFLICT

We have now developed a conceptualization of conflict by defining it and noting its characteristic phases and the levels at which it can materialize. In this section, we look at theory and research about how organizational members attempt to manage conflict. We use the term *conflict management* rather than *conflict resolution* because of the point made above about the ongoing nature of conflict and because of the complexity of most conflict situations. In discussing conflict management, we first turn to research on the various strategies that individuals use when involved in interpersonal conflict. We then discuss a more formal mode of managing conflict—negotiation. Finally, we examine the role that third parties can play in helping individuals cope with organizational conflicts.

Conflict Styles

Description   In Chapter 3, we talked about the Managerial Grid developed by Blake and Mouton (1964), who proposed that a manager's leadership style can be characterized in terms of the level of concern shown for productivity and the level of concern shown for people. For example, a manager displaying a high concern for people and a low concern for productivity was characterized as having a "country club" style of management.

Theorists studying organizational conflict have used the basic structure of the Managerial Grid as a way of exploring the styles and strategies people use when involved in interpersonal conflict. Indeed, the Managerial Grid has been described as the "conceptual grandparent" of conflict style research (Nicotera, Rodriguez, Hall, & Jackson, 1995). The analysis of conflict styles was most completely developed by Thomas (1976). In adapting the Managerial Grid for conflict situations, Thomas reconceptualized the two dimensions as *concern for self* and *concern for others*. He then identified five conflict styles that would fall at various points on this conflict grid. The conflict grid and resulting styles are presented in Figure 9.1.

These conflict styles can be illustrated by considering a specific conflict situation. Imagine that your boss has come to you with "some good news and some bad news." The good news is that the public relations firm you work for has a chance to attract an important new client. The bad news is that either you or your co-worker Wilma will have to spend a healthy portion of the weekend preparing the

Figure 9.1 | Conflict Management Styles

Adapted from Thomas, K. W. (1976). Conflict and conflict management. In M. Dunnette (Ed.), *Handbook of Industrial and Organizational Psychology*. Chicago: Rand-McNally. Used by permission of Marvin Dunnette.

proposal. Your boss has told you and Wilma to "work it out" and have a draft of the proposal ready to go on Monday morning. Neither you nor Wilma really wants to work on Saturday, but the work must get done. According to the conflict grid in Figure 9.1, you could approach this conflict in five distinct ways.

First, you could simply decide not to talk with Wilma about the problem because you know that the issue will not be easy to resolve. This strategy, *avoidance*, shows little concern for either your own needs or Wilma's. Not surprisingly, this strategy is rarely effective. Two other strategies emphasize one person's needs at the expense of the other person's needs. For example, by *accommodating*, you could simply volunteer to work on Saturday because you know Wilma wants the day off and you want to make her happy. This strategy, though, does nothing to satisfy your own needs. Or, you could pit your will against Wilma's, insisting that she must work because you cannot. This strategy, *competition*, might get you what you want, but Wilma's needs will be sacrificed in the process. A fourth strategy, *compromise*, could involve each of you working for four hours on Saturday. Although this strategy seems ideal in some ways, it means that neither you nor Wilma will be able to follow through on your weekend plans, because each of you has to work on Saturday, albeit for a shorter period of time. Finally, you might sit down with Wilma and *collaborate* to reach a solution that could benefit both of you. For example, you might find that you both have Thursday and Friday evenings free, and by working together you can write the proposal without relinquishing weekend plans.

Critique of Conflict Styles Construct The conflict styles framework has generated a great deal of research on organizational conflict, some of which we consider in the remainder of this chapter. However, this framework has also generated debate about how organizational conflict should best be studied. Knapp, Putnam, and Davis (1988) have identified four factors that limit the usefulness of the "grid" approach to organizational conflict. These factors are presented in Table 9.2.

The first criticism presented in Table 9.2 involves the extent to which a grid approach reflects the complex interactive nature of organizational conflict. By arguing that individuals possess particular conflict styles, the grid approach downplays the extent to which individuals change their tactics during interaction with others in conflict situations. For example, an individual might begin by attempting to collaborate, but having little success, might then force a solution on the other party. The second criticism presented in Table 9.2 addresses the two-dimensional nature of the conflict grid. Knapp and associates (1988) argue that issues other than concern for self and concern for others might influence a conflict interaction. For example, individuals might be worried about the political implications of communication or the impact of conflict resolution on the organization as a whole. Third, these scholars believe that research on conflict styles has downplayed the important roles that nonverbal and nonrational communication might play in conflict management. Finally, they contend that by concentrating on individual conflict style, the role of the organizational setting is ignored. An individual might deal very differently with conflict in a highly mechanistic company than in a more democratic and loosely structured one. This critique is in line with the *bona fide groups*

Table 9.2 | Criticisms of the Conflict Styles Approach

Critique 1	The conflict styles approach treats the individual communicator as the sole benchmark for conceptualizing conflict and for determining how it will develop.
Critique 2	The conflict styles approach relies too narrowly on two-dimensional theoretical models that may not be internally congruent, exhaustive, or representative of conflict-handling modes in organizations.
Critique 3	The conflict styles approach limits communication to verbal behaviors, especially those that are rational and uncomplicated, mutually exclusive across different styles, and static and unchanging.
Critique 4	The conflict styles approach treats the organization as being in the distant background rather than in the center stage of conflict activity.

Based on Knapp, M. L., Putnam, L. L., & Davis, L. J. (1988). Measuring interpersonal conflict in organizations: Where do we go from here? *Management Communication Quarterly*, 1, 414–429.

perspective discussed in Chapter 8 (Putnam & Stohl, 1996), which highlights the importance of the organizational context and culture and the interdependence of organization members in analyzing organizational communication situations.

New Directions   In recent years, communications scholars have looked beyond general issues of style in considering interpersonal conflict and have begun to pay more attention to details about message style and the perceptions of individuals in the conflict episode. For example, Jameson (2004) explored how individuals in conflict can satisfy a variety of organizational- and individual-level needs through politeness strategies in conflict interaction, and Meiners and Miller (2004) found that the level of formality in conflict interaction influenced the extent to which individuals were direct, detailed in their needs, and willing to make concessions. Gross, Guerrero, and Alberts (2004) considered perceptions of conflict management and found that people viewed controlling strategies as inappropriate when used by others and as highly effective when used by themselves.

A more comprehensive body of research has been developed by Jeffrey Kassing. Kassing is interested in a specific kind of conflict—that which occurs when an employee has a disagreement with the organization or supervisor and chooses to voice that disagreement through *dissent*. Kassing's research (1997; 2002; Kassing & Armstrong, 2002; Kassing & DiCioccio, 2004) has explored the ways in which employees choose to voice dissent in the workplace, to whom they voice that dissent, and factors that influence the likelihood of speaking up about organizational conflict.

Bargaining and Negotiation

A second general strategy for dealing with organizational conflict is bargaining (also referred to as negotiation). According to Putnam and Poole (1987),

> Bargaining constitutes a unique form of conflict management in that participants nego-
> tiate mutually shared rules and then cooperate within these rules to gain a competitive

Case in Point: Working with Jerks

For some people, conflict seems to be a way of life. If you have one of these individuals as a coworker—or even worse, as a boss—your work life can be made miserable. Conflict can shift into bullying and permeate an organizational culture. Robert Sutton, a professor of management science at Stanford University, has heard all the stories about "working with jerks," and wrote *The No A****** Rule* (2007, see references for uncensored title!).

Sutton argues that jerks who elevate the level of conflict and stress in an organization are easy to spot: "the main sign of someone who's a certified jerk is someone who leaves a trail of people feeling demeaned and de-energized. It tends to be more often associated with power dynamics—they kiss-up to those above them and kick those beneath them" ("Advice for Tackling Workplace Jerks," 2007). In the language of conflict management styles, these individuals are always confrontational and are unable to collaborate or appreciate the other person's perspective.

What to do if you find yourself working with a jerk? Sutton suggests that organizations can work to screen these individuals in the hiring process so that jerks don't enter the system. Or you could take the extreme action of quitting if you just can't work with the jerk anymore. But Sutton's best suggestion is to learn to avoid them as much as possible and learn not to care. Sutton recounts one example:

> My favorite story comes from a former CEO who told about her worst board member. When he'd call and scream, she'd lean back in her chair, put her feet on the desk, put him on speakerphone, turn off the volume and do her nails. She would check in from time to time to see if he was still screaming. When he was done; she would reason with him. She put herself in a relaxed position and did something she could control—her nails. ("Advice," 2007)

We may not all be in a position to do our nails to cope with a jerk. But the strategy of avoiding and maintaining control is certainly advice we should "file" away.

advantage over their opponent . . . Bargaining, then, differs from other forms of conflict in its emphasis on proposal exchanges as a basis for reaching a joint settlement in cooperative-competitive situations. (p. 563)

Several characteristics of bargaining are important. First, bargaining is often a *formal* activity in which disputants settle conflicts about scarce resources or policy disagreements. Formal bargaining is marked by a clear understanding of (and adherence to) the rules of the negotiation situation. For example, one rule bargainers often follow is the rule of "mutual concessions." According to this rule, if one party in the conflict gives something up, the other party should concede an issue of like value. Second, bargaining often involves individuals who serve as representatives for the parties in the dispute. Third, bargaining is the strategy often used to settle intergroup or interorganizational conflicts. For example, disputes between labor and management are typically settled through formal negotiation.

An important distinction often made about bargaining is that of *distributive* and *integrative* bargaining (Walton & McKersie, 1965). Distributive and integrative bargaining differ in terms of goals, issues, communication processes, and outcomes. These differences are summarized in Table 9.3.

In *distributive bargaining*, the two conflicting parties are working to maximize their own gains and minimize their own losses. The bargaining centers on the limited resources that must be divided in the negotiation (e.g., wages, benefits, hours).

Table 9.3 | Comparison of Distributive and Integrative Bargaining

	Distributive Bargaining	Integrative Bargaining
Goals	Maximize individual gains and minimize losses	Maximize joint gains
Issues	Fixed-sum issues with limited resources	Variable-sum issues shaped by overlapping positions
Outcomes	Compromises, trade-offs, and win–lose results	Creative solutions not attributable to specific concessions
Communication	Information seeking, withholding data, and deception in disclosures	Open sharing of information, accurate disclosure of needs and objectives

Based on Putnam, L. L., & Poole, M. S. (1987). Conflict and negotiation. In F. Jablin, L. Putnam, K. Roberts, & L. Porter (Eds.), *Handbook of Organizational Communication: An Interdisciplinary Perspective* (pp. 549–599). Newbury Park, CA: Sage.

Because bargainers are working with a "fixed pot," the only possible outcomes are win–lose solutions or compromises. Finally, because the bargainers are concerned with their own outcomes, communication is marked by withheld information, deception, and attempts to learn as much as possible about the other party's position.

In *integrative bargaining*, the conflicting parties are trying to maximize gains for both parties. Thus, the bargainers discuss issues that could lead to a more creative solution to the problem at hand. Outcomes of integrative bargaining are often solutions that allow both parties to benefit, and communication tends to be marked by open disclosure, careful listening, and multiple communication channels. In its integrative form, bargaining can serve "as a forum for identifying problems, clarifying misconceptions, signaling needs and interests, and negotiating the meaning of organizational events" (Putnam, 1995, p. 196).

Consider, for instance, a labor dispute between a nurses union and the administration of a large hospital. Often, bargainers in this situation take a distributive approach. They concentrate on issues such as salary, working hours, vacation time, and health care benefits and try to "get" as much as possible (or "give" as little as possible) in the negotiation. The actual bargaining sessions would be marked by distrust and information provided in spurts and starts. However, the parties could choose to take an integrative approach to the negotiation. In this case, the bargainers might work on developing a new organizational model in which nurses share in management and participate in fiscal decision making and profit sharing. The development of such a solution would be difficult and would involve intense communication and problem solving, but could benefit both parties in the long run.

Third-Party Conflict Resolution

There are times when the individuals (or groups) involved in a conflict are unable to resolve the disagreement on their own either through informal discussion or formal negotiation. At these times, a third party is often relied on to help resolve the conflict. Sometimes the "third party" might be a friend or coworker who is brought in to help settle the conflict or to provide support for one of the parties (Volkema, Bergmann, & Farquhar, 1997). Especially in conflicts of a relational nature, individuals often can gain important insights from those who are not directly involved in the organizational context (Myers & Larson, 2005). However, much of the research on third-party conflict resolution in the organizational context has considered the actions of a manager in resolving a conflict or the case when a mediator or an arbitrator is brought in from outside of the organization.

Managerial Conflict Resolution   Often, conflicts between coworkers stem from differences in working style or personality. Other times, disputes may arise over work processes or organizational procedures. If such differences come to a head, a supervisor might be called in to help settle the dispute.

A number of scholars have investigated the various roles that managers can play in resolving organizational conflict (Karambayya & Brett, 1989; Kolb, 1986; Kolb & Glidden, 1986; Sheppard, 1984; Thibaut & Walker, 1975). These roles, presented in Table 9.4, vary in a number of ways. For example, a manager might address a dispute by dictating both the resolution procedure and the outcome (the "inquisitor" role), by rewarding or punishing subordinates in order to facilitate a solution (the "motivator" role), or by working to change the organization in order to keep similar problems from occurring in the future (the "restructurer" role). Elangovan (1995) suggests that these strategies vary in terms of whether a manager controls procedures (e.g., what can and cannot be used as evidence in a dispute) and outcomes (e.g., how, specifically, a dispute should be resolved), and the degree to which a manager controls a dispute or shares (or cedes) control with the parties in conflict.

Research suggests that managers brought in to handle disputes do not use these third-party roles with equal frequency. For example, Karambayya and Brett (1989) and Sheppard (1984) found that managerial third parties are most likely to play the inquisitor, mediator, or motivator role. Nor, according to research, are these roles equally effective in settling disputes. Karambayya and Brett (1989) and Karambayya, Brett, and Lytle (1992) found that decisions made by a manager serving in a mediator role were perceived to be more fair by the disputants. Similarly, Weider-Hatfield and Hatfield (1996) found that managers who used collaborative techniques were evaluated much more favorably than managers who used coercive techniques.

Outside Conflict Resolution   Third parties from outside the organization also sometimes assist in settling disputes. These third parties typically serve as either *mediators* or *arbitrators*. A mediator attempts to help the parties facilitate the dispute but holds no decision power. In contrast, an arbitrator makes decisions (often binding) based on the proposals and arguments of the parties involved in the conflict. For example, major league baseball players often go to arbitration to settle

Table 9.4 | Managerial Third-Party Conflict Resolution Roles

Role	Description
Inquisitor	Third party exercises control over both the process and the outcome of conflict resolution.
Judge	Third party exercises control over the outcome but not the process of conflict resolution.
Mediator/advisor	Third party counsels parties who maintain control over both the process and the outcome.
Motivator	Third party uses threats and incentives to encourage resolution of the conflict.
Investigator	Third party ferrets out facts of dispute and presents them to relevant authority.
Restructurer	Third party uses authority to redesign the organization in a way that will resolve the conflict.
Problem solver	Third party attempts to discover underlying conditions that have led to the conflict.
Procedural marshal	Third party describes and enforces rules for conflict resolution.

contract disputes. The arbitrator hears the proposals and arguments of both the players and team management and decides on one proposal or the other without compromise.

Information sharing and persuasion are important forms of communication in arbitration. However, the role of communication is even more pronounced in mediation, as the parties in mediation are working together to develop a viable solution to the conflict at hand. There are a variety of tactics that mediators can use to facilitate effective communication in mediation. These strategies include *directive tactics*, in which the mediator initiates recommendations; *nondirective tactics*, in which the mediator attempts to secure information and clarify misunderstandings; *procedural tactics*, in which the mediator establishes an agenda and protocol for conflict resolution; and *reflexive tactics*, in which the mediator regulates the tone of the interaction by "developing rapport with participants, using humor, and speaking the language of each side" (Putnam & Poole, 1987, p. 572).

FACTORS INFLUENCING THE CONFLICT MANAGEMENT PROCESS

We have now looked at a wide array of conflict management techniques. Individuals involved in interpersonal conflict can and do use a variety of strategies that differ in terms of the attention given to self and other in the conflict. The formal give and take of bargaining and negotiation can be exercised. Or, a third party such as a manager, arbitrator, or mediator can be brought in to settle conflicts that seem intractable. But when will these various strategies be used? And when will they work to manage the conflict effectively? Although the research on these issues

Case in Point: Conflict in the Courts

In this chapter, we have considered various forms of conflict in the workplace. However, conflict can influence workplace behavior even when it is just a possibility looming in the future. Organizational behavior can be affected by the perceived threat of a lawsuit, for example, a common occurrence in a nation that many believe is becoming increasingly litigious (Taylor & Thomas, 2003). Consider the following: An automobile manufacturer can be sued for the faulty design or engineering of a car. A physician can be sued for malpractice if surgery goes wrong. A teacher can be sued if parents feel their child was disciplined inappropriately. The possibility of such lawsuits can, of course, change workplace behavior in a variety of ways.

Some see the possibility of a lawsuit as a force for good in the workplace. The threat of conflict in the courtroom is likely to improve quality control in manufacturing, encourage physicians to establish good relationships with patients, and make educators think twice before treating kids in ways that might be seen as inappropriate. But others see a dark side to increased litigation. Corporations with "deep pockets" can be blamed for the irresponsible behavior of those using their products. Physicians may have to close their practices as malpractice insurance increases or they may engage in "defensive medicine" or fail to be forthcoming about possible problems. And teachers may feel their hands are tied if they cannot maintain control in the classroom and have to worry that every comment and action could be misinterpreted. There is no straightforward solution to this thorny problem, though many remedies have been suggested (see Taylor & Thomas, 2003). What is clear, though, is that even the possibility of courtroom conflict can significantly affect communication in a wide array of organizations.

is too vast to summarize here, we will consider three factors that influence the conflict management process, specifically personal, relational, and cultural factors.

Personal Factors

It might seem that individual characteristics such as personality and gender would strongly influence how conflict is resolved. Indeed, our cultural stereotypes suggest that men are more likely to use competitive strategies, whereas women are prone to accommodate or compromise. It also seems likely that people's conflict management strategies would vary according to their personal characteristics, such as aggressiveness, introversion, or need for control.

However, Putnam and Poole's (1987) review of studies indicates that, to the contrary, personality plays a small role in conflict resolution strategies and that the findings on gender differences are mixed. Indeed, some of the research findings on gender differences contradict our stereotypical expectations. For example, Turner and Henzl (1987) found that women were very assertive when managing conflict. And Burrell, Buzzanell, and McMillan (1992) found that female managers described conflicts using the typically "male" metaphors of war and aggression. Thus, personality and gender have limited impact on conflict management tactics.

It does appear, however, that the way an individual *frames* a conflict will influence the manner in which the conflict is managed (Neale & Bazerman, 1985; Simons, 1993). The framing of a conflict can involve perceptions of self, of others, or of the conflict itself (Lewicki, Gray, & Elliott, 2003). For example, individuals

Spotlight on Scholarship

Many of the ideas in this chapter involve individuals or small groups of people working through conflicts and reaching resolutions. However, many organizational conflicts involve larger institutional entities and may continue over many years. Indeed, for some of these conflicts it seems that no resolution is in sight. It is this kind of conflict—*intractable conflict*—that Linda Putnam and Tarla Peterson consider in their examination of the "Edwards Aquifer" dispute. An intractable conflict is one that is long-standing and eludes resolution. As Putnam and Wondolleck (2003) explain,

> Intractable conflicts are messy. They are hard to pin down, manage, and analyze, and extremely difficult to resolve. They are intense, frustrating, and complex, with no readily conceivable solutions. (p. 37)

Global warming policy, the Vietnam War, abortion rights and regulations—all of these could be seen as intractable conflicts.

Putnam and Peterson (2003) consider a more regional intractable conflict—that involving the Edwards Aquifer in the south-central region of Texas. The Edwards Aquifer is an underground water formation that provides water not only to a large number of Texans (including the residents of San Antonio, the nation's seventh-largest city) but also to farms in the region and to the native flora and fauna. The aquifer is a renewable resource that is "exceptionally responsive to rainfall and drought" (Putnam & Peterson, 2003, p. 128). That is, when rainfall is plentiful, the aquifer replenishes itself, but in times of drought, the aquifer level drops to a point where the springs cease to flow. This pattern has been exacerbated by the increased use of the aquifer over time.

Not surprisingly, there has been a great deal of conflict over *who* should have control of the Edwards Aquifer and *how* that control should be exercised. Players in the conflict include local, regional, state, and federal agencies including urban municipalities,

organizations of farmers and rural residents, and environmental agencies. The conflict has involved mediation, negotiation, legislation, and litigation. It is, of course, impossible to review all of the details of the fifty-plus years of this conflict. However, after considering interviews with seventy stakeholders and the extensive media coverage of the conflict, Putnam and Peterson (2003) conclude that the way the conflict is framed contributes to its ongoing intractability.

Putnam and Peterson (2003) consider three types of conflict frames. The first, *identity frames*, refers to how stakeholders describe their own roles in the conflict. Putnam and Peterson note, for instance, that identity frames might involve interests (e.g., private property rights vs. the public good), place (e.g., urban vs. rural), or institution (e.g., coalitions formed during the conflict). A second type of frame, *characterization frames*, involves how disputants see the other parties in the conflict. In intractable conflicts, these frames often involve polarized and stereotyped categories for understanding others. Finally, disputants use *conflict management frames* to consider ways in which the conflict has been managed in the past or might be managed in the future. For example, if past efforts at mediation and negotiation are framed in negative ways, future frames for conflict negotiation may be more likely to involve resistance strategies than efforts at cooperation. In short, Putnam and Peterson believe these frames often contribute to the seemingly unresolvable nature of intractable conflicts. However, the use of frame analysis also points to the possibility for change and resolution. Indeed, efforts to reframe the conflict in more productive ways have led Putnam and Peterson to a cautiously hopeful prognosis for the Edwards Aquifer case and other seemingly intractable conflicts.

Putnam, L. L., & Peterson, T. (2003). The Edwards Aquifer Dispute: Shifting Frames in a Protracted Conflict. In R. J. Lewicki, B. Gray, and M. Elliott (eds.), *Making Sense of Intractable Environmental Conflicts: Frames and Cases* (pp. 127–158). Washington, DC: Island Press.

in conflict can frame the situation in terms of what they have to lose or in terms of what they have to gain. Neale and Bazerman (1985) found that individuals who frame conflict in terms of losses will be much more likely to take risks than those who frame conflict in terms of gains. Individuals using a frame in terms of loss are also more likely to reach an impasse and seek arbitration. Neale and Bazerman also found that negotiators who were overconfident were less likely to be successful in resolving the conflict.

Relational Factors

In contrast to personal factors, the *relationship* between the conflict parties appears to have a strong impact on conflict resolution. One important characteristic of the relationship between the conflict parties is *power*, or the hierarchical position of the individuals. Putnam and Poole (1987) have reviewed the literature on hierarchical level and conflict styles. Several findings stand out. First, it appears that organizational members generally prefer competitive styles when dealing with subordinates. However, these individuals are likely to use accommodation or collaboration when dealing with superiors and accommodating or avoiding styles when dealing with peers. Thus, conflict management style depends to a large extent on the hierarchical relationship between the conflict parties. Conflicts with supervisors and administrators are also recalled as more emotionally intense than conflicts with individuals at the same hierarchical level (Gayle & Preiss, 1998).

Another aspect of the relationship between conflict parties is how the relationship influences the interaction through which conflict is managed. For example, Jameson (2004) argued that organizations and their members often struggle with opposing needs for autonomy and connection. That is, workers depend on each other—but also want to maintain independence—and this basic relational contradiction can cause conflict. In a study of conflict between anesthesiologists and certified registered nurse anesthetists, Jameson (2004) found that individuals can use politeness strategies to keep these competing needs balanced and forge more collaborative solutions to conflict situations.

Cultural Factors

Finally, aspects of organizational, national, and ethnic culture might influence the ways in which conflict is enacted and managed in organizations. With regard to national culture, for instance, Brett and Okumura (1998) found that *intercultural* negotiations between U.S. and Japanese negotiators were far less successful than *intracultural* negotiations among these two national groups. These researchers found that U.S. and Japanese negotiators worked from different conflict "scripts," and although the Japanese negotiators understood the U.S. priorities, the U.S. negotiators did not understand the Japanese schema. Also, Japanese negotiators paid much more attention to power and hierarchical position in the negotiation, and the mismatch in approaches to power limited gains for both groups.

Ethnic and racial culture also may play a role in conflict negotiation. For example, Shuter and Turner (1997; Turner & Shuter, 2004) recently compared African American women and European American women in terms of their approaches to and perceptions of conflict. In terms of the nature of conflict, both groups viewed conflict negatively, but the perceptions of African American women were particularly negative and passive. In terms of conflict resolution, both groups saw themselves as choosing to reduce conflict in the workplace, but that perception was not shared by the other group. Further, European American women were seen as being conflict avoidant and African American women reported as using more direct means of conflict resolution.

Finally, several scholars have investigated how organizational culture can influence the conflict resolution process. This work emphasizes the extent to which conflict resolution can be difficult when organizational subcultures based on professional identity or hierarchical position do not see eye to eye. For example, Geist (1995) examined conflict within hospices, school systems, and hospitals to demonstrate how the culture built around power relationships, technology, and the interests of organizational groups can influence perceptions of conflict and how conflict is managed. Similarly, Smith and Eisenberg (1987) examined a labor dispute at Disneyland, arguing that the subcultures of the workers and management were distinct, with managers seeing Disney as "show business" or "drama" and workers seeing Disney as "family." Thus, in the labor conflict, workers looked at the contract proposals set out by management and were appalled because "this is no way to treat members of your family." In turn, management was shocked when workers went on strike because in showbiz "the show must go on."

An Alternative View of Conflict

To a great extent, the ideas we have looked at so far in this chapter are rooted in a traditional view of conflict. Oh, there are definite differences among the approaches described here. An individual using a "collaborative style" will behave differently in a conflict situation than an individual using either an "accommodating" or "competition" style. And there are clear distinctions between distributive bargaining and integrative bargaining in terms of goals, issues, outcomes, and communication processes. But in spite of these differences, all of the research considered here is based on a view of conflict rooted in the concept of *exchange*. In viewing conflict and negotiation as exchange, scholars and practitioners concentrate on goals and resources, on offers and counteroffers, on moves and concessions, and even on creating a "bigger pie" that can satisfy all parties.

Putnam and Kolb (2000) have suggested that exchange in these models of conflict and negotiation is a *gendered practice*. Specifically, they argue that negotiation:

> is gendered in that the qualities of effective bargainers (e.g., individuality and independence, competition, objectivity, analytic rationality, instrumentality, reasoning from universal principles, and strategic thinking) are linked to masculinity. Those attributes typically labeled as feminine (e.g., community, subjectivity, intuition, emotionality, expressiveness, reasoning from particulars, and ad hoc thinking) are less valued. (p. 80)

In response to the masculine exchange model of negotiation, Putnam and Kolb propose a feminist view of conflict based instead on the co-construction of the situation and relationship through collaboration, the sharing of experience and emotion, dialogic interaction, and mutual understanding. The contrast between the traditional exchange model of conflict and Putnam and Kolb's alternative model is presented in Table 9.5. Putnam and Kolb understand that "at first blush, the alternative approach may seem naive, simple, or unnatural" (p. 81). However, they

Table 9.5 | Traditional and Alternative Models of Conflict and Negotiation

Traditional Model	Alternative Model
Exchange	*Co-Construction*
Trades	Mutual inquiry
Reciprocity	Integration
Balance	Blended
Equity	Equality
Transaction	Collaboration
Goals	
Enlightened self-interest	Self-knowledge
Mutual gain	Mutual understanding
Outcomes	
Settlement	Transformation
Agreements	Jointly developed actions
Win–lose, win–win, lose–lose	Changing conflict
Relationships	
Other as distant	Other as approachable
Interdependence through desired ends	Interdependence through connectedness
Extrinsic	Intrinsic
Instrumental	Expressive
Cooperative/competitive motivation	Motivated through mutual recognition
Trust/distrust	Empathy
Rational	Emotional
Process as Activity	
Proposals/counterproposals	Offering perspectives
Making concessions	Re-sourcement/reframing
Problem solving	Dialogue
Process as Social Interaction	
Debate	Deliberation and invitational rhetoric
Information exchange	Sharing experiences
Strategies and tactics	Expressions and circular questions

From Putnam, L. L., & Kolb, D. M. (2000). Rethinking negotiation: Feminist views of communication and exchange. In P. M. Buzzanell (Ed.), *Rethinking Organizational and Managerial Communication from Feminist Perspectives*. Thousand Oaks, CA: Sage. Reproduced with permission of Sage Publications Inc. Books via Copyright Clearance Center.

convincingly argue that their feminist model is an important advance that might be particularly appropriate in situations such as "informal work negotiations, bargaining in long-term relationships, role negotiations, and even intractable disputes" (p. 104). In short, this model provides a new way to think about conflict and perhaps opens new avenues for practice in organizational communication.

SUMMARY

In this chapter, we looked at a ubiquitous facet of organizational life: conflict. We first conceptualized organizational conflict by defining conflict and considering the phases of conflict and the levels at which it can materialize. We then reviewed a number of methods for dealing with organizational conflict. We looked at the literature on conflict style and considered criticisms of the style approach. We then looked at more formal ways of settling organizational dispute: bargaining and negotiation. Then we considered third-party intervention. In the last section of the chapter, we looked at a number of factors that impinge on the conflict management process, including personal variables (personality, gender, and frames), relational variables (hierarchical position and co-orientation), and cultural variables. We concluded with a brief look at a feminist view of culture.

All of the approaches to organizational communication discussed in the first half of this textbook would view conflict as an important and interesting phenomenon, but they would do so in very different ways. As Table 9.6 indicates,

Table 9.6 | Approaches to the Conflict Management Process

Approach	How Conflict Management Would Be Considered
Classical	Conflict is viewed as a breakdown of communication. Conflict is managed (often by third parties) to the extent that existence of conflict detracts from organizational efficiency.
Human relations	Conflict is viewed negatively as evidence of faulty relationships among organizational members. Conflicting parties are encouraged to avoid conflicts or compromise in order to return to harmonious work relations.
Human resources	Conflict is viewed as a possible means for growth and development in the organization. Conflicting parties are encouraged to collaborate on solutions that will satisfy both parties and contribute to better future organizational functioning.
Systems	Conflict is conceptualized as cycles of activities that can escalate and de-escalate. Possibility for conflict varies with the interdependencies created through communication network structure.
Cultural	Conflict stems from and can be revealed through differential metaphors and value systems of individuals and groups. Organizational cultures vary in terms of their level of conflict.
Critical	Superficial organizational conflicts reflect deeper imbalances of power based on class structure, economics, or gender and are revealed and sustained through organizational discourse.

classical theorists would see conflict as something that interrupts normal organizational functioning. Thus, the classical manager would try to eliminate conflict in the most efficient way possible. The human relations manager, too, would want to eliminate conflict, but for different reasons. For this manager, conflict is an indication that relationships are not all they could be in the organization. Conflict should thus be dealt with in ways that wouldn't rock the boat—perhaps through accommodating, avoiding, or compromising. In contrast, the human resources manager would consider both the functional and dysfunctional aspects of conflict. This manager would see conflict as a pathway to organizational change and would encourage managing conflict in a collaborative manner.

We have already talked about studies that are based on the systems and cultural approaches to organizational communication. A systems approach would look at the cycles of conflict and consider the role of the larger organizational system in encouraging or discouraging conflict behavior. For example, a recent study of the ombuds system within a university considered the ways in which conflict resolution systems should take systems factors into account in the development process (Harrison & Morrill, 2004). A cultural approach would consider the extent to which cultural markers such as values and metaphors contribute to and reflect conflictual relationships in the organization. Further, cultural researchers would be particularly interested in how culture emerges through individual choices about language in interaction (Holmes & Stubbe, 2003). Finally, organizational conflict is central to the work of the critical theorist. The critical scholar, however, would see the enacted conflicts among individuals and work groups as symptomatic of deeper conflicts based on differences of class, gender, or economic conditions. For the critical theorist, then, further conflict should be encouraged to the extent that conflict serves as a pathway to the emancipation of subjugated organizational groups and individuals.

Discussion Questions

1. Conflict is defined in this chapter as requiring the "three I's": incompatible goals, interdependence, and interaction. Why are these three components necessary? What situations might arise when only one or two of these components are present?
2. Do you believe that you exhibit a typical conflict style? If so, why do you think you use that style? Are there aspects of a situation or of the other parties in a conflict that influence the conflict style you use?
3. What are the differences between integrative and distributive strategies in conflict situations? Why would you use one type of strategy over another? What are the costs of using each of these strategies?
4. Would you want to have an organization that is free of conflict? Why or why not?

CASE STUDY | **The Problem with Teamwork**

Mike Garcia and Jill Hendrickson have been butting heads for months. Mike is a manufacturing manager at Auto Safety Products, a firm in the Midwest that designs and produces automobile seat belts and infant and child safety seats. Jill is a design engineer for the same firm. Recently, top management at Auto Safety Products instituted "concurrent engineering," a new team-based system that integrates manufacturing and design processes. Concurrent engineering is intended to eliminate the problems that often occur in industry when designers are unaware of the needs of manufacturing and vice versa. Through concurrent engineering, management hopes to improve attention to all elements of the product life cycle and manufacture a quality, low-cost product that will meet user needs. The company is also hoping to decrease the amount of time it takes to move from initial conceptual design to actual production.

Mike and Jill are both on the team working on toddler booster seats. This is an important product for Auto Safety Products, as research has indicated that parents do not use safety seats once children reach toddler age, in part because they are difficult to use in cars and uncomfortable for children. As a result, many parents don't use the booster seats correctly, cancelling out any safety benefit. Thus, the team at Auto Safety Products is working to make the seats easier for parents to use by making them more comfortable, more portable, and more compatible with a range of automobiles, from small sports cars to sedans to minivans to SUVs.

Mike is 55 years old and has worked in manufacturing for most of his life, 22 years with Auto Safety Products. He has always felt some animosity toward the design side of the firm. He finds the engineers "uppity" and unwilling to listen to the problems faced in manufacturing. He has often complained that the design department generates "pie in the sky" projects that run into all sorts of practical problems once they hit manufacturing. He approached the new concurrent engineering program at Auto Safety Products with a grain of salt. He thought that it was a good idea in principle ("those guys in design could use a dose of reality"), but he was not convinced that it would ever work in actuality.

Jill is a 25-year-old mechanical engineer who has been with Auto Safety Products since her college graduation three years ago. She is assertive and strong-minded—she believes she has to be to be effective in the male-dominated world of engineering. She learned about the concurrent engineering concept when she was in school and believes it can greatly improve the effectiveness of design and manufactur-

ing. Unfortunately, it does not seem ... Auto Safety Products. The manufac...... side has not really bought into the process, and management did not take the time to introduce the team management system properly and train people to work together. Even though she tries to be open to the ideas of manufacturing, she does not feel this effort is being reciprocated. Her concerns go in one ear and out the other. She is having an especially hard time with Mike Garcia, the lead manufacturing representative on her team. Recently, the two of them have had to work together frequently on a booster seat design problem, trying to adapt the design so that it will work in a variety of minivans. Their inability to work together has gotten so bad that their supervisor has set up a meeting to help them deal with the problem.

Adam Shapiro is a project supervisor at Auto Safety Products. He oversees the booster seat project team that Mike Garcia and Jill Hendrickson work on. He knows the two of them have not hit it off on the concurrent engineering team and has decided that the conflict has gotten to the point where he must step in and help them settle it. He first asked each of them separately about the problem.

According to Jill, the problem is that Mike will not listen to her ideas and downplays the contributions that design can make to concurrent engineering. In contrast, she sees design as the most important part of the concurrent engineering process. She suspects that Mike has problems with her because she is young and a woman, and this has made her push even harder for her point of view on project disagreements.

According to Mike, the concurrent engineering system—and the booster seat team in particular—is a joke. He says that the design engineers are still trying to push their ideas down manufacturing's throat, and he's tired of the "team" facade. He would like to go back to doing things the old way. However, if he is forced to continue with the concurrent engineering system, he refuses to simply give in to every one of Jill Hendrickson's whims.

| **The Problem with Teamwork** *continued*

As Adam ponders these divergent positions, Jill and Mike enter his office. Neither of them looks particularly happy.

CASE ANALYSIS QUESTIONS

1. What kind of predispositions are Mike and Jill taking into this conflict situation? How might these predispositions influence the way they frame the conflict and the way they approach each other?

2. If Mike and Jill were to attempt to deal with this conflict on their own, what conflict style would you recommend? Given what you know about Jill and Mike, do you think they would use an effective conflict resolution style?

3. If you were Adam Shapiro, how would you approach this conflict? What third-party role should you take, and what strategies should you use to help Mike and Jill deal with their ongoing problems?

4. How would a feminist approach to conflict see this situation? Is it possible to use an alternative model that would recast this situation in a more productive frame?

Organizational Change and Leadership Processes

CHAPTER 10

AFTER READING THIS CHAPTER, YOU SHOULD . . .

- Appreciate that change is often a natural part of organizational life cycles that can appear in the guise of organizational crisis or be carefully planned and implemented
- Know the typical problems associated with planned change processes and be aware of the communication strategies that can address these problems
- Understand the stages of organizational crisis as forms of "unplanned" change
- Be able to trace the development of leadership models from trait and style theories through contingency theories to contemporary theories such as the transformational leadership model
- Appreciate the complex communicative choices that leaders must make and be able to describe specific tools for delivering leadership messages

As the old saying goes, there is nothing so constant as change. Indeed, the constancy of change becomes more and more apparent as we move further into this new millennium, and the rate of change seems to increase on a daily basis. Zorn, Page, and Cheney (2000) have argued that organizational practitioners today are "Nuts about Change," as the mantra chanted both within the organization and from management gurus is that organizations must "organize for continuous change, to become a flexible organization that can adapt quickly to environmental changes" (pp. 516–517). Zorn et al. believe that we should, perhaps, question the wisdom of this mantra, but the fact remains that in terms of rhetoric and action, change is likely to remain a central concern in organizational life.

Although change is an enduring feature of organizational life, the degree and impact of that change can vary substantially. Sometimes the change is huge and life altering. Imagine, for instance, the changes that could occur if your company merged with another organization, possibly forcing layoffs, job redefinitions, and massive shifts in company mission and processes. Sometimes the change is large but seems more manageable. For example, your work group might decide to adopt a "Six Sigma" production and management system that would influence many aspects of your work life. Most of the time, though, the changes are more mundane and simply a part of the fabric of organizational life. Your boss might ask you to write reports in a different way, or the organization might adopt new standards for customer service follow-ups.

In this chapter, then, we will consider processes of organizational change and the role of communication in these processes. We will first look at scholarship on planned and unplanned change in organizations. We will consider models of how change occurs in organizations, the roles and reactions of employees, and how communication is woven into change experiences. We will also consider times of major change when organizations face crises. And as we consider the change process, we will find that, as in much of organizational life, the success of such processes often depends on having effective leadership. The second portion of this chapter, then, will consider classic and contemporary models of leadership and look at the role of communication in the leadership process.

ORGANIZATIONAL CHANGE PROCESSES

Models of Organizational Change

No organization that remains static—stuck in particular ways of doing things and particular modes of thinking—will survive long. We can all, for example, think of products such as eight-track audiotapes and beta videotapes that have been lost to history because their makers did not anticipate changes in consumer tastes and habits or changes in the industrial marketplace. Similarly, organizations that get stuck in procedural or managerial ruts are often not long-lived. However, many organizations naturally evolve and adapt to environmental needs.

There are models of organizational life cycles (Kimberly & Miles, 1980) and the evolution of organizational populations (Hannan & Freeman, 1989) that consider the "natural" ways in which organizations and groups of organizations change with the ebb and flow of institutional life and industry history. As a highly simplistic example, the "natural" life cycle of a consulting firm might include a start-up phase in which the company develops a market and creates systems and procedures, a growth phase in which client relationships are developed and the size of the company grows, a steady "harvest" phase in which the company serves existing clients, and a decay stage in which the consulting firm's services become less relevant to the marketplace and the firm eventually folds or is bought by another company.

Other models of organizational change look at situations in which there is a *planned* change. Oftentimes organizations are confronted with problems in the environment or with internal contingencies that suggest that current "ways of doing things" are not effective. Perhaps a competitor starts cutting into the market share of a consumer products company. Or perhaps the new company president decides that it is critical to develop a new culture that emphasizes enhanced customer service. In these cases, many organizations will begin a purposeful process of change over time. This change over time may have identifiable phases (Bullock & Batten, 1985), as the organization explores the need for change and possible solutions, plans for how that change is to be instituted, implements the change and disseminates information about the change, and then integrates those changes into the day-to-day operations of the organization.

Of course, the implementation of planned change is not a simple and straightforward process. For example, Jian (2007) recently argued that there are many unintended consequences of planned change, especially because the senior managers who initiate the change might have very different ideas about the change than the employees who implement the change. Given the complicated nature of communication within each of these groups and the sometimes limited interaction between top management and employees, even a meticulously planned change can have unanticipated outcomes.

Connor and Lake (1994) have presented a model of planned change that illustrates the complexity of communication and behavior during the change process. This model is presented in Figure 10.1. This figure illustrates that planned change might involve a number of different types of change (e.g., individual behavior, organizational processes, strategic direction) and might be accomplished through a variety of methods (e.g., technical, structural, or managerial). Further, because of the interdependencies among task, structure, culture, and strategy, no change process will be straightforward.

Consider, for example, a school system that is instituting a new method for teaching reading. This change might be brought into play because of national standards such as the "No Child Left Behind" initiative, because of changes in the school population, or because of new and exciting developments in elementary school pedagogy. Regardless of the impetus for the change, factors such as individual school culture, existing textbooks and lesson plans, and community involvement and pressure will make this change process an extremely complicated undertaking. However, the model in Figure 10.1 and others like it (e.g., Dwyer, 2000; Harvey, 1995) suggest that many organizational practitioners are very concerned with ways of *managing* change rather than simply letting the "organizational life cycle" take its course. As More (1998, p. 30) argues, "successful organizations are those that initiate change, respond to change, plan change, and implement change as an ongoing way of life."

Reactions to Organizational Change

Of course, as even these idealized models of change make clear, change may not proceed in a particularly smooth fashion. Perhaps change would be easy if members of organizations were like the "cogs" described in classical and mechanistic views of organizational behavior (see Chapter 2). In such an organization, the "thinking" management could devise ideal processes for changing organizational activity and simply "tell" the workers what changes should be made. However, as we know from alternative models of organizing, such a simple process is unlikely (and probably undesirable). Instead, we now appreciate that organizations are cultural and political systems inhabited by thinking and feeling human beings. Thus, it is critical to look at how employees might react to and influence the organizational change process. For example, Kuhn and Corman (2003) have recently suggested that organizational members have "schemata," or knowledge structures, that define individual and collective beliefs about how organizations work and how change

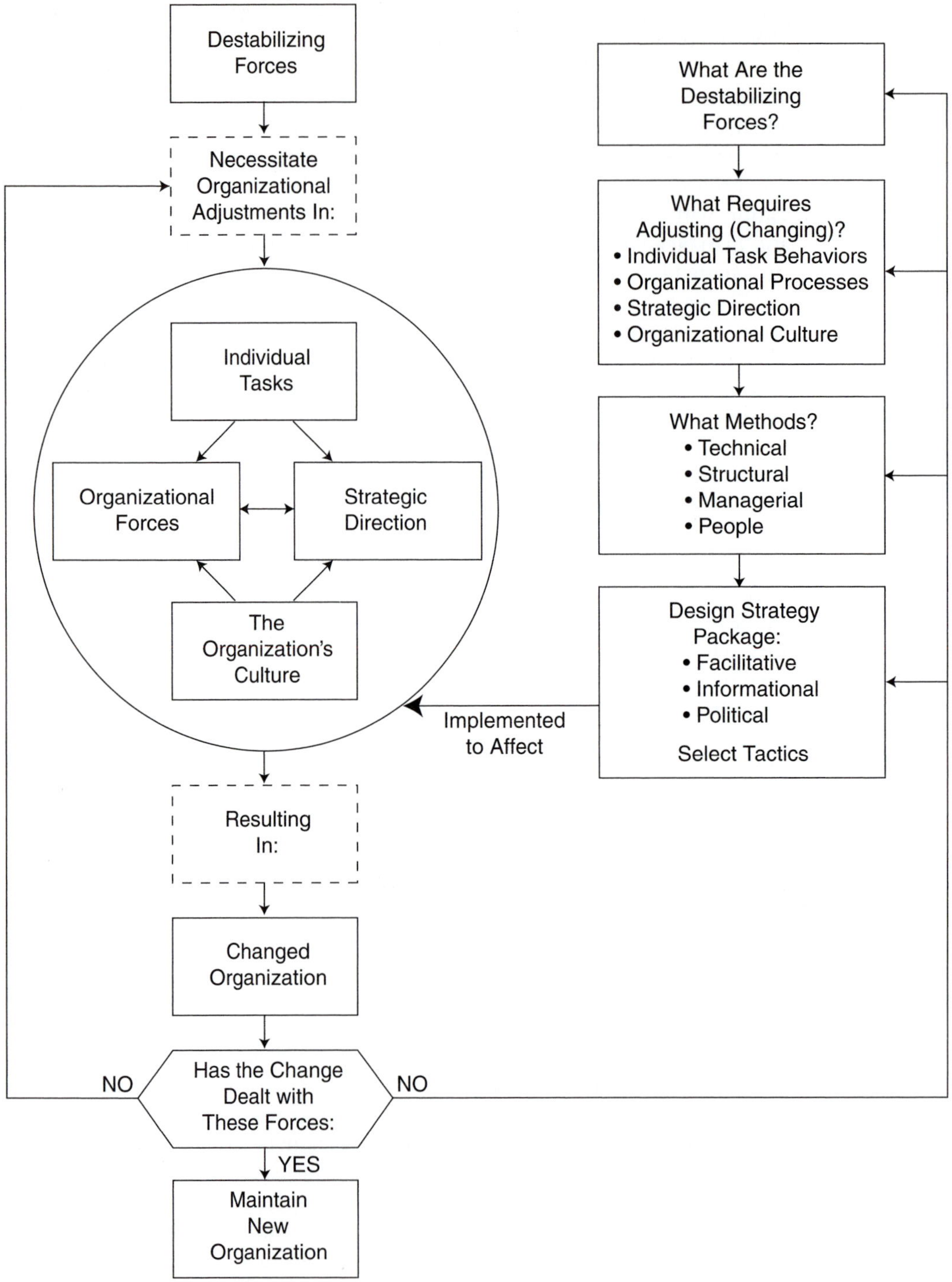

Figure 10.1 | A Model of Planned Organizational Change

From Connor, P. E., & Lake, L. K. (1994). *Managing Organizational Change* (2nd ed.). Westport, CT: Praeger, p. 7. Copyright © 1994. Reproduced with permission of Greenwood Publishing Group, Inc., Westport, CT.

happens. In organizational change processes, these schemata may be either confirmed or disrupted.

Much of the work in this area has considered typical "problems" associated with organizational change. For example, Covin and Kilmann (1990) asked managers and consultants involved in change efforts to identify factors that often have a negative impact on change. Their responses, presented in Table 10.1, indicate that change can be thwarted by a variety of obstacles at numerous levels of the organization. This suggests that responding to change at each stage of the change process (i.e., during change development, program planning, and change implementation) is critical to organizational and individual outcomes. Three themes run through much of the literature on key responses to the change process.

First, as indicated by the first three "problems" identified in Table 10.1, *management support* for the change process is critical. As Fairhurst (1993) argues, "conventional wisdom suggests that it is senior management who has the most impact on change" (p. 334). When senior management is not seen as backing the change effort or when senior management's vision is not effectively shared with others in the organization, it is unlikely that a change effort will be successful. This may be particularly true when there is an external change agent involved in the change process. For example, if change is initiated by external consultants or by government or community mandate, the perceived support for the change by organizational management can be critical.

Medved et al. (2001) call this the *ownership tension* inherent in the change process, in which the successful implementation of change efforts is contingent on ownership of the problem and ownership of the change process by those in critical positions in the organization. Consider, for instance, our school district changing to a new system of teaching reading. The new system may be mandated by a state or local board of education. If this is the case, successful change may well depend on the extent to which local administrators and school principals feel ownership of both the problem (ineffective methods for teaching reading) and the solution (the new method being proposed).

Table 10.1 | Typical Problems Identified in Organizational Change Process

Problems Identified in Change Process
Lack of management support
Top managers forcing change
Inconsistent action by key managers
Unrealistic expectations
Lack of meaningful participation
Poor communication
Purpose of program was not clear
Responsibility for change not properly identified

Based on Covin, T. J., & Kilmann, R. H. (1990). Participant perceptions of positive and negative influences on large-scale change. *Group and Organizational Studies, 15,* 233–248.

A second area of concern in the change process has been typically labeled as *resistance* to the change process (not to be confused with the more general concept of "resistance" discussed in Chapter 6). Resistance could be seen as the management "ownership" issue transplanted to lower-level employees; Markus (1983, p. 433), for example, defines resistance as "behaviors intended to prevent the implementation or use of a system or to prevent system designers from achieving their objectives." Lewis (2000) points out that resistance might also include problems such as ignorance of a change initiative, inadequate training, or fear. Resistance to change is often related to political behavior in organizations, because there are often many who have a great deal to "win" or "lose" in a change initiative. In our school district moving to a new teaching method for reading, many teachers might have a great deal invested in the "tried and true" system—lesson plans, teaching materials, ways of interacting with the class. Because of this investment and belief in existing methods, teachers might be highly resistant to change efforts.

A final important reaction to organizational change efforts is uncertainty on the part of organizational members. It has long been known that uncertainty about organizational processes can result in stress on the part of employees, and this is particularly true during times of change (Ashford & Black, 1996; Miller, Joseph, & Apker, 2000). Although complete information about organizational change might be counterproductive (e.g., Eisenberg, 1984), it is clear that uncertainty about what is happening in the change process causes heightened anxiety on the part of workers. As Harter and Krone (2001) point out, "any attempt to work with change needs to take into consideration those individual and organizational defense mechanisms against anxiety that structure and form managerial and organizational responses to change." One of the most straightforward ways to deal with this uncertainty and the anxiety it provokes is through communication and the provision of information. Indeed, Miller and Monge (1985) found that employees preferred having *negative* information about an upcoming organizational change to having *no* information about organizational change. For our school district, a great deal of stress about change might be related to a lack of information about the change itself (e.g., "What is entailed in this new teaching method?") and about how the change will be instituted (e.g., "How soon will I have to begin using this new method? Can I adapt it to my own classroom style?"). Any information about these issues can be helpful in reducing uncertainty about the upcoming change.

Communication in the Change Process

The reactions to organizational change highlighted above—ownership, resistance, and uncertainty—all point to the importance of communication in the organizational change process. For those involved in planned organizational change, there are a great many choices that must be made about communication during the change process. For example, Timmerman (2003) points out that a variety of communication media can be used when communicating with employees and people outside the organization during planned organizational change. How much communication should take place in face-to-face meetings? How much can be accomplished through written directives or the Internet? These are choices that must be

Spotlight on Scholarship

As the theory and research discussed in this chapter clearly demonstrate, change is rarely easy. In any planned change process, there are numerous roadblocks and times in the process when those in the midst of change have trouble finding their way. And, as is the case with many human processes, it is sometimes difficult to make sense of these problems when you are in the midst of them. As Karl Weick tells us in his systems theory of organization (see Chapter 4), we often have to make sense retrospectively—by "looking back" at our experiences and imbuing them with order and rationality.

Laurie Lewis explores this kind of sensemaking about change in her study of "hindsight" explanations of the change process. Lewis wanted to look at whether hindsight views of the change process matched expectations, whether perceived problems made a difference in the success of the implementation process, and whether the involvement of employees in the change process changed perceptions of difficulties. To investigate these issues, Lewis surveyed eighty-nine organizational members who had recently been involved in implementing planned change projects.

Respondents represented organizational types ranging from retailing to manufacturing to health care organizations. Respondents represented various areas of expertise on the change implementation teams (e.g., human resources, change process experts, group experts), and discussed various types of organizational change (e.g., changes in job descriptions, status, work type, performance evaluation, and organizational structure).

The results of Lewis's study confirmed conventional wisdom about change and offered new insights into the change process. Not surprisingly, a wide array of problems was identified in Lewis grouped these into categories of tudes, top management problems, communicating sion, cooperation, and problems with implementers. Not surprisingly, communication problems were ranked among the most important by implementers. As Lewis notes, "the evidence of this study suggests that implementers' sensemaking of their own planned change programs includes a view of communication as a significantly challenging aspect of implementation" (p. 63).

However, Lewis found that problems often highlighted in the literature (i.e., employee resistance, attitudes, and conflict) were not associated with the success of the change effort. Instead, Lewis found implementers reporting that the "potential 'deal-breakers' of change are their own teams and lack of cooperation from managers and from staff" (p. 63). These problems were often not anticipated by implementers and thus took them by surprise in the change process. In contrast, change agents may have been more prepared to deal with problems of resistance and "poor attitudes" among employees. Finally, Lewis found support for the general contention that "incorporation of lower-level employees in decision-making may provide a healthy antidote to many problems that commonly plague implementation efforts" (p. 64). However, small effect sizes indicated that many implementers might not perceive such participation as central to the success of organizational change efforts.

Lewis, L. K. (2000). "Blindsided by That One" and "I Saw That One Coming": The Relative Anticipation and Occurrence of Communication Problems and Other Problems in Implementers' Hindsight. *Journal of Applied Communication Research*, 28, 44–67.

made. Similarly, change agents must make decisions about whom to communicate with during the change process. Lewis, Richardson, and Hamel (2003) found that change agents communicate first and most frequently with individuals inside or close to the organization. Though this seems like an obvious choice, it might lead to "tunnel vision" about the needs of customers or other external constituents.

In addition to these general issues of media and audience, much of the research on communication in the change process has considered more specific strategies that management can use in communicating about change to employees. Clampitt,

DeKoch, and Cashman (2000) have categorized these "top-down" communication strategies, which are summarized in Table 10.2. Clampitt et al. (2000) believe that the *Underscore and Explore* strategy is most effective and that the *Spray and Pray* and *Withhold and Uphold* strategies are least effective. The two remaining strategies were seen as moderately effective. In essence, these authors argue for a strategy of involving employees in the change process in appropriate areas by providing relevant information. In support of this, Miller, Johnson, and Grau (1994) found that perceived quality of information was the strongest predictor of workers' openness to organizational change attempts. It is likely that quality of information can be enhanced most effectively by involving employees in as many aspects of the change process as possible. (See the discussion of participation in decision making in Chapter 8.)

There has also been a great deal of research investigating how change influences communication among lower-level employees in an organization. Laurie Lewis and David Seibold have taken a lead in much of this research, considering the ways in which individuals cope with organizational change. Lewis and Seibold (1993, 1996; Lewis, 1997) argue that employees are faced with numerous concerns about change, including concerns about performance (e.g., "Will I be able to teach the way I want to under the new system?"), organizational norms (e.g., "What do other teachers think about these new teaching methods?"), and uncertainty (e.g., "I know so little about these new teaching methods"). To cope with these concerns, Lewis and Seibold found that organizational members used a wide array of tactics that included information search, discussion of what the innovation would be like,

Table 10.2 | Managerial Strategies for Communicating about Change

Strategy	Definition
Spray and Pray	Management showers employees with all kinds of information in the hope that employees will be able to sort out significant and insignificant information.
Tell and Sell	Management selects a limited set of messages regarding core organizational issues. Management "tells" employees about these issues, and then "sells" employees on the wisdom of the chosen approach.
Underscore and Explore	Management focuses on fundamental issues related to change success and allows employees the creative freedom to explore various possibilities.
Identify and Reply	Management listens to and identifies key concerns of employees and then responds to those issues as they are brought up.
Withhold and Uphold	Management withholds information as much as possible. When management is confronted with questions or rumors, they uphold the party line.

Adapted from Clampitt, P. G., DeKoch, R. J., & Cashman, T. (2000). A strategy for communicating about uncertainty. *Academy of Management Executive*, 14 (4), 41–57.

exploring alternatives to the change, persuading others to support or not support the change, and formally requesting reconsideration of the change.

"Unplanned" Change: Organizational Crisis

Up to this point in the chapter, we have considered organizational change as largely a planned and manageable process. However, there are many times when change is thrust upon an organization in the wake of events such as natural disasters, ethical violations, terrorism, product failure or tampering, financial loss, or serious human error. Think, for example, of the "change" that confronted organizations coping with Hurricane Katrina and its aftermath, the 2004 and 2007 wildfires in Southern California, the space shuttle disasters, the alleged dangers presented by medications such as Vioxx, and the discovery of tainted spinach on grocery store shelves. Coombs (1999, p. 2) defines organizational crisis as "an event that is an unpredictable, major threat that can have a negative effect on the organization, industry, or stakeholders if handled improperly." In other words, crisis is unplanned change that can rock an organization and all the people associated with it.

Seeger, Sellnow, and Ulmer (2003) describe organizational crisis as evolving in three stages: precrisis, crisis, and postcrisis. In the *precrisis* stage, organizational members can work to prevent or prepare for possible problems. For example, in the "hurricane season" of 2005, many commentators noted that planners in Texas should have been better prepared for the traffic mess that occurred during Hurricane Rita—after all, they had seen what had happened during Hurricane Katrina only a few weeks before. During the *crisis* stage, there is a trigger (e.g., product failure, natural disaster) that threatens an organization's survival or reputation. During this period, there is much uncertainty, and people inside and outside the organization try to make sense of what is happening (Weick, 1988). In the *postcrisis* stage, communication focuses on determining responsibility, perhaps apologizing (Benoit, 1995), and establishing systems for coping with similar crises in the future. For example, in the fall of 2007, firefighters in the San Diego area credited their effective handling of evacuations and other crisis-related events to the lessons learned from fighting large-scale fires several years before. In all three stages, communication processes play a key role in coping with a wide range of these "unplanned" change processes.

ORGANIZATIONAL LEADERSHIP

As our discussion thus far reveals, organizational change involves a complex process of communication among a wide range of constituencies in and around the organization. For example, we found that it is critical that a wide array of organizational participants be informed about the change and feel that they are a part of the decision-making process. It is also important, however, that management in an organization is seen as clearly understanding the organization's problems, supporting appropriate change efforts, and being prepared for dealing with organizational crises. Thus, effective leadership is critical in the organizational change process.

Of course, the importance of leadership is not limited to times of change and upheaval. Indeed, we have seen many examples in recent years of how ineffective leadership during normal organizational operations has led to disastrous results for a company. For example, in the trial regarding the collapse of WorldCom, a major defense of Bernard Ebbers, the ex-CEO of the company, was that he really wasn't aware of issues of technology or finances within the organization. As Ackman (2005) reports, "Ebbers' basis for defense in the criminal case against him . . . is that he never looked at the numbers. He had people for that, and the people, his lawyers will say, let him down as much as anyone." However, many stockholders—and many scholars as well—see this not as a failure of "his people" but as a failure of his leadership. Similar arguments have been made in recent years about leadership at Tyco, Enron (see "Case in Point" below), and a host of other high-profile organizations. Thus, it is important to consider the ways in which we have come to understand leadership in organizational contexts. In this section, we will first consider some models of leadership and then look at the role that communication plays within current understandings of the leadership process.

Case in Point: Responsible Leadership at Enron

Most business analysts would agree that the most spectacular corporate collapse in history was the fall of Enron. In December 2000, Enron shares on the New York Stock Exchange hit a fifty-two-week high of $84.87. Less than a year later, Enron filed for bankruptcy and its stock was trading for less than $1. A number of factors can be pointed to that account for this monumental meltdown, but it is not surprising that many commentators have pointed to Enron's leadership to explain why the company failed so dramatically.

Seeger and Ulmer (2003) have suggested that the Enron case can be evaluated in terms of the degree to which the firm's prominent leaders—especially Ken Lay (CEO and founder), Jeffrey Skilling (president), and Andrew Fastow (chief financial officer)—exemplified qualities of "responsible leadership." Seeger and Ulmer argue that responsible leadership encompasses three related qualities. First, a responsible leader communicates appropriate values and standards to create a positive moral climate. Second, a responsible leader monitors operations at the organization to remain in-

formed. Third, a responsible leader remains open to "bad news" about the organization, which might be communicated through "whistleblowers" or others who express dissent within the organizational ranks.

It should come as no surprise that the leaders at Enron flunked these three tests of responsible leadership. Though Enron claimed to follow a set of principles known as "RICE" (Respect, Integrity, Communication, and Excellence), the leaders rarely exemplified these core ideas. Instead, Seeger and Ulmer (2003, p. 72) report that Jeffrey Skilling "modeled values of greed and excess and a view that standard notions of right and wrong and traditional business principles simply did not apply." Similarly, a radically decentralized structure led to leaders having little direct knowledge of operations, and a "no bad news" norm created an organization in which employees censored themselves and persuaded themselves and others that everything was great. In short, a great deal of the blame for Enron's collapse should go straight to the top—where those in charge failed to practice responsible leadership.

Models of Leadership

Scholars and commentators on political and organizational processes have been interested in leadership for many years. Early thinking that leaders are "born, not made" was reflected in *trait theories* of leadership. These theories propose that there are particular qualities that will tend to be associated with leaders and that will result in success in leadership activities. For example, Northouse (1997) reviews a number of studies of leadership traits and characteristics (e.g., Stogdill, 1948) and concludes that the most common traits associated with leadership are intelligence (verbal ability, perceptual ability, and reasoning), self-confidence (belief that one can make a difference), determination (the persistent desire to get the job done), integrity (honesty and trustworthiness), and sociability (being friendly and outgoing). Organizations advocating a trait approach to leadership might use personality tests to select people with the "right" combination of characteristics or might use these traits to help organization members in self-assessment. Related to trait approaches to leadership are models that suggest that leaders have particular behavioral "styles" that make them more or less effective leaders. We saw one of these *style theories* in Chapter 3 when we considered Blake and Mouton's Leadership Grid. Recall that this grid suggested evaluating leaders in terms of their "concern for production" and "concern for people," and argued that the most effective leadership style was a team management style that maximized both of these goals. Thus, this style approach is essentially a way of translating preferred traits into preferred behaviors.

There is certainly much to say for trait and style approaches to leadership—we like to think of leaders as "special" kinds of people who can do extraordinary things and we can probably think of some people who appear to be "born leaders." However, in recent years trait and style approaches have fallen into disfavor, as many scholars and practitioners are uncomfortable with the notion of a set list of specific characteristics that defines all leaders. Further, these approaches suggest that a particular leader will be effective across all situations and all followers, and this does not fit well with either research or experience. For example, we learned about the Leader-Member Exchange model in Chapter 7. The LMX model proposes that leaders develop different (and perhaps more or less effective) leadership relationships with different subordinates. Thus, the idea of having one "ideal" type of leader is contrary to much of our experience in which leaders work in different ways with different people.

The more widespread critique of trait and style approaches, though, has come with regard to the idea of leadership behaviors across situations. This critique argues that different individuals might be differently suited for various leadership situations. For example, following our discussion of organizational life cycles earlier in this chapter, the kind of leader who is good at managing a young start-up company might be different from the kind of leader who is appropriate for managing a mature organization. Or, more specifically, some leaders might be good at running structured meetings and others might be more comfortable in freewheeling brainstorming sessions or presenting large-scale public speeches. Not surprisingly, then, when many scholars rejected a trait approach to leadership, they turned to ideas that emphasized the "match" of the style of the leader to the characteristics of the situation. The best known of these theories is *contingency theory* (Fiedler & Garcia, 1987). Contingency theory would predict, for example, that a leader who likes to focus on tasks would be more effective in structured situations than a leader who likes to focus on relationships. More contemporary scholars argue that there are many situations in which a single person is not adequate for the needs of the situation and leadership functions must be shared by several individuals in a group or organization (e.g., Kramer, 2006).

Even a contingency approach to leadership, however, still emphasizes the characteristics and the style of the leader and the needs of particular situations. What is still left out of this and other classic models is the role of those *being led* in the organization. Also missing from these models is the role of communication, especially in establishing relationships between leaders and those in the organization. Thus, in recent years a variety of models that look more closely at leadership as a process of communication and as a process of establishing relationships have been proposed. Some have referred to these models as the "New Leadership" paradigm (Bryman, 1992) or the "neocharismatic" paradigm (House & Aditya, 1997). Gardner (2003) argues that models of transformational leadership and neocharismatic leadership are representative of these models in that they emphasize communication and relationship through the consideration of the ways that leaders secure "extraordinary levels of follower trust and inspire followers to emulate their behavior" (Gardner, 2003, p. 503). We'll briefly consider transformational leadership as an example of this kind of new leadership model.

Case in Point: Leader of the Free World?

In discussions of organizational communication and leadership, scholars often forget about the government organizations that make a huge difference in our everyday lives. We think about businesses in many "sectors" (manufacturing, service, financial, health care) but rarely consider political organizations like Congress or presidential administrations—or at least we don't think about these entities as organizations. But the concept of leadership is clearly as relevant to political and government organizations as to the businesses that make goods and provide services.

Jonathan Alter (2007) makes this point in arguing that in presidential elections, the winner is often determined as much by perceived leadership style as by political positions or experience. Indeed, he suggests that the United States often elects presidents that provide a shift in leadership style from the previous administration:

In 1960, young JFK was the antidote to dowdy Ike. In 1976, Jimmy ("I'll never lie to you") Carter campaigned to wipe away the stain left by Richard Nixon. In 1980, sunny Ronald Reagan tapped into disgust with the malaise of the Carter years. In 2000, George W. Bush took on not just Al Gore, but Bill Clinton and Monica Lewinsky (Alter, 2007, p. 35).

As I write these words in late 2007, it is still unclear who will take on the mantle as the next "leader of the free world." Alter argues that, in following the logic above, "Bush's successor must be a tough-minded but flexible and humble chief executive with a talent for building bridges, not burning them" (p. 35). It is clear, though, that voters' decisions depend as much on how we think a candidate will lead us through the good and bad times as on government experience or policy statements.

The *transformational leadership model* (Bass, 1985; Burns, 1978) makes a distinction between transactional leaders and transformational leaders. Transactional leadership refers to a relationship in which there is an exchange of some sort between leaders and followers. For example, a political transactional leader exchanges a promise of social security reform for the promise of a vote. A managerial transactional leader exchanges a pay raise, a promotion, or verbal praise for hard work on a project. In contrast, transformational leaders, through communication processes, create a relationship between leaders and followers that helps followers reach their full potential and has the potential for transforming both the leader and the follower. As Northouse (1997, p. 131) explains with regard to Mahatma Gandhi, "Gandhi raised the hopes and demands of millions of his people and in the process was changed himself." Gardner (2003) argues that central to transformational leadership is the concept of *exemplification*. That is, leaders who want to instill the ideals of hard work and ethical behavior would do so by exemplifying those ideals in their own behaviors. Both words and deeds are critical to the transformational leader—it is a model of "do as I say *and* as I do."

In summary, then, models of leadership have moved from relatively simplistic ideas about the traits and styles of effective leaders, through models that suggest that different styles and skills are appropriate in different situations, to models that see leadership as a process of building relationships through interaction with followers and modeling desired values. Clearly, communication processes are central to these new theories of leadership. Thus, in the next section we will briefly consider several communication factors that have been associated with effective leadership.

Communication and Leadership

The role of communication in the leadership process can be looked at in several different ways. It is important, for example, to look at what is said—the content of communication. Of course, the appropriate content of communication will vary from situation to situation, but research does give us some ideas about what effective leaders say. For example, several studies have demonstrated that leaders who use "visionary" content in their communication are more effective than those who use more pragmatic content (Awamleh & Gardner, 1999; Holladay & Coombs, 1993). Clearly, Martin Luther King's "I Have a Dream" speech would not have been as effective in motivating citizens if the content had merely listed "ten steps toward racial equality." Saying the right thing can be particularly important for leaders facing crisis situations. For example, in a study of two organizations facing the crisis of fire, Seeger and Ulmer (2003) found that effective leadership discourse was characterized by a strong commitment to stakeholders, an immediate commitment to rebuild, and the opportunity for renewal through the crisis.

Perhaps more important than what is said, though, is *how* it is said. For example, in Seeger and Ulmer's study of crisis communication, timing was critical—the leaders started talking while the fires were still burning. How a message is communicated include its delivery. Experimental studies have indicated that strong delivery styles (e.g., eye contact, appropriate use of facial expressions and gestures, increased vocal variety) led to higher ratings of leadership effectiveness (Awamleh &

Gardner, 1999; Gardner, 2003; Holladay & Coombs, 1993). These findings suggest that individuals could be trained to be more effective (or at least to be seen as more effective) through careful attention to nonverbal behaviors.

The most thorough consideration of communication and leadership, however, has come in the work of Gail Fairhurst and Robert Sarr (1996) regarding the ways in which leaders "frame" their language in interaction with a variety of constituencies. Fairhurst and Sarr see leadership as a "language game," and they argue that the most essential skill for this game is the ability to frame. Framing is a way of managing meaning in which one or more aspects of the subject at hand are selected or highlighted over other aspects. For example, in the case study examined by Seeger and Ulmer (1992) that we discussed above, the leader at one of the organizations, Malden Mills, had to find a way to "frame" a fire that destroyed a textile plant, resulted in serious injury, and placed many jobs in jeopardy. It would be easy to frame this as a disaster, an act of God, or an accident. But, in this case, the leader framed the event as a chance to demonstrate his commitment to his workers and to rebuild and renew the company. This emphasizes the notion that leadership is not about events or situations, but is, instead, a process of managing meaning (Turner, 2003).

Fairhurst and Sarr (1996) argue that effective leaders begin the framing process by having a clear understanding of their own view of reality and their own goals for the organization and for communication. That is, effective leaders know where they are and know where they want to go. Effective leaders are also those who pay attention to the context, recognizing times and situations in which there are opportunities for shaping meaning or when there are constraints that will hamper the framing process. Finally, effective leaders use language in ways that manage meaning in powerful and appropriate ways. As Fairhurst and Sarr (1996, p. 100) state, "just as an artist works from a palette of colors to paint a picture, the leader who manages meaning works from a vocabulary of words and symbols to help construct a frame in the mind of the listener." The use of language in framing can involve a variety of communicative "tools" that can help others see the world in the way you want them to see it. These linguistic tools for managing meaning are presented in Table 10.3. Of course, these tools can be overused or used in inappropriate contexts. For example, we are all well aware of the overuse of "spin" following presidential debates and other political events. However, these tools point to a variety of ways that effective leaders can shape their messages to form valued relationships with others and help them see the world in a particular way.

SUMMARY

Although it often seems that our work lives are mundane, there are change processes that permeate many aspects of organizational life. Organizations change in the "natural" course of adapting to their environments, and they change when managers or employees perceive a need to adjust things at either the individual or organizational level. Further, though many players are critically involved in these change processes, the roles of leaders become particularly pronounced. In this chapter, we have examined these related processes of organizational change and leadership. We first considered several models of how change occurs, looked at problems that often arise during planned change efforts, considered the special case of organizational crisis, and

Table 10.3 | Tools for Framing in Leadership

	Metaphors	Jargon/ Catchphrases	Contrast	Spin	Stories
Function	They show a subject's likeness with something else	They frame a subject in familiar terms	It describes a subject in terms of its opposite	It puts a subject in a positive or negative light	They frame a subject by example
Use it because	You want a subject to take on new meaning	Familiar references can enhance meaning. Jargon and catchphrases help communicate a vision's "god" and "devil" terms	It is sometimes easier to define what your subject is not than state what it is	It can reveal your subject's strengths or weaknesses	Stories attract attention and can build rapport
Avoid it when	They mask important alternative meanings	A word or phrase is in danger of overuse	Meaning can be skewed by a poor contrast	The ratio of spin to reality is excessive	They mask important alternative meanings
Example	"I feel our relationship is formal, like punching a ticket."	"We've got to break the squares today"	"It's a choice between raising my hand for the teacher to ask if it's okay or just telling it like it is."	"Which Ray will show up? The one who's cooperative and generous, or the egotist who constantly reminds others of his successes?"	"In my first three or four years here, I was a lot like you. I thought …"

From Fairhurst, G. T., & Sarr, R. A. (1996). *The Art of Framing: Managing the Language of Leadership.* San Francisco: Jossey-Bass, p. 101.

considered the role of communication in a variety of change situations. We then turned our attention to leadership, examining traditional models of leadership that emphasize traits, styles, and situations and more contemporary models that see leadership in terms of communication and the building of relationships with followers. We then considered the role of communication in leadership, looking at the role of communication content and delivery, and the importance of framing in the management of meaning.

Clearly, much of the theory and research we have considered in this chapter is rooted in classical, human resources, and systems approaches to organizational communication (see Table 10.4). Indeed, classical approaches to organizations (especially Taylor's Theory of Scientific Management) are built around the need to control the behaviors of workers in organizations and plan all changes that they encounter. The influence of systems theory can be seen in the importance of goals and communication in the organizational change process, and the human resources approach can be seen in the emphasis on maximizing the effectiveness of leaders through behavioral and communicative choices and in the belief that organizational change can be enhanced by involving employees at all organizational levels in the change process.

Table 10.4 | Approaches to Change and Leadership Processes

Approach	How Change and Leadership Would Be Considered
Classical	Change is viewed negatively, unless that change is carefully controlled by management. Leadership is seen as tied exclusively to management and based on defined traits and abilities that only managers have.
Human relations	Change is seen as a human process in which factors of employee satisfaction are taken into account. Leaders are encouraged to emphasize needs of workers to foster work satisfaction.
Human resources	Change is seen as a crucial step through which the organization can harness the skills and abilities of employees. Employees are encouraged to participate in the change process, and skills of leaders are adapted to specific situations.
Systems	Change might be viewed as part of a cybernetic system characterized by positive and negative feedback or as an outcome of chaotic systems of complex information.
Cultural	Change practices are seen as reflections of organizational values and assumptions. Effective change and effective leadership will depend on an understanding of prevailing cultural and subcultural beliefs.
Critical	Planned organizational change and leadership can be viewed as mechanisms through which management establishes and maintains a relationship of power and authority over employees. Truly democratic change, however, can enhance employee voice in the organization.

As Table 10.4 indicates, however, other approaches to the study of organizational communication could further enhance our understanding of organizational change and leadership. For example, in our discussion of leadership, we considered how effective leaders understand the context in which meaning is being created. In other words, leadership depends to a large extent on understanding organizational culture. Similarly, a cultural approach to organizational change would emphasize the norms and values of organizational members and might pay particular attention to how various subcultural groups might be affected differently by organizational change. Critical theorists also have much to say about organizational change. At a basic level, of course, critical theorists hope for emancipatory change in organizations brought on as employees realize the imbalance of power in most organizational settings. However, this emancipatory change is not the kind of change envisioned by the research discussed throughout most of this chapter. Indeed, critical theorists would be very concerned about the processes of "planned change" and "leadership" discussed here, because such processes could well perpetuate the hegemonic relationship between management and employees in organizational settings. For example, it could be argued that when employees participate in planning organizational change, they are legitimizing organizational goals at the expense of individual employee goals. In short, by adopting new approaches to the study of change processes, we gain important insights into some of the less obvious functions that these processes play in organizational life.

Discussion Questions

1. Organizational change can be an anxiety-producing process. What are ways that change can be managed to reduce the level of anxiety experienced by organizational participants? Are there times when uncertainty and anxiety about change might be a good thing?

2. What is the role of leadership in organizational change? Which of the models of leadership discussed in this chapter are most appropriate for times of change? Would the different models advocate different kinds of leadership communication during planned change?

3. In what ways is leadership a "language game" and a process of "managing meaning"? How does communication content and style influence this language game? How do leaders manage meaning through framing techniques?

CASE STUDY | **Leading Nurses through Hospital Change**

Few industries are confronted with more change and more turbulence than the health care industry. As the perusal of any newspaper or news website will indicate, there is constant pressure on health care organizations to provide quality care in a cost-controlled environment that is characterized by ever-increasing regulation. This pressure can be seen most clearly in the advent of "managed care" during the 1980s and beyond. Managed care involves integrated and comprehensive systems of health care providers, insurance companies, and government programs, coordinated around specific care plans and guidelines designed to simultaneously enhance the quality of care provided, control the cost of that care, and maintain access to care for as many people as possible. As you might guess, it's pretty much impossible to succeed in all three of these important goals of cost, quality, and access, but hospitals and other health care organizations keep on trying.

I've run into many such organizations in my research on communication in health care organizations. One of these organizations—we'll call it University Hospital—is discussed in several of my publications (Miller, 1998; Miller, Joseph, & Apker, 2000). University Hospital is a large teaching hospital that employs nearly 5,000 individuals and is responsible for half a million patient visits a year. University Hospital is acknowledged as a very high-quality medical center—for example, it typically scores extremely well on accreditation surveys. However, like all health care organizations, University Hospital needed to improve in a number of financial areas, including average length of stay and cost per discharge.

My involvement with University Hospital began when I learned of changes that were occurring in the nursing department and was asked to be a part of understanding and instituting those changes. As part of a hospital-wide effort to improve financial and care performances, the nurses were beginning a program of "differentiated nursing practice" (Hoffart & Woods, 1996) in which nursing roles were defined on a variety of specific levels of responsibility. These roles would require new training, new responsibilities, and a new orientation toward the systematized provision of care. The centerpiece of this program was the "care coordinator" role.

Care coordinators were defined as registered nurses charged with coordinating care for patients "from admissions to discharge." This coordination involved communication with relevant physicians, social workers, allied health personnel, insurance representatives, and families. The nurses selected for these roles were the "best and the brightest" that University Hospital had to offer.

Sounds like a good change, right? Coordinated care from admissions to discharge is certainly an admirable goal. However, remember that the nurses selected for these positions were trained in traditional, clinical nursing. They were then thrown into a role that required them to work with individuals from a variety of hospital disciplines (with different "turf" issues and different levels of power) within an

CASE STUDY | **Leading Nurses through Hospital Change** *continued*

incredibly complex organizational structure. And they were doing this with little or no training and with a job description that was purposefully ambiguous: Nurses were asked to design the job in the "best way possible." Indeed, the final line of the job description for care coordinators read "Role in development/work in progress"!

So imagine you are me, asked to help the leaders of the nursing department take their nurses—and especially the new care coordinators—down this path of organizational change. The department is directed by two nurses—we'll call them Hannah and Jen—who have an incredible amount of energy. Both are well liked by the nurses they supervise. Hannah has been with the hospital for many years and knows all the "ins and outs" of the system. She is the steady hand guiding the nursing department, and she feels a bit overwhelmed by all the change she is being asked to institute. Jen has been with University Hospital for only a few years, but has made quite an impact as a charismatic leader who wants University Hospital—and especially the nursing department—to be on the cutting edge of managed care initiatives. Jen is a proponent of all sorts of New Age things, and she is particularly smitten with "chaos theory" as a way to manage organizational change. She figures that they have selected the best people they can for the care coordinator roles, and she trusts that they will use their own imagination and ingenuity to craft roles that will work for the

new system. Indeed, when a care coordinator complained about the stress of the changes they were going through, Jen quoted her favorite chaos theorist, saying, "Chaos is the rich soil from which creativity is born" (Merry, 1995, p. 13). Oddly enough, the nurse did not feel comforted.

CASE ANALYSIS QUESTIONS

1. How does the nursing department at University Hospital exemplify ways that organizations often react to planned organizational change? Are there ways in which the nature of the change—or the way it is being instituted at University Hospital—differs from traditional patterns?
2. If you were taking on a "care coordinator" role at University Hospital, what kind of information would you want to have? Do you like the idea of an unstructured role that you can develop on your own? What are the advantages and disadvantages of this kind of organizational ambiguity?
3. How would you choose to lead this department through the change they are experiencing? Would you rather have Jen or Hannah as your leader in this process?
4. What are some ways that Jen and Hannah could work together to make the change process successful?

Processes of Emotion in the Workplace

CHAPTER **11**

AFTER READING THIS CHAPTER, YOU SHOULD . . .

- Appreciate the ways in which traditional organizing has been portrayed as rational and logical, and be able to provide arguments for why emotion should be considered an integral part of organizational life
- Understand the concept of "emotional labor" as communication that is in some way inauthentic and performed for the benefit of the organization
- Be able to contrast emotional labor with "emotional work," authentic emotions that are also a part of many workers' jobs
- See the ways in which emotion permeates our relationships with coworkers in both satisfying and destructive ways
- Understand the role of communication in both causing stress and burnout and in helping organizations and individuals cope with stress and burnout

There is a tradition of rationality in our consideration of organizational life. Think, for instance, of the models of organization we looked at in the first half of this book—maximizing efficiency in a machine-like factory, enhancing the effectiveness of organizational systems, making the most of human resources, even managing corporate culture—all of these models suggest that organizations run through reasoning. The same is true of the processes we've considered so far in the second half of this book, including decision making, conflict management, and organizational change. Even when we look at current trends in the popular management literature—everything from "Six Sigma" to "knowledge management" to "learning organizations"—the presumption has been that successful organizations are places where cool heads and logical thinking prevail.

Since the early 1990s, however, there has been a growing interest in the emotional side of organizational life and a growing appreciation for the tension between emotion and rationality in the workplace. Many years ago, human relations scholars advocated looking more closely at human feelings in the organization, but the only feeling considered before the last few decades was "satisfaction." However, researchers are now beginning to see just how complex emotional life in organizations is. In this chapter, we explore these issues by first considering how scholars have been moved to look at emotion in organizational life. We will examine emotion as "part of the job" and look at the ways in which emotion permeates organizational relationships. We will then consider one area of emotion in the workplace that has received a great deal of research attention—the study of stress, burnout, and social support in organizations.

EMOTION IN THE WORKPLACE

Most models of organizational life see the workplace as a setting governed by logic and rationality. According to these models, jobs consist of tasks and the cognitive functions required for those tasks. We train people in the logic and mechanics of how to do their jobs. We manage conflict and change by thinking logically about what is best for the company and employees. And when we make decisions, we carefully weigh the pros and cons of each decision and make a logical choice that will maximize gains and minimize losses.

Of course, anyone who has spent any time in an organization recognizes how inaccurate the above description really is. Our interactions are often governed by hot emotion rather than cool logic. We typically make choices about job and career based on "gut feeling" rather than a spreadsheet of pros and cons. Unfortunately, it has taken organizational theorists a while to catch up with these commonsense ideas about organizational life. But scholars are now finally beginning to appreciate the emotional nuances that are so prevalent in the workplace.

This shift in focus can be illustrated with a look back to our discussion of decision making in Chapter 8. We noted in that chapter that scholars rarely see decision making as a purely logical and data-driven process. People (in the workplace or otherwise) don't often follow the prescribed steps of defining the problem, establishing criteria, searching for information, evaluating alternatives, and reaching a decision. But even when theorists moved away from this purely logical model, they moved to models that considered the concept of *bounded rationality* in the workplace (e.g., March & Simon, 1958; Simon, 1987). Decision making couldn't be perfectly rational because of cognitive and situational limits on rationality. But rationality was still the norm; it was merely limited. More recently, however, Dennis Mumby and Linda Putnam (1992) turned this notion on its head by suggesting that instead of looking at bounded rationality we should consider *bounded emotionality*. That is, these scholars asked us to begin looking at emotional life as a central focus of organizational research and to consider the ways in which paying attention to emotion might lead to new ways of understanding the workplace.

We turn now to several areas of research that have heeded this call by looking at emotion in organizational life. We look first at scholarship that has considered emotion as part of the job. We will then look at the organizational emotion that arises through relationships with coworkers and others and consider more general ideas about emotion rules and emotional intelligence.

Emotion as Part of the Job

A wide range of occupations exists in which interaction with clients is a central aspect of the job. In many of these, communication between employee and client involves some degree of emotional or affective content (see Waldron, 1994). Some examples are obvious. Nurses and physicians interact with dying patients in a hospice, deal with stressed-out families in an intensive care unit, and share the elation of birth in a maternity ward. Ministers counsel troubled parishioners, comfort grieving families, and rejoice with newlyweds. Emotional communication is also a requirement in less obvious occupations. The flight attendant must appear happy and attentive throughout a long cross-country flight. A bill collector must remain stern and avoid any trace of sympathy in interactions. A cocktail waitress's tips depend to a large extent on maintaining a friendly and cheerful demeanor.

Arlie Hochschild was the first scholar to deal systematically with this phenomenon in her book *The Managed Heart* (1983). She uses the term *emotional labor* to refer to jobs in which workers are expected to display certain feelings in order to satisfy organizational role expectations. Hochschild argues that when performing emotional labor, workers can engage in either *surface acting* or *deep acting*. For instance, Hochschild's original study of emotional labor involved airline flight attendants. Flight attendants involved in surface acting might just "paste on a smile" to satisfy the airline's requirement of a friendly face in the cabin. However, flight attendants might also try to evoke more realistic emotional displays by using deep-acting techniques such as imagining the airplane cabin as a friendly living room or sympathizing with the stress that irate passengers might be feeling.

 ## Case in Point: Reserves of Emotion

Emotion in the workplace can take a wide variety of forms and affect individuals far removed from the job. Consider, for example, the emotional toll of those in the National Guard or Army Reserves serving during the Iraq War. There is little doubt that soldiering is an intensely emotional experience and carries additional future risks of post-traumatic stress disorder. In part because of these emotional hazards, military organizations provide soldiers with a great deal of training and psychological preparation and attempt to design systems to help soldiers cope with the psychological stress of warfare.

However, as Adler (2003) points out, it is a different situation for those in the National Guard or Army Reserves who are called up for active duty. These soldiers leave behind jobs, increasing the stress of going to war. The families of these soldiers are often isolated from others in the same situation, leading to less social support and increased stress. These soldiers have not received the same level of training as regular military personnel and thus may feel enhanced pressure in the war zone. Indeed, a recent Pentagon study indicated that post-traumatic stress disorder was much more prevalent in members of the National Guard (49 percent) than for army soldiers (38 percent) or marines (31 percent) ("VA Will Expand Mental Health Services," 2007). The employers of reservists and members of the National Guard—often "first responders" in U.S. communities—are often stretched thin in providing homeland services. And, for the reservists, their families, and their employers, there is the ongoing uncertainty of having their lives interrupted in unexpected ways and not knowing what will come next. As Adler explains, "The reservists run many of the same risks as the regular troops they support, but they pay a different price. For an active-duty soldier, foreign deployment is an expected risk, and carries benefits in pay and promotions to offset the hardships. But for reservists, this is an unexpected detour in lives and careers whose course had seemed quite predictable just a few years ago" (p. 32). The emotional toll of these interruptions—for the soldiers, for the families, for the employers—can be large, indeed.

Since Hochschild's book, the notion of emotional labor has been further developed by scholars in a variety of disciplines, including sociology, management, and communication (see Fineman, 2000; Wharton, 1999, for reviews). Some of the research has involved case studies of workers in jobs involving emotional labor, including waitresses (Leidner, 1993), flight attendants (Murphy, 1998), workers in emergency call centers (Shuler & Sypher, 2000), and cruise ship employees (Tracy, 2000). Other work has attempted to develop models of the emotional labor process (Kruml & Geddes, 2000; Morris & Feldman, 1996; Rafaeli & Sutton, 1987) that consider factors such as the antecedents of emotional labor (e.g., gender, task requirements, closeness of monitoring), dimensions of emotional labor (e.g., frequency of emotional display, variety of expressed emotion, degree of emotional dissonance), and consequences of emotional labor (e.g., burnout and job dissatisfaction).

Several generalizations can be forwarded about the body of work on emotional labor:

- Most research considers frontline service workers in organizations that sanction (and pay for) emotion in the service of customers. Thus, emotional labor is seen as a way to increase the success—and profits—of the organization.
- Most research considers emotion that is explicitly controlled through training and employee manuals. For example, Steinberg and Figart (1999, p. 9) quote an employee handbook at a gourmet deli as directing: "Under no circumstance should a customer ever wonder if you are having a bad day. Your troubles should be masked with a smile."
- Most research considers emotional displays that are created through deep acting or surface acting—in other words, emotional displays that are in some way not authentic expressions of current or enduring emotion.
- When workers enact emotional labor, they are very aware that they are acting for the purpose of managerial and (sometimes) personal profit (Miller, Considine, & Garner, 2007).

Not all job-related emotion has these characteristics, however. Ashforth and Humphrey (1993) point this out when they state: "The problem with this conception of emotional labor is that it does not allow for the instances whereby one spontaneously and genuinely experiences and expresses the expected emotion" (p. 94). Clearly, there are times when workers feel emotions on the job and express those emotions in interactions. For example, a teacher might feel joy—and express that joy—when a student finally understands long division. A nurse might feel sorrow—and express that sorrow—on the death of a patient. This kind of "genuine emotion" on the job—what Miller et al. (2007) call *emotional work*—involves people who are not in frontline service jobs, but instead hold professional positions in industries such as health care, education, or human service. Workers in these roles rarely have instructions on emotion management that are explicitly spelled out in employee handbooks or during training sessions. However, such individuals clearly do deal with a lot of emotion on the job—both of a "genuine" and "managed" variety. For example, a nurse must cope with genuine emotion (e.g., the sorrow of having a patient die) and express emotions that he may not actually feel (e.g., dealing with "difficult" patients in a cheerful or professional way).

Miller (2007) looked at a number of jobs that involve emotional work in her consideration of workers who are engaged in "compassionate communication." In her interviews with workers in a wide range of human service occupations, she found that workers communicate emotionally in ways that involve processes of noticing, connecting, and responding. Workers engaged in emotional work must *notice* the need for compassion and the details of clients' lives that will lead to appropriate communication. They must then *connect* to clients by taking the others' perspective and establishing an empathic bond. Finally, they must *respond* with verbal and nonverbal behaviors that can make a difference for troubled clients.

Emotion as Part of Workplace Relationships

Emotion is not just important when it is a prescribed part of a person's job. Indeed, individuals in *all* organizational roles feel emotion in the workplace. Several scholars have argued that we should be looking less at emotions required by the job and more at emotions that emerge from relationships in the workplace (Sandelands & Boudens, 2000; Waldron, 2000). Miller et al. (2007) have called this type of emotion in the workplace *emotion at work*, and Sandelands and Boudens (2000) make a forceful case for looking, not at the nature of the job, but at relationships with others in the workplace as the major source of organizational emotion. After reviewing many narratives of work life, these scholars conclude:

> When people talk about their work and their feelings they rarely speak about what they do on the job or the meaning of the job. They talk almost exclusively about their involvement in the life of the group . . . Feelings are not identified with evaluations of the job, even less with personal growth and development. Instead, feelings are strongly identified with a person's place and activities in the life of the group and the place of their work in the larger scheme of things. (Sandelands & Boudens, 2000, p. 52)

A number of aspects of work relationships are largely emotional. We often have coworkers (or bosses or employees) that we like or dislike, that evoke joy or irritation, that are exhilarating or maddening. Our work with these coworkers might create and sustain emotions including anger, frustration, elation, excitement, or boredom. At the most extreme level, the emotional content of workplace relationships can include psychological abuse of others through workplace bullying. As Lutgen-Sandvik (2003, p. 472) reports, bullying is a "repetitive, targeted, and destructive form of communication directed by more powerful members at work at those who are less powerful," and bullying is reportedly experienced by 90 percent of adults at some point in their work life. And beyond this extreme form of emotional abuse, feelings and emotional display—both positive and negative—are rampant in all types of organizational relationships.

Waldron (2000) has argued that there are several aspects of work relationships that create potential for intense emotion in organizations. These include:

- *The tension between the public and private in work relationships*: Consider, for example, a case where friends outside the workplace are supervisor and subordinate within the workplace. Or consider a situation in which a private disclosure is revealed in a public meeting. In short, emotion is prevalent in the

Spotlight on Scholarship

One of the most painful emotional experiences an individual can have in the workplace is to be bullied. It is easy to think that bullying is the province of boys on the playground or "mean girls" in the middle school cafeteria. But bullying is also a serious problem in the U.S. workplace, as a majority of employees are bullied at some point in their work histories and 10% are being bullied at any given time. As Sarah Tracy, Pamela Lutgen-Sandvik, and Jess Alberts note, "If 1 in 10 workers currently suffers at the hands of workplace bullies, then bullying is a pervasive problem and not just the rare experience of a few 'thin-skinned' employees" (Tracy, Lutgen-Sandvik, & Alberts, 2006, p. 149). Workplace bullying is more than just a single hostile event or a disliked coworker. Instead, "bullying at work involves situations in which employees are subjected to repeated, persistent negative acts that are intimidating, malicious, and stigmatizing" (Tracy et al., 2006, p. 152). The negative outcomes that can accrue from such bullying are also serious and pervasive and may include stress, depression, loss of productivity, and increases in health care costs.

In their article on "Nightmares, Demons, and Slaves," Sarah Tracy and her colleagues were interested in moving beyond issues of definitions and outcomes and considering the notion of what it really *feels* like to be bullied. How do individuals process the ongoing experience of behaviors that might include screaming and cursing, spreading rumors, lying, physical abuse, and social ostracism? To answer this question, these researchers conducted individual interviews and focus groups with individuals who had been (or were being) bullied. They asked these individuals to describe their experiences—and even to depict those experiences in artistic form—and they used these verbal and nonverbal responses to come to conclusions about the metaphors workers used to make sense of their bullying experiences. Tracy et al. (2006) distinguished among metaphorical themes regarding the bullying process, the bully, and the target.

Participants in the research conducted by Tracy et al. (2006) described bullying, first, as a game or a battle. However, this game is not a fair fight, because the bullies play dirty and make up their own rules. They also described the bullying process as a nightmare that couldn't be understood or escaped, as the unending drip of water torture, or as a festering and noxious substance. These descriptions of the bullying experience were related to metaphors that described the bullies. These individuals were described as dictators or self-absorbed royalty, as two-faced actors who could impress organizational superiors while tormenting others, or as evil demons whose behavior was seen as "surreal, shocking, bizarre, and inexplicable" (Tracy et al., 2006, p. 167).

Perhaps most telling, though, were the metaphors study participants used to describe themselves—the targets of workplace bullying. One metaphor highlighted the dehumanizing aspect of the bullying experience, invoking the idea of being an animal or a slave. For example, one target likened himself to a fly whose wings were being cruelly pulled off by the bully. Targets also described themselves as prisoners who were unable to escape the bully or as a child back on the schoolyard with a "kick me" sign taped to the back. Finally, the targets of bullies saw themselves in the poignant role of a heartbroken lover as the bully separated them from their jobs and from others in the workplace. These people loved their jobs, they loved their coworkers, and the bullies had torn apart those relationships. In the words and pictures of respondents, hearts were broken by the bullies. As Tracy et al. (2006, p. 171) conclude, "[t]his imagery illustrates how abused workers feel the weight, scarring, and betrayal of abuse, and the loss of a beloved job, to their very core."

Tracy, S. J., Lutgen-Sandvik, P., & Alberts, J. K. (2006). Nightmares, Demons, and Slaves: Exploring the Painful Metaphors of Workplace Bullying. *Management Communication Quarterly, 20*, 148–185.

workplace because the private and public are often in conflict in organizational life.

- *Relational networks and emotional "buzzing"*: Waldron (2000) also points out that emotions can spread like wildfire in the workplace. One negative comment in a meeting can lead to a general uprising. A rumor about a possible downsizing leads to widespread panic. In short, "the interdependent and 'nested' nature of work relationships makes certain that the emotional implications of a relational event will be distributed and magnified" (Waldron, 2000, p. 68).
- *Conflicting allegiances*: Because organizations are complex systems, workers often feel many loyalties. These conflicts might involve a distinction between what's best for the individual and what's best for the company. Or an individual might feel conflicting loyalties to various departments or individuals in an organization. Or allegiances might develop to subcultural groups that have formed in the workplace. In any of these cases, intense emotions (betrayal, dedication, jealousy) might be found.
- *Emotional rights and obligations at work*: Finally, Waldron (2000) argues that most workplaces include a strong sense of relational morality—what is fair, right, and just in workplace relationships. When these norms are disrupted, strong emotions can be seen. For instance, Waldron (2000) quotes a woman who has been accused of "sleeping her way to a promotion" by a coworker: "I took my fist and cold-cocked that little sucker, and said [to him] 'file a grievance.' I have never had another comment, to my face, about what I have done" (Waldron, 2000, p. 72).

Emotion Rules and Emotional Intelligence

Emotion, then, is a central part of organizational life both in terms of interaction with customers or clients and in terms of interaction with other members of the organization. Some scholars have recently looked across these areas by trying to understand the "rules" for emotional display in the workplace and by understanding the role that emotional intelligence might play in a wide variety of workplace interactions. For example, Kramer and Hess (2002) recently surveyed a wide range of workers to learn about the perceived rules that govern emotional life in an organization. These rules are summarized in Table 11.1. The fact that workers perceived these rules to exist clearly suggests that there are standards for emotional expression both with coworkers and with customers and clients. For example, the most often cited rule involved the need to be "professional." This rule suggests standards for emotional control while interacting with clients and coworkers. For example, expressing anger through yelling and cussing would probably be seen as a violation of this rule, as would an expression of frustration or sadness through crying. It should be noted, however, that these emotional display rules are not hard-and-fast laws, but will vary from workplace to workplace and will change over time. For example, Scott and Myers (2005) describe the ways in which rookie firefighters must be socialized into strategies for managing the emotions of their highly stressful jobs, and Morgan and Krone (2001) studied the extent to which

Table 11.1 | Emotional Display Rules

Rule	Explanation
"Express emotions in a professional way."	An individual should have *control* over emotions and maintain a "business-like" atmosphere in the workplace.
"Express emotions to improve situations."	Emotional display should be managed in order to prevent or correct problems and create a positive work climate.
"Express emotions to the right people."	Positive and negative emotions should be directed to the appropriate person in the appropriate setting.
"Express emotions to help individuals."	Emotional display should be managed to provide support and assist others.
"Do not manage emotions for personal benefit to the detriment of others."	Emotional display should not be managed in a manner that is purely for self-promotion.
"The expression of certain emotions is *always* inappropriate."	Workers should maintain role-appropriate control of positive emotions and should not abuse others.

Table developed from Kramer, M. W., & Hess, J. A. (2002). Communication rules for the display of emotions in organizational settings. *Management Communication Quarterly*, 16, 66–80.

"improvisations" in emotional behavior can lead to a bending of the rules of professional display in the workplace.

Finally, it is important to consider the concept of emotional intelligence that has recently become widely known in the popular management press (Goleman, 1995). This concept suggests that there are some people who are naturally better at understanding and managing the emotional content of workplace relationships and that emotional intelligence is also a skill that can be developed through training. Emotional intelligence involves both a clear understanding of the emotional needs of the situation and the self-awareness and self-control necessary for using the right emotional display to cope with the situation. In essence, those who have a high "emotional intelligence quotient" (EQ) have a clear understanding of the rules of emotional display and an ability to follow and adapt those rules as necessary. Though the concept of emotional intelligence has been embraced by many practicing managers, it has also been criticized by some scholars (see Dougherty & Krone, 2002; Fineman, 2000) who argue that the concept of emotional intelligence is one more example of how organizations are attempting to transform emotion into a marketable product that will enhance organizational profits—perhaps to the detriment of the authentic feelings of organizational members.

STRESS, BURNOUT, AND SOCIAL SUPPORT IN THE WORKPLACE

In this chapter so far, we have considered the centrality of emotion in the workplace. In the remainder of the chapter we will look at one area of emotion that has received a great deal of attention from organizational scholars: the consideration of stress and burnout and the role of communication in causing and coping with these critical workplace emotions.

The investigation of stress in the workplace has led to a proliferation of terms used to describe various aspects of the phenomenon. In some cases, the use of these terms can be confusing. Consider, for example, the central concept of *stress*. Some scholars use the term to refer to aspects of the workplace that are difficult to deal with, whereas others use it to refer to the negative outcomes that accrue from these work conditions. For the purposes of this chapter, we will talk about stress as a general area of investigation and use more specific terms to refer to detailed aspects of the stress process.

The stress process can best be conceptualized as one in which some aspects of the environment, called *stressors*, create a strain on the individual, called *burnout*, which can lead to negative psychological, physiological, and organizational outcomes. This basic model is illustrated in Figure 11.1. The following few sections flesh out this model by considering burnout, stressors, and outcomes. We start in the middle of the model by exploring the concept of burnout.

Burnout

The term *burnout*, which was first coined by Freudenberger (1974), refers to a "wearing out" from the pressures of work. Burnout is a chronic condition that results as daily work stressors take their toll on employees. The most widely adopted conceptualization of burnout has been developed by Maslach and her colleagues in their studies of human service workers (Maslach, 1982; see also Cordes & Dougherty, 1993). Maslach sees burnout as consisting of three interrelated dimensions. The first dimension, *emotional exhaustion*, is really the core of the burnout phenomenon. Workers suffer from emotional exhaustion when they feel fatigued,

Stressors	Burnout	Outcomes
Environmental factors that are difficult for an individual to deal with:	Strain that results from ongoing stressors:	Physiological, attitudinal, and organizational results of burnout:
workload, role conflict, role ambiguity, life events, home/work conflict	emotional exhaustion, depersonalization, decreased personal accomplishment	coronary heart disease, high blood pressure, lower job satisfaction, less commitment, turnover

Figure 11.1 | Basic Model of Stress in the Workplace

frustrated, used up, or unable to face another day on the job. The second dimension of burnout is a *lack of personal accomplishment*. This aspect of the burnout phenomenon refers to workers who see themselves as failures, incapable of effectively accomplishing job requirements. The third dimension of burnout is *depersonalization*. This dimension is relevant only to workers who must communicate interpersonally with others (e.g., clients, patients, students) as part of the job. When burned out, such workers tend to "view other people through rust-colored glasses—developing a poor opinion of them, expecting the worst from them, and even actively disliking them" (Maslach, 1982, p. 4).

Consider, for example, Rhoda, a social worker who has been working with inner-city families for more than fifteen years. Rhoda entered her occupation as a highly motivated and idealistic worker. However, over the years she has become burned out from the daily grind of her job. Rhoda exhibits all three dimensions of burnout outlined above. Over time, she has quit seeing her clients as individuals with special problems and now refers to them by case number. She has even been heard to call some particularly difficult clients "lowlifes." Not surprisingly, Rhoda has trouble motivating herself to get to work every day and is physically exhausted and mentally drained by the time she gets home. When she thinks back on what she originally wanted to accomplish as a social worker, Rhoda gets very depressed, feeling that she has made little difference to anyone she serves.

Stressors That Lead to Burnout

Researchers have investigated a wide array of organizational stressors that lead to burnout. We will look in detail at those that involve communication later in this chapter. Several other workplace stressors must also be considered to form a complete picture of the development of organizational stress. It should be noted, of course, that not all stressors will lead to burnout for all individuals.

Three of the most frequently identified workplace stressors are workload, role conflict, and role ambiguity (Miller, Ellis, Zook, & Lyles, 1990). *Workload* has been linked to burnout both quantitatively—having "too much" work to do—and qualitatively—having work that is "too difficult" (Beehr & Newman, 1978; Cooper & Marshall, 1976). Workload stress can stem from a variety of organizational sources. For example, a teacher might feel overloaded because of the number of students in his class and the need to serve on school committees and process reams of paperwork. The pressure to do more in less time is particularly prevalent in organizations that have reduced their workforces through downsizing. Role conflict and role ambiguity were first identified as stressors by Kahn, Wolfe, Quinn, Snoek, and Rosenthal (1964). *Role conflict* involves having two or more role requirements that clash with each other, and *role ambiguity* exists when there is uncertainty about role requirements (Matteson & Ivancevich, 1982). For example, if a data programmer received no instructions about job requirements or got conflicting requests from different supervisors, burnout would be the likely result.

Burnout can also result from stressors outside of the workplace. Some years ago, Holmes and Rahe (1967) demonstrated the detrimental effects of stressful life events (e.g., divorce, retirement, pregnancy, death, moving) on physiological health. These events can also have a spillover impact on burnout experienced at work.

Perhaps more important than these major life events, however, are the day-to-day hassles and the emotional strain of balancing work and home life (see, e.g., Wharton & Erickson, 1993). As any working parent knows, it is virtually impossible to maintain the home and office as separate spheres, and stressors in one domain invariably influence the other. Indeed, in her book *The Time Bind*, Hochschild argues that for some Americans, the workplace has become a refuge from the stresses of home and family life (Hochschild, 1997).

Outcomes of Burnout

Figure 11.1 indicates that burnout can have a variety of physiological, attitudinal, and organizational effects. Physiologically, burnout has been associated with such outcomes as coronary heart disease (see House & Cottington, 1986, for a review) and high blood pressure (Fox, Dwyer, & Ganster, 1993). More scholars have investigated attitudinal outcomes of burnout. For example, researchers investigating a wide range of occupations and workers have linked burnout with lowered levels of job satisfaction (Miller, Ellis, Zook, & Lyles, 1990). Similarly, burned-out workers often have lower levels of commitment as they become disenchanted with a stressful organization or occupation. As Maslach (1982) notes with respect to human service workers: "A psychiatric nurse becomes a carpenter, or a counselor turns to farming. They swear they will never return to their original occupation with its crush of people and emotional demands" (p. 81). Finally, the most prevalent behavioral outcome linked with burnout in the organization is turnover (Ellis & Miller, 1993; Shinn, 1982).

Communication as a Cause of Burnout

There are numerous ways in which communication contributes to the experience of burnout in organizations. Several workplace characteristics have already been identified—workload, role conflict, and role ambiguity—that can serve as stressors and cause burnout. One way that communication in the workplace can influence burnout is through these variables. Communicative interactions, for instance, obviously contribute substantially to an individual's workload. Communication can also influence the experience of role conflict and role ambiguity. For example, Graen's model of role development (Graen & Scandura, 1987) that we discussed in Chapter 7 describes the ways in which supervisor–subordinate interaction helps to define expectations as an individual learns about the job and the organization. If communication in this crucial stage of socialization is inadequate, role conflict and role ambiguity are likely to result.

Thus, communication can play a role in causing burnout through its influence on workplace stressors such as load, role conflict, and role ambiguity. These are not the only ways that communication plays a role in the burnout process, however. Indeed, communication also plays a role in creating stress through processes of emotional communication discussed earlier in this chapter. We will now consider two ways in which the emotional aspects of work contribute to stress and burnout.

Emotional Labor as a Contributor to Burnout   As discussed earlier in this chapter, emotional labor is the term used to describe jobs in which specific emotions are required as a part of the job. Workers in service jobs requiring emotional labor must act in ways prescribed by the organization—the cheerful checkout clerk, the stern prison guard, the sympathetic counselor. So what does emotional labor have to do with burnout? Many researchers argue that they are closely linked. For example, Hochschild's original development of the emotional labor concept suggests that workers involved in emotional labor are at serious psychological risk. It is argued that a major danger of emotional labor is the display of emotions that are not truly felt. Morris and Feldman (1996) have called this "emotional dissonance" and contend that it is the major factor leading to negative consequences such as burnout, job dissatisfaction, and turnover. Although research on the link between emotional labor and burnout is somewhat mixed (see Wharton, 1999, for review), there is clearly the possibility that the display of false emotions can, in some situations, have detrimental effects on workers.

Empathy, Communication, and Burnout   A second area of research considering emotion and burnout has considered not the "prescribed" and "managed" emotions of emotional labor, but the natural emotions that often emerge in human service work. Specifically, Miller, Stiff, and Ellis (1988) have explored the role of emotional communication and burnout by developing and testing a model of communication, empathy, and burnout for human service workers. They first noted that individuals often choose these occupations (e.g., health care, social work, teaching) because they are "people oriented" and feel a high degree of empathy for others (Pines, 1982). Miller and colleagues (1988) then draw a distinction between two kinds of empathy—*emotional contagion* and *empathic concern* (Stiff, Dillard, Somera, Kim, & Sleight, 1988). Emotional contagion is an affective response in which an observer experiences emotions parallel to those of another person. For example, a funeral director who always feels sad when talking to grieving clients is experiencing emotional contagion. In short, emotional contagion involves "feeling with" another. In contrast, empathic concern is an affective response in which an observer has a nonparallel emotional response. For example, a counselor dealing with a hysterical client might feel concerned but not share the client's hysteria. Thus, empathic concern involves "feeling for" another.

How do these two dimensions of empathy influence the communication of human service workers? Miller and her colleagues (1988) speculate that empathic concern should help an employee communicate effectively, whereas emotional contagion should hinder effective interaction. Their reasoning is similar to the argument offered by Maslach (1982):

> Understanding someone's problems and seeing things from his or her point of view should enhance your ability to provide good service or care. However, the vicarious experience of that person's emotional turmoil will increase your susceptibility to emotional exhaustion. Emotional [contagion] is really a sort of weakness or vulnerability rather than a strength. The person whose feelings are easily aroused (but not necessarily easily controlled) is going to have far more difficulty in dealing with emotionally stressful situations than the person who is less excitable and more psychologically detached. (p. 70)

Miller and colleagues (1988) further hypothesize that workers who are communicatively responsive would experience less burnout and more commitment to their occupations. The model the researchers developed is presented in Figure 11.2. In a study of hospital workers, they found support for their model, ascertaining that empathic concern enhanced communicative responsiveness, whereas emotional contagion decreased responsiveness. Furthermore, they found that communicatively responsive caregivers were less likely to experience burnout. Their model has been further supported by research on workers providing services for homeless clients (Miller, Birkholt, Scott, & Stage, 1995) and in related work considering nurses (Omdahl & O'Donnell, 1999).

This research provides evidence that emotional communication in the workplace can be detrimental, but only under certain conditions. Specifically, when an individual in a caregiving situation feels *with* the client and communicates accordingly, burnout is the likely result. In contrast, a caregiver who feels *for* the client and communicates accordingly is unlikely to suffer the effects of burnout. This pattern has led some scholars to recommend that physicians and other human service workers attempt to adopt a stance of "detached concern" in which concern for clients can be maintained independent of strong emotional involvement (Lief & Fox, 1963).

Coping with Burnout

Thus far, we have looked at the genesis of burnout in the workplace, painting a somewhat bleak picture of organizational life. However, there are ways of coping with burnout. In this section, we first look briefly at individual and organizational strategies for handling burnout, then we expand on the role of participation in decision making and social support as communicative strategies to reduce burnout.

Individual and Organizational Coping Strategies There are many ways an individual might react to burnout. Some of these reactions—such as excessive drinking, drug use, and absenteeism—are clearly dysfunctional. However, an

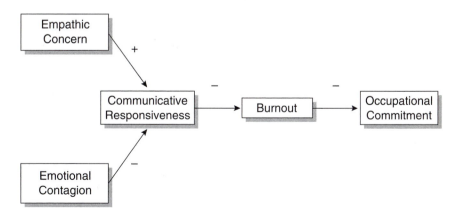

Figure 11.2 | Model of Empathy, Communication, and Burnout

individual might also cope in ways that could serve to ameliorate the experience of burnout and its negative outcomes. For example, some scholars have pointed to different types of coping for dealing with life stress and organizational stress (Billings & Moos, 1981; Folkman, Lazarus, Gruen, & DeLongis, 1986). Three types of coping have been identified. *Problem-focused coping* involves dealing directly with the causes of burnout. *Appraisal-focused coping* involves changing the way one thinks about the stressful situation. *Emotion-centered coping* involves dealing with the negative affective outcomes of burnout.

Consider Peter, an engineer who feels overwhelmed by the amount of work he must accomplish. His job leaves him no time for his family, and he is under constant pressure from his supervisor to do more and more on the job. There are several ways Peter could cope with this situation. He might employ emotion-centered coping by using relaxation techniques designed to release job-related tension. Or, he might use appraisal-centered coping by convincing himself that he needs to work hard in order to advance in the company and that short-term family sacrifices are necessary for long-term security. Or, he might use problem-centered coping by delegating some of his responsibilities, talking to his supervisor about work reduction, or using time-management techniques. These strategies would probably vary in their effectiveness in reducing Peter's stress. However, it is likely that problem-centered coping will generate the most enduring and satisfying reduction in job-related burnout.

The organization can also play a role in reducing burnout (see Pines, Aronson, & Kafry, 1981). Socialization programs can be designed to enhance the clarity of employee role definitions. Workload can be carefully monitored and controlled. Workers involved in high-stress or emotional occupations can be provided "time-outs" during the workday or occasional sabbaticals to recharge. The conflict between home and work can be acknowledged through the provision of flextime and on-site day care. All of these organizational strategies can serve to eliminate the causes of burnout or lessen its negative effects. Perhaps the most important ways of coping with burnout, however, arise through communicative interactions. Let's look at two important communicative ways of dealing with burnout: participation in decision making and social support.

Communicative Coping: Participation in Decision Making   A first communicative strategy for coping with workplace burnout is participation in decision making (PDM). We have already looked extensively at the participation process in Chapter 8. Specifically, we noted that PDM can improve both worker satisfaction and productivity through enhanced information flow (cognitive model) and the satisfaction of workers' higher-order needs (attitudinal model). Research has also indicated that PDM can decrease burnout in the workplace. Miller and colleagues (1990) found that perceived participation reduced burnout in a sample of hospital employees. Ray and Miller (1991) reached similar conclusions in their study of elementary school teachers. In an experimental study, Jackson (1983) found that employees who had an opportunity to participate in decisions experienced lower levels of strain and fewer intentions to leave their jobs.

Why should PDM work to reduce job-related burnout? Several explanations are feasible. First, it is possible that PDM serves to reduce two of the workplace stressors we talked about earlier in this chapter—role conflict and role ambiguity. As Jackson (1983) notes, PDM should lead to "more accurate knowledge of (a) the formal and informal expectations held by others for the worker, and (b) the formal and informal policies and procedures of the organization, as well as the discrepancies between the two" (p. 6). In addition to this effect on role definition, it is also possible that employees who participate feel more valued by the organization and feel a greater sense of influence and control in the workplace.

Communicative Coping: Social Support   A second communicative avenue for coping with workplace stress and burnout is social support. Voluminous research exists on social support as a means of protecting individuals from the major and minor stresses of life (see Albrecht, Burleson, & Goldsmith, 1995, for a review). In this section, we focus on the role of social support as a means of coping with job-related stress and burnout by considering the functions social support can play, the sources of social support for reducing strain in the workplace, and the mechanisms through which social support reduces burnout.

A wide variety of typologies have been proposed to categorize social support (see, e.g., House, 1981). Most typologies involve three major functions of social support:

- *Emotional support* involves letting another person know that they are loved and cared for. Emotional support might involve a message that boosts another's self-esteem ("I know you're bright enough to do well on the test") or a message that indicates unconditional regard ("You know I'll be proud of you no matter what you do"). Or emotional support might involve the provision of

Case in Point: Stretched Thin in the ER

As the scholarship discussed in this chapter makes clear, workers in human service careers such as health care face emotionally burdensome jobs. These workers interact with the sick and their families, dealing with stressed-out people during the most troubling times of their lives. Obviously, this is never an easy task, and it can be the source of both great rewards and intense burnout. However, the struggles of this kind of work become increasingly difficult when the load of health care workers increases.

Paul Duke (2004) makes this argument with regard to workers in his career—emergency room nursing. Duke points out that the load of ER nurses has increased substantially in recent years. This increase can be traced to a variety of sources—fewer qualified nurses, an aging population, more underinsured people using the ER as their first-line source of health care. For all of these reasons, ER nurses now must deal with many more patients than in the past, and those patients often have increasingly serious needs. Duke reports that he, like many nurses, is pulled apart emotionally by the stress. He says, "After all this you must wonder why I don't quit. The truth is, I love nursing. It's what I am good at. I love the challenge of not knowing what will come crashing through the doors. Emergency-room nurses rise to the occasion. But we are being steamrolled, stretched thin and beaten down, and the best of us are frustrated" (p. 12).

In this emotional struggle between the love of nursing and the frustration of increasing patient loads, we can only hope that the love of nursing continues to win out or that we find a way to cope with the pressures of an increasingly congested health care system.

a shoulder to cry on or a friend to gripe to ("You can always come to me when you have problems").

- *Informational support* involves the provision of facts and advice to help an individual cope. Several types of informational support could be helpful in the workplace. First, information might serve to decrease job-related stressors such as role conflict and workload (e.g., clarifying a job description or providing strategies for time management). Second, informational support might provide suggestions for dealing with the strain of burnout (e.g., suggesting a good health club for exercise).

- *Instrumental support* involves physical or material assistance that helps an individual cope with stress and strain. For example, a coworker might pitch in to help someone finish a project when that person is fighting a tight deadline. A supervisor might send an employee to a management seminar for extra job-related training. One's spouse might cook dinner. In short, instrumental support involves providing the resources and labor employees need to cope with workplace burnout.

A variety of people can provide individuals the support they need to cope with burnout. The three most common sources are supervisors, coworkers, and friends and family:

- *Support from supervisors* is most likely to come in the form of instrumental and informational support. A supervisor has the knowledge to provide informational support and the access to resources to provide instrumental support. For example, a supervisor can reduce role ambiguity by sitting down with an employee and clarifying job expectations (informational support). A supervisor could also reduce workload by informing management of the need for additional workers (instrumental support).

- *Support from coworkers* is most likely to come in the form of informational and emotional support. Coworkers (especially long-term employees) can often provide valuable information about how to deal with organizational stressors. Coworkers are also crucial as sources of emotional support because they have a clear understanding of the workplace context. Ray (1987) quotes a day care center worker on this topic: "When I try to tell my husband or friends what it's like at work, to deal with 15 screaming, fighting, attention-demanding kids for 8 hours straight, they don't really understand. The only people who really feel like I do are the people I work with" (p. 174).

- *Support from friends and family* will typically come in the form of emotional and instrumental support. Friends and family know an individual well enough to provide esteem support and a shoulder to lean on. Friends and family can also provide instrumental support by freeing an individual from home responsibilities. For example, a woman might take charge of the children for an evening to allow her husband to put in some extra time catching up with an office project.

SUMMARY

In this chapter, we have looked at an important emerging area of scholarship in organizational communication—the consideration of emotion in the workplace. We first looked at several areas of scholarship that emphasize the role of emotion in organizations. These include the consideration of emotional labor, the consideration of emotion in human service occupations, and the investigation of emotion in ongoing organizational relationships. We then turned to a consideration of a specific area of workplace emotion and communication: research on stress, burnout, and social support. We first looked at the burnout syndrome and then at workplace antecedents and outcomes of burnout and the role of commu-

nication in both causing and helping individuals cope with burnout.

As in previous chapters, it is instructive to look at our topic in the light of the various approaches to organizational communication (see Table 11.2). The classical approach to organizational communication largely ignores emotion, in general, and burnout, in particular. Indeed, a burned-out employee is simply a cog in the machine that must be replaced. Emotion has similarly been ignored by many scholars in the human relations, human resources, and systems approaches. Although human relations theorists consider "feelings" such as job satisfaction, and all of these theorists would see burnout as a

Table 11.2 | Approaches to the Emotion Process

Approach	How Emotion Would Be Considered
Classical	Emotions are not seen as an issue except to the extent that they lower worker productivity. Working conditions of classical organizations are likely to cause burnout, but burned-out employees will be replaced quickly.
Human relations	The only emotion considered is job satisfaction. Stress and burnout are likely to be dealt with through provision of emotional support or other means of boosting employee self-esteem.
Human resources	Emotions are rarely considered while rationally designing the organization. Stress and burnout are likely to be dealt with through participative decision making or structural changes designed to enhance employee control.
Systems	Emotions are seen as sensemaking opportunities. Stress scholars might consider the impact of communication network participation on stress and cybernetic models of burnout control in the work place.
Cultural	Expressed emotions are seen as one aspect of the values and assumptions held by organizational members. Conditions that breed stress and burnout are socially created through the interaction of organizational participants.
Critical	Emotions are seen as one indicator of strain in the relationship between employees and owners in the organizational context. Goal of the critical researcher is to educate workers to resist acceptance of conditions that create stress and burnout.

"problem" to be solved, emotion takes a backseat in the work of all of these approaches.

Much of the emerging work on emotion in organizations has developed from cultural and critical approaches to organizational scholarship. For example, Meyerson (1994, 1998) has contrasted the cultures of two health care settings with regard to stress and burnout. Her analysis points to differences in organizational culture (e.g., one culture saw burnout as a "disease" whereas the other saw it as a natural outcome of social work) that highlighted emotional aspects of organizational culture. Further, much of the research considering emotion and communication in the workplace has come from feminist scholars, who are particularly concerned with the experience of women in frontline service roles. Indeed, some researchers have argued that the performance of emotional labor is a "gendered" process (e.g., Hall, 1993). Finally, in the area of social support, Kirby (2006) has argued that many organizational programs and policies now take on the support tasks that were once the purview of family and friends. This development points to the increasing ways in which organizations maintain control over ever-increasing areas of our lives. Work such as this points to the important role that both cultural and critical researchers play in our consideration of emotion in the workplace.

Discussion Questions

1. How does a consideration of emotion change the way we view basic processes of organizational life such as conflict, decision making, socialization, and organizational change? Is it possible to balance concerns for rationality and emotion? How can this be accomplished?
2. How is the experience and expression of emotion different in different types of jobs? Compare, for example, emotion in the work of a minister, a store clerk, and a data processor. Are the emotional demands of some jobs more challenging than others?
3. As a student, you sometimes experience stress and burnout. How do your experiences compare with the discussion of stress and burnout in this chapter? How do you cope with stress and burnout as a student?

CASE STUDY | Inexplicable Events

- On November 18, 1999, on the campus of Texas A&M University, the Aggie bonfire collapsed, killing 12 students and injuring many more. The collapse of the bonfire was a hugely emotional event for students at Texas A&M, for faculty and staff, and for members of the surrounding community. Investigations regarding the decades-old tradition followed, and no on-campus bonfire has been burned since.
- On September 11, 2001, planes piloted by terrorists were flown into the twin towers of the World Trade Center in New York and the Pentagon in Washington, D.C. Another plane crashed in a rural Pennsylvania field. Thousands were killed, and 9/11 will forever be a dividing day in history, marking the beginning of an era in which terms such as "war on terror" and "homeland security" became common parlance. The emotional toll of September 11 on our individual, national, and global psyches will last for untold years to come.
- On August 29, 2005, Hurricane Katrina made landfall along the gulf coast of the United States. Hours later, many levees were breached

in New Orleans, leading to the flooding of over 80 percent of the city. For days, New Orleans residents sought refuge in shelters, in the ill-prepared Superdome, and in neighboring and distant states. Over 1,800 people died, and many more lost homes or were displaced for many months. Criticisms of local and national authorities for their handling of the storm were widespread.

- On April 16, 2007, the deadliest school shooting in U.S. history occurred on the campus of Virginia Tech University in Blacksburg, Virginia. In shootings two hours apart, Seung-Hui Cho, a mentally ill English major at the school, shot 32 people before committing suicide. The campus community mourned the loss of both students and faculty, and the incident led to national discussions regarding issues ranging from gun control to campus security to the treatment of the mentally ill.

These events—spread over less than a decade—took place in various locations of the U.S. geography. These events can be attributed to very different causes—terrorism, a natural disaster, a deranged student, a tragic accident. These events varied in terms of their long-term influence on our national and global consciousness—from a ripple in the aftermath of the bonfire collapse to the huge changes in both institutional systems and individual mind-sets brought on by the 9/11 terrorist attacks. But these events also share important characteristics. Though in retrospect they can be "explained" to a greater or lesser extent, at the time they occurred, the events were seen as somehow inexplicable. They were a breach to our beliefs about how things happened in a rational and predictable world. They shifted our organized ways of coping—sometimes for a few days or a few weeks and sometimes forever. Thus, individuals working with and around these events can shed important light on the role of emotion in organizational communication. Consider just a few of the possibilities.

EMOTION IN THE MIDST OF THE INEXPLICABLE

In each of these events, there were "first responders" who worked with the immediate onset of the disaster. Firefighters rushed to the World Trade Center and the Pentagon. Rescue teams hovered in helicopters, plucking New Orleans residents off of rooftops. Campus police worked to secure the safety of students on the Virginia Tech campus. Emergency medical personnel worked in the early morning hours to pull injured students out of "the stack" in College Station, Texas. These first responders were, in one sense, just doing their jobs. These were highly trained men and women who understood the needs of individuals in disasters and understood the ways that the work needed to be accomplished. First responders understand the emotional aspects of their jobs, and have special education to deal with stress. However, that does not mean they are immune to the emotional effects of working in the midst of a disaster. Indeed, recent research suggests that social workers who work with disaster victims have a heightened chance of experiencing post-traumatic stress disorder (Adams, 2007).

EMOTION IN THE AFTERMATH OF THE INEXPLICABLE

In the days and weeks following these events, a variety of workers had to cope with a huge number of organizational problems. In my experience as a professor at Texas A&M University following the bonfire collapse, I found that instructors and staff members were asked to deal with an incredible range of student emotions, and we weren't trained for it. As I wrote afterwards, "As professional academics, we were prepared to impart knowledge, to conduct research, to serve on committees, to provide career counseling, and so on . . . We weren't prepared to deal with the emotional turmoil that ensued when

12 young people were wrenched from a community in the prime of their lives" (Miller, 2002, p. 589). And there are a myriad of other "job tasks" that must be accomplished in the aftermath of a disaster. In New Orleans, thousands of people needed to be housed and fed, paperwork needed to be processed to provide money for immediate needs and long-term relief, funds needed to be solicited from donors around the country, planning needed to be started to consider ways in which the "next" hurricane could be coped with in a better way. Many of these tasks are bureaucratic and, on the surface, highly rational. However, in the aftermath of the inexplicable, even these rational tasks can be overridden by emotion.

EMOTION IN THE "NEW NORMAL"

And finally, we move past the disaster and beyond the inexplicable. Or do we? Can our personal and organizational lives ever return to the rationality of the times before the inexplicable? Do we just recreate new sets of logic to encompass that which we do not want to accept? Or was any of it ever all that logical to begin with? In the years since the 9/11 terrorist attacks, we have, in many ways, returned to a new normal. But this is a new normal in which media reports regarding war and terrorism are commonplace. It is a new normal in which we know that we need to take off our shoes in airport security lines. It is a new normal in which a widespread power outage causes rampant speculation about what group might be attacking us. It is a new normal in which the possibility

of surveillance from our government—and the organizations we work for—is much more conceivable than it was a decade ago. In all of these ways in which the inexplicable has somehow been made "explicable," we find the tight weaving of emotion and rationality in our lives and in our work.

CASE ANALYSIS QUESTIONS

1. In what ways do the "special cases" of organizational life discussed in this case bring processes of rationality and emotion into sharp relief? Is emotion more "present" in these cases? Are different kinds of emotion brought to the forefront? How does the everyday nature of most of our work lives blind us to processes of emotion?

2. How are the specific processes of emotion discussed in this chapter—emotional labor, emotional work, and compassion, stress, and burnout—illustrated in these examples of the inexplicable? Are particular processes of emotion in the workplace especially apparent in the midst of the inexplicable, in the aftermath of the inexplicable, or in living in the new normal?

3. How could organizations and employees in those organizations be better prepared to cope with the emotion of these inexplicable events? And could those lessons be translated into practices that lead to more healthy and happy organizational life during the more mundane days, as well?

Organizational Diversity Processes

CHAPTER 12

AFTER READING THIS CHAPTER, YOU SHOULD . . .

- Be able to describe how the workplace is changing in terms of the representation and participation of women and minorities
- Appreciate how the experiences of women and minorities in the workplace might differ from the experiences of white males
- Understand how prejudice, discrimination, and relational barriers contribute to the experiences of women and minorities in the workplace
- Be able to explain various approaches to the multicultural workplace and consider the ways in which diversity can make organizations more effective and better places to work
- Know about the challenges of the diverse and multicultural organization, including sexual harassment and balancing work and home, and be familiar with specific diversity management programs

As we move further into the twenty-first century, the workforce continues to reflect the dramatic demographic changes that began many years ago. Women continue to join the workforce in increasing numbers and are now entering careers that were once the exclusive bastions of men. The number of women in the workforce is anticipated to increase by 10.9 percent between 2004 and 2014, with women representing 46.8 percent of the workforce by 2014 ("The American Workforce: 2004–14"). Various factors have contributed to these changes over the last several decades, including increased career aspirations, changes in educational systems, and the creation of workplace support schemes such as child care and flextime (Goldstein & Gilliam, 1990). Changes in workforce demographics are also found along racial and ethnic lines. Indeed, it is estimated that by the year 2050 the U.S. population will be 24 percent Hispanic, 15 percent African American, and 15 percent Asian (Bryan, 1999), and this balance will be represented in the workforce, as well. In short, the organizations of today and tomorrow are, and will continue to be, populated by men and women from a wide range of racial, ethnic, and cultural groups.

What is it like to be a woman or a person of color in today's workplace? What factors contribute to their organizational experiences? What are the benefits and challenges of a culturally diverse workplace? And what strategies can be instituted to enhance the effectiveness of culturally diverse organizations? In this chapter, we discuss these issues and consider the implications of the changing workplace. First, we examine the experiences of people of color and women in the workplace and attempt to answer questions about how those experiences are changing. Then, we discuss the notion of a "multicultural organization" and consider the advantages and challenges of such a workplace. Finally, we look at some strategies for developing, managing, and celebrating a culturally diverse organization.

Before we delve into these topics, however, it is worthwhile to briefly consider the terminology that will be used in this chapter. Writing about organizational diversity can be a challenge, as terms used to describe people can be viewed as having a variety of meanings depending on who is involved in the conversation and the norms of particular contexts of time and place. In this chapter I will use the term *white* rather than the term *Euro-American*, which was used in a previous edition of this textbook. I use this terminology both because this is the term typically used in conversations about race and because "whiteness" has become a concept of theoretical interest to scholars in recent years (see, e.g., Grimes, 2002; Nakayama & Martin, 1999). I will use the terms *people of color* and *minorities* in this discussion, as well, though it is certainly true that "white" is also a color (see Grimes, 2002) and that the term *minority* might at times be misleading when we consider sheer numbers. What is more important than the terminology, of course, is an understanding of the communication and experiences of a wide range of individuals and groups within increasingly diverse organizational settings.

WOMEN AND MINORITIES IN TODAY'S ORGANIZATIONS

As noted above, women and people of color are entering the workforce in increasing numbers. But what are their experiences in the workplace? Are these experiences similar to those of white males? The consistent answer to this question is that the workplace experiences of women and people of color are vastly different from that of white men (Allen, 2000; Gates, 2003).

Consider first the case of women. For several decades, commentators have talked about the phenomenon that has come to be known as the *glass ceiling*. As Morrison and Von Glinow (1990) explain, "The glass ceiling is a concept popularized in the 1980s to describe a barrier so subtle that it is transparent, yet so strong that it prevents women and minorities from moving up in the management hierarchy" (p. 200). Heilman (1994) laid out the relevant statistics from fifteen years ago: "While women occupy 36% of the management positions in the United States . . . less than 3% of the top executives in *Fortune* 500 companies are women" (p. 126). Have things improved since then? Hardly. As Anna Quindlen noted in 2006, "it seems like a classic dance of two steps forward, one back. Indra Nooyi, an Indian-born numbers cruncher, was recently named CEO of Pepsi. But that makes her one of only 11 women now running a Fortune 500 company, which works out to slightly more than 2 percent" (Quindlen, 2006, p. 84).

The situation is even grimmer for people of color. The Equal Employment Opportunity Commission reports that "color discrimination in employment seems to be on the rise" ("Why Do We Need E-Race?" 2007). For example, in a 2005 Gallup poll, 26 percent of African Americans and 31 percent of Asian Americans reported that they had witnessed or experienced incidents of discrimination ("New Gallup Poll," 2005). Further, recent studies have found that black job applicants with lighter skin were more likely to be hired than those with darker skin, even when identical qualifications were presented (Cazares, 2007). There are also differences in various sectors of the labor market. For example, though black men are now less likely to be discriminated against in jobs requiring technical skills, discrimination still exists in jobs that require more social skills (Kim & Tamborini, 2006). Thus, two aspects defining the experience of women and minorities in today's organizations are a relatively greater difficulty in getting jobs and in climbing the corporate ladder to join the ranks of upper management.

There are other difficulties as well. We talked earlier about the "glass ceiling" that hampers advancement for women. Additional buzzwords describe further problems in the workplace. Several decades ago, Schwartz (1989) differentiated between women on a career track and women on a "mommy track" who were assumed to want flexible work arrangements and family support in exchange for fewer opportunities for advancement. The newest catchphrases in this area suggest enhanced flexibility for women as they choose to "opt-in" and "opt-out" of work (Conant, 2007), or as they take the "off-ramp" from the workplace to have children and then take the "on-ramp" back into a career several years later (McGinn, 2006). However, these transitions aren't always easy. For example, Hewlett (2007)

Case in Point: Working (and Fighting) in a Man's World

In recent decades, women have become commonplace in occupations that were traditionally seen as "men's work." For example, today no one thinks twice about a woman working as a doctor or a lawyer. However, there are still some workplaces in which the presence of women—particularly in the top echelons—remains unusual. Consider police work. For many years, women have "worn the uniform" and "walked the beat," but it is only quite recently that women have been appointed chief of police in some of the nation's tough urban police departments (Tyre, 2004). Women now head departments in Detroit, Boston, and San Francisco. The "bulletproof glass ceiling" has been shattered because these women are tough, competent officers who embody some of the skills increasingly valued for a chief of police—education, management and administration skills, and strong ties to the community.

Violet Palmer also works in a man's workplace. As the only female referee in the National Basketball Association, Palmer initially encountered the doubts of players and coaches, and still endures the jeers of some fans (Juarez, 2004). However, Palmer has made her way like all workplace pioneers. She said, "You know what, this is because it's different, because I'm a woman, and they just don't know any better." She countered with her philosophy that "if I prove myself, credibility will follow" (Juarez, 2004, p. 38).

Perhaps the most important area in which women now work in a man's world, however, is that of the military. Women have served in the military for decades, but there has always been a clear dividing line —women were not allowed to serve in combat roles and this limited the number of deaths of women in war. However, the nature of the wars in Iraq and Afghanistan have blurred this dividing line and added combat to the arenas in which women work. As Ephron and Wingert (2006) note, "Although in some circles the unprecedented role women are playing in combat zones is still contentious, the real surprise is how easily we've come to accept women's fighting and dying in war—and, with an overstretched military, how indispensable they've become" (Ephron & Wingert, 2006, p. 43).

reports that when women wanted to "on-ramp" back to work, only about three-quarters found a job and only 40 percent returned to full-time work. Finally, both women and people of color are often hampered by restricted access to power and by being assigned suboptimal tasks in the workplace (see, e.g., Ohlott, Ruderman, & McCauley, 1994); and many women and people of color find themselves marginalized, taking on the role of the "outsider within" established organizational systems (Allen, 2000; Collins, 1990).

Thus, women and people of color do indeed have different organizational experiences than white men. In the next few sections we'll explore those differences further by considering the concepts of discrimination and relational barriers in the organization and by looking at some of the unexpected experiences brought on by gender diversity in the workplace.

Stereotyping and Discrimination

One of the most basic ways that the experiences of women and people of color differ from those of white men is in the perceptions and attitudes that many people have about the two former groups—and in the behavior that sometimes results from these perceptions and attitudes. In essence, others often view women and people of color in biased ways, and these biases may result in significantly different treatment within the organization. Such bias in the organization has two components: "*Prejudice* refers to negative attitudes toward an organization member based on his/her culture group identity, and *discrimination* refers to observable behavior for the same reason" (Cox, 1991, p. 36). For example, a manager may believe, based on cultural stereotypes, that Japanese American workers are unassertive or that Mexican American workers are lazy. A patient might believe that only men have the mental capacity to be physicians. A customer might think that an elderly salesperson must be senile. These attitudes are all examples of prejudice. If these beliefs result in differential treatment of people in the organization, discrimination has occurred.

Research suggests that both prejudice and discrimination exist in the organizational context. Morrison and Van Glinow (1990) observe that:

> There is growing concern that differential treatment of women and blacks is not related to performance alone. Some studies suggest that deficiencies are presumed even when no differences exist because stereotypes based on historical roles persist . . . Ambiguity or lack of specific information about an individual contributes to bias against women and minorities because judgments are based on negative stereotypes of the group as a whole. (p. 202)

The stereotyping of women and minorities in the workplace is not always overt and simplistic, however. Osland and Bird (2000), for instance, note that people in organizations often move beyond irrational stereotypes such as "The (fill in the blank) are lazy, dirty thieves, and their women are promiscuous" (p. 66) but still engage in stereotyping that might be seen as more sophisticated (e.g., "gays and lesbians tend to be politically progressive") or as helpful (e.g., "individuals who are in wheelchairs prefer to be treated no differently than others"). However, even this sophisticated stereotyping can be dangerous, because it is typically incomplete and misleading (and often just plain wrong) when applied to individual members of a cultural group.

Unfortunately, there is little evidence that problems of prejudice and discrimination are decreasing in today's workplace. In 1992, the Equal Employment Opportunity Commission received 374 charges of color-based discrimination; in 2006, these filings increased to 1,241 ("Why Do We Need E-Race?" 2007). Further, new forms of discrimination and prejudice are emerging, as interracial marriages, increased immigration, and increased openness about homosexuality lead to the possibility of additional prejudice. Indeed, one of the most disturbing recent trends has been the discovery of the noose in the workplace, showing a return to a decades-old symbolic means of communicating hatred ("Employees Find Noose Hanging at Work," 2007).

Relational Barriers in Organizational Systems

The experiences of stereotyping, prejudice, and discrimination are typically seen as individual-level phenomena. That is, these are problems based on the mental models of individuals, though these mental models are often shared by large segments of the organizational population. However, there are also aspects of organizational relationships and systems that lead to differential experiences for women and minorities in organizations. Four of these issues will be discussed in this section.

First, there is compelling evidence that women and ethnic minorities experience limited access to or exclusion from informal communication networks (see Ibarra,

Case in Point: Working (and Teaching) in a Woman's World

The previous "Case in Point" considered several ways in which women are now working in occupations that were previously seen as the bastion of men. However, there are also jobs that are seen as "women's work." These include a variety of human service jobs such as nursing and social work, but perhaps the most female profession around is that of elementary school teacher. Sadly, though many women are now working in typically male occupations, the same cannot be said of men working in typically female occupations, such as primary school. Indeed, 18 percent of elementary school teachers in 1981 were men, as of 2007 that percentage is down to 9 (Scelfo, 2007). And this problem is likely to be self-perpetuating, as boys who might think about teaching see few role models in the classroom.

Why are there so few men teaching our young children? Several factors can explain the situation. First, pay is very low for elementary school teachers, and though this is a problem that affects everyone, men are still more likely than women to earn the primary salary in a family. But there are other more subtle barriers. Cultural stereotypes portray men as less nurturing than women and less able to connect with small children. Sadly, this stereotype sometimes leads to accusations that an affectionate male teacher is a pedophile. Scelfo (2007) recounts the story of a male first-grade teacher who, when his students "need help undoing buckles or rebuttoning pants when using the toilet, insists they step into the public hallway before he will help them" (Scelfo, 2007, p. 44). Luckily, there are programs underway trying to recruit additional male elementary teachers and provide important support and mentoring for current teachers. Unfortunately, these programs may have limited success if we retain our beliefs about the "natural" abilities and tendencies of men and women.

1993, for a review). This is critical because of the widespread importance of informal communication networks in such processes as socialization, decision making, and conflict management. Thus, as Ibarra (1993) notes, "Limited network access, therefore, produces multiple disadvantages, including restricted knowledge of what is going on in their organizations and difficulty in forming alliances, which, in turn are associated with limited mobility and 'glass ceiling' effects" (p. 56). Ibarra (1995) found that minority employees experience the most success when they develop a differentiated network consisting of both majority and minority members and of individuals on a wide range of hierarchical levels (Ibarra, 1995).

It is not always easy to fit into these networks, however. Ragins, Townsend, and Mattis (1998) report that successful executive women often had to develop an interpersonal communication style that men were comfortable with in order to be successful. One vice president reported that she had to learn "how to act with men who had never dealt with women before, and how to be heard, and how to get past what you looked like, and what sex you were, and into what kind of brain you had" (Ragins et al., 1998, p. 30). These difficulties can be particularly challenging in fields that are typically dominated by males such as engineering and the sciences (Kantrowitz & Scelfo, 2006).

A second relational experience that is different for white men and women and people of color involves that of establishing mentor–protégé relationships (Noe, 1988; Ragins & Cotton, 1991). Kram (1985) was one of the first researchers to discuss the importance of mentoring relationships, defining a mentor as "an experienced, productive manager who relates well to a less-experienced employee and facilitates his or her personal development for the benefit of the individual as well as that of the organization" (Noe, 1988, p. 65). Indeed, research indicates that women who have been successful in breaking into the executive ranks of large companies rank "having an influential mentor" as a critical component for career advancement (Ragins et al., 1998).

Because the mentor–protégé relationship is a close one that involves both career and psychosocial benefits (Kram, 1985), many women would prefer to develop such a relationship with another woman. Unfortunately, there is often a shortage of women in the upper-management ranks to serve as mentors (Ragins et al., 1998). Thus, a potential female protégé often must establish a mentoring relationship with a male, and this can be extremely difficult. Noe (1988) has reviewed some of the barriers to establishing cross-gender mentorships, such as lack of access to information networks, socialization practices, and norms regarding cross-gender relationships. For example, if "Diedra" were looking for a mentoring relationship, she might be hampered because she knows few people in the management ranks, because her upbringing makes her reluctant to initiate relationships with men, and because she is worried about how others might construe a mentoring relationship between herself and a man.

Mentoring can also be a challenge for minority employees trying to move into the executive suite. For example, research by Thomas (1993) considered communication in cross-ethnic mentorship. He found that successful mentorship could be achieved in relationships in which ethnicity was either openly discussed or suppressed, as long as the mentor and protégé agreed on the appropriateness of

Spotlight on Scholarship

In spite of increasing diversity in the workplace, scholars studying organizational communication have "typically used knowledge about one group (white males) as a reference point in their discussions of all organizational participants" (Orbe, 1998, p. 230). Orbe finds this "monocultural assumption" extremely problematic, because it diminishes and marginalizes the experiences of others in the organization. Orbe uses the label "co-cultural group" to categorize these others (e.g., women, people of color, people with disabilities, gays/lesbians/bisexuals) and explores the communicative experiences of co-cultural group members in his article on an "outsider within" perspective.

Orbe draws on theory from several sources (e.g., standpoint theory, muted group theory, phenomenology) and considers data from interviews with a wide array of co-cultural group members. From this theory and data, Orbe develops a model that explores "the everyday communicative experiences of a variety of co-cultural group members as they function in a variety of organizational contexts" (Orbe, 1998, p. 232).

Orbe's model of co-cultural communication is organized around two dimensions: the preferred outcome of interaction and the communication approach used in interaction. In terms of preferred outcome, Orbe discusses three possibilities:

- *Assimilation* involves the attempt to fit into dominant society through the elimination of cultural differences. Consider the comments of an African American man: "I think that for some of us there is a specific tendency to turn our radios down, take up golf, and other things like that to say that 'Oh, okay, I fit in.'" (Orbe, 1998, p. 244).
- *Accommodation* involves the promotion of multiculturalist collaboration. Orbe notes that this preferred outcome strives to "change the organizational culture so that many cultural experiences are reflected in it" (Orbe, 1998, p. 244).

- *Separation* involves the creation and maintenance of unique group identities outside or within dominant structures. Orbe notes that many with separation goals see themselves as being not extremists, but realists about intergroup relations.

Following this discussion of goals, Orbe considers three communication approaches. These are:

- *Nonassertive communication* that puts the needs of others before self. Orbe notes that this kind of communication can be strategically used to achieve goals in organizational settings.
- *Aggressive communication* might involve confronting, attacking, or sabotaging others. Aggressive styles might be used when more nonassertive stances are unsuccessful.
- *Assertive communication* takes the middle road through collaboration, but is often perceived as more aggressive by dominant group members. Consider the comments of one woman: "So I try to say my piece without stepping on any toes but sometimes it just comes across as 'we are going to do it this way, no if's and and's about it'" (Orbe, 1998, p. 247).

Orbe then takes these dimensions of communicative interaction and considers specific practices that are often instituted by co-cultural group members with varying goals and styles. These practices range from "manipulating stereotypes" to "educating others" to "intragroup networking." Through the consideration of these practices, Orbe opens a window onto the communicative experiences of "outsiders within" in organizational settings.

Orbe, M. P. (1998). An Outsider Within Perspective to Organizational Communication: Explicating the Communicative Practices of Co-Cultural Group Members. *Management Communication Quarterly*, 12, 230–279.

the chosen interaction style. However, establishing such a relationship can be difficult.

A third systemic aspect of organizational life that confronts women and minorities is tokenism. In many organizations, white males represent the vast majority of employees, especially among the ranks of management. Thus, women and people of color in managerial positions are often "tokens" or highly visible representatives of their gender or ethnic minority (Ilgen & Youst, 1986; Kanter, 1977). According to Morrison and Von Glinow (1990), "Tokens' performances are hindered because of the pressure to which their visibility subjects them and because members of the dominant group exaggerate differences according to stereotypes" (p. 203). That is, the only African American in a work group might be pressured to always represent the "black viewpoint," or men in a workgroup might joke about having to curb their language because there is a "lady" in the room. For example, Janna Levin, an astronomist who studies the origin of the universe, was asked for years about what it was like to be a woman scientist. She's now rejected that role as a spokesperson: "It took me 10 years to get back the confidence I had at 19 and to realize that I didn't want to deal with gender issues. And I didn't have to. Why should curing sexism be yet another terrible burden on every female scientist?" (Levin, 2006, p. 72).

Finally, there is evidence that the types of work experiences available to women and minorities may hamper their ability to advance in organizations. In a study of female executives, Mainiero (1994) found that their success was marked by such factors as getting assigned to a high-visibility project and demonstrating critical skills needed for effective job performance. Similarly, Ragins et al. (1998) found that women ranked the availability of "difficult or high visibility assignments" as crucial to career advancement. However, other research (e.g., Ohlott et al., 1994) has demonstrated that these kinds of job opportunities are often unavailable to women in the workplace. This, in addition to the tendency for men to be concentrated in "line" positions and women in "staff" positions, serves as an additional barrier to career advancement.

Summary of Women and Minorities in Organizations

In summary, then, the organizational experiences of women and people of color are likely to differ substantially from the experiences of white men. To varying degrees, women and minorities are confronted with stereotyping and prejudice, and with relational and systemic barriers, such as lack of access to networks and mentoring relationships and problems of tokenism in organizational groups. Thus, today's organizations can be an unfriendly place for women and people of color.

But what will tomorrow's organizations look like? Can these difficulties be overcome? In the next few sections, we will explore the notion of a multicultural organization by considering what such an organization looks like, the opportunities and challenges of a multicultural organization, and steps for developing one.

THE MULTICULTURAL ORGANIZATION

Moving beyond the stereotyping and discrimination found in many of today's organizations is a difficult task. To illustrate this, Morrison and Von Glinow (1990) have described three phases of workplace development in the area of cultural and gender diversity. In the first stage, *first-generation affirmative action*, the organization is concerned with meeting legally mandated requirements for gender and ethnic diversity. Unfortunately, "simply responding to legislative mandates does not seem to automatically result in greater minority inclusion" (Gilbert & Ivancevich, 2000, p. 93). Indeed, the focus on numbers and quotas in these firms can lead to intergroup conflict, distrust, and hostility. In the second stage of development, organizations reach *second-generation affirmative action*. At this stage, the firm has met affirmative action goals in terms of numbers, and the emphasis shifts to supporting female and minority employees. Finally, a *multicultural organization* moves beyond the concept of support for minority members to the institution of policies that deliberately capitalize on cultural and gender diversity. As Gilbert and Ivancevich (2000, p. 93) contend, "[R]ather than simply making a commitment to valuing diversity, creating an atmosphere of inclusion requires change on many fronts, including fairness, empowerment, and openness."

Cox (1991) provides a detailed description of a multicultural organization in terms of six dimensions: acculturation, structural integration, informal integration, cultural bias, organizational identification, and intergroup conflict. These dimensions are defined in Table 12.1.

According to Cox (1991), a multicultural organization is marked by the full structural integration of women and people of color. Women and minorities are proportionally represented at all levels of an organization and in all work groups. A multicultural organization is also marked by full informal integration. That is, people of color and women are not excluded from social activities or from mentoring and other developmental processes. A multicultural organization is also marked by an absence of discrimination, low levels of intergroup conflict, and high levels of organizational identification for all gender and ethnic groups.

Perhaps the most distinguishing characteristic of a multicultural organization, though, is the form of acculturation used. Cox (1991) distinguishes among three

Table 12.1 | Dimensions for Describing a Multicultural Organization

Dimension	Definition
1. Acculturation	Modes by which two groups adapt to each other and resolve cultural differences
2. Structural integration	Cultural profiles of organization members, including hiring, job placement, and job status profiles
3. Informal integration	Inclusion of minority-culture members in informal networks and activities outside of normal working hours
4. Cultural bias	Prejudice and discrimination
5. Organizational identification	Feelings of belonging, loyalty, and commitment to the organization
6. Intergroup conflict	Friction, tension, and power struggles between cultural groups

From Cox, T. H. (1991). The multicultural organization. *Academy of Management Executive*, 5(2), 34–47. Reproduced with permission of Academy of Management (NY) via Copyright Clearance Center.

processes through which differences between the dominant culture and minority cultures can be treated. The first of these, *assimilation*, is "a unilateral process by which minority culture members adopt the norms and values of the dominant group in the organization" (p. 35). The second, *cultural separatism*, is "a situation where there is little adaptation on either side" (p. 35). Finally, *pluralism* is "a process by which both minority and majority culture members adopt some norms of the other group" (p. 35). Cox believes that the pluralistic form of acculturation is the defining feature of a multicultural organization. It is only through pluralism that organizational members can come to understand and truly value cultural and gender diversity.

It should be noted, however, that developing this kind of diversity does not necessarily mean that members of the diverse organization will always agree with each other. Hafen (2003), for instance, talks about how the dominant metaphor of pluralistic diversity involves having a wide range of voices singing together in a single organizational chorus. However, Hafen believes that this chorus might not always be harmonious and she argues for "letting all voices on and (arguably) off key, into the choir, without flinching at discordant notes, without wishing that they would just be silent" (Hafen, 2003). In other words, a diverse organization provides both opportunities and challenges, some of which will be considered in the following sections.

The Diverse Organization: Opportunities

Probably few organizations today would meet Cox's (1991) description of a multicultural organization. The achievement of full structural and informal integration is the first difficult step. Attitudinal and behavioral changes following integration pose even greater difficulty. However, a number of organizations are moving toward this goal (see Gilbert & Ivancevich, 2000, for examples). Diversity, of course, should be valued in and of itself not simply as a means to an end (Ashcraft & Allen, 2003). However, it is also useful to consider the outcomes that can arise from diversity in the workplace. We have already talked about some of the advantages that might accrue to the individual in a multicultural organization (e.g., opportunities for advancement, equitable job opportunities). Organizations can also realize a number of opportunities as they move toward the multicultural model.

Cox and Blake (1991) argue for six important competitive advantages that can be gained through the insightful management of cultural diversity. These competitive advantages are detailed in Table 12.2.

Research and anecdotal evidence exist to support all of these competitive advantages. For example, Weaver (1999) indicates that the high turnover of women and minorities may be spurred by factors such as stereotyping, the absence of mentors, and the high costs associated with recruiting and training new employees. Robinson and Dechant's (1997) survey of human resources managers at Fortune 100 companies also points to many "bottom-line" advantages of a diverse workforce. Several of the competitive advantages highlighted in Table 12.2 have particularly interesting implications in terms of communication within organizations. These are the advantages to be gained through increased creativity and enhanced

Table 12.2 | Opportunities Realized through Diversity

1. Cost argument	As organizations become more diverse, the cost of a poor job in integrating workers will increase. Companies who handle diversity well will create cost advantages over those that do not.
2. Resource-acquisition argument	Companies develop reputations as prospective employers for women and ethnic minorities. Those with the best reputations for managing diversity will win the competition for the best personnel. As the labor pool shrinks and changes composition, this edge will become increasingly important.
3. Marketing argument	For multinational organizations, the insight and cultural sensitivity that members with roots in other countries bring to the marketing effort should improve that effort in important ways. The same rationale applies to marketing in subpopulations within domestic operations.
4. Creativity argument	Diversity of perspectives and less emphasis on conformity to norms of the past (which characterize the modern approach to management of diversity) should improve the level of creativity.
5. Problem-solving argument	Heterogeneity in decision-making and problem-solving groups potentially produces better choices through a wider range of perspectives and more critical analysis of issues.
6. Systems flexibility argument	An implication of the multicultural model for managing diversity is that the system will become less determinant, less standardized, and therefore more fluid. The increased fluidity should create greater flexibility to react to environmental changes (i.e., reactions should be faster and at less cost).

From Cox, T. H. (1991). The multicultural organization. *Academy of Management Executive*, 5(2), 34–47. Reproduced with permission of Academy of Management (NY) via Copyright Clearance Center.

problem solving and decision making, advantages that Milliken and Martins (1996) label the "cognitive" consequences of diversity.

Arguments for increased creativity and enhanced problem solving through diversity both rest on the contention that a diversity of employees will translate into a diversity of viewpoints. That is, men and women from different ethnic and cultural backgrounds will bring ideas to the organization that would not be available from a homogeneous workforce of white males. Considerable evidence supports this argument. For example, Kanter (1983) found that innovative companies employed more women and people of color than less innovative companies. Innovative companies also worked to establish heterogeneous work teams in order to "create a marketplace of ideas, recognizing that a multiplicity of points of view needs to be brought to bear on a problem" (Kanter, 1983, p. 167). The value of a diverse workforce has also become especially apparent in today's global marketplace in which a variety of backgrounds and viewpoints are needed to cope with increasingly complex problems stemming from many national and cultural locations (see, e.g., Carroll, 2007).

Managing these culturally diverse groups poses communicative challenges, however. For example, Watson, Kumar, and Michaelsen (1993) found that realizing the advantages of diversity takes time and effort. Specifically, these researchers found that when first formed, diverse groups were inferior to homogeneous groups in both performance and in managing the process of group interaction. However, over time, the diverse groups developed communicative strategies for encouraging participation and eventually generated a wider range of alternatives and perspectives on a problem than homogeneous groups. As noted earlier, however, a critical facet of this process is allowing for many voices to be heard (Hafen, 2003). Indeed, Kirby and Harter (2001) suggest that the concept of "managing" diversity—with the implication of management on the bottom line—can be problematic if it leads to valuing the profit-driving impact of diversity more than the people involved.

The Diverse Organization: Challenges

The challenges of managing and working in culturally diverse organizations are just beginning to be understood. For example, we have already talked about the glass-ceiling phenomenon, the "off-ramps" and "on-ramps" of careers, and the difficulty of managing cultural diversity in a way that values, rather than minimizes or ignores, differences. In this section, we consider three challenges that face organizations as the workplace becomes more diverse. The first of these is instituting diversity management programs (e.g., affirmative action) in ways that avoid the negative consequences associated with these programs. The second two challenges are associated with gender diversity: the challenge of dealing with sexual harassment and of achieving a balance between work and home.

Avoiding Negative Impacts of Diversity Management Programs   The Civil Rights Act of 1964 marked the beginning of programs designed to ensure equal opportunity in the workplace. The affirmative action programs that stemmed from this act aimed "to remedy discrimination and increase the representation of designated disadvantaged groups, namely, women and ethnic minorities" (Heilman, 1994, p. 126). However, debates continue about the efficacy of these programs, their impact on workers and organizations, and indeed their future as policy in the United States.

But what *are* the impacts of affirmative action programs? Heilman and her associates (Heilman, 1994; Heilman, Block, & Stathatos, 1997) have discovered a number of negative consequences for those the programs is trying to help, for those who feel "victimized" by the programs, and for others in the organization. Although the research on this issue is complicated, several generalizations are possible. First, affirmative action programs can affect how an individual benefiting from the program views his or her competence, and this *self-view of competence* can in turn impact their work behavior and communication. Second, affirmative action leads others in the workplace to *stigmatize* as incompetent those individuals assumed to have benefited from these programs. Third, individuals who feel they have been unfairly bypassed by affirmative action programs perceive injustice in hiring and promotion procedures.

To deal with these possible negative consequences, Heilman (1994) recommends that organizations emphasize the use of merit criteria in addition to some preferential criteria in making hiring and promotion decisions. She argues that the more a program emphasizes preferential treatment and quotas at the expense of merit criteria, "the more likely it is to exacerbate the negative self-view of competence of beneficiaries, to fuel the discounting process whereby beneficiaries are stigmatized by others, and to increase the perception of unfairness on the part of those who believe themselves to have been bypassed in the selection process" (p. 160). She notes that these "softer" forms of affirmative action might involve programs that specify minimum qualifications as a screen or ones that specify that minority status should be taken into account only with equally qualified applicants. Further, Heilman et al. (1997) conclude that it is critical for organizations to provide "unambiguous, objective, and public information regarding the job qualifications and performance of individuals associated with affirmative action" (Nye, 1998, p. 89). Such information can serve to minimize or eliminate problems associated with victimization and stigmatization.

Sexual Harassment   In 1980, the Equal Employment Opportunity Commission (EEOC) specified that sexual harassment is a kind of sex discrimination under Title VII of the Civil Rights Act of 1964:

> Unwelcome sexual advances, requests for sexual favors, and other verbal or physical conduct of a sexual nature constitute sexual harassment when (1) submission to such conduct is made either explicitly or implicitly a term or condition of an individual's employment, (2) submission to or rejection of such conduct by an individual is used as the basis for employment decisions affecting such individual, or (3) such conduct has the purpose or effect of substantially interfering with an individual's work performance or creating an intimidating, hostile, or offensive working environment. (*Federal Register*, 1980, p. 25025)

As is clear from this definition, a wide range of communicative behaviors can constitute sexual harassment, although many women and men see only serious offenses (e.g., requests of sexual favors in exchange for career opportunities) as harassment (see Solomon & Williams, 1997, for more detailed analysis). However, a person need not suffer severe psychological damage or extensive adverse work outcomes to be a victim of sexual harassment. It is enough to believe that sexual comments or behaviors create a work environment that is clearly hostile. Thus, understanding and recognizing sexual harassment in the workplace is rarely clear-cut. This is because "sexual harassment is not a purely objective phenomenon but one based on an individual's perception of another's behavior, which may be affected by any of a number of factors that make up a situational context" (York, 1989, p. 831). That is, one person may be offended by "girlie" calendars hanging on the wall, another might not even notice them. What one person sees as an innocent flirtation, another may construe as sexual harassment. Although quid pro quo harassment is probably much more rare than hostile work environment harassment, the Civil Rights Act of 1964 makes it clear that all forms of harassment must be taken seriously.

Several studies have specifically looked at sexual harassment as a communicative phenomenon. Taylor and Conrad (1992), in an analysis of narratives about sexual harassment, argue that sexual harassment is an expression of power, not of sexuality. "It is the antithesis of intimacy, self-knowledge and growth" (Taylor & Conrad, 1992, p. 414). Dougherty (1999) agrees with this assessment, but further argues that men and women see sexual harassment differently because of different experiences with power and fear. Indeed, Dougherty's (2001) study of perceptions of harassment in a hospital found that men and women might view the very same behaviors in very different ways. In her study, men viewed sexual joking and innuendo as a way to release tension in their stressful jobs. Women often viewed the same behavior as harassment. These findings suggest that in today's diverse organizations, dealing with harassment will not be a simple and straightforward task, as the standpoints of men and women may lead to very different conclusions about communicative behavior.

Finally, Bingham (1991) has looked at communicative strategies for dealing with sexual harassment in the workplace. Bingham notes that women (and, less often, men) who are being harassed face multiple communicative goals. The desire to deal with the harassment sometimes competes with the goal of keeping a good job and saving face. Thus, Bingham suggests that there is rarely an ideal way of dealing with harassment. Directly confronting the harasser in an assertive fashion is often the best strategy, but there are times when a victim of sexual harassment should use other strategies (e.g., directly reporting the harassment or dealing with the harasser in a less confrontational manner).

Balancing Work and Home   Finally, individuals and organizations are increasingly faced with the daunting challenge of balancing the needs of work and home. More and more women are entering in the workforce—some for their entire lives and others for shorter time periods throughout the lifespan. The needs of older women in the workplace might be quite different from those of younger women or of midlife men. For example, younger women have serious concerns with the logistics of child care and the creation of flexible work plans. For older women, the concerns often shift to balancing the needs of child care, elder care, and self-care, and to planning for future retirement. Further, both women and men may now find themselves trying to make sense of the "work" of staying at home with children. For example, Medved and Kirby (2005) argue that women who have taken an "off-ramp" from work construct "corporate mothering discourses" that see a stay-at-home mother as a "professional, well-educated, highly skilled, irreplaceable worker who is able to choose this supposed career path" (Medved & Kirby, 2005, p. 465).

For both organizations and individuals, the challenges of achieving balance between work and home are myriad. For the organization, the first challenge rests in the institution of programs that are "family friendly," such as flextime, on-site day care, job sharing, family leave policies, and telecommuting (see Friedman, 1987) and in making these policies usable by employees (Kirby & Krone, 2002). The second challenge for the organization involves the creation of a culture that values various aspects of employees' lives. The development and maintenance of such a culture can be extremely difficult in a diverse workplace. For example, employees who do *not* have children may resent the special benefits provided for "familied" employees and may feel bitter about needing to work late or on holidays so that others can be with children (Flynn, 1996).

For the individual, the challenges of balancing work and home are both personal and interpersonal. At the personal level, there are challenges of identity and defining self in both work and home roles. For example, Gregory (2001) found that individuals in the "new economy" often shape identities with values such as "family first" and "don't sweat the small stuff" as defining principles. Buzzanell and Liu (2005) found that negotiating identity was particularly difficult for women during the process of negotiating and experiencing maternity leave. For example, one respondent in this study noted the contrast between a "working" self and a "mothering" self: "You don't feel like the same . . . you're used to working every-day . . . you're cleaning, cooking and stuff and that's not you" (Buzzanell & Liu, 2005, p. 12). There are also interpersonal challenges for workers, as they attempt to negotiate tasks and identities with others in the workplace and with family members (Golden, 2001). These negotiations are complicated by culturally defined notions of gender and work that may limit choices. As Kirby et al. (2003) argue,

> If women are (or want to be) the primary caretakers—especially because new mothers nurse babies, women "intuitively" know how to do household chores, and women who fail to enact caregiving are derided as selfish—then women should downscale their careers, be "stay-at-home" mothers, or expect to participate in a second shift that may include eldercare.

Expectations such as these can make the negotiation of both job and home roles fraught with difficulty.

Managing (and Celebrating) Cultural Diversity

We have now talked about a number of advantages and challenges that can accrue from an organization with cultural and gender diversity. Demographic trends indicate that most organizations will have no choice but to become more diverse in the future, and many organizations are already working on ways to increase and capitalize on the benefits that come from a diverse workforce. However, this is not an easy task. In this section, we briefly consider some strategies organizations can use to gain effectiveness as a multicultural organization. Most of the scholarly and popular writing on this issue uses the term *managing* diversity to talk about these issues. For example, this is the term used in Figure 12.1 to discuss cultural diversity in the organizational setting. However, as we noted earlier, if management becomes equated solely with bottom-line concerns with profit, the people who make the organization diverse can get lost in the shuffle (Kirby & Harter, 2001). Thus, some scholars have suggested that we think not about the management of diversity but about the celebration of diversity in organizational and cultural life (Said, 2001).

Cox and Blake (1991) identify a number of "spheres of activity" that must be dealt with when living life in a culturally diverse organization (see Figure 12.1).

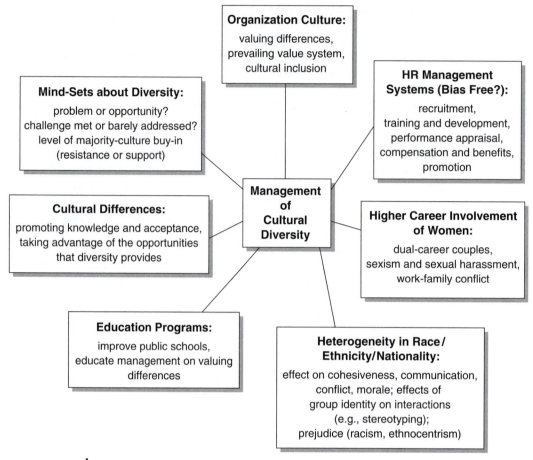

Figure 12.1 | Spheres of Activity in the Management of Cultural Diversity

Based on Cox, T. H., & Blake, S. (1991). Managing cultural diversity: Implications for organizational effectiveness. *Academy of Management Executive*, 5(3), 45–56. Reproduced with permission of Academy of Management (NY) via Copyright Clearance Center.

These spheres of activity highlight several points. First, life in a diverse organization involves both attitude and action. Managers and employees must view diversity as a challenge and an opportunity rather than as a problem that must be dealt with, and must become knowledgeable about the needs and contributions of diverse organizational members. But knowledge and attitude change are not enough; specific action must also be taken to ensure an educated workforce, the elimination of discrimination, a bias-free human resources system, and work options that ease the conflict between job and family. Second, as illustrated in Figure 12.1, managing different national and ethnic cultures requires an adjustment of the organizational culture.

How can an organization work to change its culture to embrace diversity as a core value? Cox and Blake (1991) suggest that five steps are needed to transform a traditional organization into a multicultural one: leadership, training, research, analysis and change of culture and human resources management systems, and follow-up.

First, in terms of leadership, Cox and Blake (1991) point out that top management must have a true commitment to diversity. Gilbert and Ivancevich (2000) note that "at several organizations recognized for managing diversity, a major organizing force is the CEO, who alone has the authority to make diversity part of the organizational mission." Second, employees must receive both awareness training and skill-building training. Third, research should be conducted to identify problem areas in the organizational culture and build appropriate educational programs. Finally, the culture of the organization must be audited to reveal ways in which diverse members could be hampered by current organizational values. Cox and Blake (1991) explain:

> To identify ways that corporate culture may put some members at a disadvantage, consider a scenario where a prominent value in the organization culture is "aggressiveness." Such a value may place certain groups at a disadvantage if the norms of their secondary or alternative culture discouraged this behavior. This is indeed the case for many Asians and for women in many countries including the United States. While it is conceivable that the preservation of this value may be central to organizational effectiveness (in which case the solution may be to acknowledge the differential burden of conformity that some members must bear and to give assistance to them in learning the required behaviors), it may also be that the organizational values need to change so that other styles of accomplishing work are acceptable and perhaps even preferred. The point is that the prevailing values and norms must be identified and then examined critically in light of the diversity of the workforce. (p. 54)

SUMMARY

In this chapter, we have looked at the changing face of organizations by considering the explosion of diversity in today's workplace. We began this chapter by considering several aspects of the experiences of women and minorities in organizations today. We found that women and people of color often deal with stereotyping and discrimination, as well as systemic and relational barriers in the workplace. We then considered the concept of a "multicultural organization" and discussed the opportunities and challenges posed by diversity. We concluded by outlining steps organizations can take in moving toward multiculturalism.

As seen in Table 12.3, the notion of diversity would be viewed very differently by different types of organizational communication scholars and practitioners. Managers taking a classical approach would probably go to great lengths to avoid diversity. After all, the classical approach is based on the concept of standardization, and there is nothing standardized about a diverse work population. Human relations proponents would strive to meet the needs of a diverse workforce, but would probably do little to either encourage or discourage diversity. In contrast, individuals from the human resources school would embrace diversity if they were convinced that a diverse workforce could provide a competitive advantage. The arguments we discussed regarding increased creativity and improved decision making would probably convince human resources managers to work toward the goal of an effective multicultural organization.

A systems researcher would be particularly interested in the structural challenges facing diverse employees. As mentioned earlier, women and people of color are often excluded from formal and informal communication networks, and a systems approach would be a viable avenue for

Table 12.3 | Approaches to Organizational Diversity

Approach	How Diversity Would Be Considered
Classical	Because diversity would limit the homogeneity of the workforce and hence be distracting or detrimental to morale, diversity would be strongly discouraged.
Human relations	Diversity would be neither encouraged nor discouraged. Emphasis would be placed on meeting the needs of women and ethnic minorities, even if those needs diverged from those of majority employees.
Human resources	Diversity would be encouraged because increased creativity and new ideas would increase the competitive advantage of the organization. Emphasis would be placed on maximizing the potential of women and minorities to contribute to the goals of the organization.
Systems	Diversity would be seen as one important avenue for the organization to adapt effectively to a turbulent global environment. Systems scholars might address the integration of women and minorities into formal and informal communication networks.
Cultural	Diverse organizations would be seen as important places where organizational culture intersects with national, ethnic, and gender-based culture. Emphasis would be placed on the process through which the intersection of cultural values is negotiated through communicative interaction.
Critical	Diverse organizations would be seen as the arena in which subjugated groups (e.g., women and people of color) must deal with the dominant class. Emphasis would be placed on the ways in which interaction among members of various cultures serves to perpetuate hegemonic relationships.

explaining and rectifying this problem. Scholars taking a cultural approach to the study of organizational communication would also be vitally interested in diversity. An organization with employees representing a variety of ethnic groups can be viewed as an intersection of cultural values. Thus, the creation and re-creation of organizational culture require the negotiation of many disparate value systems. Finally, critical scholars have already taken an interest in some of the power discrepancies that can arise in a diverse organization, and critical organizational communication researchers have shown intense interest in sexual harassment as a hegemonic relationship in the organizational context.

Discussion Questions

1. What have your experiences told you about the differences in organizational life for white men and for women and people of color? If you are a white male, do you believe these differences are real and viable? If you are a woman or a person of color (or

both), do you think your workplace experiences are influenced by your gender, culture, or ethnicity? In what ways?

2. What is the difference between "managing" diversity and "celebrating" diversity? Is this a valuable distinction to make, or merely a matter of semantics?

3. What do you think about affirmative action programs, both at the university level and in the workplace? Are these programs important to increasing diversity? Is affirmative action an equitable way of dealing with this issue?

4. Has the challenge of balancing home and work life been an issue in your family? If you are a "traditional" college-age student, how did this issue play out as you were growing up? Will the way your parents dealt with this issue influence your career and work choices?

CASE STUDY | **Perspectives on Encouraging Cultural Diversity**

The San Lucas Unified School District has a very aggressive affirmative action program. San Lucas, a midsize city in the Southwest, has a population that is approximately 50 percent white, 10 percent African American, and 40 percent Hispanic (mostly Mexican American). School district officials are strongly committed to recruiting and retaining teachers who represent this diverse population. They believe that students should have positive role models from their own ethnic groups and also think that a diverse teaching staff is best able to deal with student differences stemming from unique cultural backgrounds. The school district's goal is to achieve a teaching staff that has the same proportion of minority groups as in the local population. District officials realized early on that achieving this goal would be no easy task, so they instituted a set of hiring procedures that they hoped would attract minority applicants. Then they worked to make especially attractive offers to these candidates and instituted special programs (mostly seminars and workshops) designed to aid in these recruits' adjustment and to decrease turnover.

The officials hoped that Maria Sanchez would be one of their early "success stories." Maria was hired straight out of the state university into a position at San Lucas High School. She specialized in the science curriculum, teaching mostly courses in biology and general science. Hired at the highest salary possible for a new graduate, Maria also negotiated several conditions that were not part of the traditional employment contract. She felt she needed a computer at home to prepare exercises and graphics for her classes, and the school board provided one. She also asked for an extra free period each day for class preparation. She felt this was necessary, because much of her after-school time would be taken up by extracurricular activities and counseling the Hispanic students at the high school. The school board also complied with this request, agreeing that Maria's role in providing social support for the students was an important one.

Some rough times marked the first two years of Maria's contract with San Lucas High School. Her teaching evaluations were uneven because she had trouble maintaining control in the classroom and had difficulty explaining basic concepts to her first-year classes. She was much more effective in her advanced biology classes, where she could use extended simulations and exercises to illustrate complex processes. In general, the students liked her, but some complained that she "played favorites." She also ran into problems with her coworkers. Most of the teachers were friendly with her on an interpersonal level, but they were concerned that she was rarely willing to serve on curriculum, planning, or special-events committees.

After two years, Maria's probationary period was over, and it was time to make a decision about a long-term contract. Three representatives of the school district were meeting to discuss this issue: Jan Dobos, director of minority recruitment for the district; Raul Rivera, the principal at San Lucas High

School; and Zoe Grainger, head of the teachers' union.

Jan opened up the discussion. "It looks like Ms. Sanchez is doing a reasonably good job at the high school, and I definitely think she should be given a long-term contract. She's doing great work providing advice for many of the Mexican American girls who have no one else to talk to. And her teaching is beginning to shape up. I think with a bit more support from the district, she can develop into a really valuable contributor."

"We've got a problem here if you're talking about giving Maria even more support," Zoe interrupted. "There's already some discontent among the high school teachers about the special perks Maria got when she signed on here. None of the other teachers got a computer for home use, and they resent the fact that she only has four classes a day while they're teaching five. It's not that they don't support the diversity program here, but they see it coming out of their own hides. Maria's not pulling her weight at the school, and it's going to be tough to swallow if she gets any more special treatment."

"And aren't we forgetting something here?" added Raul. "What about what's best for Maria?"

Zoe laughed. "Most of the teachers don't think Maria's needs are being forgotten! Quite the contrary, it seems that Maria's needs are being considered over everyone else's—other teachers' and the students'!"

"That's just what I'm getting at," said Raul. "I've talked to Maria a lot about this, and I don't think you've taken her perspective at all. She's in a tough situation here. She feels like she's expected to be the perfect cultural role model for students and the school board alike. And she doesn't have anyone to serve as a role model for her; she's just feeling her way through the system. Maria's under a microscope—expected to advise minority students as well as serve in outreach programs. You may not think she pulls her weight with school committees, but you don't know the half of what she does with community programs."

"So what do we do?" asked Jan. "We need to make an immediate recommendation to the school board. Does she get a long-term contract, and if so, what should it look like?"

CASE ANALYSIS QUESTIONS

1.   What do you think of the cultural diversity program in the San Lucas school district? Are the goals of this program reasonable? Are good systems in place for reaching these goals? What alternative ideas could you suggest to the school district for improving its program?

2.   What should this committee recommend to the school board with respect to retaining Maria Sanchez? What other recommendations should they make to the board given what they have learned from their experiences so far?

3.   How can you explain the very different experiences of Maria and other teachers at the high school? Is there an avenue that could be taken to cope with these differences? How could this situation be managed to improve the situation for Maria, for other teachers, for the students, and for the community?

Technological Processes

CHAPTER 13

AFTER READING THIS CHAPTER, YOU SHOULD . . .

- Be familiar with new forms of communication technology in the workplace and appreciate how these technologies might differ from more traditional modes of communication
- Be able to explain the process of technology adoption in an organizational setting, including those processes presented by the media richness theory, the social information processing model, and the dual-capacity model
- Be familiar with how technologies might change the content of communication in the workplace
- Appreciate how technology shifts communication patterns, including patterns of power, participation, and social networking
- Understand how technology can radically change organizational structures, especially in the form of telework and virtual teams; you should also understand the paradoxical effects of these new organizational forms

Consider the changes that have taken place in workplace communication over the past hundred years. To create a simple document, we have moved from handwriting to typing to word processing. To produce multiple copies of that document, we have moved from copying the document by hand to carbon paper to high-speed copying machines. To store those documents, we have moved from boxes to file cabinets to floppy disks to hard drives, servers, CDs and flash drives. To send those documents over long distances, we have moved from stagecoaches to airmail to express mail to facsimile to PDF files. To exchange messages over long distances, we have moved from messengers to telegraph to telephone to voice mail and electronic mail. To get together as a group, we have moved from formal meeting rooms to conference calls to video conferencing to computer conferencing and online chat rooms. To make a decision we have moved from meetings run by parliamentary procedure to the use of computerized group decision support systems. To prepare presentations we have moved from charts to overheads to PowerPoint. In short, the workplace in the early twenty-first century bears little resemblance to the workplace of 100 years ago, and many of the workplace changes we observe are the result of technological innovations.

When I was finishing up graduate school more than twenty years ago, my fiancé and I were excited to buy our first computer. We went top-of-the-line, spending almost $7,000. But we felt we were getting our money's worth, because the computer had a dot matrix printer that worked at three different speeds, an internal dial-up modem (it was $500 just for that feature), and 10 megabytes' worth of storage capacity. We couldn't imagine ever using up that much space on the hard drive. My, how times have changed in twenty years. For one-tenth of the cost, you can now get a computer that is a thousand times better. And, of course, the basic PC is only the beginning. Twenty years ago, I couldn't have imagined the world I live in today, with e-mail, cell phones, Web shopping, fantasy football drafts via online chat rooms . . . And I'm not technologically advanced. Of course, for most of you reading this book, many of these technologies have been a part of your lives for as long as you can remember—so it's difficult to imagine what changes you may experience twenty years from now.

In this chapter, we examine some technological changes that have influenced organizational communication in recent years. We first look at some of these communication technologies and differentiate them from more traditional communication media. We then consider models that attempt to explain the process through which organizational members come to adopt these communication technologies. Finally, we examine the effects of communication technology on a variety of organizational communication outcomes. Before we begin our discussion, however, several caveats are in order. First, any discussion of "new" communication technologies is sure to be quickly outdated as innovations replace what is currently in vogue. Indeed, each new edition of this book requires the consideration of additional "new" technologies as well as new ways of using more dated technologies. Second, the introduction of new technologies does not always lead to the demise of older technologies. Although the copy machine largely eliminated carbon paper and the computer did away with, for most practical purposes, the typewriter, there are also counterexamples. The existence of video conferencing technology has not made the old-fashioned meeting obsolete, nor has the fax machine put the postal service out of business. And though experts were predicting the advent of the "paperless office" with the increased use of computer technology, most businesses go through more paper now than ever before. With these caveats in mind, let us move on to a discussion of technologies that have made an important impact on organizational communication processes.

TYPES OF ORGANIZATIONAL COMMUNICATION TECHNOLOGY

The range of technologies introduced to the workplace in recent years is mind-boggling. A number of these technologies are described in Table 13.1. This is not, of course, an exhaustive summary of organizational communication technologies, but many representative technologies are listed. In this section, we will briefly consider some facets of two of these technologies: electronic mail and the World Wide Web. Electronic mail has clearly changed both personal and organizational life in the last fifteen years. Indeed, it is likely that most people reading this page have "checked their e-mail" at least once already today. Jones (2002) reports that there were approximately 400 million e-mail messages sent daily in 1995 and almost

Table 13.1 | Examples of Organizational Communication Technology

Technology	Description
Electronic mail	User creates a written document at a computer and sends the document via computer to other user(s). Messages may be answered, filed, and/or discarded.
Instant messaging (IM)	Allows immediate communication with others online via the keyboard.
Voice mail	Messages are left and retrieved via voice synthesis technology on telephone. Messages can be edited, stored, and forwarded.
Facsimile (fax)	Document images are transmitted to another location by telephone and communication technology.
Audio and video conferencing	Allows participation in group meeting by participants at many locations. The conference can involve voice, image, and graphic material.
Computer conferencing	Allows synchronous or asynchronous participation in a conference on a specified topic. Typically includes the ability to poll participants and to maintain a transcript of proceedings.
Management information system	Computer system that stores and integrates information from throughout the organization for retrieval and use in decision making.
Group decision support system (GDSS)	Computer and communication technologies configured to maintain data sources, enhance information capacity, and provide decision-making structures for individuals and groups.
Internet and World Wide Web (WWW)	The Internet is a complex system of telecommunications linkages among major computer facilities worldwide. The World Wide Web is the sophisticated application on the Internet that allows widespread access to graphics and information, gateways to other Web sites, and interactivity for chat and customer service.
Wireless networks	Cellular telephones are the most familiar form of wireless communication. Computers and handheld computing devices (e.g., personal digital assistants) can also be connected in wireless networks for a variety of business applications.

16 billion sent daily in 2001, an exponential increase. By 2006, some estimates placed the daily total at over 60 billion. In short, e-mail is a ubiquitous form of organizational communication that can be used to send instant messages to targeted individuals, to "broadcast" information to a large organizational group, to chat with collaborators across the country or world, and to exchange and revise long, complex documents.

The World Wide Web is another aspect of Internet technology that has radically changed the way organizations operate. For the individual worker, the web can be used to gather relevant technical or policy information, to check on the activities of partners and competitors, to access timely news on a minute-by-minute basis, or to shop for just about anything. For the organization, the web serves as a forum to promote a desired image, to communicate with customers, and to conduct business of all kinds. Indeed, research conducted by Aikat (2000) suggests that even large corporations have barely begun to make use of the technological possibilities of the World Wide Web. But, of course, the web can also serve to drain organizational productivity. For example, the Monday after Thanksgiving is now popularly referred to as "cyber Monday," as individuals return to work and surf the web for holiday shopping bargains. Cyber Monday is one of the busiest online shopping days of the year, and if that much shopping is occurring, there is also some work that is not occurring.

What features make these and the other technologies considered in Table 13.1 different from more traditional organizational communication options? A number of characteristics do set these new technologies apart, although these characteristics vary from technology to technology. First, many of these technologies allow *faster* message transmission than that of traditional organizational communication media. Electronic and voice messages are delivered in seconds, and facsimile machines have provided a high-speed alternative to overnight mail delivery. Second, these new technologies often allow communication among *geographically dispersed* participants. For example, audio, video, and computer conferencing systems allow participants at many locations to take part in meetings that formerly would have required hours or days of travel. Similarly, with electronic mail and fax machines, individuals can be productive at home and avoid long commutes to and from the office. Third, new technologies allow *asynchronous* communication; that is, communication between individuals at different points in time. For example, communication by means of electronic mail can be accomplished effectively even if the two people communicating are never logged on to the computer at the same time. Indeed, many people see voice mail as a particularly efficient form of communication and may purposefully make phone calls when they know the other person will not be there to answer the phone. As Schulman (2000) ruefully notes, "talk into a recording and you expediently do the job: cancel a dinner reservation, terminate an employee, send a message of condolence after a death."

Some other features of new organizational communication media are less obvious. For example, new media often change ways of addressing messages. With most communication channels, the sender must specifically address a particular receiver (or group of receivers). However, media such as electronic "bulletin boards" and chat rooms allow communication to an unknown group of people who are interested in a particular topic. This anonymity can provide comfort for those uncomfortable sharing information. For example, Group Decision Support System (GDSS) technologies allow for the anonymous contribution of ideas to a decision-making process and thus may allow for a more egalitarian sharing of ideas (see Chapter 8). However, anonymity in other settings—for example, on some websites—can also serve as a shield for those engaged in criminal or unethical activities. New communication technologies also differ from traditional organizational communication forms in terms of *memory, storage*, and *retrieval* features. For example, GDSS technologies allow decision-making groups to create a full written transcript of meeting proceedings.

Finally, many new technologies differ in terms of the cues that are available in the communication process (Short, Williams, & Christie, 1976). Compare, for example, a traditional meeting with an audio conference. In an audio conference, participants are unable to assess nonverbal communication cues that are available in face-to-face settings. In a computer conference, even more communication cues are "filtered out," as participants look only at typed messages and are unable to gain information from vocal or visual channels. Sometimes, the elimination of cues is intentional, as users work to use the technology as efficiently as possible. For example, many older parents would have a difficult time deciphering the text messages of their teenage children, as such messages are written with a very specific code. And, of course, users of technologies can often enhance the content of their messages through codes developed specifically for the technology (☺).

In summary, new communication technologies offer organizational participants a wide array of interaction and decision-making options that can differ substantially from traditional ways of working. In considering the impact of these technologies on the workplace, two important questions must be answered (Yates & Orlikowski, 1992). First, what are the factors that will lead organizational members to choose particular types of technologies for their communication needs? Second, once these technologies are used, do they have a discernible impact on organizational communication processes? The remainder of this chapter will address

Case in Point: Caring at a Distance

We often think about the ways in which communication technology can influence business organizations, service companies, or even educational endeavors. However, in the field of medicine, the "technology" advances we think of more often are advances in surgical procedures, pharmaceuticals, or biotechnology. But communication technologies can make a huge difference in the provision of quality care, as well. For example, for many years, individuals in rural communities have been able to discuss diagnoses, have tests analyzed, and have X-rays read by physicians who are many miles away. In recent years, though, even the highly involved care provided by an intensive care unit has been assisted by communication technology.

Stern (2007) examines such a system of "eICU" that has been adopted at several hospitals in the United States. In this system, critical care nurses and doctors can monitor patients from afar, relying on multiple monitors and webcams. These remote caregivers supplement the on-floor staff, relying on tracking software that allows for early detection of possible problems. These systems are expensive to license and install, but Setara Healthcare in Virginia reports that they are worthwhile both for the bottom line and for patient care. Stern (2007, p. E18) notes that in this hospital system, there was a "27 percent reduction in the ICU's mortality rate, a 17 percent reduction in length of stay and savings of $2,150 per patient—or $3 million systemwide." These systems have not met with total enthusiasm, however, as some hospitals have not found them to be a cost-effective way to provide care. And even though there has been little criticism of these systems from the medical community, it's clear that long-distance medicine still requires lots of direct contact between physicians and patients. As Stern (2007, p. E18) concludes, "even in the digital age, the need for good bedside manners remains."

these two fundamental questions. After examining models that predict the adoption and use of communication media, we will discuss the effects of these media on organizational functioning.

THEORIES OF COMMUNICATION MEDIA USAGE

Once a new organizational communication technology hits the scene, most users do not quickly and automatically embrace it. Although their ranks are becoming increasingly thin, there are still people who are reticent to use a computer and many more who cringe at the thought of creating a personal web page. There are others, of course, who adopt each new technology with great enthusiasm. Consider, for example, the explosion in recent years of blogs and bloggers on the web. What factors predict the extent to which various communication media will be used in accomplishing organizational tasks or perhaps distracting workers from those tasks? Several theoretical positions have been offered on this question. For example, Markus (1990) suggests that new communication technologies will not be widely embraced until there is a "critical mass" of individuals who use the technology. The idea of critical mass is particularly important for communication technologies that require connectivity. For example, instant messaging did not take off until a critical mass of individuals were online with the technology for IM-ing available. However, the adoption of technologies involves more than just numbers. This section presents three important theoretical positions on factors that predict organizational communication media use: The *media richness model* was first on the scene and has engendered considerable research; the *social information processing model* and the *dual-capacity model* were proposed later to address perceived weaknesses in the media richness model.

The Media Richness Model

The media richness model was proposed by Daft and Lengel (1984, 1986) as a framework for understanding the choices organizational members make about communication media use. Daft, Lengel, and their colleagues were interested in how managers choose one communication medium over another for an array of organizational tasks. For example, if a manager were faced with the task of reminding employees about an upcoming meeting, what communication medium would be used to send the message: face-to-face communication, the phone, a memo, or an electronic mail message? Or, what would be the preferred communication medium for firing an employee or for resolving a conflict between two subordinates?

To explain such communication choices, these theorists first suggested that organizational communication tasks vary in their level of ambiguity. *Ambiguity* refers to the existence of conflicting and multiple interpretations of an issue. Consider, for instance, the examples described above. The manager informing employees about an upcoming meeting is faced with a relatively unambiguous task because multiple interpretations about a simple reminder are unlikely. In contrast, the manager who must resolve a conflict between two subordinates is faced with a communicative situation that has great potential for misunderstanding and emergent meaning.

Thus, this communicative interaction would be characterized as much more ambiguous.

Daft, Lengel, and Trevino (1987) then argue that communication channels available to the organizational manager differ markedly in their capability to convey information. These theorists use four criteria to distinguish the information-carrying capacity of media: (1) the availability of instant feedback, (2) the use of multiple cues, (3) the use of natural language, and (4) the personal focus of the medium. Communication channels that have all or many of these characteristics (e.g., face-to-face communication) are called *rich* media, whereas channels that have none or few of these characteristics (e.g., a mailbox flyer) are called *lean* media. Between these two endpoints would fall media including telephone, electronic mail, voice mail, written letters and memos, and others.

Media richness theorists then combine the notion of task ambiguity with the notion of media richness and argue that managers will choose media that *match* the ambiguity of the message. That is, when dealing with highly ambiguous tasks, managers will choose to use a rich communication medium (e.g., face-to-face interaction), but when dealing with a communication message low in ambiguity, managers will opt for a lean communication medium (e.g., a memo or flyer). These theorists further argue that managers will be more effective if they choose a communication medium that is a proper match for the ambiguity of the task at hand. These ideas regarding communicative effectiveness are illustrated in Figure 13.1.

	Unambiguous Task	Ambiguous Task
Rich Media	***Communication failure.*** Data glut. Rich media used for routine tasks. Excess cues cause confusion and surplus meaning.	***Effective communication.*** Communication success because rich media match ambiguous tasks.
Lean Media	***Effective communication.*** Communication success because media low in richness match routine messages.	***Communication failure.*** Data starvation. Lean media used for ambiguous messages. Too few cues to capture message complexity.

Figure 13.1 | Effective Media Selection Predictions

Adapted with permission of the publisher, from Lengel, R. H., & Daft, R. L. (1988). The selection of communication media as an executive skill. *Academy of Management Executive, 2,* 225–232. Reproduced with permission of Academy of Management (NY) via Copyright Clearance Center.

In general, there has been support for the basic tenets of the media richness model. Research has found that managers tend to choose rich media to deal with ambiguous tasks and lean media to deal with unambiguous tasks (see, e.g., Russ, Daft, & Lengel, 1990; Trevino, Lengel, Bodensteiner, Gerloff, & Muir, 1990); furthermore, there is some evidence that managers who follow this trend are more effective (Daft, Lengel, & Trevino, 1987). Recent research has also supported the basic ideas of media richness theory for the operation of organizational teams that relied heavily on communication technology. Maznevski and Chudoba (2000) found that the effectiveness of the team depended on matching complex tasks with face-to-face meetings or conference calls and relying on e-mail for simpler messages.

However, scholars still debate whether the media richness model provides a thorough explanation for the process of technology use in organizations (see Mennecke, Valacich, & Wheeler, 2000). Several studies have not found support for the model (see Fulk, Steinfield, Schmitz, & Power, 1987). Even in studies that generally support the model, there is a great deal of media-use behavior that is *not* accounted for by a match between task ambiguity and channel richness, and it is clear that organizational members may have goals in addition to task ambiguity (e.g., relationship maintenance) when making communication choices (Sheer & Chen, 2004). Scholars have also debated the extent to which managers are rational in their media choice behavior and the degree to which the characteristics of various media are objective and stable. Thus, several alternative models have been proposed to explain more fully the usage of organizational communication technologies.

The Social Information Processing Model

Janet Fulk and her colleagues have proposed that the adoption of organizational technologies (and the use of all organizational communication media) can be more fully explained by looking at the social environment of the organization (Fulk, Schmitz, & Steinfield, 1990; Fulk, Steinfield, Schmitz, & Power, 1987). In adopting a social information processing model (Salancik & Pfeffer, 1978), these theorists argue that communication between coworkers, supervisors, customers, and others affects media usage.

Consider, for example, an academic department that wants to increase the use of Web-based curricular offerings. A media richness approach would suggest that this communication channel would be adopted whenever it provides a proper "match" for the ambiguity of the communicative task. However, a social information processing approach suggests that an individual's use of Web-enhanced instruction will also be influenced by interaction with others in the department. Let's look at Rebecca, an instructor in our example department. Rebecca may have heard a great deal through the grapevine about how difficult Web instruction is to set up and maintain. This social information influences her perception of the medium's characteristics. Similarly, she might talk a great deal with students who have hated Internet instruction in other courses. Because of these and other social influences, Rebecca might not choose to use Web-based instruction, even if it provides an appropriate match to the ambiguity of the task at hand.

The social information processing model is depicted in Figure 13.2. As this figure illustrates, this approach sees the use of a communication technology as a complex function of (1) the objective characteristics of the task and media, (2) past experience and knowledge, (3) individual differences, and (4) social information. Because the model shows the objective characteristics of task and media (i.e., task ambiguity and media richness) as influencing media use, it can be seen as an extension of the media richness theory. In support of the social information processing model, evidence to date suggests that communication patterns do have an influence on technology adoption (Fulk, 1993; Rice & Aydin, 1991; Schmitz & Fulk, 1991; but see Rice, 1993, for contrary evidence). For example, a study by Contractor, Seibold, and Heller (1996) found that perceptions of a GDSS were more strongly influenced by the attitudes of others than by demographic characteristics or system attributes. Similarly, Carlson and Zmud (1999) found that perceptions of electronic mail were influenced both by the opinions of others and by experience and knowledge with the system.

The Dual-Capacity Model

In addition to the social information processing model, a second alternative to the media richness theory has been proposed. The dual-capacity model of media choice in organizations (Sitkin, Sutcliffe, & Barrios-Choplin, 1992) posits that com-

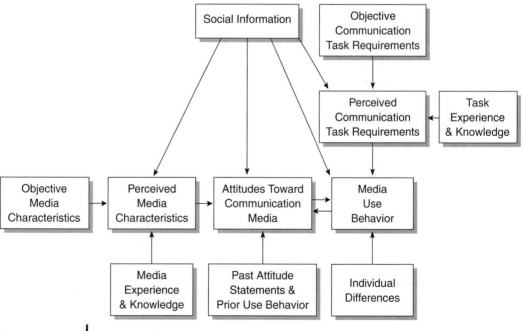

Figure 13.2 | A Social Information Processing Model of Media Use

From Fulk, J., Steinfield, C. W., Schmitz, J., & Power, J. G. (1987). A social information processing model of media use in organizations. *Communication Research*, 14, 529–552. Reproduced with permission of Sage Publications Inc. Journals via Copyright Clearance Center.

munication media are not simply "rich" or "lean," as proposed by media richness theorists. Rather, the dual-capacity model proposes that every organizational medium has the ability to carry two kinds of messages. The first of these is the medium's *data-carrying capacity*, defined as "the degree to which a medium is able to effectively and efficiently convey task-relevant data" (Sitkin et al., 1992, p. 566). Data-carrying capacity is analogous to media richness and relatively invariant across organizations. That is, voice mail will have approximately the same data-carrying capacity in all organizational settings.

Sitkin and associates (1992) propose that organizational communication media also have *symbol-carrying capacity*. The symbol-carrying capacity of a medium can be manifest in several ways. First, media can be more or less able to convey the core values and assumptions that constitute the organization's culture (see Chapter 5). For example, in an organization that values a "personal touch," a formal letter will not provide a communicator with the option to personalize a message in line with the company's culture. Second, a communication medium can attain the status of a symbol apart from the actual message being transmitted. For example, a meeting conducted via video conferencing can carry symbolic messages about the importance and technological sophistication of the meeting participants.

According to the dual-capacity model, the choice of communication channel will depend on *both* the data-carrying capacity and the symbol-carrying capacity of the medium. For example, a manager who needs to remind subordinates about an upcoming meeting is faced with a relatively unambiguous task. Media richness theory would predict that media choice will be based on the data-carrying capacity of media and that the manager will choose a lean medium such as a memo. However, the organizational culture in question might include a strong value for daily interpersonal contact. Thus, face-to-face communication has strong symbolic value, and our manager might decide to stop by the offices of subordinates to remind them about the meeting.

We have now considered three models that offer explanations for the process through which new communication technologies are used in organizations. The first, the media richness model, proposes that effective managers will match the richness of the medium to the ambiguity of the task. The other two models add complexity to this model by considering communicative influences on media perception and choice (social information processing model) and by considering the symbolic value of communication media (dual-capacity model). It is likely that organizational media choices are determined by a complex combination of all of these factors: the richness of the medium, the ambiguity of the task, the symbolic value of the medium, and the social information received from others in the organizational setting. It is also worth noting that individuals in organizations often have little choice about the adoption of new technologies, especially given the technological sophistication of many organizations. However, these models are useful in helping us understand the attitudes of people using technologies in the workplace and in understanding various patterns of media use.

Spotlight on Scholarship

The Internet and World Wide Web have changed our personal lives in many ways, and these technologies are also revolutionizing organizational functioning. In addition to the prevalence of electronic mail, the Internet is changing organizations through the development of organizational websites that serve functions including public relations, marketing, advertising, and direct sales. However, not all organizations have been quick to develop and adopt websites, and Andrew Flanagin (2000) conducted a study to pinpoint factors that influence the adoption of this important technology.

Flanagin proposed three sets of factors that might influence website adoption and use: (1) features of the organization, including size, age, and reliance on advanced technology; (2) perceived benefits of the technology, including benefits to profit and reputation, improved communication flow, and technical complexity; and (3) social pressures to adopt the technology, including the existence of others in the same industry who had adopted the technology, organizational visibility, and the perceived "faddishness" of the technology. Flanagin tested his model by surveying executives at 288 organizations and asking them about their use of company websites and the factors that influenced their adoption.

Flanagin noted that in predicting adoption most previous research has considered only the characteristics of the organization or those of the technology. However, Flanagin's research found that social pressures were key in distinguishing those who had adopted website technology from those who hadn't.

As Flanagin notes, "the single most important factor in separating adopters from nonadopters was institutional pressure: If organizations believed that other organizations in similar businesses or fields had a website, they were likely to have adopted one themselves" (p. 637). Thus, there seems to be a bit of a "bandwagon" effect in considering the adoption of new technologies.

However, Flanagin found other factors at play, as well. Specifically, his research suggested that the bandwagon effect was only in play for a limited time in the adoption cycle. As he argues, "social pressures may be most pronounced shortly after the achievement of a critical mass of users, because of the new viability of the innovation and corresponding pressure to take advantage" (Flanagin, 2000, p. 644). After this critical point in the adoption curve was past, however, Flanagin found that the likelihood of adopting and developing a website was more dependent on factors such as beliefs about the benefits of the technology and the technological sophistication of the organization. In conclusion, Flanagin found that the adoption of website technology—and doubtless the adoption of many new technologies yet to come—depended on a complex mix of factors that included the nature of the organization, the nature of the technology, the social interaction of individuals within the organization, and the institutions surrounding the organization.

Flanagin, A. J. (2000). Social Pressures on Organizational Website Adoption. *Human Communication Research*, 26, 618–646.

EFFECTS OF ORGANIZATIONAL COMMUNICATION TECHNOLOGY

The second general question to be answered with regard to technological innovations concerns the impact that those technologies can have on communication in organizations. We now examine this question by considering the effects of organizational communication technology on communication content, communication patterns, and organizational structure (see Rice & Gattiker, 2001, for summary). It is important to remember, however, that technologies do not *determine* particular outcomes and that the effects of any communication technology will depend on the manner in which it is employed or appropriated by the users (Poole & DeSanctis, 1992). For example, the user of an Apple iPhone has an incredible range of functions available—surfing the Internet, accessing music and videos, getting directions to a restaurant, organizing appointments. Yet it is also still possible to use the phone just to make and receive phone calls. Thus, the effects of a particular technology will depend both on its features and on how those features are used by the individual.

It is also important to note that the effects of technological advances can take many years to come to fruition and may be counterintuitive. For example, many commentators were puzzled when the U.S. economy came out of a recession in 2001–2003 but did not show any employment gains. Much of this paradox could be attributed to technology, as fewer workers were needed to generate productivity increases. For example, the technology for self-service at the grocery store has been around for years, but it is only recently that productivity gains have been realized through this technology. Similar effects (i.e., taking organizations a while to "get up to speed" with and to realize the effects of a technology in the workplace) are true for a great many communication technologies. With these caveats in mind, we will now consider the effects of technology on communication content, communication patterns, and organizational structure.

Effects on Communication Content

We noted earlier that many communication media "filter out" cues that would be available in face-to-face interactions. For example, when communicating by electronic mail, vocal cues and many nonverbal cues are unavailable in the interaction. How does this filtering out of cues impact message content? Several effects are possible. First, electronic media may *inhibit* the communication of social and emotional content because many of the cues often associated with such content are unavailable. For example, many people communicate anger through facial expressions or tone of voice rather than through words. Because these nonverbal cues are unavailable when using many electronic media, it seems reasonable that socioemotional communication content would be inhibited. In general, however, research has not supported this idea (Rice & Love, 1987). However, the socioemotional messages sent via technological channels may be more difficult to interpret than those sent face-to-face. One commentator noted: "I can't always read messages with emotional clarity . . . Is the writer of this e-mail argument taking on an angry tone? An ironic one? Conciliatory? Only the most highly skilled writers can make these nuances clear" (Schulman, 2000, p. 14). Over time, though, frequent users of electronic media may develop codes for socioemotional content that are widely shared (e.g., abbreviated messages sent in text messaging) and those codes may eventually be built into the technology itself. For example, on many word processing systems, the typing of a colon followed by a parenthesis will automatically turn into a smiley face (☺).

It is also possible that the distance and anonymity afforded by many electronic media will lead users to be less inhibited in their communication of socioemotional messages. Some research (Sproull & Kiesler, 1986) has supported this notion, finding that computer-mediated communication includes many instances of *flaming* (name-calling, sarcasm, obscene language, emotional outbursts). Although other researchers have questioned the prevalence of flaming (Matheson & Zanna, 1989), it is clear that both task and socioemotional content are prevalent when electronic communication technologies are used.

Effects on Communication Patterns

Extensive attention has been given to the effects of communication technologies on patterns of communication within the organization. The first finding in this area stems from our earlier observation that new technologies augment existing technologies rather than replace them. Because of this, organizations that adopt new communication technologies are marked by an overall increase in the amount of communication (Kraemer, 1982; Rice & Case, 1983). For example, when video conferencing is available, it will be used in addition to face-to-face meetings (not instead of them), increasing the overall level of organizational communication.

One disturbing result of this information increase is that we often feel that we are "drowning in data" (Tanaka, 1997). Shenk (1997) writes about the "data smog" that can result when we are constantly besieged with information from e-mail, pagers, cell phones, the web, faxes, and assorted mass-media sources. Jones (2002) reports that even CEOs of major corporations often spend hours a day writing and responding to e-mail. Further, the proliferation of junk e-mail, also known as "spam" (Branscum, 1997), has implications for individual irritation, for organizational productivity, and for the ability of computer systems to process the proliferation of data on the information highway. One research group reports that spam now accounts for 60 percent of all e-mail, putting a $9 billion dent in U.S.

Case in Point: BlackBerry Meetings

Cell phones, pagers, iPods, PDAs. It's amazing what kind of technology you can fit in your backpack, briefcase, or pocket these days. Technological advances in communication systems have made it possible to always be "in touch" with the office, home, and friends. One of the most popular communication technologies of the last decade is the BlackBerry, a device that combines electronic mail with the convenience of a pager. No longer do you need to find a computer to check your e-mail; you can pull your BlackBerry (or now, iPhone) out of your pocket and send and receive to your heart's content.

A friend of mine who works at a large corporation on the West Coast tells a story from a few years ago when BlackBerries were just becoming all the rage. He would attend meetings and everyone would pull out their BlackBerries, along with their legal pads and pens. During lulls in the meeting (and what meeting doesn't have its share of lulls) people could surreptitiously check their e-mail to be sure they weren't missing anything. Thus, attendees could be at the meeting and attending to other work at the same time. But the most interesting thing about these "BlackBerry meetings" is the influence of the technology on the meeting itself: the BlackBerries were also used to e-mail others sitting around the conference table. An individual who wants to put something on the table but doesn't think he's in a good political position to make a suggestion could e-mail a colleague to raise the issue. If the meeting is getting bogged down, e-mails could be sent to the convener to get it to "move along" without the embarrassment of an overt suggestion. In essence, the BlackBerry creates a distinct level of communication during the meeting available only to those who have the technology and choose to use it.

productivity "as workers peck away at the delete button every time another Nigerian dictator with a sob story crashes their IN box" (Stone, 2003, p. 66).

More specific issues regarding communication patterns have also been investigated. For example, Rice and Case (1983) found that an electronic message system increased the prevalence of upward communication in an organization, and Huber (1984) found that communication contacts were more diverse with communication technology. Similarly, there is some evidence that computer technology will lead to greater equality of participation in group interactions (Fulk & Collins-Jarvis, 2001), and there is other evidence indicating that establishing rules enhances trust in virtual groups (Walther & Bunz, 2005). Not surprisingly, one of the most widespread effects of communication technology is the increased prominence of individuals knowledgeable about the technology (Aydin, 1989; Ducheneaut, 2002). For example, Soukup (2003) reports the growing importance of consultants who secretly teach CEOs the basics of computer technology. The importance of "computer experts" becomes even more pronounced when there are concerns about system security. For example, in many organizations, only people with "administrator status" can make simple software changes on a computer. This can often result in frustration and lost productivity on the part of workers.

One of the most interesting new Web technologies with the potential to change organizational communication patterns is the increasing prevalence of social networking sites such as MySpace and FaceBook. For example, though FaceBook started as a site devoted to college students, its expansion has led to incredible levels of access to others' personal information and connection to "friends" of "friends" and so on. There are positive and negative implications of these social networking sites. On the negative side, individuals looking for a job should be very careful of the information (and perhaps photos!) available through these sites. On the positive side, these sites provide important ways to make contact with others about a wide range of work-related issues. Indeed, networking services are now available (e.g., LinkedIn, Ryze, and Tribe.net) that offer a work parallel to the social networking sites of MySpace and FaceBook (Jardin, 2007; Jones, 2007).

Effects on Organizational Structure

Finally, it is becoming increasingly clear that technology can change the very way we structure work and design organizations (Huber, 1990). Because technologies allow communication at great distances and at asynchronous times, it is often not necessary for people working together to be in the same place. Grantham (1995) has examined these issues in his discussion of *distributed work*. By examining both the time and place at which work is accomplished, four variations of work distribution become apparent. When work is accomplished by people in the same time and the same place, we have a classic example of a *central office*. When work is accomplished at the same time in a different place, we have *telework*, whereas work done at the same place and different time exemplifies *flextime*.

The most radical new form of organizations created through technology is the *virtual organization* that has no brick-and-mortar presence at all (Cooper & Rousseau, 1999; Igbaria & Tan, 1998). Rather, virtual work is accomplished at different times and different places through the use of multiple information and computer technologies. Shockley-Zalabak (2002) calls these virtual organizations "protean places" after Proteus, a being in Greek mythology who could transform his shape to meet the changing requirements of a situation. There are several ways to think about virtual work. First, for many, virtual work involves working from home, and this kind of arrangement is on the rise, especially given increasing concerns about the environment and work–family balance. For example, according to the International Telework Association and Council, in 2004 more than 44.4 million Americans worked from home at least one day a week (an increase of 7.5% from the year before) and 12 million workers were full-time telecommuters (Hansen, 2007).

A second way to think about the virtual organization is to consider virtual teams (sometimes called "geographically dispersed teams") that work across borders of time, space, and often, organizational boundaries. Virtual teams might be groups of individuals working on a particular project, parallel teams working in different locations, or service teams providing around-the-clock technical help. Virtual teams, with the help of advanced technology, work across time zones and across cultures, and this makes virtual teamwork particularly challenging. For example, Snyder (2003) provides some "tips from the trenches" of virtual teams, including suggestions to maximize face time, be considerate, make sure communication flows through a shared database, utilize appropriate technologies, and handle serious conflicts face-to-face whenever possible.

Cascio (2000) lays out advantages and disadvantages to both types of virtual work. Reasons for moving into this new way of doing business include reduced real

 ## Case in Point: Newspapers on the Way Out?

Technology changes not just the structure and communication patterns of single organizations—technology can also shift entire industries. Robert Samuelson (2007) presents the case for how this is happening in the newspaper business. He notes that as the Internet steals both the audience that reads the news and the advertising that pays for the news, the business of print journalism is in big trouble. For example, he notes that editorial staffs at U.S. daily newspapers dropped 7 percent from 2000 to 2006 and he estimates that the staff at *Newsweek* is now half as large as it was in 1983. Samuelson is frustrated by these changes (as traditional journalists probably are generally), as he sees journalism moving from a craft concerned with reporting and writing to a business run by multinational corporations that are largely concerned with multimedia presentations. Samuelson discusses several concerns with this trend. First, he worries that as traditional newspapers are taken over by large conglomerates (he uses Rupert Murdoch's 2007 purchase of the *Wall Street Journal* as an illustration), "journalistic integrity" could surrender to "the almighty buck" (p. 40). On an individual level, he raises the concern that "journalists are expected to be multimedia utility players, feeding Web sites, posting videos and doing TV" (p. 40), and he worries that these responsibilities will detract from reporting.

In the end, though, Samuelson is less pessimistic. For one thing, he notes that Murdoch has pledged to respect the *Journal*'s independence, and he hopes that this will be the case. He also notes that there is value in journalists finding new ways to inform and he notes the endurance of journalistic values such as respect for facts and an effort to be fair. So, though Samuelson acknowledges that, "If the Internet permanently crashed tomorrow, I'd be thrilled" (p. 40), he concludes that the news business is not really collapsing under the weight of technology. "It's merely changing" (Samuelson, 2007, p. 40).

estate expenses, access to global markets, and environmental benefits, as well as the possibility of increased productivity, improved customer service, and enhanced profits. However, there are also inherent challenges in managing a virtual organization—set-up and maintenance costs can be formidable, there are often losses of cost-efficiencies that can be secured in a traditional business, and tele-workers often feel isolated and cut off from the culture of the organization. For example, a recent report on National Public Radio pointed to the increasing trend of telecommuters gathering at private homes to work on their own projects but to share space and social interaction ("Work Groups," 2007). In summing up these advantages and challenges, Pearlson and Saunders (2001) discuss three important paradoxes that illustrate the difficulties of telework and virtual organizations:

- *Paradox 1: Increased Flexibility and Increased Structure.* One of the attractions of telework is the increased flexibility afforded to the employee. However, telework also requires the manager to keep better track of schedules and meetings, because "chance encounters and informal discussions do not occur" (Pearlson & Saunders, 2001, p. 118).
- *Paradox 2: Greater Individuality and More Teamwork.* Teleworkers are isolated on an individual basis, but they are also required to coordinate work to a high degree. For example, Hylmo and Buzzanell (2002) report that the telecommuters they studied often saw basic procedures as "mysterious" because they were expected to be independent and yet still adapt to the rules and regulations of the central organization.
- *Paradox 3: More Responsibility and Less Control.* The nature of telework requires tasks that can be accomplished independently. However, managers often fear losing control of workers who are out of sight (Fritz, Narashim, & Rhee, 1998). Similarly, teleworkers fear that if they are "out of sight" they will be less likely to be considered for promotions (Hylmo & Buzzanell, 2002).

As these paradoxes illustrate, virtual work opens up new avenues and new concerns for both individuals and organizations. Indeed, this uncertainty characterizes many of our predictions about the impact of communication technology in the workplace. Some forecasters ("utopians") are quite hopeful about the positive impacts of technology on organizations, whereas others ("dystopians" or "Luddites") are more pessimistic. As Turnage (1990) observes:

> The optimists view technology as increasing both productivity and employee quality of work life. They see the computer as freeing employees to work on more challenging tasks by taking over the routine aspects of jobs, thus increasing productivity and competition and creating more employment in the long run. The pessimists . . . associate automation with loss of employment, de-skilling (i.e., lowering the skill requirements for job incumbents), physical and mental problems, and a tightly controlled work environment. (pp. 171–172)

SUMMARY

In this chapter, we have examined the role of communication technologies in organizational life.

We began by considering a wide array of communication technologies and differentiated these technologies from traditional organizational communication media. We then considered three models of organizational communication media adoption. The first of these models, the media richness model, views media choice as a rational process of matching the richness of the medium to the ambiguity of the task. The second model, the social information processing model, expands on the media richness model by considering the role of communication in creating and sustaining attitudes and behaviors relating to communication technology. The third model, the dual-capacity model, highlights the ability of communication media to carry both data and symbolic meaning. After considering these models of media choice, we reviewed research on the effects of organizational communication technology. We discussed technological impacts on communication content, patterns, and outcomes, and paid particular attention to the ways technology has influenced organizational structure through telework and virtual workplaces.

As we have done with other topics, it is useful to consider how different theoretical approaches would consider the issue of organizational communication technology (see Table 13.2). Early classical theorists such as Taylor and Fayol would probably be amazed at the technological advancements in today's workplace. These classical theorists would see these technologies as tools through which the efficiency and productivity of workers could be maximized. In contrast, human relations

Table 13.2 | Approaches to Communication Technology Processes

Approach	How Communication Technology Would Be Considered
Classical	Organizational communication technology is seen as a tool that can be used to enhance the efficiency of organizations by supplementing or replacing efforts of human workers. Little concern is paid to other effects of technology.
Human relations	Organizational communication technology is seen as a tool that can free workers from mundane tasks and allow them to engage in activities that satisfy higher-order needs. Emphasis is placed on technological impacts on worker attitudes.
Human resources	Organizational communication technology is seen as a tool that could enhance organizational effectiveness when used in combination with human workers. Decision-making technologies are particularly relevant to the extent that they maximize the knowledge potential of employees.
Systems	Organizational communication technology is seen as a way to link organizational subsystems and to link the organization with the environment. Special attention is paid to the impact of technologies on communication networks and on the unintended effects of technologies.
Cultural	Organizational communication technology is seen as a symbolic manifestation of organizational culture and as a medium through which cultural values are developed and communicated.
Critical	Organizational communication technology is seen as a means for repressing workers through deskilling of jobs and control of information. Alternatively, technologies could serve as channels for democratization by allowing more open communication.

theorists would be concerned with the extent to which technologies could free employees from the drudgery of mundane work and offer them more intrinsically rewarding work. Human resources theorists would be most interested in how communication technologies could enhance information flow and how decision-making technologies could maximize workers' effectiveness.

A great deal of the research conducted to date on organizational communication technology has taken a systems point of view. The ability of these technologies to link disparate parts of the organization and to transform organizational processes makes a systems perspective especially appropriate. We have also already noted the impact of cultural theorists on the study of communication technology. When we considered the dual-capacity model of media adoption, we indicated the important role of technologies as symbols and as carriers of organizational values.

Finally, critical theorists could make valuable contributions to our understanding of communication technologies by considering the impact of these technologies on the distribution of power within the organization. As Huber (1990) has pointed out, there are mixed ideas about the impact of technologies on power distribution within the organization. Some scholars argue that technologies allow top managers to exercise greater power, whereas others believe that technologies serve to decentralize decision making and power as lower-level employees have greater access to information. There is little doubt, though, that technological innovations will lead to shifts in information access and resulting shifts in organizational power. Thus, a central role for critical theorists is the study of technologies in their capacity as tools for both oppression and emancipation.

Discussion Questions

1. Reflect on changes in communication technology during your lifetime. Are there communication technologies you use now that were not available when you were a child? What about changes experienced by your parents or grandparents? Do you think the pace of technological change is increasing or decreasing?
2. Which theory of communication media use seems most appropriate for describing the process through which you choose what technology to use? Are you rational in your

choices? Are you swayed by what others say about a technology or the symbolic value of the technology?
3. Consider all of the effects of communication technology discussed in this chapter. What do you see as the most positive effects? What effects are indicative of a "dark side" to communication technology? Given your beliefs about technology, would you consider yourself to be a "utopian" or a "Luddite"?

CASE STUDY | High-Tech Gardening

Hank Pembrook is the owner of The Greenery, a chain of a dozen plant nurseries in a large western metropolitan area. The Greenery has been very successful and has the largest market share of any nursery in the area. Not surprisingly, Hank is pleased

with his nurseries. They stock a wide selection of trees, plants, and gardening supplies, and Greenery customers come back because the staff is highly knowledgeable and extremely helpful. Hank has never been one to sit on his laurels (even box laurels!), though, so he has been looking at ways to improve customer service and enhance the overall profitability of his nurseries.

Hank has a good friend, Felipe, who is a bit of a "computer nerd." For years, Felipe has bombarded Hank with ideas about how he could improve Hank's business through the wonders of technology. Hank has finally agreed and has instituted two cutting-edge systems designed to improve business at The Greenery.

The first is a wireless information system designed to improve communication and inventory control among the various branches of The Greenery. All associates at The Greenery now have personal digital assistants that allow them to schedule appointments and send and receive e-mail. In addition, the system allows for immediate updating of inventory and pricing, which can be shared at all branches of The Greenery. Adopting this system required outfitting each person with his or her own PDA, as well as purchasing the complex business software for inventory control. It cost Hank about $25,000 for the necessary hardware and software.

The second system is one designed to enhance customer service. This system includes a touch-screen computer for each store equipped with software that helps customers select plants appropriate for their particular landscaping needs. For example, if a customer is looking for a small flowering bush that requires little water and would thrive in full sunlight, the computer would provide a list of plants that might fit the bill. Further, a full-color picture of each plant would appear on the screen so customers could actually see the variety of plants that might work for their needs. With the touch-screen computer, the menu-driven program is easy to use, and pilot tests with consumers have indicated that most gardeners find it helpful, educational, and fun to use. It cost Hank more than $5,000 per store to install these computer assistance centers.

Although Hank has spent a lot of money on the wireless data system and computer assistance cen-

ters, he is confident that the investments will pay off. The wireless data system has the potential to make the entire chain work more effectively, because information can be easily disseminated to all stores, individual branches can transfer data and messages with minimum hassle, and individuals can keep track of appointments and contacts and share that information easily with others. Further, the computer assistance centers promise to give The Greenery an important edge over the competition. No other nurseries in the area can provide such detailed information and advice for clients at the touch of a fingertip.

There are only two problems. First, managers and employees are not using the wireless data system. Instead, they continue to keep in contact by phone, track inventory via paper forms, and keep relevant contact and scheduling information stored in day-planners or in their heads. Second, customers are not using the new assistance centers. Some customers try the computers out of curiosity, but few go beyond the stage of "checking it out." Clearly, neither system is being used to its full potential. Because Hank has sunk nearly $90,000 into the new systems, he is understandably concerned.

Well, perhaps "concerned" is an understatement: Hank is panicked. The next time he sees Felipe, he flies off the handle: "Felipe, what am I going to do? My staff doesn't use their PDAs, my customers don't use the assistance centers! What should I do? More documentation? More training? More advertising? Bonuses for use? New software? New hardware? New employees? New customers? Should I just dump the whole idea?"

Felipe leans back in his chair. "Gee, Hank. I'm more of a systems guy. You've got good technology, but you're gonna have to talk to a people person to figure out how to get folks to use it."

CASE ANALYSIS QUESTIONS

1. As a "people person," how would you advise Hank? What can he do to increase the use of his

CASE STUDY | **High-Tech Gardening** *continued*

wireless data system and his customer assistance centers?

2. What different kinds of suggestions for increased adoption of these systems might be made by supporters of the media richness model, the social information processing model, and the dual-

capacity model? Is there a way to combine these approaches to help Hank out of his bind?

3. Was Hank realistic in his assessment of the possible advantages of these systems? What would research tell us about the likely outcomes of wireless data systems and the customer assistance centers?

The Changing Landscape of Organizations

CHAPTER 14

AFTER READING THIS CHAPTER, YOU SHOULD . . .

- Be able to distinguish between *modern* organizations stemming from the Industrial Revolution and *postmodern* organizations stemming from the Information Revolution
- Understand the nature of a global organizational environment and appreciate the practical and cultural challenges of working within such an environment
- Be familiar with the role of organizational and personal identity in postmodern organizations, especially during times of change and crisis
- Recognize the contemporary shift from a manufacturing to a service economy and be familiar with the communication challenges of providing service
- Recognize the move from a permanent to a contingent workforce and see how temporary workers (and the organizations they work for) are both challenged and rewarded

We began, in Chapter 1, with a consideration of the ways in which our organizational world of today is complicated. This complexity was illustrated with such issues as globalization, terrorism, climate change, and shifting demographics. I suggested that equally complex views of organizational communication are needed to effectively address these issues. In the following twelve chapters, our journey introduced you to ways of approaching organizational communication as well as to specific processes such as conflict, socialization, and emotion that are vital to considering organizational communication.

This journey began, in Chapter 2's discussion of classical approaches to organizational communication, with a consideration of the organizational world brought on by the Industrial Revolution. This was the *modern era*, ushered in by the logic and rationality of science and technology and nurtured by the managerial search for effectiveness and efficiency. This modern era or *industrial age* spawned many of the corporations and organizations with which we are most familiar and was the basis for many of the ideas about organizational communication that you have encountered in this book. These ideas about approaches ranging from human relations to systems to culture, and about processes including decision making, conflict, change, emotion, diversity, and technology, are highly relevant in today's organizations. But the world of organizations is changing, and in this chapter we conclude our journey with a look at some of the major alterations to the organizational landscape.

If the Industrial Revolution ushered in the modern era of efficient organization and society, many would say that the *Information Revolution* has ushered in the *postmodern era* where everything moves fast and life is more fragmented and less consistent. A number of years ago, Kenneth Gergen described these societal changes in the opening of his book *The Saturated Self* (1991):

> An urgent fax from Spain lay on the desk, asking about a paper I was months late in contributing to a conference in Barcelona. Before I could think about answering, the office hours I had postponed began. One of my favorite students arrived and began to quiz me about the ethnic biases in my course syllabus. My secretary came in holding a sheaf of phone messages, and some accumulated mail . . . My conversations with my students were later interrupted by phone calls from a London publisher, a colleague in Connecticut on her way to Oslo for the weekend, and an old California friend wondering if we might meet during the summer travels to Holland. By the morning's end I was drained. (p. 1)

Although Gergen felt drained by these multiple contacts around the world, his morning seems relatively sedate by today's standards. Where are the e-mail, the PalmPilot, and the cell phone? Why is Gergen merely concerned about work and not checking on stock prices, on turmoil in the Middle East, on his parents' move to an assisted living facility, and on his child's rescheduled soccer game? In short, we now seem to be living in a frenetic, multi-tasking, quickly changing, immense, and fragmented world. As we demonstrated in Chapter 1—this world is complicated. In this concluding chapter, then, we will again look squarely at our present and future lives and consider those issues that directly influence our work experiences. To do this, we will revisit one of the issues examined in Chapter 1: how work itself is directly affected by our global economy and related societal shifts. We will also focus on three aspects of our postmodern world that are key to a consideration of organizational communication. These are the increasing importance of image and identity, the shift to a predominantly service economy, and the prevalence of new employment relationships such as the "disposable worker."

COMMUNICATION IN THE GLOBAL WORKPLACE

Most likely many of us have recently called a help line for information about a product or help with computer software or perhaps government benefits. It is also likely that our helper was someone located in a call center in another corner of the world. In recent years, for example, when citizens in New Jersey and a number of other states have called for help with their welfare benefits, they found themselves talking to someone in Ireland. Service technicians for one Mexican tourism hotline are located in Oregon. A recent article offering assistance for businesses choosing an offshore call center location noted that though India is currently the preferred outsourcing site, there are important advantages for locations such as the Philippines and South Africa (Asangi & Sathe, 2007). The proliferation of companies choosing to locate call centers in such far-reaching locations is just one example of globalization, or "the rapidly developing processes of complex interconnections between societies, cultures, institutions, and individuals worldwide" (Tomlinson, 1997, p. 170).

Other examples abound. As we discussed in Chapter 1, as political changes have broken down many boundaries that once divided countries, business practices have changed, too. Many countries that were once considered unable to compete in the global marketplace have developed modernization programs that are helping them meet new challenges. As Zahra argues, "[T]hese countries have come to realize that in tomorrow's global economies there is room for all, assuming they have something to share with the rest of humanity" (1998, p. 10). Corporations in developed nations now have branches and manufacturing plants worldwide, as "[e]ven the best performing companies in these advanced economies have not escaped scrutiny in the face of the massive globalization of the world economy" (Zahra, 1998, p. 10).

A number of factors have contributed to the rise of globalization. Conrad and Poole (2002) argue that the intellectual impetus for the global economy is *laissez-faire capitalism*, or "the assumption that a free-market economic system has sufficient checks and balances in place to ensure that the legitimate interests of all members of a society will be met" (Conrad & Poole, 2002, p. 392). This economic philosophy—which minimizes the role of government—advocates the creation of wealth through free trade and has contributed to the globalization of business during the past few decades. With this globalization movement has come the increasing democratization of many world governments.

Of course, the economic and political impetus toward globalization has been helped along by many technological factors. Foremost among these are the ease of travel and the advent of advanced communication technologies. Through low-cost air travel, it is possible for companies to employ many "road warriors" to span the globe. And through technologies such as the Internet, the World Wide Web, facsimile, and video conferencing, it is possible to conduct business across great distances. (See Chapter 13 for a review of technological advances and their impact on virtual teams and virtual organizing.) As a result, we have moved from a landscape in which companies are largely associated with one country to a landscape where there is a mix of domestic organizations, multicultural organizations, multinational organizations, international organizations, and global organizations (see Table 14.1).

As Table 14.1 indicates, the global marketplace contains an array of organizational types. These organizations differ not only in their geographical identity (do they operate in one country? several countries? around the globe?) but also in how they manage the interests and concerns of their employees, customers, and clients.

Effects of Globalization

Clearly, economic globalization has substantially changed how we live and how organizations do business. As we noted in Chapter 1, there is considerable debate as to whether these are changes we should applaud or dread. And as Zahra (1999) points out, there are utopian and dystopian views on this subject. In the utopian view:

Table 14.1 | Organization Types in the Global Marketplace

Organization Type	Description
Domestic	An organization that identifies with a single country and predominant culture.
Multicultural	An organization that identifies predominantly with one country, but recognizes the needs of a culturally diverse workforce and diverse contacts outside the company.
Multinational	An organization that identifies with one nationality while doing business across several or many nations. Management recognizes the needs of a multinational workforce, customer base, and institutional environment.
International	An organization that identifies with two or more countries with distinct cultural qualities. Distinct national interests are assumed to exist within the company's management, clients, customers, and institutional environment.
Global	An organization that identifies with the global system rather than any particular nation. In a global workplace, organizational membership takes precedence over national allegiances.

Adapted from Stohl, C. (2001). Globalizing organizational communication. In F. M. Jablin & L. L. Putnam (Eds.), *The New Handbook of Organizational Communication: Advances in Theory, Research, and Methods* (pp. 323–375). Thousand Oaks, CA: Sage.

> Globalization will continue to escalate, transferring technologies, bringing cultures and societies closer, and creating a community of peace loving, intelligent citizens. In this vision of the future, globalization will foster cooperation among nations and create good will. Globalization will be an instrument of peace, growth, progress and prosperity. Competitiveness is viewed as a marathon to achieve and sustain excellence. (Zahra, 1999, p. 36)

For example, Taylor and Doerfel (2003) have described how an interorganizational network of nongovernmental organizations (NGOs) came together in Croatia during that country's transformation from a totalitarian state into the initial phases of a civil society. In contrast, a variety of dystopian views see globalization in dramatically different terms:

> Conservatives fear that globalization will undermine the integrity of a country's political and social institutions and may weaken its cultural fabric. Leftists are concerned about the prospect of political, technological and economic dependence. Others are concerned over our growing reliance on technology to address complex social and cultural problems. (Zahra, 1999, p. 36)

Of course, we will not be able to decide here which of these views will ultimately prevail. However, it is possible to consider some general effects of globalization and to examine how some organizations adapt to the global workplace. For example, Monge (1998) proposes several ways that globalization influences organizational communication. First, globalization results in *time and space compression*, changing communication patterns and perceptions. In the global workplace, every-thing moves quickly—you can be in Tokyo one day and Cleveland the next, and it's always the beginning of the workday somewhere around the globe. Space and time are no longer directly connected. Second, globalization enhances our sense of *global consciousness and reflexivity*. When we work in an organization that is global, multinational, or multicultural, we must be aware of the cultures of others and of our own attitudes, beliefs, and behaviors. This cultural consciousness and self-reflexivity is a requirement for organizational and individual well-being. Third, globalization leads to *disembedded* organizations and people. In a global society, behavior and interaction are often lifted from their local context and restructured across time and space. Monge, for instance, talks about how "the introduction of 'cybercafes' has altered the worldview of the younger generation in Kuwait and other Islamic Persian Gulf nations, where strong traditions for local values and considerable restrictions on the flow of information create inward-oriented socie-ties" (Monge, 1998, p. 146).

In addition to these specific effects, there are general patterns to consider in how people view the process and outcomes of globalization. Stohl (2001) has noted two such patterns for viewing the challenges and outcomes of globalization within organizational communication research and practices. The first of these, *conver-gence*, is an approach that emphasizes the need of organizations to adapt their practices to a global marketplace. A convergence approach considers how an orga-nization might adapt its practices to "a global system that requires flexibility, re-sponsiveness, speed, knowledge production, and knowledge dissemination" (Stohl, 2001, p. 325). In this approach, communication is seen as "a conduit for the acqui-sition of resources, capital, information, and expertise" (Stohl, 2001, p. 325). For example, Roberts, Kossek, and Ozeki (1998) have discussed management chal-lenges in the global workplace and advocated specific strategies for coping with such management challenges. Their ideas about instituting structures such as aspa-tial careers, awareness-building assignments, corporate SWAT teams, and virtual solutions (see Table 14.2) illustrate a convergence approach to globalization in which the goal is to enhance organizational performance in the worldwide marketplace.

In contrast, the *divergence* approach to the globalizing workplace emphasizes the cultural distinctiveness found around the world. The divergence perspective is less interested in exploring strategies for organizational success than in exploring how meaning is constructed in various cultural settings and the impact of organiza-tional norms and functioning on that construction of meaning. Stohl (2001) argues that "[t]he environmental and technological pressure on contemporary organiza-tions to become more and more similar clash with the proprietary pull of cultural identifications, traditional values, and conventional practices of social life" (p. 326). Thus, it is critical to look at the competing forces of convergence and di-vergence in examining communication within global organizations.

It is also vital to consider the human effects of globalization as more indivi-duals are working in unfamiliar cultures with people who hold different values and goals. For example, English-Lueck, Darrah, and Saveri (2002) found that it was not only crucial but also quite challenging for high-technology workers to es-tablish trusting relationships in global organizations where workers are separated

Table 14.2 | Strategies for Managing in a Global Marketplace

Strategy	What?	Who?	How?
Aspatial Careers	A corps of experts with borderless careers on long-term overseas assignments	Mobile and globally oriented employees with proven ability and loyalty	Deploy employees in leadership positions across sites, and rotate to develop human resources
Awareness-Building Assignments	3- to 12-month assignments in various global locations	High-potential employees who are early in their careers	Deploy employees in global positions to enhance global perspective and skills. Screen employees for ability to function in other cultures
SWAT Teams	Short-term project-length assignments in worldwide locations	Technical specialists	Provide specialized skills and the transfer of technical processes and systems to global locations on an "as-needed" basis
Virtual Solutions	Allow employees in a wide variety of locations to work together on global solutions to problems	Employees assigned throughout the organization in need of overseas connections	Use electronic communication such as the Web, intranets, and distance learning to disperse information across locations

Adapted from Roberts, K., Kossek, E. E., & Ozeki, C. (1998). Managing the global workforce: Challenges and strategies. *Academy of Management Executive*, 12(4), 93–106.

by great distances and are working under severe time constraints. Similarly, Mattson and Stage (2001) describe a variety of ethical dilemmas faced by workers who confront different cultural norms while working for global organizations. For example, Stage (1999) found that American companies in Thailand had an especially difficult time adapting to the national custom of gift giving at New Year's. Gifts were expected by clients from the Thai culture but were seen as unethical by many U.S. organizations.

In summary, a variety of economic, political, and technological forces have begun to transform the workplaces of organizations competing in the global marketplace. In the global marketplace, our perceptions of time and space change, as does our understanding of others and ourselves. Communication in these global organizations will depend largely on balancing the forces of convergence (making us more alike in our search for workplace efficiency) with the forces of divergence (making us appreciate our cultural differences).

Case in Point: Off-Shoring, On-Shoring, or Right-Shoring

Economists say that the United States emerged from recession in late 2001. However, for many months that recovery was characterized as a "jobless recovery" in which productivity increased but the jobless rate remained steady. What accounted for this pattern? In part, the jobless recovery was due to businesses becoming more productive with current workers because of technology (e.g., self-scanners at supermarkets) and other increases in efficiency (McGinn, 2004). However, globalization—and "outsourcing" in particular—is another reason why corporations were thriving but not hiring additional U.S. workers.

In the early days of outsourcing, most jobs sent overseas by U.S. corporations were either production or semi-skilled service jobs. Indeed, it is now commonplace to call a help center about a U.S. product and talk with a company worker in India, Thailand, or Bangladesh. However, in recent years, more skilled high-tech jobs have been sent overseas. Stories abound of computer programmers required to train their foreign-born replacements before being laid off (McGinn, 2004). Yet, the tide may be turning on the outsourcing craze. Stone (2004) details a number of problems encountered by organizations outsourcing skilled labor, including rising wages and office rents, high turnover of overseas workers, and shaky quality control. Thus, U.S. organizations are now struggling with decisions about which jobs are profitable to send offshore and how to best manage offshore operations. As Stone (2004, p. 53) concludes, "The latest term making its way through corporate America . . . [is] 'right-shoring.'"

COMMUNICATION IN AN ERA OF SHIFTING IDENTITY

As our economy becomes more global, the names of some corporations have become known worldwide. Some critics have talked about the "McDonaldization" of the world (Ritzer, 2000; Smart, 1999), and other names such as Disney, Ford, Nike, and CNN are brand names that are clearly recognizable around the globe. The worldwide spread of these corporate monikers suggests the increasing importance of organizational identity—knowing an organization, what it sells, and where it stands on relevant issues of the day. Indeed, Cheney and Christensen (2001, p. 233) argue that "[i]n the contemporary activities of public relations, issue management, marketing, advertising, and the like . . . the ongoing rhetorical struggle for organizations of most kinds is to establish a clearly distinctive identity and at the same time connect with more general concerns so as to be maximally persuasive and effective."

In addition to worldwide recognition, there are many other reasons for the increased importance of organizational identity in today's economy. For example, with widespread mergers and acquisitions, there is the shifting landscape of "who belongs to whom," causing confusion for a great many individuals and organizations. These mergers and acquisitions are often contentious. Consider the merger between technology giants Hewlett-Packard and Compaq in 2002. The very public fight between management at Hewlett-Packard (which favored the merger) and members of the Hewlett family (who opposed the merger) clearly influenced the opinions of many stakeholders, including customers, competitors, government regulators, and shareholders (Vance, 2002). Even mergers that are seen as "matches made in heaven" can run into serious problems when they are implemented. For example, the 1998 merger between Daimler-Benz and Chrysler was initially seen as a perfect match, but the merger soon ran into trouble as the corporate (and national) cultures of the two organizations clashed (Naughton, 2000). No one was particularly surprised when DaimlerChrysler sold Chrysler to a private equity firm in May 2007. Thus, today more than ever, many organizations are concerned with creating and presenting an image to their various publics. In this section, we will look at the communication that plays a central role in this effort.

Heath (1994) has noted that "[c]ompanies try to impose themselves on their environments, rather than merely adapt to them. They attempt to shape their environment by their presence in it, by what they do and say" (p. 228). This shaping of the environment involves creating and maintaining an organizational image or a "mental picture that is descriptive, evaluative, and predisposing" (Crable & Vibbert, 1983, p. 56). Organizations seek to create and maintain positive images in order to achieve long-term goals. As Cheney and Frenette (1993) explain, "The presumed circle of influence runs thus: corporation to public to policy makers to corporation" (p. 50). For example, a pharmaceutical company may attempt to enhance its image in a number of ways: by providing free AIDS drugs in sub-Saharan Africa, by distributing prescription discount cards for senior citizens who rely on Medicaid, or by promoting concern for the long-term health of Americans. It is then hoped that this positive image will engender public support that could eventually be parlayed into favorable policy decisions at various levels of government.

It is important to note, however, that organizational images are not always created and maintained through purposive campaigns. Members of the organizational environment form perceptions of an organization's image based on a wide array of messages. Further, sometimes the style or means of communication can be more important than the actual message. As Cheney and Christensen (2001, p. 241) suggest, "the principal management problem in today's marketplace of goods and ideas is not so much to provide commodities and services or to take stands on the salient issues of the day, but to do these things with a certain distinctiveness that allows the organization to create and legitimize itself." For example, Abercrombie and Fitch has positioned itself as a clothier for ultrahip, cutting-edge young adults, even in the midst of public relations debates regarding the appropriateness of certain images on clothing and in advertising (Kong, 2002).

Examples of organizational image creation and maintenance abound and illustrate the various communication avenues through which this process occurs. In the late 1970s, Mobil Oil enhanced its image through an advertising campaign that advocated positions on a wide range of public issues (Crable & Vibbert, 1983). Vibbert and Bostdorff (1993) recount how the insurance industry created and legitimated a "lawsuit crisis" through a well-orchestrated public information campaign. In more recent examples, the accounting firm Arthur Andersen attempted to distance itself from employees who might have been involved in illegal activity while serving its major client, Enron Corporation. In the fall of 2001, the travel industry as a whole attempted to link its image with patriotism in a post–September 11 public relations campaign. Federal and state government agencies (especially the Federal Emergency Management Association, FEMA) suffered from severe image concerns in the aftermath of hurricanes Katrina and Rita in 2005. And in 2006, California's agriculture industry worked to rebuild its reputation when fresh

Spotlight on Scholarship

This chapter argues that developing a business identity has become a critical aspect of organizational communication. However, recent trends also advocate the importance of packaging identity at the individual level. This is the "personal branding" movement in which "the concepts of product development and promotion are used to market persons for entry into or transition within the labor market" (Lair, Sullivan, & Cheney, 2005). Authors and consultants who are part of the personal branding movement ask individuals to sell themselves by determining (or creating) an identity that is notable and distinguishable, arguing that "Everybody is a package . . . The trick is making sure you control your package and the message it sends" (Peters, 1999, p. 46). Daniel Lair, Katie Sullivan, and George Cheney have recently described and critiqued the rhetoric of the personal branding movement.

Lair and his colleagues first situate the branding movement within the organizational world of the late twentieth and early twenty-first centuries. They note several ways in which the personal branding phenomenon is a response to the complexities encountered by today's workers. For example, they show ways in which personal branding is seen as an "inevitable" response to today's economic environment: "The argument goes that, because the economic environment is out of the control of the individual, the individual must be ready to respond to that turbulence" (Lair et al., p. 321). Further, personal branding is sold as a return to the American myth of self-reliance in which everyone was responsible for creating opportunities and realizing the American dream. Further, personal branding is portrayed as a way to combat the cynicism that might be an easy response to a boring work world of mundane tasks in cubicles. Lair et al. contend that "Taken together, each of these general appeals works to form an interlocking series of arguments insulating personal branding from criticism" (p. 324).

However, Lair and his colleagues *do* level several important critiques against the branding movement. First, they argue that the exhortation toward personal branding implies a model of work and life in which individuals are told to put their "brands" above their relationships. They quote Peters (1999, p. 72), who tells his readers that "We all know folks who are going to . . . start a business . . . write a book . . . learn to skydive . . . build a house . . . as soon as they 'find the time.' *BULLSHIT!* When you CARE you MAKE the time . . . and if that means saying 'NO!' to your friends, your spouse, your kids (hey, I never said there would be no sacrifices), well, there it is!" Lair et al. also argue that the personal branding movement provides few tenable options for women and almost no acknowledgement of people of color or working class individuals. This sends a dangerous message to many. According to Lair et al. (2005, p. 333), "By invoking the rags-to-riches Alger (1990) myth through its emphasis on the individual's ability to succeed if only they can find the right way to promote themselves, personal branding discourse leaves those who are economically marginalized as responsible for their own lot. Their economic failures become simply a result of their inability or unwillingness to package themselves correctly." In other words, though the personal branding movement traces its genesis to the complexity of today's organizational world, the solutions this movement offers (primarily to white, professional men) ignore—or magnify—some of the most vexing aspects of that complex world.

Lair, D. J., Sullivan, K., & Cheney, G. (2005). Marketization and the Recasting of the Professional Self: The Rhetoric and Ethics of Personal Branding. *Management Communication Quarterly*, 18, 307–343.

spinach contaminated by *E. coli* bacteria infected more than one hundred people and caused at least one death.

As many of these examples illustrate, image becomes particularly critical during times of organizational crisis. Classic examples include Exxon after the Valdez oil spill, Johnson & Johnson after the discovery of tainted Tylenol tablets, Union Carbide after the energy plant disaster in Bhopal, India, and NASA after the explosion of the *Challenger* space shuttle. More recent examples include a wide variety of food safety issues, concerns with toy safety dealt with by Mattel, the rollover accidents linked to Ford sport utility vehicles equipped with Firestone tires, and NASA's renewed problems with the *Columbia* space shuttle disaster, which suggested that the organizational culture may not have changed much (see Chapter 5 "Case Study"). The messages sent by organizational representatives in the face of such events could predict both the short-term image and long-term survival of the organization. Ginzel, Kramer, and Sutton (1993) have proposed that image management in these situations is a reciprocal process in which organizational members (especially top management) create and adapt accounts of the event in response to both sympathetic and antagonistic organizational audiences. They use the case of Dow Corning and questions about breast implants as an example of how a top management team provides an account of what happened and then "actively scans the environment for signs of audience reaction" (p. 244). Through active monitoring and spin control, the organization attempts to create an optimal image in light of changing environmental conditions.

In sum, then, there are a variety of forces that have recently enhanced the importance of organizational identity and image. These include globalization and the increased occurrence of organizational mergers and acquisitions. In this environment—and especially during times of crisis—organizations engage in public relations, marketing, advertising, and issues management to create and maintain a preferred public image.

COMMUNICATION IN A SERVICE ECONOMY

A third aspect of the changing landscape for organizational communication involves the type of business we conduct in today's organizational world. In the years following the Industrial Revolution (see Chapter 2), most organizations counted the creation of "things" as a primary goal. The U.S. economy (and other world economies) was based primarily on manufacturing. Today, however, our economy can largely be characterized as a service economy. Meyer and DeTore (1999, p. 64) laid out some relevant statistics and projections a decade ago, noting that "the service-producing sector continues to lead projected employment growth, and . . . the 10 leading industries, accounting for 60 percent of all projected job growth over the coming decade, are all service producers." A recent publication of the U.S. Department of State bears out many of these predictions, noting that in 2006, 67.8 percent of the U.S. gross domestic product could be accounted for by services produced by private industry, especially in the areas of banking, insurance, investment, wholesale and retail sales, transportation, and health care ("A Service Economy," 2007).

Indeed, it is hard to deny the importance of service in our daily lives as employees, students, customers, and clients in a wide range of organizational settings. Even a trip to the grocery store involves a service encounter that has implications both for the grocer's profits and for your mood for the rest of the day. Thus, it is little surprise that popular business publications tout the importance of service. As Pederson (1997) notes, "We were supposed to be enjoying a fabulous experience with every retail transaction by now—at least according to all those books about super-duper getting-close-to-your-customer excellence" (p. 57). However, surveys indicate that, with a few exceptions (e.g., parcel delivery and express mail), people's perceptions are that the quality of service is generally declining. For example, in one market research survey nearly 45 percent of respondents said most companies simply do not provide good customer service ("New Study Reveals," 2004).

The airline industry is a case in point. Flying was a luxury afforded only to a few in the middle part of the twentieth century, but by the 1990s air travel was a part of everyday life for many. Deregulation had lowered prices, thus increasing the prevalence of business and leisure travel and with the rising number of travelers came declining service standards. Indeed, in April 2001, *Newsweek* ran an in-depth story entitled "Why Flying Is Hell" (Bryant, 2001). Surveys in subsequent years, however, indicated a slight turnaround in perceptions of airline service ("Study: U.S. Airline Quality Improving" in 2002 and Peraino reporting on "Good Times in the Skies" in 2003), but in 2007, dissatisfaction spiked again. There were many reasons for this renewed dissatisfaction (e.g., delays in arrival, cutting back services such as meals on flights, difficulties with security lines, etc.). It is clear that in the airline industry—as in other sectors of the service economy—attention to improving service while keeping costs in line is a never-ending and demanding battle.

Why are there problems with service? Part of the answer may lie in organizational moves such as corporate downsizing and retrenchment. As Pederson (1997) notes, "While manufacturers can often replace workers with machines, that's usually not an option for services. Some companies—FedEx, UPS, Nordstrom—kept customers happy despite the new pressures. Many others just got surlier" (p. 57). Thus, in a turbulent environment, an organization may choose to sacrifice customer service in the belief that such a move will enhance profits and keep the company economically competitive.

Another answer to problems with service may lie in the type of service that is provided and the match of that service communication to the needs of the customers. Ford and Etienne (1994) have suggested that service comes in many guises. For example, a supermarket clerk may strive to be courteous, auto dealers have the reputation of providing manipulative service, and retailers like Nordstrom take great pride in providing personalized service. Ford (1995) has found that these forms of service can have a significant impact on customers' satisfaction and behavior. When customers develop expectations about service, violations of those expectations can either be highly gratifying (e.g., when personalized service is not expected but received) or highly dissatisfying (e.g., when manipulation is encountered in a sales presentation). Indeed, Ford (2003) found that

> professionals who do not spend sufficient time listening to customers, advising them of their options, sharing technical information in simple terms, giving encouragement and support, and engaging in additional communication behaviors that allow them to tailor service to each customer, are likely to have less satisfied customers who will not return or refer family or friends in the future. (Ford, 2003, p. 203)

Third, as noted in Chapter 11, the provision of service often involves emotional labor and accompanying stress for the service provider. Undoubtedly, worker stress can lead to service that is less than optimal. This problem can be accentuated when service providers are "stretched thin" by understaffing and unrealistic

Table 14.3 | Communication Strategies for E-Commerce Customer Service

General Communication Strategies	Specific Communication Tactics
Provide information to customers on a regular and frequent basis.	Update customers via channels, including both electronic (e.g., e-mail) and traditional (e.g., direct mail, advertising) communication modes.
Use one-way sources for providing information, but don't violate trust by invading privacy.	Use websites, e-magazines, electronic kiosks, and other strategies as a continual source of information.
Offer technologies with high levels of interactivity to keep current with customer needs.	Interactive communication channels can include both traditional (phone) and electronic (e-mail, live chat) modes.
Foster community among customers to enhance customer base, loyalty, and understanding of product or service.	Customers can stay in touch with each other through technologies such as newsgroups, online forums, and chat rooms.

Adapted from Scott, C. R. (2001). Establishing and maintaining customer loyalty and employee identification in the new economy: A communicative response. *Management Communication Quarterly*, 14, 629–636; and Newell, F. (2000). *Loyalty.com*. New York: McGraw-Hill.

expectations. For example, poor service at a restaurant might be related both to servers trying to handle more tables than they should and to the strain of trying to deal cheerfully with unrealistic customer demands.

The challenges of communication in a service environment can be particularly pronounced in our economy, which is increasingly dominated by electronic transactions ("e-commerce"). Scott (2001) reports on the difficulties of maintaining quality communication in e-commerce transactions, noting reports that only 1.3 percent of a typical e-commerce website's customers return for additional purchases (Cross, 2000). Because there is no face-to-face interaction and much of the service is provided through "self-service transactions" (see Johnson, 2001), enhancing service for e-commerce can be particularly challenging. Clearly, service in these instances is taking place along a "lean media" conduit (see Chapter 13) with limited opportunities for complex messages and immediate feedback. However, some of the communicative strategies that can be used to enhance customer service during these e-commerce transactions are illustrated in Table 14.3.

In sum, then, we now live in a service economy and hence an organizational world that is dominated by service encounters. Communication in service encounters—whether an ongoing service relationship with a valued massage therapist or a point-and-click encounter when ordering flowers online—can influence customer attitudes and satisfaction as well as organizational profits and the satisfaction and health of service providers.

Communication in the Age of the Disposable Worker

A final factor to consider in the changing landscape of the workplace involves the roles that individuals play in the new global economy. In the past, many people stayed with one or perhaps two organizations throughout their working lives. As Reich (2000, pp. 93–94) notes, "two-thirds of senior executives surveyed in 1952 had been with the same company for more than twenty years." And most people working at a given company were permanent, full-time employees of that organization. These circumstances created strong connections between an individual and the company with which he or she worked—what William Whyte called *The Organization Man* (Whyte, 1956). As Holstein and Gubrium (2000, p. 45) explain, "the Organization Man (and presumably woman) . . . puts the organization's interests above individual goals and priorities." And in exchange for that loyalty, the organization was supposed to take care of all of the organizational men and women.

But times have changed. The global economy, increased technology, weakened labor unions, and an extremely competitive organizational environment have all contributed to what Robert Reich calls "the end of employment as we knew it" (Reich, 2000) and what Conrad and Poole (1997) call "the age of the disposable worker." Conrad and Poole note that there are a number of explanations for why this age is upon us. Some see this change in employment relationships as an inevitable outcome of the success of American capitalism. As one commentator explains:

> We have gotten competitive and yet have the lowest unemployment we have ever had. This shows very strongly that what's happening is good, not bad. Yes, there are dislocations of people. It's hard in the interim, but an awful lot of people are getting better jobs than they had before . . . The American dream is alive and well. ("Does America Still Work?" 1996, 12:42:44)

Others have different explanations for the disposable workforce. Robert Reich (2000) argues that managers have made decisions in the "new economy" that have led to a disposable workforce, rather than taking a "high road" approach in which they encourage employee participation, invest in the workforce, and make good decisions about scarce capital (see Conrad & Poole, 1997). Still others argue that the disposable workforce is part of an "overall strategy to minimize worker incomes and eliminate labor power to the benefit of management and shareholders" (Conrad & Poole, 1997). Workers' choices could also be contributing to this trend, as some people (especially younger workers) might prefer more fluid work situations to the commitment of permanent, fixed employment. Whichever of these explanations is correct—be it an inevitable outgrowth of capitalism, bad choices on the part of management, a conscious strategy to disempower workers, or individuals exercising agency in their employment decisions—it is clear that members of today's workforce hold very different relationships to organizations than did workers in the mid-twentieth century.

What are the characteristics of this disposable workforce? How has the nature of the employment relationship changed? A number of descriptors can be cited.

First, today's workforce is increasingly made up of contingent workers. Contingent workers are temporary workers such as independent consultants, day laborers, temporary clerical workers, or home health workers. Gossett (2001) notes that in the United States, temporary employment nets $60 billion a year, and temps are no longer just "fill-ins" for permanent workers. Instead, "[j]obs are being created specifically for temps to perform" (Gossett, 2001, p. 116).

Second, many in the workforce have been forced into temporary work or self-employment or into an underemployment situation through corporate layoffs, downsizing, and mergers. For example, in a *Newsweek* article entitled "How Safe Is Your Job?" McGinn and Naughton (2001, p. 38) note that "after years of near-continuous downsizings (many due to mergers), many workers have come to accept the risk of layoffs as the price of admission to the New Economy." Further, in some areas of the economy, the jobs simply "aren't there" and there is a great deal of underemployment. For example, McGinn (2000) explains how people graduating with PhDs in the humanities are often unable to find university positions and instead take jobs as consultants, in corporations, or as truck drivers. As McGinn (2000, p. 70) notes, "their status illustrates how pockets of the work force can miss out on a boom—and how a low unemployment rate doesn't measure 'underemployed' people doing jobs for which they are vastly overqualified."

Third, many workers are not forced into alternative work arrangements but intentionally opt for an employment situation that bears little resemblance to Whyte's "Organization Man" (or woman). Individuals may choose to work as temps, telecommute, work part time, or enter and exit the workforce at various stages of their lives. These choices can be motivated by a variety of factors. Some workers want to concentrate on an avocation rather than a vocation. Some workers simply enjoy the liberty of being "temporary." One major motivation for becoming more "disposable" is a concern for putting the needs of family ahead of (or at least on equal

Case in Point: Generation Y in the Workplace

Part of the changing landscape of work stems from younger workers arriving in organizations. The most recent influx of workers has come from Generation Y, often defined as those born in the 1980s and 1990s. These new workers are seen as different from the preceding baby boomers and Gen-Xers. Tim Irvin, a corporate psychologist, explains: "They come in with very high expectations . . . Their parents have told them from the moment they were born that they were special. These Gen Y'ers believe it. The thought of having to pay dues for a long time to get into a corner office is kind of jarring to them" (Osburn, p. D1, 2007).

Now, if you are someone born in the 1980s or 1990s—a member of Generation Y—this description might seem a bit insulting. Perhaps you would not agree with the assessment that indulgent parents have produced "workers without a sense of responsibility, accountability, or commitment" (Osburn, 2007, p. D6). However, these generational differences can clearly influence relationships in the workplace,

and the prevailing perception of younger workers can be seen as a disturbing trend for both employers and for workers. However, there's another side of the story. For example, Generation Y workers are also seen as being highly motivated, willing to stay with a company if they are challenged and given opportunities, and very aware of the technology options that are vital to today's workplace. One of these Gen Y'ers, Anthony Oni, describes it this way: "For the 76 million or so Gen Y'ers in the world, we are trying to find our place in the business community. Sometimes it doesn't always happen the first time. Young people are graduating college and exploring and finding their niche in a community and taking advantage of great opportunities. This may be confused with impatience" (Osburn, 2007, p. D6). Indeed, these words might describe you: exploring, looking for opportunity, finding your place, perhaps impatient. Difficult and challenging tasks in the changing world of work.

footing with) the requirements of work. Greenberg (2001) explains this motivation with regard to young women entering the workplace:

> Today's young women have seen enough harried superwomen to recognize that blending full-time work with raising children is hardly "having it all." At the same time, the idea of not working is unfathomable to many of them. So they have invented their own compromise: having some of it all. Many plan to work hard for a few years, take time off to have children, then return to a less demanding or part-time job. (p. 54)

For these reasons, then, the nature of the workforce is rapidly changing. We are now increasingly temporary, part-time, independent, freelancing, e-lancing, and telecommuting workers. What are the implications of these basic changes in work as we know it? A few issues are highlighted below.

There are, of course, financial implications for the disposable worker (see, especially, Reich, 2000, for analysis). Those who are unemployed, underemployed, working in temporary jobs, or in and out of the workforce will most often earn less money over their lifetimes than will a lifetime corporate employee. A second financial implication involves employment benefits. For example, Reich (2000, p. 99) notes that "in 1980, more than 70 percent of workers received some form of health benefit from their employers. By the late 1990s, that percentage had slipped to about 60 percent. And even when employees have some coverage, it has become less generous." A recent report indicates that the percentage of employees receiving health benefits had slipped to under 60 percent by 2005 ("Health Insurance Coverage," 2007).

A disposable workforce feels less connection to the organization and vice versa. For example, Gossett (2002) found that many contemporary companies could be described as "organizations of free agents," where lack of interaction and purposeful organizational policies limited the extent to which temporary workers felt connected to the organization. A lack of employee identification has implications for personal and organizational decision making (see the discussion in Chapters 6 and 8) and for job satisfaction and turnover. The implications of an employer's lack of commitment to the worker is also clear: "Part-time jobs are . . . the first to go in an economic downturn" (Greenberg, 2001, p. 55). Further, in addition to feeling a limited connection to the organization, contingent workers often receive directives from both the staffing agency and the organization that contracts for their work. This situation can lead to role conflict and the need for temporary workers to choose between the desires of these competing organizations (Gossett, 2007).

Finally, and clearly on the positive side, a contingent workforce has the potential to continuously breathe new life into organizations. As Conrad and Poole (1997, p. 590) argue, "[t]emporary or part-time workers bring new ideas and new ways of doing things . . . they may also bring a useful candor; they may be less strategically motivated and less concerned with impression management than employees with their future at stake."

SUMMARY

In this chapter, we have considered a number of factors critical to a continuing understanding of organizational communication. The landscape of the work world has shifted substantially in the last twenty years, and it continues to change. First, the organizational landscape has become global. Second, this globalization—along with other aspects of the "new economy"—has heightened the importance of understanding the creation and maintenance of organizational image. Third, the economy is increasingly dominated by organizations that provide services rather than products. Finally, workers in today's economy increasingly hold temporary and contingent positions that make them more "disposable" and that change the basic relationship between workers and organizations.

This changing nature of the organizational world does not diminish the value of other concepts we have considered in this text. People still enter and leave organizations, make decisions, manage conflict, deal with change, balance emotional and rational needs, and organize in the midst of diversity and technological change. And these processes can still be understood through lenses that include the systemic, the cultural, and the critical. But knowing about the changes in our organizational landscape helps to highlight areas of increasing importance in the workplace, such as managing diversity in a multicultural organization or understanding the comings and goings of temporary workers. And knowing about the changing nature of organizations provides a new lens for the consideration of organizational communication processes.

CASE STUDY | Charting the Changing Nature of Work

In this final case study, we turn away from looking at fictional (or occasionally factual) organizations for information and inspiration. Instead, as we close our examination of organizational communication, I ask you to look at yourself and others close to you as a way of understanding how the work world—and communication within that world—has changed in recent years and will continue to change in the future.

Throughout this chapter, we have highlighted ways that society has been transformed in recent decades and the implications of those transformations for organizational communication. Our economy is now primarily a service economy. We live in a global village dominated by business conducted in the global marketplace. Many workers are "disposable," moving in and out of organizations, as temporary and contract work become more common. These workers are sometimes (but certainly not always) disposable by choice. At a more macro level, companies merge and acquire with such frequency that the question of "who owns whom" is often difficult to answer, and loyalties toward organizations are not at all straightforward. In short, we live in an organizational world that is far different from the one inhabited by workers one hundred, fifty, or even twenty years ago.

As you conclude this course in organizational communication, then, I would like you to first take a look at those who have worked in organizations for many years. Talk to your parents and grandparents, aunts and uncles, brothers and sisters, or old family friends. Ask these people how the work world has changed in the years they have been employed. Here are some issues you might raise with them:

- Have they worked for one or two organizations throughout their lives, or have they changed jobs frequently? What kind of loyalty do they feel to their organizations and occupations?
- Has technology transformed the nature of their work? Do they feel these shifts are for the better or worse?
- Do they feel the impact of globalization in their work? How do other nations and cultures influence their work lives and the flow of business in their organizations?
- How have economic shifts affected them? Have they ever been laid off or downsized? Have they chosen alternative work arrangements like contract work or temporary work? Have they started their own businesses as a result of economics (or other factors)? And how have all of

CASE STUDY | **Charting the Changing Nature of W**

these alternative work arrangements influenced the quality of their work and family lives?

- Are the people you talk to happy with their work lives? Do they enjoy their work? Do they like the amount of time they spend working? If they could go back in time and make different choices about work, what would those choices be?

These questions—and the stories they spur in the people you talk with—will help you understand the changing nature of work in a very personal way. Consider the brief stories of my family as an example. My grandparents labored during the early part of the twentieth century in working-class jobs typical of the time. One grandfather was a printer, the other a bookkeeper. They worked to keep food on the table during the Great Depression and the time surrounding it, and they thought little about the intrinsic rewards of work. The question of whether work made them feel "happy" would seem quite ludicrous to them. My grandmothers both cared for their families, although one grandmother was trained as a schoolteacher. My parents—born in the 1920s—both went to college and worked as journalists. My father worked for a large daily newspaper for more than thirty years and felt a strong connection to the organization and to the union. And the corporation he worked for (with some prodding from the union) reciprocated through steady employment, a pension, and retirement benefits. My mother was a journalist during World War II; in the decade after, she dropped out of the workforce to have her children. She returned to a newspaper job when the youngest was in school and continued to work for many years. Her career trajectory was typical of working women of her generation.

My parents' children (fo career paths, which are typ children. One daughter is teaches music in several rural school districts; another, originally trained as a computer engineer, returned to school to earn a teaching degree and now teaches fifth grade; and another also returned to school, after her children entered elementary school, and, after completing her education degree with high honors, is now a sixth grade teacher. None of us feels tied to a particular organization as our parents did. All of us define ourselves more in terms of our profession and our family. Add in the stories of my husband (a former college professor who left academia for consulting and now runs his own consulting company), his family (ten children and their families engaged in work ranging from manufacturing to truck driving to lawyering to social work), and my daughter (a 15-year-old who has as many career options at this point as the day is long), and you can see that the notion of there being a single way to work and communicate in organizations is as outdated as an eight-track tape player.

So what are the stories of the people you know? And what do you think your own story will be? Will you stay in one career or explore various options throughout your life? Will your job take you to various parts of the globe, or will others from worldwide cultures be an important part of your work life at your home base? Will you work in a manufacturing industry, a service industry, an information age industry, or perhaps an industry we have not yet dreamed of? How will you fit family into the mix of your work life? These questions will take many years to explore. Hence, these questions serve as a fitting end to our consideration of organizational communication.

REFERENCES

"A Service Economy" (2007). USA Economy in Brief, International Information Programs. Retrieved December 8, 2007, from http://usinfo.state.gov/products/pubs/economy-in-brief/page3.html.

Abrahamson, E., & Freedman, D. H. (2007). *A Perfect Mess: The Hidden Benefits of Disorder*. New York: Little, Brown, & Co.

Ackman, D. (2005, January 18). Will the Jury Believe Bernie the Believer? Retrieved December 20, 2007, from www.forbes.com.

Adams, J. S. (1980). Interorganizational Processes and Organization Boundary Activities. *Research in Organizational Behavior, 2*, 321–355.

Adams, W. L. (2007, February 19). PTSD for Social Workers, the Price of Caring. *Newsweek*, p. 12.

Adler, J. (2003, November 17). The Hearts Left Behind. *Newsweek*, pp. 31–33.

——— (2007, September 3). Era of the Super Cruncher. *Newsweek*, p. 42.

"Advice for Tackling Workplace Jerks" (2007, April 11). *Associated Press*. Retrieved October 29, 2007, from http://www.msnbc.msn.com/id/17629928/.

Aikat, D. (2000). A New Medium for Organizational Communication: Analyzing Web Content Characteristics of Fortune 500 Companies. *Electronic Journal of Communication, 10*. Retrieved December 20, 2007, from www.cios.org/www/ejcmain.htm.

Albrecht, T. L., Burleson, B. R., & Goldsmith, D. (1995). Supportive Communication. In M. Knapp & G. R. Miller (eds.), *Handbook of Interpersonal Communication* (pp. 419–449). Thousand Oaks, CA: Sage.

Alger, H. (1990). *Ragged Dick or, Street Life in New York with the Boot-Blacks*. New York: Signet.

Allen, B. J. (1996). Feminist Standpoint Theory: A Black Woman's (Re)View of Organizational Socialization. *Communication Studies, 47*, 257–271.

——— (2000). "Learning the Ropes": A Black Feminist Critique. In P. Buzzanell (ed.), *Rethinking Organizational and Managerial Communication from Feminist Perspectives* (pp. 177–208). Thousand Oaks, CA: Sage.

Allen, D. (2001). *Getting Things Done*. New York: Penguin.

Alter, J. (2007, March 12). Wrong Time for an Urban Cowboy? *Newsweek*, p. 35.

Alvesson, M. (1993). *Cultural Perspectives on Organizations*. Cambridge: Cambridge University Press.

Alvesson, M., & Deetz, S. (1996). Critical Theory and Postmodernism Approaches to Organizational Studies. In S. R. Clegg, C. Hardy, & W. R. Nord (eds.), *The Handbook of Organization Studies* (pp. 191–217). Newbury Park, CA: Sage.

Alvesson, M., & Willmott, H. (1992). On the Idea of Emancipation in Management and Organization Studies. *Academy of Management Review, 17*, 432–464.

Amason, A. C. (1996). Distinguishing the Effects of Functional and Dysfunctional Conflict in Strategic Decision Making: Resolving a Paradox for Top Management Teams. *Academy of Management Journal, 39*, 123–148.

Apker, J., Propp, K. M., & Ford, W. S. Z. (2005). Negotiating Status and Identity Tensions in Healthcare Team Interactions: An Exploration of Nurse Role Dialectics. *Journal of Applied Communication Research, 33*, 93–115.

275

Argyris, C., & Schon, D. A. (1978). *Organizational Learning*. Reading, MA: Addison-Wesley.

Asangi, S., & Sathe, D. (2007). Choosing an Offshore Call Center. Retrieved February 19, 2008, from www.sourcingmag.com/content/c060619a.asp.

Ashcraft, K. L. (2000). Empowering "Professional" Relationships: Organizational Communication Meets Feminist Practice. *Management Communication Quarterly, 13,* 347–392.

——— (2005). Feminist Organizational Communication Studies: Engaging Gender in Public and Private. In S. May & D. K. Mumby (eds.), *Engaging Organizational Communication Theory and Research* (pp. 141–169). Thousand Oaks, CA: Sage.

——— (2005). Resistance through Consent? Occupational Identity, Organizational Form, and the Maintenance of Masculinity among Commercial Airline Pilots. *Management Communication Quarterly, 19,* 67–90.

Ashcraft, K. L., & Allen, B. J. (2003). The Racial Foundation of Organizational Communication. *Communication Theory, 13,* 5–38.

Ashcraft, K. L., & Mumby, D. K. (2004). *Reworking Gender: A Feminist Communicology of Organization*. Thousand Oaks, CA: Sage.

Ashford, S. J., & Black, J. S. (1996). The Role of Proactivity during Organizational Entry. *Journal of Applied Psychology, 81,* 199–215.

Ashforth, B. E., & Humphrey, R. H. (1993). Emotional Labor in Service Roles: The Influence of Identity. *Academy of Management Review, 18,* 88–115.

Awamleh, R., & Gardner, W. L. (1999). Perceptions of Leader Charisma and Effectiveness: The Effects of Vision Content, Delivery, and Organizational Performance. *Leadership Quarterly, 10,* 343–375.

Aydin, C. (1989). Occupational Adaptation to Computerized Medical Information Systems. *Journal of Health and Social Behavior, 30,* 163–179.

Ayres, I. (2007). *Super Crunchers: Why Thinking-by-Numbers Is the New Way to Be Smart*. New York: Bantam.

Babbitt, L. V., & Jablin, F. M. (1985). Characteristics of Applicants' Questions and Employment Screening Interview Outcomes. *Human Communication Research, 11,* 507–535.

Bales, R. F., & Strodtbeck, F. L. (1951). Phases in Group Problem-Solving. *Journal of Abnormal and Social Psychology, 46,* 485–495.

Bantz, C. R. (1993). *Understanding Organizations: Interpreting Organizational Communication Cultures*. Columbia: University of South Carolina Press.

Barker, J. R. (1993). Tightening the Iron Cage: Concertive Control in Self-Managing Teams. *Administrative Science Quarterly, 38,* 408–437.

——— (1999). *The Discipline of Teamwork: Participation and Concertive Control*. Thousand Oaks, CA: Sage.

Barker, J. R., & Cheney, G. (1994). The Concept and the Practices of Discipline in Contemporary Organizational Life. *Communication Monographs, 61,* 19–43.

Barker, J. R., Melville, C. W., & Pacanowsky, M. E. (1993). Self-Directed Teams at XEL: Changes in Communication Practices during a Program of Cultural Transformation. *Journal of Applied Communication Research, 21,* 297–312.

Barling, J., Rogers, K., & Kelloway, E. K. (1995). Some Effects of Teenagers' Part-Time Employment: The Quantity and Quality of Work Make the Difference. *Journal of Organizational Behavior, 16,* 143–154.

Barnard, C. I. (1938). *The Functions of the Executive*. Cambridge, MA: Harvard University Press.

Bass, B. M. (1985). *Leadership and Performance Beyond Expectations*. New York: Free Press.

Becker, S. (1993). TQM Does Work: Ten Reasons Why Misguided Efforts Fail. *Management Review, 82,* 30–34.

Beehr, T. A., & Newman, J. E. (1978). Job Stress, Employee Health, and Organizational Effectiveness: A Facet Analysis, Model, and Literature Review. *Personnel Psychology, 31,* 665–699.

Bell, E., & Forbes, L. (1994). Office Folklore in the Academic Paperwork Empire: The Interstitial Space of Gendered (Con)Texts. *Text and Performance Quarterly, 38,* 181–196.

Bennis, W. G. (1986). *Leaders and Visions: Orchestrating the Corporate Culture*. New York: Conference Board.

Bennis, W. G., & Nanus, B. (1985). *Leaders: The Strategies for Taking Charge*. New York: Harper & Row.

Benoit, W. L. (1995). *Accounts, Excuses and Apologies*. Albany, NY: SUNY Press.

Bernard, T. S. (2004, August 29). Examine Your Finances—or Your Head. *The Bryan-College Station Eagle,* p. E5.

Bernstein, R. J. (1976). *The Restructuring of Social and Political Theory*. Philadelphia: University of Pennsylvania Press.

Beyer, J., & Trice, H. (1987). How an Organization's Rites Reveal Its Culture. *Organizational Dynamics, 15,* 4–35.

Billings, A. G., & Moos, R. H. (1981). The Role of Coping Responses and Social Resources in Altering the Stress of Life Events. *Journal of Behavioral Medicine, 4,* 157–189.

Bingham, S. G. (1991). Communication Strategies for Managing Sexual Harassment in Organizations: Understanding Message Options and Their Effects. *Journal of Applied Communication Research, 19,* 88–115.

Blake, R., & McCanse, A. A. (1991). *Leadership Dilemmas: Grid Solutions*. Houston: Gulf.

Blake, R., & Mouton, J. (1964). *The Managerial Grid*. Houston: Gulf.

Boje, D. (1991). The Storytelling Organization: A Study of Story Performance in an Office-Supply Firm. *Administrative Science Quarterly, 36,* 106–126.

Bormann, E. G. (1996). Symbolic Convergence Theory and Communication in Group Decision-making. In R. Y. Hirokawa & M. S. Poole (eds.), *Communication and Group Decision Making*, 2nd ed. (pp. 81–113). Thousand Oaks, CA: Sage.

Bowes, J. M., & Goodnow, J. J. (1996). Work for Home, School, or Labor Force: The Nature and Sources of Changes in Understanding. *Psychological Bulletin, 119*, 300–321.

Branscum, D. (1997, May 12). King of "Spam" and Proud of It. *Newsweek*, p. 90.

Branson, R. (2006, December 18). Making the Skies Green. *Newsweek*, p. 48.

Braverman, H. (1974). *Labor and Monopoly Capital: The Degradation of Work in the Twentieth Century*. New York: Monthly Review Press.

Brett, J. M., & Okumura, T. (1998). Inter- and Intracultural Negotiation: U.S. and Japanese Negotiators. *Academy of Management Journal, 41*, 495–510.

Brief, A. P. (1998). *Attitudes in and around Organizations*. Thousand Oaks, CA: Sage.

Brown, M. H., & McMillan, J. (1991). Culture as Text: The Development of an Organizational Narrative. *Southern Communication Journal, 57*, 49–60.

Browning, L. B., & Shetler, J. (2000). *Sematech: Saving the U.S. Semiconductor Industry*. College Station, TX: Texas A&M University Press.

Bryan, J. H. (1999). The Diversity Imperative. *Executive Excellence, 16*, 6.

Bryant, A. (2001, April 23). Why Flying Is Hell. *Newsweek*, pp. 34–47.

Bryman, A. (1992). *Charisma and Leadership in Organizations*. London: Sage.

Buckley, W. (1967). *Sociology and Modern Systems Theory*. Englewood Cliffs, NJ: Prentice-Hall.

Bullis, C. (1993a). Organizational Socialization Research: Enabling, Constraining, and Shifting Perspectives. *Communication Monographs, 60*, 10–17.

—— (1993b). Organizational Values and Control. In C. Conrad (ed.), *Ethical Nexus* (pp. 75–102). Norwood, NJ: Ablex.

Bullis, C., & Bach, B. W. (1989). Socialization Turning Points: An Examination of Change in Organizational Identification. *Western Journal of Speech Communication, 53*, 273–293.

Bullock, R. J., & Batten, D. (1985). It's Just a Phase We're Going Through: A Review and Synthesis of OD Phase Analysis. *Group and Organization Studies, 10*, 383–412.

Burke, K. (1966). *Language as Symbolic Action*. Berkeley: University of California Press.

Burke, L., & Miller, M. K. (1999). Taking the Mystery Out of Intuitive Decision Making. *Academy of Management Executive, 13* (4), 91–99.

Burns, J. M. (1978). *Leadership*. New York: Harper & Row.

Burrell, G., & Morgan, G. (1979). *Sociological Paradigms and Organizational Analysis*. London: Heinemann.

Burrell, N. A., Buzzanell, P. M., & McMillan, J. J. (1992). Feminine Tensions in Conflict Situations as Revealed by Metaphoric Analyses. *Management Communication Quarterly, 6*, 115–149.

Buzzanell, P. M. (1994). Gaining a Voice: Feminist Organizational Communication Theorizing. *Management Communication Quarterly, 7*, 339–383.

Buzzanell, P. M., & Liu, M. (2005). Struggling with Maternity Leave Policies and Practices: A Poststructuralist and Feminist Analysis of Gendered Organizing. *Journal of Applied Communication Research, 33*, 1–25.

Buzzanell, P. M., & Turner, L. H. (2003). Emotion Work Revealed by Job Loss Discourse: Backgrounding-Foregrounding of Feelings, Construction of Normalcy, and (Re)Instituting of Traditional Masculinities. *Journal of Applied Communication Research, 31*, 27–57.

Campion, M. A., Palmer, D. K., & Campion, J. E. (1997). A Review of Structure in the Selection Interview. *Personnel Psychology, 50*, 655–702.

Carbaugh, D. (1988). Cultural Terms and Tensions at a Television Station. *Western Journal of Speech Communication, 52*, 216–237.

Carey, A. (1967). The Hawthorne Studies: A Radical Criticism. *American Sociological Review, 32*, 403–416.

Carlson, J. R., & Zmud, R. W. (1999). Channel Expansion Theory and the Experimental Nature of Media Richness Perceptions. *Academy of Management Journal, 42*, 153–170.

Carroll, C. (2007, January 29). Why Different Is Better. *Newsweek*, p. E4.

Cascio, W. F. (2000). Managing a Virtual Workplace. *Academy of Management Executive, 14* (3), 81–90.

Casey, C. (1999). "Come Join Our Family": Discipline and Integration in Corporate Organizational Culture. *Human Relations, 52*, 155–178.

Cazares, L. (2007). Study Reveals Skin Color Influences Wages. Retrieved November 24, 2007, from http://media.californiaaggie.com/media/storage/paper981/news/2007/02/02/CityNews/Study.REV-2693981.shtml.

Chatman, J. A., Polzer, J. T., Barsade, S. G., & Neale, M. A. (1998). Being Different yet Feeling Similar: The Influence of Demographic Composition and Organizational Culture on Work Processes and Outcomes. *Administrative Science Quarterly, 43*, 749–780.

Cheney, G. (1995). Democracy in the Workplace: Theory and Practice from the Perspective of Communication. *Journal of Applied Communication Research, 23*, 167–200.

Cheney, G., & Christensen, L. T. (2001). Organizational Identity: Linkages between Internal and External Communication. In F. M. Jablin & L. L. Putnam (eds.), *The New Handbook of Organizational Communication: Advances in Theory, Research, and Methods* (pp. 231–269). Thousand Oaks, CA: Sage.

Cheney, G., & Frenette, G. (1993). Persuasion and Organization: Values, Logics, and Accounts in Contemporary Corporate Public Discourse. In C. Conrad (ed.), *The Ethical Nexus* (pp. 49–73). Norwood, NJ: Ablex.

Childress, S. (2006, October 30). Signs of Trouble. *Newsweek*, p. 44.

Chiles, A. M., & Zorn, T. E. (1995). Empowerment in Organizations: Employees' Perceptions of the Influences on Empowerment. *Journal of Applied Communication Research, 23*, 1–25.

Choi, T. Y., & Behling, O. C. (1997). Top Managers and TQM Success: One More Look after All These Years. *Academy of Management Executive, 11* (1), 37–47.

Cissna, K. (1984). Phases in Group Development: The Negative Evidence. *Small Group Behavior, 14*, 3–32.

Clair, R. P. (1993a). The Bureaucratization, Commodification, and Privatization of Sexual Harassment through Institutional Discourse: A Study of the "Big Ten" Universities. *Management Communication Quarterly, 7*, 123–157.

——— (1993b). The Use of Framing Devices to Sequester Organizational Narratives: Hegemony and Harassment. *Communication Monographs, 60*, 113–136.

——— (1996). The Political Nature of the Colloquialism, "A Real Job": Implications for Organizational Socialization. *Communication Monograhs, 63*, 249–267.

Clampitt, P. G., DeKoch, R. J., & Cashman, T. (2000). A Strategy for Communicating about Uncertainty. *Academy of Management Executive, 14* (4), 41–57.

Clegg, S. R. (1990). *Modern Organizations*. Newbury Park, CA: Sage.

Clegg, S. R., & Dunkerley, D. (1980). *Organization, Class and Control*. London: Routledge & Kegan Paul.

"Climate Change" (2007). Environmental Protection Agency. Retrieved September 17, 2007, from http://epa.gov/climatechange/basicinfo.html.

Coch, L., & French, J. R. P. (1948). Overcoming Resistance to Change. *Human Relations, 1*, 512–532.

Cohen, M. D., March, J. G., & Olson, J. P. (1972). A Garbage Can Model of Organizational Choice. *Administrative Science Quarterly, 17*, 1–25.

Collins, D. (1997). The Ethical Superiority and Inevitability of Participatory Management as an Organizational System. *Organization Science, 8*, 489–507.

Collins, J. (2004). *Good to Be Great*. New York: Harper Business.

Collins, P. H. (1990). *Black Feminist Thought: Knowledge, Consciousness, and the Politics of Empowerment*. Boston: Unwin Hyman.

"*Columbia* Spouse: Report a Prescription for Change" (2003, August 26). *CNN.com*. Retrieved October 11, 2007.

Comer, D. R. (1991). Organizational Newcomers' Acquisition of Information from Peers. *Management Communication Quarterly, 5*, 64–89.

Conant, E. (2007, May 28). Trying to Opt Back In. *Newsweek*, p. 42.

"Concerns Raised that Changes in NASA Won't Last" (2003, August 26). *CNN.com*. Retrieved October 11, 2007.

Connor, P. E., & Lake, L. K. (1994). *Managing Organizational Change*, 2nd ed. Westport, CT: Praeger.

Conrad, C. (1985). *Strategic Organizational Communication*. New York: Holt, Rinehart & Winston.

——— (ed.) (1993). *Ethical Nexus*. Norwood, NJ: Ablex.

Conrad, C., & Poole, M. S. (1997). Introduction: Communication and the Disposable Worker. *Communication Research, 24*, 581–592.

——— (2002). *Strategic Organizational Communication in a Global Economy*, 5th ed. Orlando, FL: Harcourt.

Conrad, C., & Ryan, M. (1985). Power, Praxis, and Self in Organizational Communication Theory. In R. D. McPhee & P. K. Tompkins (eds.), *Organizational Communication: Traditional Themes and New Directions* (pp. 235–257). Beverly Hills, CA: Sage.

Contractor, N. S. (1994). Self-Organizing Systems Perspective in the Study of Organizational Communication. In B. Kovacic (ed.), *New Approaches to Organizational Communication* (pp. 39–66). Albany: State University of New York Press.

Contractor, N. S., & Seibold, D. R. (1993). Theoretical Frameworks for the Study of Structuring Processes in Group Decision Support Systems: Adaptive Structuration Theory and Self-Organizing Systems Theory. *Human Communication Research, 19*, 528–563.

Contractor, N. S., Seibold, D. R., & Heller, M. A. (1996). Interactional Influence in the Structuring of Media Use in Groups: Influence of Members' Perceptions of Group Decision Support System Use. *Human Communication Research, 22*, 451–481.

Coombs, W. T. (1999). *Ongoing Crisis Communication: Planning, Managing, and Responding*. Thousand Oaks, CA: Sage.

Cooper, C. L., & Marshall, J. (1976). Occupational Sources of Stress: A Review of the Literature Relating to Coronary Heart Disease and Mental Ill Health. *Journal of Occupational Psychology, 49*, 11–28.

Cooper, C. L., & Rousseau, D. M. (1999). *The Virtual Organization*. New York: Wiley.

Cooper, M. H. (1996). Background: A History of U.S. Intelligence Gathering. *The CQ Researcher, 6* (5), 108–09.

Cordes, C. L., & Dougherty, T. W. (1993). A Review and Integration of Research on Job Burnout. *Academy of Management Review, 18*, 621–656.

Cote, S. (1999). Affect and Performance in Organizational Settings. *Current Directions in Psychological Science, 8*, 65–68.

Cotton, J. L. (1993). *Employee Involvement: Methods for*

Improving Performance and Work Attitudes. Newbury Park, CA: Sage.

Cotton, J. L., Vollrath, D. A., Froggatt, K. L., Lengnick-Hall, M. L., & Jennings, K. R. (1988). Employee Participation: Diverse Forms and Different Outcomes. *Academy of Management Review, 12,* 8–22.

Coveney, P., & Highfield, R. (1995). *Frontiers of Chaos: The Search for Order in a Chaotic World.* New York: Fawcett Columbine.

Covey, S. (1994). *First Things First.* New York: Simon & Schuster.

Covin, T. J., & Kilmann, R. H. (1990). Participant Perceptions of Positive and Negative Influences on Large-Scale Change. *Group and Organizational Studies, 15,* 233–248.

Cox, S. A. (1999). Group Communication and Employee Turnover: How Coworkers Encourage Peers to Voluntarily Exit. *Southern Communication Journal, 64,* 181–192.

Cox, T. H. (1991). The Multicultural Organization. *Academy of Management Executive, 5* (2), 34–47.

Cox, T. H., & Blake, S. (1991). Managing Cultural Diversity: Implications for Organizational Effectiveness. *Academy of Management Executive, 5* (3), 45–56.

Crable, R. E., & Vibbert, S. L. (1983). Mobil's Epideictic Advocacy: "Observations" of Prometheus-Bound. *Communication Monographs, 50,* 380–394.

Craig, R. T. (1999). Communication Theory as a Field. *Communication Theory, 9,* 119–161.

Cross, K. (2000). @ Your Service. *Business 2.0, 5,* 427–428.

Daft, R. L., & Lengel, R. H. (1984). Information Richness: A New Approach to Managerial Information Processing and Organizational Design. In B. Staw & L. L. Cummings (eds.), *Research in Organizational Behavior, Vol. 6* (pp. 191–233). Greenwich, CT: JAI Press.

——— (1986). Organizational Information Requirements, Media Richness and Structural Design. *Management Science, 32,* 554–571.

Daft, R. L., Lengel, R. H., & Trevino, L. K. (1987). Message Equivocality and Media Selection: Implications for Information Systems. *MIS Quarterly, 11,* 355–366.

Dallimore, E. J. (2003). Memorable Messages as Discursive Formations: The Gendered Socialization of New University Faculty. *Women's Studies in Communication, 26,* 214–265.

Dandridge, T. (1986). Ceremony as an Integration of Work and Play. *Organization Studies, 7,* 159–170.

Daniels, T. D., Spiker, B. K., & Papa, M. J. (1997). *Perspectives on Organizational Communication,* 4th ed. Dubuque, IA: Brown & Benchmark.

Deal, T., & Kennedy, A. (1982). *Corporate Cultures: The Rites and Rituals of Corporate Life.* Reading, MA: Addison-Wesley.

DeBell, C. S., Montgomery, M. J., McCarthy, P. R., & Lanthier, R. P. (1998). The Critical Contact: A Study of Recruiter Verbal Behavior during Campus Interviews. *Journal of Business Communication, 35,* 202–223.

Deetz, S. (1992). *Democracy in an Age of Corporate Colonization.* Albany: State University of New York Press.

——— (1995). *Transforming Communication, Transforming Business.* Albany: State University of New York Press.

——— (2005). Critical Theory. In S. May and D. K. Mumby (eds.), *Engaging Organizational Communication Theory and Research* (pp. 85–111). Thousand Oaks, CA: Sage.

Deetz, S., & Kersten, S. (1983). Critical Models of Interpretive Research. In L. Putnam & M. Pacanowsky (eds.), *Communication and Organizations* (pp. 147–171). Beverly Hills, CA: Sage.

Deetz, S., & Mumby, D. K. (1990). Power, Discourse, and the Workplace: Reclaiming the Critical Tradition. In J. Anderson (ed.), *Communication Yearbook 13* (pp. 18–47). Newbury Park, CA: Sage.

DeLong, D. W. (2004). *Lost Knowledge: Confronting the Threat of an Aging Workforce.* Oxford: Oxford University Press.

Derrida, J. (1976). *Speech and Phenomenon.* Evanston, IL: Northwestern University Press.

Deutsch, M. (1973). *The Resolution of Conflict: Constructive and Destructive Processes.* New Haven, CT: Yale University Press.

Dienesch, R. M., & Liden, R. C. (1986). Leader-Member Exchange Model of Leadership: A Critique and Further Development. *Academy of Management Review, 11,* 618–634.

Doerfel, M. L., & Taylor, M. (2004). Network Dynamics of Interorganizational Cooperation: The Croation Civil Society Movement. *Communication Monographs, 71,* 371–394.

"Does America Still Work?" (1996, May 21). *Frontline.* Public Broadcasting System.

Dougherty, D. S. (1999). Dialogue through Standpoint: Understanding Women's and Men's Standpoints of Sexual Harassment. *Management Communication Quarterly, 12,* 436–468.

——— (2001). Sexual Harassment as [Dys]Functional Process: A Feminist Standpoint Analysis. *Journal of Applied Communication Research, 29,* 372–402.

Dougherty, D. S., & Krone, K. J. (2002). Emotional Intelligence as Organizational Communication: An Examination of the Construct. In William B. Gudykunst (ed.), *Communication Yearbook 26* (202–229). Mahwah, NJ: Lawrence Erlbaum Associates.

Doyle, K. (1992). Who's Killing Total Quality? *Incentive, 16,* 12–19.

Ducheneaut, N. B. (2002). The Social Impacts of Electronic Mail in Organizations: A Case Study of Electronic Power Games Using Communication Genres. *Information Communication & Society, 5,* 153–188.

Duke, P. (2004, February 2). If ER Nurses Crash, Will Patients Follow? *Newsweek,* p. 12.

D'Urso, S. C. (2006). Who's Watching Us at Work? Toward a Structural-Perceptual Model of Electronic Monitoring and Surveillance in Organizations. *Communication Theory, 16*, 281–303.

Dwyer, T. (2000). *The Change Agent: The Executive Manifesto for Managing Change.* Irving, TX: Fusion.

Edley, P. P. (2000). Discursive Essentializing in a Woman-Owned Business: Gender Stereotypes and Strategic Subordination. *Management Communication Quarterly, 14*, 271–306.

Edwards, R. C. (1981). The Social Relations of Production at the Point of Production. In M. Zey-Ferrell & M. Aiken (eds.), *Complex Organizations: Critical Perspectives* (pp. 156–182). Glenview, IL: Scott, Foresman.

Eisenberg, E. M. (1984). Ambiguity as Strategy in Organizational Communication. *Communication Monographs, 51*, 227–242.

Eisenberg, E. M., Farace, R. V., Monge, P. R., Bettinghaus, E. P., Kurchner-Hawkins, R., Miller, K. I., & Rothman, L. (1985). Communication Linkages in Interorganizational Systems: Review and Synthesis. In B. Dervin & M. Voigt (eds.), *Progress in Communication Sciences, Vol. 6* (pp. 231–258). Norwood, NJ: Ablex.

Eisenberg, E. M., & Goodall, H. L. (1997). *Organizational Communication: Balancing Creativity and Constraint,* 2nd ed. New York: St. Martin's Press.

Eisenberg, E. M., Murphy, A., & Andrews, L. (1998). Openness and Decision Making in the Search for a University Provost. *Communication Monographs, 65*, 1–23.

Eisenberg, E. M., & Riley, P. (2001). Organizational Culture. In F. M. Jablin & L. L. Putnam (eds.), *The New Handbook of Organizational Communication: Advances in Theory, Research, and Methods* (pp. 291–322). Thousand Oaks, CA: Sage.

Elangovan, A. R. (1995). Managing Third-Party Dispute Intervention: A Prescriptive Model of Strategy Selection. *Academy of Management Review, 20*, 800–830.

Ellingson, L. L. (2003). Interdisciplinary Health Care Teamwork in the Clinic Backstage. *Journal of Applied Communication Research, 31*, 93–117.

Ellis, B. H., & Miller, K. I. (1993). The Role of Assertiveness, Personal Control, and Participation in the Prediction of Nurse Burnout. *Journal of Applied Communication Research, 21*, 327–342.

"Employees Find Noose Hanging at Work" (2007, January 5). *CNN .com.* Retrieved November 24, 2007.

English-Lueck, J. A., Darrah, C. N., & Saveri, A. (2002). Trusting Strangers: Worker Relationships in Four High-Tech Communities. *Information Communication & Society, 5*, 90–108.

Ephron, D., & Wingert, P. (2006, October 9). Top of Her Class. *Newsweek,* p. 43.

"Equal Employment Opportunity Guidelines on Sexual Harassment." (1980). *Federal Register, 45* (72), 25025.

Everbach, T. (2007). The Culture of a Women-Led Newspaper: An Ethnographic Study of the *Sarasota Herald-Tribune. Journalism and Mass Communication Quarterly, 83*, 477–493.

Fairhurst, G. T. (1993). Echoes of the Vision: When the Rest of the Organization Talks Total Quality. *Management Communication Quarterly, 6*, 331–371.

Fairhurst, G. T., & Chandler, T. A. (1989). Social Structure in Leader-Member Exchange. *Communication Monographs, 56*, 215–239.

Fairhurst, G. T., & Sarr, R. A. (1996). *The Art of Framing: Managing the Language of Leadership.* San Francisco: Jossey-Bass.

Fairhurst, G. T., & Wendt, R. F. (1993). The Gap in Total Quality: A Commentary. *Management Communication Quarterly, 6*, 441–451.

Farace, R. V., Monge, P. R., & Russell, H. M. (1977). *Communicating and Organizing.* Reading, MA: Addison-Wesley.

Fayol, H. (1949). *General and Industrial Management,* C. Storrs, trans. London: Pitman.

Fein, M. (1974). Job Enrichment: A Reevaluation. *Sloan Management Review,* 69–88.

Ferguson, K. E. (1984). *The Feminist Case against Bureaucracy.* Philadelphia: Temple University Press.

Fiedler, F. E., & Garcia, J. E. (1987). *New Approaches to Effective Leadership: Cognitive Resources and Organizational Performance.* New York: Wiley.

Fineman, S. (2000). Commodifying the Emotional Intelligent. In S. Fineman (ed.), *Emotion in Organizations,* 2nd ed. London: Sage.

——— (2000). Emotional Arenas Revisited. In S. Fineman (ed.), *Emotion in Organizations,* 2nd ed. (pp. 1–24). London: Sage.

Fisher, B. A. (1970). Decision Emergence: Phases in Group Decision-Making. *Communication Monographs, 37*, 53–66.

Fisher, K., & Duncan, M. D. (1998). *The Distributed Mind: Achieving High Performance through the Collective Intelligence of Knowledge Work Teams.* New York: AMACOM.

Flanagin, A. J. (2000). Social Pressures on Organizational Website Adoption. *Human Communication Research, 26*, 618–646.

Flynn, G. (1996). No Spouse, No Kids, No Respect: Backlash. Why Single Employees Are Angry. *Personnel Journal,* 59–69.

Folger, R., & Skarlicki, D. P. (1998). When Tough Times Make Tough Bosses: Managerial Distancing as a Function of Layoff Blame. *Academy of Management Journal, 41*, 79–87.

Folkman, S., Lazarus, R. S., Gruen, R. J., & DeLongis, A. (1986). Appraisal, Coping, Health Status, and Psychological Symptoms. *Journal of Personality and Social Psychology, 50*, 571–579.

Ford, W. S. Z. (1995). Evaluation of the Indirect Influence of Courteous Service on Customer Discretionary Behavior. *Human Communication Research, 22*, 65–89.

——— (2003). Communication Practices of Professional Service Providers: Predicting Customer Satisfaction and Loyalty. *Journal of Applied Communication Research, 31*, 189–211.

Ford, W. S. Z., & Etienne, C. N. (1994). Can I Help You? A Framework for the Interdisciplinary Research on Customer Service Encounters. *Management Communication Quarterly, 7*, 413–441.

Foroohar, R. (2006, September 18). Are They Worthy? *Newsweek*. Retrieved September 25, 2007, from http://www.msnbc.msn.com/id/14752519/site/newsweek/.

Forrester, R. (2000). Empowerment: Rejuvenating a Potent Idea. *Academy of Management Executive, 14* (3), 67–80.

Forrester, R., & Drexler, A. B. (1999). A Model for Team-Based Organization Performance. *Academy of Management Executive, 13* (3), 36–49.

Foucault, M. (1976). *Discipline and Punish*, A. Sheridan, trans. New York: Vintage.

Fox, M. L., Dwyer, D. J., & Ganster, D. C. (1993). Effects of Stressful Job Demands and Control on Physiological and Attitudinal Outcomes in a Hospital Setting. *Academy of Management Journal, 36*, 289–318.

Franke, R. H., & Kaul, J. (1978). The Hawthorne Experiments: First Statistical Interpretation. *American Sociological Review, 43*, 623–643.

Freidman, T. J. (2005). *The World Is Flat: A Brief History of the Twenty-First Century*. New York: Farrar, Straus, & Giroux.

French, J. R. P., Israel, J., & As, D. (1960). An Experiment in a Norwegian Factory: Interpersonal Dimensions in Decision-Making. *Human Relations, 13*, 3–19.

Freudenberger, H. J. (1974). Staff Burn-Out. *Journal of Social Issues, 30*, 159–165.

Friedman, D. (1987). *Family Supportive Policies: The Corporate Decision Making Process*. New York: The Conference Board.

Fritz, M. B. W., Narashim, S., & Rhee, H.-S. (1998). Communication and Coordination in the Virtual Office. *Journal of Management Information Systems, 14* (4), 7–28.

Frost, P. J., Moore, L. F., Louis, M. R., Lundberg, C. C., & Martin, J. (1991). *Reframing Organizational Culture*. Newbury Park, CA: Sage.

Fulk, J. (1993). Social Construction of Communication Technology. *Academy of Management Journal, 36*, 921–950.

Fulk, J., & Collins-Jarvis, L. (2001). Wired Meetings: Technological Mediation of Organizational Gatherings. In F. M. Jablin & L. L. Putnam (eds.), *The New Handbook of Organizational Communication: Advances in Theory, Research, and Methods* (pp. 624–663). Thousand Oaks, CA: Sage.

Fulk, J., Schmitz, J., & Steinfield, C. W. (1990). A Social Influence Model of Technology Use. In J. Fulk & C. W. Steinfield (eds.), *Organizations and Communication Technology* (pp. 117–140). Newbury Park, CA: Sage.

Fulk, J., Steinfield, C. W., Schmitz, J., & Power, J. G. (1987). A Social Information Processing Model of Media Use in Organizations. *Communication Research, 14*, 529–552.

Galloway, R. (2005). *Why Wal*Mart Works and Why This Makes Some People C-R-A-Z-Y!* DVD-Video, Hannover House.

Ganesh, S., Zoller, H., & Cheney, G. (2005). Transforming Resistance, Broadening Our Boundaries: Critical Organizational Communication Meets Globalization from Below. *Communication Monographs, 72*, 169–191.

Gardner, W. L. (2003). Perceptions of Leader Charisma, Effectiveness, and Integrity: Effects of Exemplification, Delivery, and Ethical Reputation. *Management Communication Quarterly, 16*, 502–527.

Garner, J. T. (2006). Masters of the Universe? Resource Dependency and Interorganizational Power Relationships at NASA. *Journal of Applied Communication Research, 34*, 368–385.

Garr, D. (2004, June 21). Sick, and Tired of the Endless Paperwork. *Newsweek*, p. 19.

Gates, D. (2003). Learning to Lay the Game: An Exploratory Study of How African American Women and Men Interact with Others in Organizations. *Electronic Journal of Communication, 13* (2–3).

Gayle, B. M., & Preiss, R. W. (1998). Assessing Emotionality in Organizational Conflicts. *Management Communication Quarterly, 12*, 280–302.

Geertz, C. (1973). *The Interpretation of Cultures*. New York: Basic Books.

Geist, P. (1995). Negotiating Whose Order? Communicating to Negotiate Identities and Revise Organizational Structures. In A. M. Nicotera (ed.), *Conflict and Organizations: Communicative Processes* (pp. 45–64). Albany: State University of New York Press.

Gergen, K. (1991). *The Saturated Self: Dilemmas of Identity in Contemporary Life*. New York: Basic Books.

Gersick, C. (1991). Revolutionary Change Theories: A Multilevel Exploration of the Punctuated Equilibrium Paradigm. *Academy of Management Review, 16*, 10–36.

Gibson, M. K., & Papa, M. J. (2000). The Mud, the Blood, and the Beer Guys: Organizational Osmosis in Blue-Collar Work Groups. *Journal of Applied Communication Research, 28*, 68–88.

Giddens, A. (1979). *Central Problems in Social Theory: Action, Structure and Contradiction in Social Analysis*. Berkeley: University of California Press.

Gilbert, J. A., & Ivancevich, J. M. (2000). Valuing Diversity: A Tale of Two Organizations. *Academy of Management Executive, 14* (1), 93–105.

Ginzel, L. E., Kramer, R. M., & Sutton, R. I. (1993). Organizational Impression Management as a Reciprocal Influence Process: The Neglected Role of the Organizational Audience. In L. L. Cummings & B. M. Staw (eds.), *Research in Organizational Behavior, Vol. 15* (pp. 227–266). Greenwich, CT: JAI Press.

Glaser, B., & Strauss, A. (1967). *The Discovery of Grounded Theory*. Chicago: Aldine.

Golden, A. G. (2001). Modernity and the Communicative Management of Multiple Role-Identities: The Case of the Worker-Parent. *The Journal of Family Communication, 1,* 233–264.

Goldstein, E. L., & Gilliam, P. (1990). Training System Issues in the Year 2000. *American Psychologist, 45,* 134–143.

Goleman, D. P. (1995). *Emotional Intelligence.* New York: Bantam Books.

Golitz, S. M., & Giannantonio, C. M. (1995). Recruiter Friendliness and Attraction to the Job: The Mediating Role of Inferences about the Organization. *Journal of Vocational Behavior, 46,* 109–118.

Goodall, H. L. (1989). *Casing a Promised Land: The Autobiography of an Organizational Detective as Cultural Ethnographer.* Carbondale: Southern Illinois University Press.

——— (1991). *Living in the Rock 'n' Roll Mystery: Reading Context, Self, and Others as Clues.* Carbondale: Southern Illinois University Press.

——— (2000). *Writing the New Ethnography.* Walnut Creek, CA: AltaMira Press.

Gordon, J. (2007, September 7–13). Parkland Slashes ER Admission Wait Time. *Dallas Business Journal,* p. 13.

Gore, A. (2006). *An Inconvenient Truth.* New York: Rodale.

Gossett, L. M. (2001). The Long-Term Impact of Short-Term Workers: The Work Life Concerns Posed by the Growth of the Contingent Workforce. *Management Communication Quarterly, 15,* 115–120.

——— (2002). Kept at Arm's Length: Questioning the Desirability of Organizational Identification. *Communication Monographs, 69,* 385–404.

——— (2007). Falling Between the Cracks: Control and Communication Challenges of a Temporary Workforce. *Management Communication Quarterly, 19,* 376–415.

Gossett, L. M., & Kilker, J. (2006). My Job Sucks: Examining Counterinstitutional Web Site as Locations for Organizational Member Voice, Dissent, and Resistance. *Management Communication Quarterly, 20,* 63–90.

Gouran, D. S., & Hirokawa, R. Y. (1996). Functional Theory and Communication in Decision-Making and Problem-Solving Groups: An Expanded View. In R. Y. Hirokawa and M. S. Poole (eds.), *Communication and Group Decision Making,* 2nd ed. (pp. 55–80). Thousand Oaks, CA: Sage.

Gouran, D. S., Hirokawa, R. Y., Julian, K. M., & Leatham, G. B. (1993). The Evolution and Current Status of the Functional Perspective on Communication in Decision-Making and Problem-Solving Groups: A Critical Analysis. In S. A. Deetz (ed.), *Communication Yearbook 16* (pp. 573–600). Newbury Park, CA: Sage.

Gouran, D. S., Hirokawa, R. Y., & Martz, A. E. (1986). A Critical Analysis of Factors Related to Decisional Processes in the *Challenger* Disaster. *Central States Speech Journal, 37,* 119–135.

Graen, G. B. (1976). Role-Making Processes within Complex Organizations. In M. D. Dunnette (ed.), *Handbook of Industrial and Organizational Psychology* (pp. 1201–1245). Chicago: Rand McNally.

Graen, G. B., & Scandura, T. A. (1987). Toward a Psychology of Dyadic Organizing. In B. Staw & L. L. Cummings (eds.), *Research in Organizational Behavior, Vol. 9* (pp. 175–208). Greenwich, CT: JAI Press.

Graham, L. (1995). *On the Line at Subaru-Isuzu.* Ithaca, NY: ILR Press.

Gramsci, A. (1971). *Selections from the Prison Notebooks,* Q. Hoare & G. Nowell Smith, trans. New York: International Publishers.

Grantham, C. (1995, September/ October). The Virtual Office. *At Work: Stories of Tomorrow's Workplace,* pp. 12–14.

"Green Your Getaway" (2007, July 9). *Newsweek.* Retrieved September 18, 2007, from http://www.msnbc.msn.com//id/19376385/site/newsweek/.

Greenberg, S. H. (2001, January 8). Time to Plan Your Life. *Newsweek,* pp. 54–55.

Greenberger, E., Steinberg, L. K., Vaux, A., & McAuliffe, S. (1980). Adolescents Who Work: Effects of Part-Time Employment on Family and Peer Relations. *Journal of Youth and Adolescence, 9,* 189–202.

Greenwald, R. (2005). *Wal-Mart: The High Cost of Low Price.* DVD-Video, Brave New Films.

Gregory, K. W. (2001). "Don't Sweat the Small Stuff": Employee Identity Work in the New Economy. Unpublished doctoral dissertation. Department of Communication, University of South Florida.

Grimes, D. S. (2002). Challenging the Status Quo? Whiteness in the Diversity Management Literature. *Management Communication Quarterly, 15,* 381–409.

Gronn, P. (1983). Talk as the Work: The Accomplishment of School Administration. *Administrative Science Quarterly, 28,* 1–21.

Gross, M. A., Guerrero, L. K., & Alberts, J. K. (2004). Perceptions of Conflict Strategies and Communication Competence in Task-Oriented Dyads. *Journal of Applied Communication Research, 32,* 249–270.

Gutek, B. A., & Welsh, T. (2000). *The Brave New Service Strategy: Aligning Customer Relationships, Market Strategies, and Business Structures.* New York: American Management Association.

Habermas, J. (1971). *Knowledge and Human Interests,* J. J. Shapiro, trans. Boston: Beacon Press.

Hafen, S. (2003). Cultural Diversity Training: A Critical (Ironic) Cartography of Advocacy and Oppositional Silences. In G. Cheney and G. Barnett (eds.), *Organization Communication: Emerging Perspectives.* Cresskill, NJ: Hampton Press.

Hall, E. J. (1993). Smiling, Deferring, and Flirting: Doing Gender by Giving "Good Service." *Work and Occupations, 20,* 452–471.

Hall, S. (1985). Signification, Representation, Ideology: Althusser and the Post-Structuralist Debates. *Critical Studies in Mass Communication, 2,* 91–114.

Hannan, M., & Freeman, J. (1989). *Organizational Ecology.* Cambridge, MA: Harvard University Press.

Hansen, K. (2007). Making Your Case for Telecommuting: How to Convince the Boss. Retrieved February 19, 2008, from www .quitcareers.com/telecommuting_ options.html.

Hardy, C., & Clegg, S. R. (1996). Some Dare Call It Power. In S. R. Clegg, C. Hardy, & W. R. Nord (eds.), *The Handbook of Organization Studies* (pp. 622–641). Newbury Park, CA: Sage.

Harrison, T. (1994). Communication and Interdependence in Democratic Organizations. In S. Deetz (ed.), *Communication Yearbook 17* (pp. 247–274). Beverly Hills, CA: Sage.

Harrison, T. R., & Morrill, C. (2004). Ombuds Processes and Disputant Reconciliation. *Journal of Applied Communication Research, 32,* 318–342.

Harrop, F. (2007). The High Price of Low Prices. *The Providence Journal.* Retrieved September 20, 2007, from http://www.creators .com/print/opinion/froma-harrop/ the-high-price-of-low-prices.html.

Harter, L. M., & Krone, K. J. (2001). The Boundary-Spanning Role of a Cooperative Support Organization: Managing the Paradox of Stability and Change in Non-Traditional Organizations. *Journal of Applied Communication Research, 29,* 248–277.

Harvey, T. R. (1995). *Checklist for Change: A Pragmatic Approach to Creating and Controlling Change.* Lancaster, PA: Technomic.

"Health Insurance Coverage" (2007). National Coalition on Health Care. Retrieved December 8, 2007, from http://www.nchc.org/facts/coverage .html.

Heath, R. L. (1994). *Management of Corporate Communication: From Interpersonal Contacts to External Affairs.* Hillsdale, NJ: Erlbaum.

Heaton, L. H. (2008). Knowledge Management. *International Encyclopedia of Communication.* Boston: Blackledge.

Heaton, L., & Taylor, J. R. (2002). Knowledge Management and Professional Work: A Communication Perspective on the Knowledge-Based Organization. *Management Communication Quarterly, 16,* 210–236.

Heilman, M. E. (1994). Affirmative Action: Some Unintended Consequences for Working Women. In B. M. Staw & L. L. Cummings (eds.), *Research in Organizational Behavior, Vol. 16* (pp. 125–169). Greenwich, CT: JAI Press.

Heilman, M. E., Block, C. J., & Stathatos, P. (1997). The Affirmative Action Stigma of Incompetence: Effects of Performance Information Ambiguity. *Academy of Management Journal, 40,* 603–625.

Held, D., et al. (2005). *Debating Globalization.* Malden, MA: Polity Press.

Herrmann, A. F. (2007). Stockholders in Cyberspace: Weick's Sensemaking Online. *Journal of Business Communication, 44,* 13–35.

Herzberg, F. (1966). *Work and the Nature of Man.* Cleveland, OH: World.

Hewlett, S. A. (2007). *Off-Ramps and On-Ramps: Keeping Talented Women on the Road to Success.* Cambridge, MA: Harvard Business School Press.

Hirokawa, R. Y., & Salazar, A. J. (1999). Task-Group Communication and Decision-Making Performance. In L. R. Frey, D. S. Gouran, & M. S. Poole (eds.), *The Handbook of Group Communication Theory and Research* (pp. 167–191). Thousand Oaks, CA: Sage.

Hirokawa, R. Y., & Scheerhorn, D. R. (1986). Communication in Faulty Group Decision-Making. In R. Y. Hirokawa & M. S. Poole (eds.), *Communication and Group Decision-Making* (pp. 63–80). Beverly Hills, CA: Sage.

Hochschild, A. (1983). *The Managed Heart.* Berkeley: University of California Press.

——— (1997). *The Time Bind.* New York: Metropolitan.

Hoffart, N., & Woods, C. Q. (1996). Elements of a Professional Practice Model. *Journal of Professional Nursing, 12,* 354–364.

Hoffman, M. F. (2002). "Do All Things with Counsel": Benedictine Women and Organizational Democracy. *Communication Studies, 53,* 203–218.

Holladay, S. J., & Coombs, W. T. (1993). Communicating Visions: An Exploration of the Role of Delivery in the Creation of Leader Charisma. *Management Communication Quarterly, 6,* 405–427.

Holmes, J., & Stubbe, M. (2003). Doing Disagreement at Work: A Sociolinguistic Approach. *Australian Journal of Communication, 30,* 53–77.

Holmes, T., & Rahe, R. (1967). The Social Readjustment Rating Scale. *Journal of Psychosomatic Research, 11,* 213–218.

Holstein, J. A., & Gubrium, J. F. (2000). *The Self We Live By: Narrative Identity in a Postmodern World.* New York: Oxford University Press.

Horgan, J. (1996). *The End of Science: Facing the Limits of Knowledge in the Twilight of the Scientific Age.* Reading, MA: Addison-Wesley.

House, J. S. (1981). *Work Stress and Social Support.* Reading, MA: Addison-Wesley.

House, J. S., & Cottington, E. M. (1986). Health and the Workplace. In L. H. Aiken & D. Mechanic (eds.), *Application of Social Science to Clinical Medicine and Health Policy* (pp. 392–415). New Brunswick, NJ: Rutgers University Press.

House, R. J., & Aditya, R. N. (1997). The Social Scientific Study of Leadership: Quo Vadis? *Journal of Management, 23,* 409–473.

Houston, R., & Jackson, M. H. (2003). Technology and Context within Research on International Development Programs: Positioning an Integrationist Perspective. *Communication Theory, 13,* 57–77.

Howard, L. A., & Geist, P. (1995). Ideological Positioning in Organizational Change: The Dialectic of Control in a Merging Organization. *Communication Monographs, 62*, 110–131.

Huber, G. P. (1984). Issues in the Design of Group Decision Support Systems. *MIS Quarterly, 8*, 195–204.

——— (1990). A Theory of the Effects of Advanced Information Technologies on Organizational Design, Intelligence, and Decision Making. *Academy of Management Review, 15*, 47–71.

Hughes, E. C. (1958). *Men and Their Work*. Glencoe, IL: Free Press.

Huspek, M. (1997). Toward Normative Theories of Communication with Reference to the Frankfurt School: An Introduction. *Communication Theory, 7*, 265–276.

Hylmo, A., & Buzzanell, P. M. (2002). Telecommuting as Viewed through Cultural Lenses: An Empirical Investigation of the Discourses of Utopia, Identity, and Mystery. *Communication Monographs, 69*, 329–356.

Ibarra, H. (1993). Personal Networks of Women and Minorities in Management: A Conceptual Framework. *Academy of Management Journal, 18*, 56–87.

——— (1995). Race, Opportunity, and Diversity of Social Circles in Managerial Networks. *Academy of Management Journal, 38*, 673–703.

Igbaria, M., & Tan, M. (1998). *The Virtual Workplace*. Hershey, PA: Idea Group Publishing.

Ilgen, D. R., & Youst, M. A. (1986). Factors Affecting the Evaluation and Development of Minorities in Organizations. In K. M. Rowland & G. R. Ferris (eds.), *Research in Personnel and Human Resource Management, Vol. 4* (pp. 307–337). Greenwich, CT: JAI Press.

Isikoff, M. (2004, July 19). The Dots Never Existed. *Newsweek*, pp. 36–38.

Iverson, J. O., & McPhee, R. D. (2002). Knowledge Management in Communities of Practice: Being True to the Communicative Character of Knowledge. *Management Communication Quarterly, 16*, 259–266.

Jablin, F. M. (2001). Organizational Entry, Assimilation, and Disengagement/Exit. In F. M. Jablin & L. L. Putnam (eds.), *The New Handbook of Organizational Communication: Advances in Theory, Research, and Methods* (pp. 732–818). Thousand Oaks, CA: Sage.

Jablin, F. M., & Kramer, M. W. (1998). Communication-Related Sense-Making and Adjustment during Job Transfers. *Management Communication Quarterly, 12*, 155–182.

Jablin, F. M., & Krone, K. J. (1987). Organizational Assimilation. In C. R. Berger & S. H. Chaffee (eds.), *Handbook of Communication Science* (pp. 711–746). Newbury Park, CA: Sage.

Jablin, F. M., & Miller, V. D. (1990). Interviewer and Applicant Questioning Behavior in Employment Interviews. *Management Communication Quarterly, 4*, 51–86.

Jabs, L. B. (2005). Communicative Rules and Organizational Decision Making. *Journal of Business Communication, 42*, 265–288.

Jackson, M. (1989). *Paths toward a Clearing*. Bloomington: Indiana University Press.

Jackson, S. E. (1983). Participation in Decision Making as a Strategy for Reducing Job-Related Strain. *Journal of Applied Psychology, 68*, 3–19.

Jameson, J. K. (2004). Negotiating Autonomy and Connection through Politeness: A Dialectical Approach to Organizational Conflict Management. *Western Journal of Communication, 68*, 257–277.

Janis, I. L. (1972). *Victims of Groupthink*. Boston: Houghton Mifflin.

——— (1982). *Groupthink*. Boston: Houghton Mifflin.

Jardin, X. (2007). Online Social Networks Go to Work. Retrieved December 1, 2007, from http://www.msnbc.com/id/5488683.

Jassawalla, A. R., & Sashittal, H. C. (1999). Building Collaborative Cross-Functional New Product Teams. *Academy of Management Executive, 13* (3), 50–63.

Jenkins, B.M. (2007). *Basic Principles for Homeland Security*. Santa Monica, CA: RAND Corporation.

Jian, G. (2007). Unpacking the Unintended Consequences in Planned Organizational Change: A Process Model. *Management Communication Quarterly, 21*, 5–28.

Johnson, D. T. (2001). Is This a Real Person? Communication and Customer Service in E-Commerce. *Management Communication Quarterly, 14*, 659–665.

Jones, D. (2002, January 4–6). E-Mail Avalanche Even Buries CEOs. *USA Today*, 1–2.

Jones, M. (2007). Leveraging Social Networking Sites to Generate Business. Retrieved December 1, 2007, from http://entrepreneurs.about.com/od/onlinenetworking/a/socinetsites.htm.

Juarez, V. (2004, March 8). Out of Bounds. *Newsweek*, pp. 38–39.

Kahn, R. L., Wolfe, D. M., Quinn, R. P., Snoek, J. D., & Rosenthal, R. A. (1964). *Organizational Stress*. New York: Wiley.

Kamalanabhan, T. J., Uma, J., & Vasanthi, M. (1999). A Delphi Study of Motivational Profile of Scientists in Research and Development Organisations. *Psychological Reports, 85*, 743–749.

Kanter, R. M. (1977). *Men and Women of the Corporation*. New York: Basic Books.

——— (1983). *The Change Masters*. New York: Simon & Schuster.

Kantrowitz, B., & Scelfo, J. (2006, September 25). Science and the Gender Gap. *Newsweek*, pp. 67–72.

Karambayya, R., & Brett, J. M. (1989). Managers Handling Disputes: Third-Party Roles and Perceptions of Fairness. *Academy of Management Journal, 32*, 687–704.

Karambayya, R., Brett, J. M., & Lytle, A. (1992). Effects of Formal Authority and Experience on Third-Party Roles, Outcomes, and Perceptions of Fairness. *Academy of Management Journal, 35*, 426–438.

Kassing, J. W. (1997). Articulating, Antagonizing, and Displacing: A

Model of Employee Dissent. *Communication Studies, 48,* 311–332.

——— (2002). Speaking Up: Identifying Employees' Upward Dissent Strategies. *Management Communication Quarterly, 16,* 187–209.

Kassing, J. W., & Armstrong, T. A. (2002). Someone's Going to Hear about This: Examining the Association between Dissent-Triggering Events and Employees' Dissent Expression. *Management Communication Quarterly, 16,* 39–65.

Kassing, J. W., & DiCioccio, R. L. (2004). Testing a Workplace Experience Explanation of Displaced Dissent. *Communication Reports, 17,* 113–120.

Katz, D., & Kahn, R. L. (1978). *The Social Psychology of Organizations,* 2nd ed. New York: Wiley. (First published in 1966.)

Kim, C., & Tamborini, C. R. (2006). The Continuing Significance of Race in Occupational Attainment of Whites and Blacks: A Segmented Labor Market Analysis. *Sociological Inquiry, 76,* 23–51.

Kimberly, J. R., & Miles, T. H. (1980). *The Organizational Life Cycle: Issues in the Creation, Transformation, and Decline of Organizations.* San Francisco: Jossey-Bass.

Kinlaw, D. C. (1991). *Developing Superior Work Teams: Building Quality and the Competitive Edge.* Lexington, MA: Lexington Books.

Kirby, E. L. (2006). "Helping You Make Room in Your Life for Your Needs": When Organizations Appropriate Family Roles. *Communication Monographs, 73,* 474–480.

Kirby, E. L., Golden, A. G., Medved, C. E., Jorgenson, J., & Buzzanell, P. M. (2003). An Organizational Communication Challenge to the Discourse of Work and Family Research: From Problematics to Empowerment. In Pamela J. Kalbfleisch (ed.), *Communication Yearbook 27* (1–43). Mahwah, NJ: Lawrence Erlbaum Associates.

Kirby, E. L., & Harter, L. M. (2001). Discourses of Diversity and the Quality of Work Life: The Char-

acter and Costs of the Managerial Metaphor. *Management Communication Quarterly, 15,* 121–127.

Kirby, E. L., & Krone, K. J. (2002). "The Policy Exists but You Can't Really Use It": Communication and the Structuration of Work-Family Policies. *Journal of Applied Communication Research, 30,* 50–77.

Knapp, M. L., Putnam, L. L., & Davis, L. J. (1988). Measuring Interpersonal Conflict in Organizations: Where Do We Go from Here? *Management Communication Quarterly, 1,* 414–429.

Kolb, D. M. (1986). Who Are Organizational Third Parties and What Do They Do? In R. J. Lewicki, B. H. Sheppard, & M. H. Bazerman (eds.), *Research on Negotiations in Organizations, Vol. 1* (pp. 207–278). Greenwich, CT: JAI Press.

Kolb, D. M., & Glidden, P. (1986). Getting to Know Your Conflict Options. *Personnel Administrator, 31,* 77–90.

Kong, D. (2002, April 18). Abercrombie and Fitch Pulls T-Shirts. *Associated Press.*

Koontz, H., & O'Donnell, C. (1976). *Management: A Systems and Contingency Analysis of Managerial Functions.* New York: McGraw-Hill.

Kraemer, K. L. (1982). Telecommunications/Transportation Substitution and Energy Conservation. *Telecommunications Policy, 6,* 39–59.

Kram, K. E. (1985). *Mentoring at Work: Developmental Relationships in Organizational Life.* Glenview, IL: Scott Foresman.

Kramer, M. W. (1993a). Communication after Job Transfers: Social Exchange Processes in Learning New Roles. *Human Communication Research, 20,* 147–174.

——— (1993b). Communication and Uncertainty Reduction during Job Transfers: Leaving and Joining Processes. *Communication Monographs, 60,* 178–198.

——— (1995). A Longitudinal Study of Superior-Subordinate Com-

munication during Job Transfers. *Human Communication Research, 22,* 39–64.

——— (1996). A Longitudinal Study of Peer Communication during Job Transfers: The Impact of Frequency, Quality, and Network Multiplexity on Adjustment. *Human Communication Research, 23,* 59–86.

——— (2006). Shared Leadership in a Community Theater Group: Filling the Leadership Role. *Journal of Applied Communication Research, 34,* 141–162.

Kramer, M. W., & Berman, J. E. (2001). Making Sense of a University's Culture: An Examination of Undergraduate Students' Stories. *Southern Communication Journal, 66,* 297–311.

Kramer, M. W., & Hess, J. A. (2002). Communication Rules for the Display of Emotions in Organizational Settings. *Management Communication Quarterly, 16,* 66–80.

Kreps, G. L. (1990). *Organizational Communication: Theory and Practice.* New York: Longman.

Kruml, S. M., & Geddes, D. (2000). Exploring the Dimensions of Emotional Labor: The Heart of Hochschild's Work. *Management Communication Quarterly, 14,* 8–49.

Kuhn, T., & Corman, S. R. (2003). The Emergence of Homogeneity and Heterogeneity in Knowledge Structures during a Planned Organizational Change. *Communication Monographs, 70,* 198–229.

Kuhn, T., & Poole, M. S. (2000). Do Conflict Management Styles Affect Group Decision Making? Evidence from a Longitudinal Field Study. *Human Communication Research, 26,* 558–590.

Lair, D. L., Sullivan, K., & Cheney, G. (2005). Marketization and the Recasting of the Professional Self: The Rhetoric and Ethics of Personal Branding. *Management Communication Quarterly, 18,* 307–343.

Lawler, E. E., & Finegold, D. (2000). Individualizing the Organization:

Past, Present, and Future. *Organizational Dynamics, 29*, 1–15.

Leidner, R. (1993). *Fast Food, Fast Talk: Service Work and the Routinization of Everyday Life.* Berkeley: University of California Press.

Lengel, R. H., & Daft, R. L. (1988). The Selection of Communication Media as an Executive Skill. *Academy of Management Executive, 2*, 225–232.

Levin, J. (2006, September 25). 'This Topic Annoys Me.' *Newsweek,* p. 72.

Levy, S. (2004, June 7). A Future with Nowhere to Hide? *Newsweek,* p. 76.

Lewicki, R. J., Gray, G., & Elliott, M. (eds.) (2003). *Making Sense of Intractable Environmental Conflicts: Frames and Cases.* Washington, DC: Island Press.

Lewin, R. (1992). *Complexity: Life at the Edge of Chaos.* New York: Macmillan.

Lewis, L. K. (1997). Users' Individual Communicative Responses to Intraorganizationally Implemented Innovations and Other Planned Changes. *Management Communication Quarterly, 10*, 455–490.

——— (2000). "Blindsided by That One" and "I Saw That One Coming": The Relative Anticipation and Occurrence of Communication Problems and Other Problems in Implementers' Hindsight. *Journal of Applied Communication Research, 28*, 44–67.

Lewis, L. K., Richardson, B. K., & Hamel, S. A. (2003). When the "Stakes" Are Communicative: The Lamb's and the Lion's Share during Nonprofit Planned Change. *Human Communication Research, 29*, 400–430.

Lewis, L. K., & Seibold, D. R. (1993). Innovation Modification during Intraorganizational Adoption. *Academy of Management Review, 18*, 322–354.

——— (1996). Communication during Intraorganizational Innovation Adoption: Predicting Users' Behavioral Coping—Responses to Innovations in Organizations. *Communication Monographs, 63*, 131–157.

Lief, H. I., & Fox, R. C. (1963). Training for "Detached Concern" in Medical Students. In H. I. Lief, V. F. Lief, & N. R. Lief (eds.), *The Psychological Basis of Medical Practice.* New York: Harper & Row.

Likert, R. (1961). *New Patterns of Management.* New York: McGraw-Hill.

——— (1967). *The Human Organization: Its Management and Value.* New York: McGraw-Hill.

Lim, V. K. G. (1996). Job Insecurity and Its Outcomes: Moderating Effects of Work-Based and Nonwork-Based Social Support. *Human Relations, 49*, 171–194.

Linstead, S. (1993). Deconstruction in the Study of Organizations. In M. Parker & J. Hassard (eds.), *Postmodernism and Organizations* (pp. 49–70). Newbury Park, CA: Sage.

Liu, M. (2007, July 16). The Toxic Republic. *Newsweek,* p. 44.

Louis, M. R. (1980). Surprise and Sense-Making: What Newcomers Experience When Entering Unfamiliar Organizational Settings. *Administrative Science Quarterly, 23*, 225–251.

——— (1985). An Investigator's Guide to Workplace Culture. In P. J. Frost, L. F. Moore, M. R. Louis, C. C. Lundberg, & J. Martin (eds.), *Organizational Culture* (pp. 73–93). Beverly Hills, CA: Sage.

Lutgen-Sandvik, P. (2003). The Communicative Cycle of Employee Emotional Abuse: Generation and Regeneration of Workplace Mistreatment. *Management Communication Quarterly, 16*, 471–501.

Mael, F., & Ashforth, B. E. (1992). Alumni and Their Alma Mater: A Partial Test of the Reformulated Model of Organizational Identification. *Journal of Organizational Behavior, 13*, 103–123.

Mainiero, L. A. (1994). Getting Anointed for Advancement: The Case of Executive Women. *Academy of Management Executive, 8* (2), 53–63.

March, J. G., & Simon, H. A. (1958). *Organizations.* New York: Wiley.

Markus, M. L. (1983). Power Politics and MIS Implementation. *Communications of the ACM, 26*, 430–444.

——— (1990). Toward a "Critical Mass" Theory of Interactive Media. In J. Fulk & C. W. Steinfield (eds.), *Organizations and Communication Technology* (pp. 194–218). Newbury Park, CA: Sage.

Marschall, D. (2002). Internet Technologists as an Occupational Community: Ethnographic Evidence. *Information Communication & Society, 5*, 51–69.

Marshall, A. A., & Stohl, C. (1993). Being "In the Know" in a Participative Management System. *Management Communication Quarterly, 6*, 372–404.

Marshall, J. (1993). Viewing Organizational Communication from a Feminist Perspective: A Critique and Some Offerings. In S. Deetz (ed.), *Communication Yearbook 16* (pp. 122–141). Newbury Park, CA: Sage.

Martin, J. (1992). *Cultures in Organizations: Three Perspectives.* New York: Oxford University Press.

——— (2002). *Organizational Culture: Mapping the Terrain.* Thousand Oaks, CA: Sage.

Martin, J., & Frost, P. (1996). The Organizational Culture War Games: A Struggle for Intellectual Dominance. In S. R. Clegg, C. Hardy, & W. R. Nord (eds.), *The Handbook of Organization Studies* (pp. 599–621). Newbury Park, CA: Sage.

Maruyama, M. (1963). The Second Cybernetics: Deviation-Amplifying Mutual Causal Processes. *American Scientist, 51*, 52–64.

Marx, K. (1967). *Writings of the Young Marx on Philosophy and Society,* (L. D. Easton & K. H. Guddat, eds. and trans. New York: Anchor Books.

Maslach, C. (1982). *Burnout: The Cost of Caring.* Englewood Cliffs, NJ: Prentice-Hall.

Maslow, A. H. (1943). A Theory of Human Motivation. *Psychology Review, 50*, 370–396.

—— (1954). *Motivation and Personality*. New York: Harper & Row.

Matheson, K., & Zanna, M. (1989). Impact of Computer-Mediated Communication on Self-Awareness. *Computers in Human Behavior, 4,* 221–233.

Matteson, M. T., & Ivancevich, J. M. (1982). *Managing Job Stress and Worker Health*. New York: Free Press.

Mattson, M., & Stage, C. W. (2001). Toward an Understanding of Intercultural Ethical Dilemmas as Opportunities for Engagement in New Millennium Global Organizations. *Management Communication Quarterly, 15,* 103–109.

Maznevski, M. L., & Chudoba, K. M. (2000). Bridging Space over Time: Global Virtual-Team Dynamics and Effectiveness. *Organization Science, 11,* 473–492.

McComb, K. B., & Jablin, F. M. (1984). Verbal Correlates of Interviewer Empathic Listening and Employment Interview Outcomes. *Communication Monographs, 51,* 353–371.

McCurdy, H. E. (1992). NASA's Organizational Culture. *Public Administration Review, 52,* 189–192.

McDaniel, M. A., Whetzel, D. L., Schmidt, F. L., & Maurer, S. D. (1994). The Validity of Employment Interviews: A Comprehensive Review and Meta-Analysis. *Journal of Applied Psychology, 79,* 599–616.

McGinn, D. (2000, November 13). A Ph.D. Hits the Road. *Newsweek,* pp. 70–72.

—— (2004, March 1). Help Not Wanted. *Newsweek,* pp. 31–33.

—— (2004, April 19). Faster Food. *Newsweek,* pp. E20–E22.

—— (2006, September 25). Getting Back on Track. *Newsweek,* pp. 62–66.

—— (2007, March 19). You Need to Get to Work! *Newsweek,* pp. E8–E15.

McGinn, D., & Naughton, K. (2001, February 25). How Safe Is Your Job? *Newsweek,* pp. 36–43.

McGregor, D. (1957). The Human Side of Enterprise. *Management Review, 46,* 22–28, 88–92.

—— (1960). *The Human Side of Enterprise*. New York: McGraw-Hill.

McMillan, J. J., & Northern, N. A. (1995). Organizational Co-dependency: The Creation and Maintenance of Closed Systems. *Management Communication Quarterly, 9,* 6–45.

McPhee, R. D., & Babrow, A. (1987). Causal Modeling in Communication Research: Use, Disuse, and Misuse. *Communication Monographs, 54,* 344–366.

McPhee, R. D., & Poole, M. S. (2001). Organizational Structure and Configurations. In F. M. Jablin & L. L. Putnam (eds.), *The New Handbook of Organizational Communication: Advances in Theory, Research, and Methods* (pp. 503–543). Thousand Oaks, CA: Sage.

Medved, C. E., & Kirby, E. L. (2005). Family CEOs: A Feminist Analysis of Corporate Mothering Discourses. *Management Communication Quarterly, 18,* 435–478.

Medved, C. E., Morrison, K., Dearing, J., Larson, R. S., Cline, G., & Brummans, B. H. J. M. (2001). Tensions in Community Health Improvement Initiatives: Communication and Collaboration in a Managed Care Environment. *Journal of Applied Communication Research, 29,* 137–152.

Meiners, E. B., & Miller, V. D. (2004). The Effect of Formality and Relational Tone on Supervisor/Subordinate Negotiation Episodes. *Western Journal of Communication, 68,* 302–321.

Mennecke, B. E., Valacich, J. S., & Wheeler, B. C. (2000). The Effects of Media and Task on User Performance: A Test of the Task-Media Fit Hypothesis. *Group Decision & Negotiation, 9,* 507–529.

Merry, U. (1995). *Coping with Uncertainty: Insights from the New Sciences of Chaos, Self-Organization, and Complexity*. Westport, CT: Praeger.

Meyer, J. (1995). Tell Me a Story: Eliciting Organizational Values from Narratives. *Communication Quarterly, 43,* 210–224.

Meyer, J. W., & Scott, W. R. (1983). *Organizational Environments: Ritual and Rationality*. Beverly Hills, CA: Sage.

Meyer, M. H., & DeTore, A. (1999). Product Development for Services. *Academy of Management Executive, 13* (3), 64–76.

Meyerson, D. E. (1994). Interpretations of Stress in Institutions: The Cultural Production of Ambiguity and Burnout. *Administrative Science Quarterly, 39,* 628–653.

—— (1998). Feeling Stressed and Burned Out: A Feminist Reading and Re-Visioning of Stress-Based Emotions within Medicine and Organizational Science. *Organizational Science, 8,* 103–118.

Miles, R. (1965). Human Relations or Human Resources. *Harvard Business Review, 43,* 21–29.

Miller, K. (1995). *Organizational Communication: Approaches and Processes*. Belmont, CA: Wadsworth.

—— (1998). Nurses at the Edge of Chaos: The Application of "New Science" Concepts to Organizational Systems. *Management Communication Quarterly, 12,* 112–127.

—— (2001). Quantitative Research Methods in Organizational Communication: Practices and Challenges. In F. M. Jablin & L. L Putnam (eds.), *The New Handbook of Organizational Communication: Advances in Theory, Research, and Methods*. Newbury Park, CA: Sage.

—— (2002). The Experience of Emotion in the Workplace: Professing in the Midst of Tragedy. *Management Communication Quarterly, 15,* 571–600.

—— (2005). *Communication Theories: Perspectives, Processes, and Contexts*, 2nd ed. New York: McGraw-Hill.

—— (2007). Compassionate Communication in the Workplace: Exploring Processes of Noticing, Connecting, and Responding.

Journal of Applied Communication Research, 35, 223–245.

Miller, K. I., Birkholt, M., Scott, C., & Stage, C. (1995). Empathy and Burnout in Human Service Work: An Extension of a Communication Model. *Communication Research, 22,* 123–147.

Miller, K. I., Considine, J., & Garner, J. (2007). "Let Me Tell You about My Job": Exploring the Terrain of Emotion in the Workplace. *Management Communication Quarterly, 20,* 231–260.

Miller, K. I., Ellis, B. H., Zook, E. G., & Lyles, J. S. (1990). An Integrated Model of Communication, Stress, and Burnout in the Workplace. *Communication Research, 17,* 300–326.

Miller, K. I., Joseph, L., & Apker, J. (2000). Strategic Ambiguity in the Role Development Process. *Journal of Applied Communication Research, 28,* 193–214.

Miller, K. I., & Monge, P. R. (1985). Social Information and Employee Anxiety about Organizational Change. *Human Communication Research, 11,* 365–386.

———— (1986). Participation, Satisfaction, and Productivity: A Meta-Analytic Review. *Academy of Management Journal, 29,* 727–753.

———— (1987). The Development and Test of a System of Organizational Participation and Allocation. In M. McLaughlin (ed.), *Communication Yearbook 10* (pp. 431–455). Beverly Hills, CA: Sage.

Miller, K. I., & Ryan, D. J. (2001). Communication in the Age of Managed Care: Introduction to the Special Issue. *Journal of Applied Communication Research, 29,* 91–96.

Miller, K. I., Stiff, J. B., & Ellis, B. H. (1988). Communication and Empathy as Precursors to Burnout among Human Service Workers. *Communication Monographs, 55,* 250–265.

Miller, V. D., & Jablin, F. M. (1991). Information Seeking during Organizational Entry: Influences, Tactics, and a Model of the Process. *Academy of Management Review, 16,* 92–120.

Miller, V. D., Jablin, F. M., Casey, M. K., Lamphear-Van Horn, M., & Ethington, C. (1996). The Maternity Leave as a Role Negotiation Process. *Journal of Managerial Issues, 8,* 286–309.

Miller, V. D., Johnson, J. R., & Grau, J. (1994). Antecedents to Willingness to Participate in a Planned Organizational Change. *Journal of Applied Communication Research, 22,* 59–80.

Milliken, F. J., & Martins, L. L. (1996). Searching for Common Threads: Understanding the Multiple Effects of Diversity in Organizational Groups. *Academy of Management Review, 21,* 402–433.

Miner, J. B. (1980). *Theories of Organizational Behavior.* New York: Dryden Press.

———— (1982). *Theories of Organizational Structure and Process.* New York: Dryden Press.

Mintzberg, H. (1973). *The Nature of Managerial Work.* New York: Harper & Row.

Mohrman, S. A., with Cohen, S. G, & Mohrman, A. M. (1995). *Designing Team-Based Organizations.* San Francisco: Jossey-Bass.

Monge, P. R. (1982). Systems Theory and Research in the Study of Organizational Communication: The Correspondence Problem. *Human Communication Research, 8,* 245–261.

———— (1990). Theoretical and Analytical Issues in Studying Organizational Processes. *Organization Science, 1,* 406–430.

———— (1998). Communication Structures and Processes in Globalization. *Journal of Communication, 48* (4), 142–153.

Monge, P. R., & Contractor, N. S. (2001). Emergence of Communication Networks. In F. M. Jablin & L. L. Putnam (eds.), *The New Handbook of Organizational Communication: Advances in Theory, Research, and Methods* (pp. 440–502). Thousand Oaks, CA: Sage.

Monge, P. R., & Eisenberg, E. M. (1987). Emergent Communication Networks. In F. M. Jablin, L. L. Putnam, K. H. Roberts, & L. W. Porter (eds.), *Handbook of Organizational Communication: An Interdisciplinary Perspective* (pp. 304–342). Newbury Park, CA: Sage.

Monge, P. R., Farace, R. V., Eisenberg, E. M., White, L., & Miller, K. I. (1984). The Process of Studying Process in Organizational Communication. *Journal of Communication, 34,* 22–43.

Monge, P. R., & Miller, K. I. (1988). Participative Processes in Organizations. In G. M. Goldhaber & G. A. Barnett (eds.), *Handbook of Organizational Communication* (pp. 213–229). Norwood, NJ: Ablex.

Mooney, C. (2007). *Storm World: Hurricanes, Politics, and the Battle over Global Warming.* Orlando, FL: Harcourt.

More, E. (1998). *Managing Change: Exploring State of the Art.* Greenwich, CT: JAI Press.

Morgan, G. (1986). *Images of Organization.* Beverly Hills, CA: Sage.

———— (1997). *Images of Organization,* 2nd ed. Newbury Park, CA: Sage.

Morgan, J. M., & Krone, K. J. (2001). Bending the Rules of "Professional" Display: Emotional Improvisation in Caregiver Performances. *Journal of Applied Communication Research, 29,* 317–340.

Morley, D. D., & Shockley-Zalabak, P. (1991). Setting the Rules: An Examination of Organizational Founders' Values. *Management Communication Quarterly, 4,* 422–449.

Morley, I. E., & Stephenson, G. M. (1977). The Social Psychology of Bargaining. London: Allen & Unwin.

Morris, J. A., & Feldman, D. C. (1996). The Dimensions, Antecedents, and Consequences of Emotional Labor. *Academy of Management Review, 21,* 986–1010.

Morrison, A. M., & Von Glinow, M. A. (1990). Women and Minorities in Management. *American Psychologist, 45,* 200–208.

Morrison, E. W. (1993). Newcomer Information Seeking: Exploring Types, Modes, Sources, and

Outcomes. *Academy of Management Journal, 36,* 557–589.

——— (2003). Information Seeking within Organizations. *Human Communication Research, 28,* 229–242.

Morrow, R. A. (1994). *Critical Theory and Methodology.* Thousand Oaks, CA: Sage.

Muchinsky, P. (1977). Organizational Communication: Relationships to Organizational Climate and Job Satisfaction. *Academy of Management Journal, 20,* 592–607.

Mumby, D. K. (1987). The Political Functions of Narrative in Organizations. *Communication Monographs, 54,* 113–127.

——— (1988). *Communication and Power in Organizations: Discourse, Ideology, and Domination.* Norwood, NJ: Ablex.

——— (1989). Ideology and the Social Construction of Meaning: A Communication Perspective. *Communication Quarterly, 37,* 291–304.

——— (1993). *Narrative and Social Control.* Newbury Park, CA: Sage.

——— (1996). Feminism, Postmodernism, and Organizational Communication Studies: A Critical Reading. *Management Communication Quarterly, 9,* 259–295.

——— (2000). Common Ground from the Critical Perspective: Overcoming Binary Oppositions. In S. R. Corman & M. S. Poole (eds.), *Perspectives on Organizational Communication: Finding Common Ground* (pp. 68–86). New York: Guilford.

——— (2001). Power and Politics. In F. M. Jablin & L. L. Putnam (eds.), *The New Handbook of Organizational Communication: Advances in Theory, Research, and Methods* (pp. 585–623). Thousand Oaks, CA: Sage.

——— (2005). Theorizing Resistance in Organization Studies: A Dialectical Approach. *Management Communication Quarterly, 19,* 19–44.

Mumby, D. K., & Putnam, L. L. (1992). The Politics of Emotion: A Feminist Reading of Bounded Rationality. *Academy of Management Review, 17,* 465–486.

Murphy, A. G. (1998). Hidden Transcripts of Flight Attendant Resistance. *Management Communication Quarterly, 11,* 499–535.

——— (2001). The Flight Attendant Dilemma: An Analysis of Communication and Sensemaking during In-Flight Emergencies. *Journal of Applied Communication Research, 29,* 30–53.

Myers, K. K. (2005). A Burning Desire: Assimilation into a Fire Department. *Management Communication Quarterly, 18,* 344–384.

Myers, K. K., & McPhee, R. D. (2006). Influences on Member Assimilation in Workgroups in High-Reliability Organizations: A Multilevel Analysis. *Human Communication Research, 32,* 440–468.

Myers, K. K., & Oetzel, J. G. (2003). Exploring the Dimensions of Organizational Assimilation: Creating and Validating a Measure. *Communication Quarterly, 51,* 438–457.

Myers, L. L., & Larson, R. S. (2005). Preparing Students for Early Work Conflict. *Business Communication Quarterly, 68,* 306–317.

Nakayama, T., & Martin, J. (eds.) (1999). *Whiteness: The Communication of Social Identity.* Thousand Oaks, CA: Sage.

Naughton, K. (2000, December 11). A Mess of a Merger. *Newsweek,* pp. 54–56.

Neale, M. A., & Bazerman, M. H. (1985). The Effects of Framing and Negotiator Overconfidence on Bargaining Behaviors and Outcomes. *Academy of Management Journal, 28,* 34–49.

"New Gallup Poll" (2005, December 8). *U.S. Equal Employment Opportunity Commission.* Retrieved November 24, 2007, from http://www.eeoc.gov/press/12-8-05.html.

Newell, F. (2000). *Loyalty.com.* New York: McGraw-Hill.

"New Study Reveals Sweeping Dissatisfaction with Customer Service" (2004, July 19). Retrieved February 19, 2008, from www.instantservice.com/news/20040719_2.html.

Nicotera, A. M., Rodriguez, A. J., Hall, M., & Jackson, R. L. (1995). A History of the Study of Communication and Conflict. In A. M. Nicotera (ed.), *Conflict and Organizations: Communicative Processes* (pp. 17–41). Albany: State University of New York Press.

Noe, R. A. (1988). Women and Mentoring: A Review and Research Agenda. *Academy of Management Review, 13,* 65–78.

Nonaka, I., & Takeuchi, H. (1995). *The Knowledge-Creating Company.* Oxford: Oxford University Press.

Northouse, P. G. (1997). *Leadership.* Thousand Oaks, CA: Sage.

Nutt, P. C. (1984). Types of Organizational Decision Processes. *Administrative Science Quarterly, 29,* 414–450.

——— (1999). Surprising but True: Half the Decisions in Organizations Fail. *Academy of Management Executive, 13* (4), 75–90.

Nye, D. (1998). Affirmative Action and the Stigma of Incompetence. *Academy of Management Executive, 12* (1), 88–89.

O'Connell, C. J., & Mills, A. J. (2003). Making Sense of Bad News: The Media, Sensemaking, and Organizational Crisis. *Canadian Journal of Communication, 28,* 323–339.

Ohlott, P., Ruderman, M., & McCauley, C. (1994). Gender Differences in Managers' Developmental Job Experiences. *Academy of Management Journal, 37,* 46–67.

O'Kane, R. H. T. (2007). *Terrorism: A Short History of a Big Idea.* Harlow, England: Pearson Longman.

Oliver, J. K. (2007). U.S. Foreign Policy after 9/11: Context and Prospect. In M. J. Miller & B. Stefanova (eds.), *The War on Terror in Comparative Perspective: U.S. Security and Foreign Policy after 9/11* (pp. 19–45). New York: Palgrave MacMillan.

Omdahl, B. L., & O'Donnell, C. (1999). Emotional Contagion, Empathic Concern and Communicative Responsiveness as Variables Affecting Nurses' Stress and Occupational Commitment. *Journal of Advanced Nursing, 29,* 1351–1359.

Orbe, M. P. (1998). An Outsider within Perspective to Organizational Communication: Explicating the Communicative Practices of Co-Cultural Group Members. *Management Communication Quarterly, 12,* 230–279.

Orlitzky, M., & Hirokawa, R. Y. (2001). To Err Is Human, to Correct for It Divine: A Meta-Analysis of Research Testing the Functional Theory of Group Decision-Making Effectiveness. *Small Group Research, 32,* 313–341.

Osburn, L. (2007, September 17). Expecting the World on a Silver Platter. *Houston Chronicle,* pp. D1, D6.

Osland, J. S., & Bird, A. (2000). Beyond Sophisticated Stereotyping: Cultural Sensemaking in Context. *Academy of Management Executive, 14* (1), 65–79.

Ouchi, W. G. (1981). *Theory Z.* New York: Avon Books.

Pacanowsky, M. (1988). Communication in the Empowering Organization. In J. A. Anderson (ed.), *Communication Yearbook 11* (pp. 356–379). Newbury Park, CA: Sage.

Pacanowsky, M., & O'Donnell-Trujillo, N. (1983). Organizational Communication as Cultural Performance. *Communication Monographs, 50,* 126–147.

Papa, M. J., Auwal, M. A., & Singhal, A. (1995). Dialectic of Control and Emancipation in Organizing for Social Change: A Multitheoretic Study of the Grameen Bank in Bangladesh. *Communication Theory, 5,* 189–223.

Parker, P. S. (2003). Control, Resistance, and Empowerment in Raced, Gendered, and Classed Work Contexts: The Case of African American Women. In Pamela J. Kalbfleisch (ed.),

Communication Yearbook 27, (257–291). Mahwah, NJ: Lawrence Erlbaum Associates.

Pearlson, K. E., & Saunders, C. S. (2001). There's No Place like Home: Managing Telecommuting Paradoxes. *Academy of Management Executive, 15* (2), 117–128.

Pederson, D. (1997, June 23). Dissing Customers: Why the Service Is Missing from America's Service Economy. *Newsweek,* pp. 56–57.

Penelope, J. (1990). *Speaking Freely: Unlearning the Lies of the Fathers' Tongues.* New York: Pergamon Press.

Penn, M. J. (2007). *Microtrends: The Small Forces behind Tomorrow's Changes.* New York: Hachette Book Group.

Pepper, G. L., & Larson, G. S. (2006). Cultural Identity Tensions in a Post-Acquisition Organization. *Journal of Applied Communication Research, 34,* 49–71.

Peraino, K. (2003, September 8). Good Times in the Skies. *Newsweek,* p. 58.

Peters, T. (1999). *The Brand You 50.* New York: Knopf.

Peters, T. J., & Waterman, R. H. (1982). *In Search of Excellence: Lessons from America's Best-Run Companies.* New York: Harper & Row.

Pfeffer, J. (1998). *The Human Equation: Building Profits by Putting People First.* Boston: Harvard Business School Press.

Pfeffer, J., & Veiga, J. F. (1999). Putting People First for Organizational Success. *Academy of Management Executive, 13* (2), 37–48.

Pierce, T., & Dougherty, D. S. (2002). The Construction, Enactment, and Maintenance of Power-as-Domination through an Acquisition: The Case of TWA and Ozark Airlines. *Management Communication Quarterly, 16,* 129–164.

Pines, A. M. (1982). Changing Organizations: Is a Work Environment without Burnout an Impossible Goal? In W. S. Paine (ed.), *Job Stress and Burnout: Research, Theory and Intervention*

Perspectives (pp. 172–191). Newbury Park, CA: Sage.

Pines, A. M., Aronson, E., & Kafry, D. (1981). *Burnout: From Tedium to Personal Growth.* New York: Free Press.

Pondy, L. R. (1967). Organizational Conflict: Concepts and Models. *Administrative Science Quarterly, 12,* 296–320.

Poole, M. S. (1983). Decision Development in Small Groups II: A Study of Multiple Sequences in Decision-Making. *Communication Monographs, 50,* 206–232.

——— (1996, February). Another Turn of the Wheel: A Return to Systems Theory in Organizational Communication. Paper presented at the Conference on Organizational Communication and Change, Austin, TX.

Poole, M. S., & DeSanctis, G. (1992). Microlevel Structuration in Computer-Supported Group Decision Making. *Human Communication Research, 19,* 5–49.

Poole, M. S., & Doelger, J. A. (1986). Developmental Processes in Group Decision-Making. In R. Y. Hirokawa & M. S. Poole (eds.), *Communication and Group Decision-Making* (pp. 35–61). Beverly Hills, CA: Sage.

Poole, M. S., & Roth, J. (1989a). Decision Development in Small Groups IV: A Typology of Group Decision Paths. *Human Communication Research, 15,* 323–356.

——— (1989b). Decision Development in Small Groups V: Test of a Contingency Model. *Human Communication Research, 15,* 549–589.

Popovich, P., & Wanous, J. P. (1982). The Realistic Job Preview as a Persuasive Communication. *Academy of Management Review, 7,* 570–578.

Poundstone, W. (2003). *How Would You Move Mount Fuji? Microsoft's Cult of the Puzzle.* New York: Little, Brown, & Company.

Powell, G. N., & Goulet, L. R. (1996). Recruiters' and Applicants' Reactions to Campus Interviews and Employment Decisions.

Academy of Management Journal, 39, 1619–1640.

Pugh, D. S., & Hickson, D. J. (1989). *Writers on Organizations.* Newbury Park, CA: Sage.

Putnam, L. L. (1983). The Interpretive Perspective: An Alternative to Functionalism. In L. L. Putnam & M. E. Pacanowsky (eds.), *Communication and Organizations: An Interpretive Approach* (pp. 31–54). Beverly Hills, CA: Sage.

—— (1995). Formal Negotiations: The Productive Side of Organizational Conflict. In A. M. Nicotera (ed.), *Conflict and Organizations: Communication Processes* (pp. 183–200). Albany: State University of New York Press.

Putnam, L. L., & Kolb, D. M. (2000). Rethinking Negotiation: Feminist Views of Communication and Exchange. In P. M. Buzzanell (ed.), *Rethinking Organizational and Managerial Communication from Feminist Perspectives* (pp. 76–104). Thousand Oaks, CA: Sage.

Putnam, L. L., & Peterson, T. (2003). The Edwards Aquifer Dispute: Shifting Frames in a Protracted Conflict. In R. J. Lewicki, B. Gray, and M. Elliott (eds.), *Making Sense of Intractable Environmental Conflicts: Frames and Cases* (pp. 127–158). Washington, DC: Island Press.

Putnam, L. L., & Poole, M. S. (1987). Conflict and Negotiation. In F. M. Jablin, L. L. Putnam, K. H. Roberts, & L. W. Porter (eds.), *Handbook of Organizational Communication: An Interdisciplinary Perspective* (pp. 549–599). Newbury Park, CA: Sage.

Putnam, L. L., & Stohl, C. (1996). Bona Fide Groups: An Alternative Perspective for Communication and Small Group Decision Making. In R. Y. Hirokawa & M. S. Poole (eds.), *Communication and Group Decision Making,* 2nd ed. (pp. 147–178). Thousand Oaks, CA: Sage.

Putnam, L. L., & Wondolleck, J. M. (2003). Intractability: Definitions, Dimensions, and Distinctions. In R. J. Lewicki, B. Gray, and M. Elliott (eds.), *Making Sense of Intractable Environmental Conflicts: Frames and Cases* (pp.

35–59). Washington, DC: Island Press.

Quindlen, A. (2003, October 20). Still Needing the F Word. *Newsweek,* p. 74.

—— (2006, September 25). Everyday Equality. *Newsweek,* p. 84.

Quinn, J. B. (2006, December 18). Giving Freely and Wisely. *Newsweek,* p. 51.

Quinn, R. E., & McGrath, M. R. (1985). The Transformation of Organizational Cultures: A Competing Values Perspective. In P. J. Frost, L. F. Moore, M. R. Louis, C. C. Lundberg, & J. Martin (eds.), *Organizational Culture* (pp. 315–334). Beverly Hills, CA: Sage.

Rafaeli, A., & Sutton, R. I. (1987). Expression of Emotion as Part of the Work Role. *Academy of Management Review, 12,* 23–37.

Ragins, B. R., & Cotton, J. L. (1991). Easier Said than Done: Gender Differences in Perceived Barriers to Gaining a Mentor. *Academy of Management Journal, 34,* 939–951.

Ragins, B. R., Townsend, B., & Mattis, M. (1998). Gender Gap in the Executive Suite: CEOs and Female Executives Report on Breaking the Glass Ceiling. *Academy of Management Executive, 12* (1), 28–42.

Rains, S. A. (2005). Leveling the Organizational Playing Field—Virtually: A Meta-Analysis of Experimental Research Assessing the Impact of Group Support System Use on Member Influence Behaviors. *Communication Research, 32,* 193–234.

Ralston, S. M. (1993). Applicant Communication Satisfaction, Intent to Accept Second Interview Offers, and Recruiter Communication Style. *Journal of Applied Communication Research, 21,* 53–65.

Ralston, S. M., & Kirkwood, W. G. (1995). Overcoming Managerial Bias in Employment Interviewing. *Journal of Applied Communication Research, 23,* 75–92.

Ramer, S. (2003, August 18). It's More than the Economy, Stupid. *Newsweek,* p. 14.

Ray, E. B. (1987). Supportive Relationships and Occupational

Stress in the Workplace. In T. L. Albrecht & M. B. Adelman (eds.), *Communicating Social Support* (pp. 172–191). Beverly Hills, CA: Sage.

—— (1993). When the Links Become Chains: Considering Dysfunctions of Supportive Communication in the Workplace. *Communication Monographs, 60,* 106–111.

Ray, E. B., & Miller, K. I. (1991). The Influence of Communication Structure and Social Support on Job Stress and Burnout. *Management Communication Quarterly, 4,* 506–527.

Reich, R. B. (2000). *The Future of Success: Working and Living in the New Economy.* New York: Vintage Books.

Reichers, A. E. (1987). An Interactionist Perspective on Newcomer Socialization Rates. *Academy of Management Review, 12,* 278–287.

Reichers, A. E., Wanous, J. P., & Austin, J. T. (1997). Understanding and Managing Cynicism about Organizational Change. *Academy of Management Executive, 11* (1), 48–59.

Rice, R. E. (1993). Media Appropriateness: Using Social Presence Theory to Compare Traditional and New Organizational Media. *Human Communication Research, 19,* 451–484.

Rice, R. E., & Aydin, C. (1991). Attitudes toward New Organizational Technology: Network Proximity as a Mechanism for Social Information Processing. *Administrative Science Quarterly, 36,* 219–244.

Rice, R. E., & Case, D. (1983). Computer-Based Messaging in the University: A Description of Use and Utility. *Journal of Communication, 33,* 131–152.

Rice, R. E., & Gattiker, U. E. (2001). New Media and Organizational Structuring. In F. M. Jablin & L. L. Putnam (eds.), *The New Handbook of Organizational Communication: Advances in Theory, Research, and Methods* (pp. 544–581). Thousand Oaks, CA: Sage.

Rice, R. E., & Love, G. (1987). Electronic Emotion: Socioemotional

Content in a Computer-Mediated Communication Network. *Communication Research, 14,* 85–108.

Risberg, A. (1999). *Ambiguities Thereafter.* Lund, Sweden: Lund University Press.

Ritchie, J. B., & Miles, R. E. (1970). An Analysis of Quantity and Quality of Participation as Mediating Variables in the Participative Decision Making Process. *Personnel Psychology, 23,* 347–359.

Ritzer, G. (2000). *The McDonaldization of Society.* Thousand Oaks, CA: Pine Forge Press.

Roberts, K., Kossek, E. E., & Ozeki, C. (1998). Managing the Global Workforce: Challenges and Strategies. *Academy of Management Executive, 12* (4), 93–106.

Robinson, G., & Dechant, K. (1997). Building a Case for Diversity. *Academy of Management Executive, 11,* 21–31.

Roethlisberger, F. J., & Dickson, W. J. (1939). *Management and the Worker.* Cambridge, MA: Harvard University Press.

Roloff, M. E. (1987). Communication and Conflict. In C. R. Berger & S. H. Chaffee (eds.), *Handbook of Communication Science* (pp. 484–534). Newbury Park, CA: Sage.

Rosenfeld, L. B., Richman, J. M., & May, S. K. (2004). Information Adequacy, Job Satisfaction and Organizational Culture in a Dispersed-Network Organization. *Journal of Applied Communication Research, 32,* 28–54.

Roth, N. L. (1991, February). Secrets in Organizations: Addressing Taboo Topics at Work. Paper presented at the annual meeting of the Western Speech Communication Association, Phoenix, AZ.

Russ, G. S., Daft, R. L., & Lengel, R. H. (1990). Media Selection and Managerial Characteristics in Organizational Communications. *Management Communication Quarterly, 4,* 151–175.

Russo, T. C. (1998). Organizational and Professional Identification: A Case of Newspaper Journalists. *Management Communication Quarterly, 12,* 72–111.

Rybicki, M. (2003, March 10). Temporary Worker, Permanent Loser? *Newsweek,* p. 18.

Rynes, S. L. (1990). Recruitment, Job Choice, and Post-Hire Consequences: A Call for New Research Directions. In M. D. Dundee & L. Hugh (eds.), *Handbook of Industrial and Organizational Psychology,* 2nd ed. (pp. 399–444). Palo Alto, CA: Consulting Psychologists Press.

Said, E. (2001). The Clash of Ignorance. *The Nation, 273* (12), 11–13.

Salancik, G. R., & Pfeffer, J. (1978). A Social Information Processing Approach to Job Attitudes and Task Design. *Administrative Science Quarterly, 23,* 224–253.

Samuelson, R. J. (2006, September 4). Wal-Mart's a Diversion. *Newsweek,* p. 39.

———— (2007, May 28). Long Live the News Business. *Newsweek,* p. 40.

Sandelands, L. E., & Boudens, C. J. (2000). Feeling at Work. In S. Fineman (ed.), *Emotion in Organizations,* 2nd ed. (pp. 46–63). London: Sage.

Scelfo, J. (2007, September 17). Come Back, Mr. Chips. *Newsweek,* p. 44.

Schall, M. (1983). A Communication-Rules Approach to Organizational Culture. *Administrative Science Quarterly, 28,* 557–581.

Schein, E. H. (1985). *Organizational Culture and Leadership.* San Francisco: Jossey-Bass.

———— (1992). *Organizational Culture and Leadership,* 2nd ed. San Francisco: Jossey-Bass.

———— (2004). The Culture of Media as Viewed from an Organizational Culture Perspective. *International Journal on Media Management, 5,* 171–172.

Schmitz, J., & Fulk, J. (1991). Organizational Colleagues, Media Richness, and Electronic Mail: A Test of the Social Influence Model of Technology Use. *Communication Research, 18,* 487–523.

Schulman, C. (2000, December 18). E-Mail: The Future of the Family Feud? *Newsweek,* p. 14.

Schuman, H., & Scott, J. (1989). Generations and Collective Memories. *American Psychological Review, 54,* 359–381.

Schwartz, E. I. (2004). *Juice: The Creative Fuel That Drives World-Class Inventors.* Cambridge, MA: Harvard Business School Press.

Schwartz, F. N. (1989). Management Women and the New Facts of Life. *Harvard Business Review,* January/February, 65–76.

Schwartz, N. D. (2001, December 24). Enron Fallout: Wide, but Not Deep. *Fortune,* pp. 71–72.

Scott, C., & Myers, K. K. (2005). The Socialization of Emotion: Learning Emotion Management at the Fire Station. *Journal of Applied Communication Research, 33,* 67–92.

Scott, C. R. (2001). Establishing and Maintaining Customer Loyalty and Employee Identification in the New Economy: A Communicative Response. *Management Communication Quarterly, 14,* 629–636.

———— (2003). New Communication Technologies and Teams. In R. Y. Hirokawa, R. S. Cathcart, L. A. Samovar, & L. D. Henman (eds.), *Small Group Communication Theory and Practice: An Anthology,* 8th ed. (pp. 134–147). Los Angeles, CA: Roxbury.

Scott, J. (1990). *Domination and the Arts of Resistance: Hidden Transcripts.* New Haven, CT: Yale University Press.

Seeger, M. W., Sellnow, T. L., & Ulmer, R. R. (2003). *Communication and Organizational Crisis.* Westport, CT: Praeger.

Seeger, M. W., & Ulmer, R. R. (2003). Explaining Enron: Communication and Responsible Leadership. *Management Communication Quarterly, 17,* 58–84.

Seibold, D. R., & Shea, B. C. (2001). Participation and Decision Making. In F. M. Jablin & L. L. Putnam (eds.), *The New Handbook of Organizational Communication: Advances in Theory, Research, and Methods* (pp. 664–703). Thousand Oaks, CA: Sage.

Senge, P. (1991). *The Fifth Discipline: The Art and Practice of the Learning Organization.* New York: Doubleday/Currency.

Senge, P., Roberts, C., Ross, R., Smith, B., & Kleiner, A. (1994). *The Fifth Discipline Fieldbook*. New York: Doubleday/Currency.

Sheer, V. C., & Chen, L. (2004). Improving Media Richness Theory: A Study of Interaction Goals, Message Valence, and Task Complexity in Manager–Subordinate Communication. *Management Communication Quarterly, 18*, 76–93.

Shenk, D. (1997). *Data Smog*. New York: Harper-Edge.

Sheppard, B. H. (1984). Third Party Conflict Intervention: A Procedural Framework. In B. M. Staw & L. L. Cummings (eds.), *Research in Organizational Behavior, Vol. 6* (pp. 141–190). Greenwich, CT: JAI Press.

Shinn, M. (1982). Methodological Issues: Evaluating and Using Information. In W. S. Paine (ed.), *Job Stress and Burnout: Research, Theory and Intervention Perspectives* (pp. 61–79). Beverly Hills, CA: Sage.

Shockley-Zalabak, P. (2002). Protean Places: Teams across Time and Space. *Journal of Applied Communication Research, 3*, 231–250.

Shockley-Zalabak, P., & Morley, D. D. (1994). Creating a Culture: A Longitudinal Examination of the Influence of Management and Employee Values on Communication Rule Stability and Emergence. *Human Communication Research, 20*, 334–355.

Short, J., Williams, E., & Christie, B. (1976). *The Social Psychology of Telecommunications*. New York: Wiley.

Shuler, S., & Sypher, B. D. (2000). Seeking Emotional Labor: When Managing the Heart Enhances the Work Experience. *Management Communication Quarterly, 14*, 50–89.

Shultz, K. S., Morton, K. R., & Weckerle, J. R. (1998). The Influence of Push and Pull Factors on Voluntary and Involuntary Early Retirees' Retirement Decision and Adjustment. *Journal of Vocational Behavior, 53*, 45–58.

Shumate, M., Fulk, J., & Monge, P. (2005). Predictors of the International HIV-AIDS INGO Network over Time. *Human Communication Research, 31*, 482–510.

Shuter, R., & Turner, L. H. (1997). African American and European American Women in the Workplace: Perceptions of Conflict Communication. *Management Communication Quarterly, 11*, 74–96.

Sias, P., & Jablin, F. (1995). Differential Superior–Subordinate relations, Perceptions of Fairness, and Coworker Communication. *Human Communication Research, 22*, 5–38.

Simon, H. A. (1960). *Administrative Behavior*, 2nd ed. New York: Macmillan.

——— (1987). Making Management Decisions: The Role of Intuition and Emotion. *Academy of Management Executive, 1*, 57–64.

Simons, T. (1993). Speech Patterns and the Concept of Utility in Cognitive Maps: The Case of Integrative Bargaining. *Academy of Management Journal, 36*, 139–156.

Sitkin, S. B., Sutcliffe, K. M., & Barrios-Choplin, J. R. (1992). A Dual-Capacity Model of Communication Media Choice in Organizations. *Human Communication Research, 18*, 563–598.

Sloan, A. (2002, January 21). Who Killed Enron? *Newsweek*, pp. 18–24.

Smart, B. (ed.) (1999). *Resisting McDonaldization*. London: Sage.

Smith, F. L., & Keyton, J. (2001). Organizational Storytelling: Metaphors for Relational Power and Identity Struggles. *Management Communication Quarterly, 15*, 149–182.

Smith, N. (ed.) (2002). *Changing U.S. Demographics*. New York: H. W. Wilson.

Smith, R. C., & Eisenberg, E. M. (1987). Conflict at Disneyland: A Root Metaphor Analysis. *Communication Monographs, 54*, 367–380.

Solomon, D. H., & Williams, M. L. M. (1997). Perceptions of Social-Sexual Communication at Work as Sexually Harassing. *Management Communication Quarterly, 11*, 147–184.

Snyder, B. (2003, May). Teams That Span Time Zones Face New Work Rules. *Stanford Business Magazine*. Retrieved December 1, 2007, from http://www.gsp.stanford.edu/news/bmag/sbsm0305/feature.

Soukup, E. (2003, September 22). CEOs: That's What That Is. *Newsweek*, p. 10.

Sproull, L., & Kiesler, S. (1986). Reducing Social Context Cues: The Case of Electronic Mail. *Management Science, 32*, 1492–1512.

Stacey, R. D. (1996). *Complexity and Creativity in Organizations*. San Francisco: Berrett-Koehler.

Stage, C. W. (1999). Negotiating Organizational Communication Cultures in American Subsidiaries Doing Business in Thailand. *Management Communication Quarterly, 13*, 245–280.

Starr, M. (2004, April 19). Reversing the Curse. *Newsweek*, pp. E10–E16.

"Statistics on Aging" (2007). Administration on Aging. Retrieved September 14, 2007, from http://www.aoa.gov/prof/Statistics/statistics.asp.

Steinberg, R. J., & Figart, D. M. (1999). Emotional Labor Since *The Managed Heart*. *Annals of the American Academy of Political and Social Science, 561*, 8–26.

Stern, L. (2007, September 17). Care from Afar. *Newsweek*, p. E18.

Stiff, J. B., Dillard, J. P., Somera, L., Kim, H., & Sleight, C. (1988). Empathy, Communication, and Prosocial Behavior. *Communication Monographs, 55*, 198–213.

Stiglitz, J.E. (2002). *Globalization and Its Discontents*. New York: Norton.

——— (2006). *Making Globalization Work*. New York: Norton.

Stogdill, R. M. (1948). Personal Factors Associated with Leadership: A Survey of the Literature. *Journal of Psychology, 25*, 35–71.

Stohl, C. (1986). The Role of Memorable Messages in the Process of Organizational Socialization. *Communication Quarterly, 34,* 231–249.

——— (2001). Globalizing Organizational Communication. In F. M. Jablin & L. L. Putnam (eds.), *The New Handbook of Organizational Communication: Advances in Theory, Research, and Methods* (pp. 323–375). Thousand Oaks, CA: Sage.

Stohl, C., & Cheney, G. (2001). Participatory Processes/Paradoxical Practices: Communication and the Dilemmas of Organizational Democracy. *Management Communication Quarterly, 14,* 349–407.

Stohl, C., & Sotirin, P. (1990). Absence as Workplace Control: A Critical Inquiry. In J. Anderson (ed.), *Communication Yearbook 13* (pp. 59–68). Newbury Park, CA: Sage.

Stohl, C., & Stohl, M. (2007). Networks of Terror: Theoretical Assumptions and Pragmatic Consequences. *Communication Theory, 17,* 93–124.

Stone, B. (2003, November 24). Soaking in Spam. *Newsweek,* pp. 66–69.

——— (2004, April 19). Should I Stay or Should I Go? *Newsweek,* pp. 52–54.

Strauss, A., & Corbin, J. (1990). *Basics of Qualitative Research: Grounded Theory Procedures and Techniques.* Newbury Park, CA: Sage.

"Study: U.S. Airline Quality Improving" (2002, April 8). *CNN.com.*

Surber, J. P. (1998). *Culture and Critique: An Introduction to the Critical Discourses of Cultural Studies.* Boulder, CO: Westview.

Susskind, A.M. (2007). Downsizing Survivors' Communication Networks and Reactions: A Longitudinal Examination of Information Flow and Turnover Intentions. *Communication Research, 34,* 156–184.

Sutton, R. I. (2007). *The No Asshole Rule: Building a Civilized Workplace and Surviving One That Isn't.* New York: Warner Business Books.

Sypher, B. D. (ed.) (1997). *Case Studies in Organizational Communication 2: Perspectives on Contemporary Work Life.* New York: Guilford.

Tanaka, J. (1997, April 28). Drowning in Data. *Newsweek,* p. 85.

Taylor, B., & Conrad, C. (1992). Narratives of Sexual Harassment: Organizational Dimensions. *Journal of Applied Communication Research, 20,* 401–418.

Taylor, B. C., & Trujillo, N. (2001). Qualitative Research Methods. In F. M. Jablin & L. L. Putnam (eds.), *The New Handbook of Organizational Communication: Advances in Theory, Research, and Methods* (pp. 161–194). Thousand Oaks, CA: Sage.

Taylor, F. W. (1911). *The Principles of Scientific Management.* New York: Harper & Row.

Taylor, M., & Doerfel, M. L. (2003). Building Interorganizational Relationships That Build Nations. *Human Communication Research, 29,* 153–181.

Taylor, S., & Thomas, E. (2003, December 15). Civil Wars. *Newsweek,* pp. 43–51.

Teboul, J. C. B. (1995). Determinants of New Hire Information-Seeking during Organizational Encounter. *Western Journal of Communication, 59,* 305–325.

Teboul, J. C. B., & Cole, T. (2005). Relationship Development and Workplace Integration: An Evolutionary Perspective. *Communication Theory, 15,* 389–413.

Tengler, C. D., & Jablin, F. M. (1983). Effects of Question Type, Orientation, and Sequencing in the Employment Screening Interview. *Communication Monographs, 50,* 243–263.

"The American Workforce: 2004–14" (2007). Retrieved November 24, 2007, from http://careers.stateuniversity.com/pages/838/American-Workforce-2004-14.html.

Therborn, G. (1980). *The Ideology of Power and the Power of Ideology.* London: Verso.

Thibaut, J. W., & Walker, L. (1975). *Procedural Justice: A Psychological Analysis.* New York: Erlbaum/Halstead.

Thomas, D. (1993). Racial Dynamics in Cross-Race Developmental Relationships. *Administrative Science Quarterly, 38,* 169–194.

Thomas, K. W. (1976). Conflict and Conflict Management. In M. Dunnette (ed.), *Handbook of Industrial and Organizational Psychology* (pp. 889–936). Chicago: Rand McNally.

Thompson, J. D. (1967). *Organizations in Action.* New York: McGraw-Hill.

Tichy, N., Tushman, M., & Fombrun, C. (1979). Social Network Analysis for Organizations. *Academy of Management Review, 4,* 507–519.

Timmerman, C. E. (2003). Media Selection during the Implementation of Planned Organizational Change: A Predictive Framework Based on Implementation Approach and Phase. *Management Communication Quarterly, 16,* 301–340.

Tjosvold, D., & Tjosvold, M. M. (1991). *Leading the Team Organization.* New York: Lexington Books.

Tobin, D. R. (1998). *The Knowledge-Enabled Organization.* New York: AMACOM.

Tomlinson, J. (1997). Cultural Globalization and Cultural Imperialism. In A. Mohammadi (ed.), *International Communication and Globalization* (pp. 170–190). Thousand Oaks, CA: Sage.

Tompkins, P. K., & Cheney, G. (1985). Communication and Unobtrusive Control in Contemporary Organizations. In R. D. McPhee & P. K. Tompkins (eds.), *Organizational Communication: Traditional Themes and New Directions* (pp. 179–210). Beverly Hills, CA: Sage.

Tracy, S. J. (2000). Becoming a Character for Commerce: Emotional Labor, Self-Subordination, and Discursive Construction of Identity in a Total Institution. *Management Communication Quarterly, 14,* 90–128.

Tracy, S. J., Lutgen-Sandvik, P., & Alberts, J. K. (2006). Nightmares,

Demons, and Slaves: Exploring the Painful Metaphors of Workplace Bullying. *Management Communication Quarterly, 20,* 148–185.

Trethewey, A. (1999). Disciplined Bodies: Women's Embodied Identities at Work. *Organization Studies, 20,* 423–450.

——— (2000). Revisioning Control: A Feminist Critique of Disciplined Bodies. In P. M. Buzzanell (ed.), *Rethinking Organizational and Managerial Communication from Feminist Perspectives* (pp. 107–127). Thousand Oaks, CA: Sage.

Tretheway, A., & Ashcraft, K. L. (2004). Practicing Disorganization: The Development of Applied Perspectives on Living with Tension. *Journal of Applied Communication Research, 32,* 81–88.

Trevino, L. K., Lengel, R. H., Bodensteiner, W., Gerloff, E. A., & Muir, N. K. (1990). The Richness Imperative and Cognitive Style: The Role of Individual Differences in Media Choice Behavior. *Management Communication Quarterly, 4,* 176–197.

Trevino, L. K., Lengel, R. H., & Daft, R. L. (1987). Media Symbolism, Media Richness, and Media Choice in Organizations: A Symbolic Interactionist Perspective. *Communication Research, 14,* 553–574.

Trist, E. L. (1969). On Socio-Technical Systems. In W. G. Bennis, K. D. Benne, & R. Chin (eds.), *The Planning of Change* (pp. 269–282). New York: Holt, Rinehart & Winston.

Tubbs, S. (1978). *A Systems Approach to Small Group Interaction.* Reading, MA: Addison-Wesley.

Turnage, J. J. (1990). The Challenge of New Workplace Technology for Psychology. *American Psychologist, 45,* 171–178.

Turner, L. H., & Henzl, S. A. (1987). Influence Attempts in Organizational Conflict: The Effects of Biological Sex, Psychological Gender, and Power Position. *Management Communication Quarterly, 1,* 32–57.

Turner, L. H., & Shuter, R. (2004). African American and European

American Women's Visions of Workplace Conflict: A Metaphorical Analysis. *Howard Journal of Communications, 15,* 169–183.

Turner, P. K. (2003). Paradox of Ordering Change: I Insist that We Work as a Team. *Management Communication Quarterly, 16,* 434–439.

Tyre, P. (2004, April 12). Ms. Top Cop. *Newsweek,* pp. 48–49.

"VA Will Expand Mental Health Services" (2007, July 16). *Associated Press.* Retrieved November 19, 2007, from msnbc.com.

Vance, A. (2002, January 21). HP Slams Hewlett in Letter to Shareholders. Retrieved December 20, 2007, from http://www.itworld .com/Tech/2428/IDG020121hpmemo/.

Van Maanen, J. (1975). Breaking In: Socialization to Work. In R. Dubin (ed.), *Handbook of Work, Organization and Society* (pp. 67–120). Chicago: Rand McNally.

——— (1988). *Tales of the Field: On Writing Ethnography.* Chicago: University of Chicago Press.

Van Maanen, J., & Schein, E. H. (1979). Toward a Theory of Organizational Socialization. In B. M. Staw & L. L. Cummings (eds.), *Research in Organizational Behavior, Vol. 1* (pp. 209–264). Greenwich, CT: JAI Press.

Vibbert, S. L., & Bostdorff, D. M. (1993). Issue Management in the "Lawsuit Crisis." In C. Conrad (ed.), *Ethical Nexus* (pp. 103–120). Norwood, NJ: Ablex.

Volkema, R. J., Bergmann, T. J., & Farquhar, K. (1997). Use and Impact of Informal Third-Party Discussions in Interpersonal Conflicts at Work. *Management Communication Quarterly, 11,* 185–216.

Von Bertalanffy, L. (1968). *General Systems Theory.* New York: Braziller.

Wagner, J. A. (1994). Participation's Effect on Performance and Satisfaction: A Reconsideration of Research Evidence. *Academy of Management Review, 19,* 312–330.

Waldron, V. R. (1994). Once More, with Feeling: Reconsidering the Role of Emotion in Work. In S. Deetz (ed.), *Communication Yearbook 17* (pp. 388–416). Thousand Oaks, CA: Sage.

——— (2000). Relational Experiences and Emotion at Work. In S. Fineman (ed.), *Emotion in Organizations,* 2nd ed. (pp. 64–82). London: Sage.

Walther, J. P., & Bunz, U. (2005). The Rules of Virtual Groups: Trust, Liking, and Performance in Computer-Mediated Communication. *Journal of Communication, 55,* 828–846.

Walton, R. E., & McKersie, R. B. (1965). *A Behavioral Theory of Labor Negotiations: An Analysis of a Social Interaction System.* New York: McGraw-Hill.

Wanous, J. P. (1992). *Organizational Entry: Recruitment, Selection, Orientation, and Socialization of Newcomers,* 2nd ed. Reading, MA: Addison-Wesley.

Wanous, J. P., & Colella, A. (1989). Organizational Entry Research: Current Status and Future Directions. In K. M. Rowland & G. R. Ferris (eds.), *Research in Personnel and Human Resource Management, Vol. 7* (pp. 59–120). Greenwich, CT: JAI Press.

Wanous, J. P., Poland, T. D., Premack, S. L., & Davis, K. S. (1992). The Effects of Met Expectations on Newcomer Attitudes and Behaviors: A Review and Meta-Analysis. *Journal of Applied Psychology, 77,* 288–297.

Watson, W. E., Kumar, K., & Michaelsen, L. K. (1993). Cultural Diversity's Impact on Interaction Progress and Performance: Comparing Homogeneous and Diverse Task Groups. *Academy of Management Journal, 36,* 590–602.

Weaver, V. J. (1999, May/June). If Your Organization Values Diversity, Why Are They Leaving? *Mosaics, 4.*

Weber, M. (1946). *From Max Weber: Essays in Sociology,* H. H. Gerth & C. Wright Mills, trans. and eds. New York: Oxford University Press.

———— (1947). *Max Weber: The Theory of Social and Economic Organization,* T. Parsons & A. M. Henderson, trans. and eds. New York: Free Press.

———— (1968). *Economy and Society,* G. Roth & C. Wittich, trans. and eds. New York: Bedminster.

Weick, K. E. (1969). *The Social Psychology of Organizing.* Reading, MA: Addison-Wesley.

———— (1979). *The Social Psychology of Organizing,* 2nd ed. Reading, MA: Addison-Wesley.

———— (1993). The Collapse of Sensemaking in Organizations: The Mann Gulch Disaster. *Administrative Science Quarterly, 38,* 628–652.

———— (1995). *Sensemaking in Organizations.* Newbury Park, CA: Sage.

———— (1998). Enacted Sensemaking in Crisis Situations. *Journal of Management Studies, 25,* 305–317.

Weider-Hatfield, D., & Hatfield, J. D. (1996). Superiors' Conflict Management Strategies and Subordinate Outcomes. *Management Communication Quarterly, 10,* 189–208.

Wendt, R. (1994). Learning to "Walk the Talk": A Critical Tale of the Micropolitics at a Total Quality Management University. *Management Communication Quarterly, 8,* 5–45.

Wendt, R. F. (1998). The Sound of One Hand Clapping: Counterintuitive Lessons Extracted from Paradoxes and Double Binds in Participative Organizations. *Management Communication Quarterly, 11,* 323–371.

Wharton, A. S. (1999). The Psychosocial Consequences of Emotional Labor. *Annals of the American Academy of Political and Social Science, 561,* 158–176.

Wharton, A. S., & Erickson, R. J. (1993). Managing Emotions on the Job and at Home: Understanding the Consequences of Multiple Emotional Roles. *Academy of Management Review, 18,* 457–486.

Wheatley, M. (1992). *Leadership and the New Science.* San Francisco: Berrett-Koehler.

"Why Do We Need E-Race?" (2007, July 17). U.S. Equal Employment Opportunity Commission. Retrieved November 24, 2007, from http://www.eeoc.gov/initiatives/e-race/why_e-race.html.

Whyte, G. (1989). Groupthink Reconsidered. *Academy of Management Review, 14,* 40–56.

Whyte, W. H. (1956). *The Organization Man.* Garden City, NY: Doubleday.

Wiener, N. (1948). *Cybernetics: On Control and Communication in the Animal and the Machine.* New York: Wiley.

———— (1954). *The Human Side of Human Beings: Cybernetics and Society.* Garden City, NY: Doubleday/Anchor.

Williamson, A. P. (1994). Executive Commentary to "Getting Anointed for Advancement: The Case of Executive Women." *Academy of Management Executive, 8* (2), 64–66.

Woodburn, S. (2007, March 19). The Cookie Hustler. *Newsweek,* p. E4.

"Work Groups Make Telecommute a Social Affair" (2007, September 12). *Morning Edition,* National Public Radio.

Yates, J., & Orlikowski, W. J. (1992). Genres of Organizational Communication: A Structurational Approach to Studying Communication and Media. *Academy of Management Review, 17,* 299–326.

York, K. M. (1989). Defining Sexual Harassment in Workplaces: A Policy-Capturing Approach. *Academy of Management Journal, 32,* 830–850.

Young, R. (2004). *Frontline: Is Wal-Mart Good for America?* DVD-Video, PBS.

Zahra, S. A. (1998). Competitiveness and Global Leadership in the 21st Century. *Academy of Management Executive, 12* (4), 10–12.

———— (1999). The Changing Rules of Global Competitiveness in the 21st Century. *Academy of Management Executive, 13* (1), 36–42.

Zey, M. (1991). *The Mentor Connection.* Homewood, IL: Dow Jones-Irwin.

Zoller, H. M. (2003). Health on the Line: Identity and Disciplinary Control in Employee Occupational Health and Safety Discourse. *Journal of Applied Communication Research, 31,* 118–139.

Zorn, T. E., Page, D. J., & Cheney, G. (2000). Nuts about Change: Multiple Perspectives on Change-Oriented Communication in a Public Sector Organization. *Management Communication Quarterly, 13,* 515–566.

Name Index

Note: Italic page numbers indicate material in tables or figures.

A

Abrahamson, E., 26
Ackman, D., 188
Adams, J. S., 161
Adams, W. L., 215
Aditya, R. N., 190
Adler, J., 142, 199
Adorno, Theodor, 101
Aikat, D., 240
Alberts, J. K., 165, 202
Albrecht, T. L., 211
Alger, H., 265
Allen, B. J., 136, 218, 220, 226
Allen, D., 26
Alter, J., 190
Alvesson, M., 85, 101, 107, 116
Amason, A. C., 146
Apker, J., 69, 132, 184, 195
Argyris, C., 92
Armstrong, T. A., 165
Aronson, E., 210
As, D., 149
Asangi, S., 258
Ashcraft, K. L., 11, 12, 109, 112, 113, 114, 226
Ashford, S. J., 184

Ashforth, B. E., 111, 200
Austin, J. T., 54
Auwal, M. A., 112
Awamleh, R., 191–192
Aydin, C., 245, 250
Ayres, I., 142

B

Babbitt, L. V., 128, 129
Babrow, A., 75
Bach, B. W., 121
Bales, R. F., 143
Bantz, C. R., 95
Barker, J. R., 110, 111, 112, 156
Barling, J., 123
Barnard, C. I., 141, 142
Barrios-Choplin, J. R., 245
Bass, B. M., 191
Batten, D., 180
Bazerman, M. H., 170, 172
Becker, S., 54
Beehr, T. A., 206
Behling, O. C., 53
Bell, E., 109
Benoit, W. L., 187
Bergmann, T. J., 168
Berman, J. E., 86

Bernard, T. S., 141
Bernstein, R. J., 100, 106, 108
Beyer, J., 84
Billings, A. G., 210
Bingham, S. G., 230
Bird, A., 220
Birkholt, M., 209
Black, J. S., 184
Blake, Robert R., 43, 46, 47, 48, 163, 189
Blake, S., 226, 227, 231, 232, 232, 233
Block, C. J., 228
Bloodworth-Thomason, Linda, 104
Bodensteiner, W., 244
Boje, D., 84
Bormann, E. G., 147
Bostdorff, D. M., 264
Boudens, C. J., 201
Bowes, J. M., 123
Branscum, D., 249
Branson, R., 7
Braverman, H., 103
Brett, J. M., 168, 172
Brief, A. P., 44
Brown, M. H., 94

297

Subject Index

Note: Italic page numbers indicate material in tables or figures.

Employee involvement, 52
Employees
  change processes and, 184,
    185–187
  concertive control and,
    111–112
  disposable workers and, 258,
    268–271
  efficiency of, 25–26, 35
  globalization and, 268–271
  human resources approaches
    and, 52
  monitoring of, 27, 105
  renumeration of, 21
  replaceability of, 18
  resistance of, 108–110
  satisfaction of, 38, 41, 42, 44,
    49, 148, 149, 207, 271
  socialization and, 124
Employment interview
  anticipatory socialization and,
    123, 126, 127
  assimilation processes and,
    126–129
  as information-gathering tool,
    128–129
  as recruiting and screening tool,
    127–128
  as socialization tool, 129
Enactment, 67
Encounter phase of socialization,
  123–125, 129–131
Enrollment management systems
  case study, 156–158
Enron case example, 188
Episodic performances, 85
EQ (emotional intelligence
  quotient), 204
Equal Employment Opportunity
  Commission (EEOC), 218,
  221, 229
Equifinality, 63
Equity, 21, 113
Equivocality, 68
ER waiting times case example, 45
Esprit de corps, 21
Esteem needs, 39, 148
Ethnicity and race
  affirmative action programs
    and, 228–229

conflict management process
  and, 172–173
demographics and, 9, 217
mentor–protégé relationships
  and, 222–223
opportunities of, 226–228
relational barriers and, 221–224
See also People of color
Ethnography, 94–96
European Union, 2
Evaluation stage of decision
  making, 140
Evolutionary theory, 67
Excellent cultures, 81–83, 82
Exchange processes, 61, 71, 173
Exemplification, 191
Explanatory approaches, 13, 22,
  81, 83, 100
Explicit knowledge, 154
Exploitive authoritative
  organization, 48

F

Facebook, 1, 250
Face-to-face communication, 30,
  50–51, 72, 243, 246, 248
Family leave policies, 230
Family metaphor, 41
Fax machines, 240
Fayol's bridge, 20, 29
Fayol's Theory of Classical
  Management, 17, 18–22
Feedback processes
  cybernetic systems theory and,
    65, 66
  media richness model and, 243
  system approaches and, 61–62,
    64, 71
Felt conflict, 162
Feminist theories
  conflict management processes
    and, 159–160, 173–175
  of organizational communica-
    tion, 112–116
See also Gender issues; Women
First-generation affirmative action,
  224–225
First Things First (Covey), 26
Flaming, 248–249
Flextime, 250

Flow of communication
  channels and, 30
  in classical approaches, 29
  direction of, 28, 29, 50
  in human relations approaches, 50
  in human resources approaches, 50
Formal bargaining, 166
Formal communication, 30, 51, 165
Formulation stage of decision
  making, 140
Fragmentation perspective, 87, 93
Framing devices
  conflict management processes
    and, 170, 171, 172
  leadership and, 192, 193
  sexual harassment and, 114, 115
Frankfurt school of critical
  theory, 101
Frontline (Young), 109
Functional theory, 146–147
Functional Theory of Group
  Decision Making (Hirokawa
  and Gouran), 146

G

Gaia Capitalism (R&D project), 7
Gallaudet University case example,
  87
Garbage can model of decision
  making, 143
GDSSs (Group Decision Support
  Systems), 147, 240, 241, 245
Gender issues
  affirmative action programs
    and, 228–229
  conflict management processes
    and, 170, 173–175
  disciplined bodies and, 115–116
  feminist theories and, 112–116
  mentor–protégé relationships
    and, 222
  multicultural organizations and,
    224–226
  organizational culture and, 86
  sexual harassment and, 114,
    115, 229–230
  stereotypes and, 220–221, 224, 226
  work/home life balance and,
    230–231
See also Women